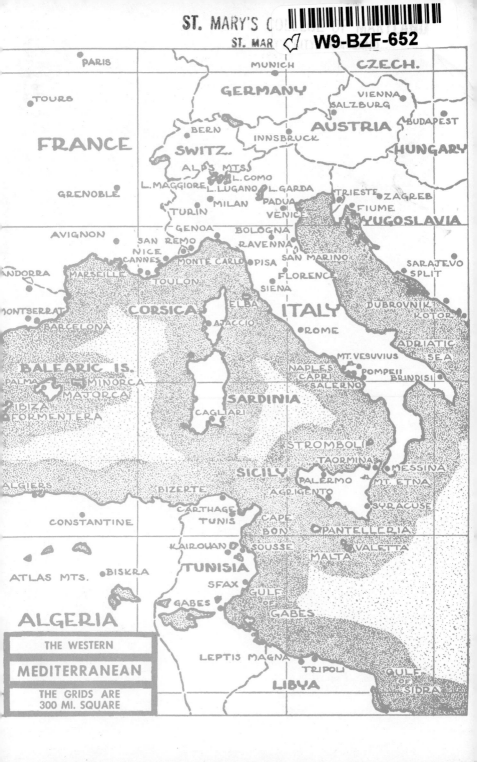

PARIS

TOURS

FRANCE

GRENOBLE

AVIGNON

ANDORRA

MONTSERRAT

BARCELONA

BALEARIC IS.

PALMA
MINORCA
MAJORCA
IBIZA
FORMENTERA

ALGIERS

CONSTANTINE

ATLAS MTS. BISKRA

ALGERIA

MUNICH

GERMANY

BERN

SWITZ.

ALPS MTS.
L.COMO
L.MAGGIORE
L.LUGANO L.GARDA
MILAN
TURIN PADUA
VENICE
GENOA
BOLOGNA
SAN REMO
RAVENNA
NICE
CANNES
MONTE CARLO PISA
MARSEILLE
TOULON
FLORENCE
SIENA
CORSICA
ELBA
AJACCIO
ROME

MT. VESUVIUS
NAPLES
CAPRI POMPEII
SALERNO
SARDINIA
CAGLIARI

STROMBOLI
TAORMINA
SICILY MESSINA
PALERMO MT. ETNA
AGRIGENTO
SYRACUSE
BIZERTE
CARTHAGE
TUNIS CAPE
BON PANTELLERIA
KAIROUAN SOUSSE VALETTA
MALTA
TUNISIA
SFAX GULF
GABES OF
GABES

LEPTIS MAGNA
TRIPOLI GULF
OF
LIBYA SIDRA

CZECH.

VIENNA
SALZBURG
BUDAPEST
AUSTRIA
INNSBRUCK
HUNGARY

TRIESTE ZAGREB
FIUME
YUGOSLAVIA

SAN MARINO
SARAJEVO
SPLIT

ITALY
DUBROVNIK
KOTOR

ADRIATIC
SEA

BRINDISI

The Pageant of the Mediterranean

THE PAGEANT OF
The
Mediterranean

by Sheridan H. Garth

With a Prologue by
JAMES W. KIRK

HASTINGS HOUSE PUBLISHERS

New York 22

Completely Revised Edition

Reprinted March 1966

Copyright © 1952, 1962 by Sheridan H. Garth

Library of Congress Catalog Card Number : 52–8630

Printed in the United States of America

To

VICTORIA GARTH ~-

My Mother, whose pioneering in the travel field,
and whose unfailing inspiration, have made this
work possible.

SCENES OF THE PAGEANT

PROLOGUE

I. The Mediterranean Theatre and Its Unique Stage

The Setting

Most historic areas of the world are land masses surrounded by seas: Asia, Africa, the Americas. Yet the most historic of all—the Mediterranean area—is a shallow, almost tideless sea, surrounded by land.

In fact, this unique aqua-stage is so interspersed with islands and peninsulas that one can sail only a few hours in any given direction without sighting some historic landmark.

This indeed was a setting fit to nurture the rise of navigation and commerce, as well as the growth of the arts and sciences; across this stage, what we know as civilization, born in Egypt and the Levant, has been carried relentlessly westward through Greece, Rome and Europe to the Americas of the Western Hemisphere.

Location and Dimensions

Often thought of as tropical because of its associations with Egypt and the Nile, the great Mediterranean stage is actually in the North Temperate Zone. As far as the sea itself is concerned, the range is from 30° at Alexandria to 45° in Venice, or the difference in latitude between Jacksonville, Florida, and Bangor, Maine, here in the United States. On the wide side, Gibraltar is just west of the Greenwich Meridian, and the Suez Canal bottleneck at the eastern extremity is near the fortieth parallel on a line with Ankara and Moscow (see maps).

Neither is the Mediterranean aqua-stage large in area nor lengthy in mileage. Considered only as a sea, its 1,145,000 square miles is less than the size of the Caribbean and the Gulf of Mexico, or about 1% of the water surface of the earth (the Atlantic Ocean covers 25 times as much area). Its east to west length is only 2300 miles and from south to north it averages less than 500 miles. Superimposed on the map of the United States, the Mediterranean Sea area would cover the width of our Great Lakes and extend eastward to Maine and westward to Montana.

Its Strategic Situation

Although representing such a small part of the now known world, this classic area has played a tremendous role in shaping world events. Historically in the middle of the ancient world, hence its name, the Mediterranean Sea became the maritime crossroads for the development of the continents of Europe, Asia, and Africa; it carried the torch of civilization from East to West, and for 3000 years until the discovery of the New Worlds in 1492, it was the world's busiest highway.

The Mediterranean stage, in its larger sense, came to embrace the land areas around it where nations rose and fell through the ages. By the time Columbus set sail for the west, the influence of this strategic area reached from the Azores in the Atlantic to the borders of India, and north from Ethiopia, the source of the Nile, to the latinized domain of Rumania on the Danube.

Eclipsed for a few centuries by the discovery of new routes to the west and to the Indies, the Mediterranean theatre came back again into the center of global strategy with the opening of the world's longest canal (104.5 miles) through the Isthmus of Suez in 1869. And now, in our 20th Century Air Age, the Mediterranean has become a major crossroads for world airlines. It has been transformed into a major stopover region for the growing numbers of round-the-world air travelers.

Important Physical Features

The dawn of history found the Mediterranean a huge finger bowl bequeathed by the geological eons, an inland sea in a vast depression filled with the ocean waters of the nearby Atlantic.

This placid blue sea was left surrounded by mountains on the north and west and hemmed in by impassable deserts on the south and east—a welcome protection from neighboring hordes.

Few rivers penetrated into the basin of the Mediterranean, but from the center of Africa came the world's longest inland waterway, the Nile, covering 4000 miles in its course and creating a belt of fertile soil that enabled the Egyptians to set up the first real agricultural system in a stable society.

Finally, few regions on earth offer such a variety of altitudes for its inhabitants, ranging from the lowest point on the world's surface in the Dead Sea Rift, to the two-mile-high active volcanic peak of Mount Etna, in Sicily.

Climate and the Elements

As stated above, the Mediterranean stage is not in the Tropical Zone. Yet, due to the effect of the desert winds, the protection of the mountains, and the ever present sea, the climate is extremely moderate. Seasons fade away in the protected surroundings of southern Spain, Sicily and the Nile belt, while they are scarcely perceptible along the entire littoral.

The Mediterranean climate is characterized by warm days with clear blue skies, exceptional luminosity and bright light; however, the nights are cool even on the desert, and snow is not unknown in Rome and Istanbul. The sun is an outstanding feature of any Mediterranean setting, from the French Riviera to the Lebanon, but it never becomes oppressive, owing to the dryness of the atmosphere. Rainstorms of any length are rare, although sometimes violent. For the most part the Mediterranean has suffered more from drought than from excessive rains.

The typical Mediterranean climate covers those limits in which the olive tree grows, which include the entire perimeter of the great sea and from 10 to 200 miles inland, depending upon the altitude.

Soil and Resources

The physical aspects of the Mediterranean area have not produced fertility of soil sufficient for agricultural purposes, except in scattered districts such as the Nile Valley, a few choice spots in Africa, and narrow coastal strips along the European shores. Agricultural methods have thus always remained primitive and small scale.

Neither was the area blessed even in small portion by the Hercynian chain, which geologists explain encircled the globe in the Primary Era. This chain, identifying most of the great coal and metallurgical deposits in the world today, bypassed our Mediterranean theatre to the north, ushering in the industrial revolution in Europe and America but leaving to the Mediterranean the practices of trade and barter and craftsmanship.

In short, Nature's greatest contribution here was in bringing the sea and land together in such a way as to promote the growth of seamanship, communications and small business. The Mediterranean nevertheless became a great amphitheatre, upon the stage of which paraded the peoples of many nations in the everlasting pageant leading to modern civilization.

II. *The Mediterranean Cast of Many Peoples*

The Great Lost Mediterranean Valley

While our pageant of peoples begins, for our purpose, with the time when dates can be fairly well approximated, a word should be said of the primitive Mediterranean species.

There is evidence upon which to speculate that during the Glacial Age, when the waters of the oceans receded, much of the present Mediterranean Sea was blocked at Gibraltar, and a land bridge connected Italy with Africa via Malta, dividing the Mediterranean depression into a western salt sea and an eastern fresh-water lake fed by the Nile and probably by the rivers of the Po and Red Sea valleys.

In these great valleys primitive men wandered through on their migrations among the land masses of Europe, Asia and Africa for thousands of years before the breaking of the Gibraltar barrier raised the Mediterranean basin to the levels we know at the beginnings of recorded history.

The Parade of Peoples Through Five Thousand Years

Since the comparatively recent era began in which definite dates can be verified (about 3000 B.C.), the Mediterranean stage has remained physically inert except for an occasional volcanic eruption.

However, across this strategic stage in the last 4000 years have paraded most of the interesting peoples of the world. Our cast is concerned with peoples and cultures rather than with races or individuals, as the Mediterranean area today is a mixture of many races, and its cultures have been passed along from one people to another, while the individuals were playing mostly minor, if at times interesting, roles.

For the twenty Scenes in the Pageant to follow, we have not only verified documents as a source of our inspiration, but the historic relics of man's genius left before our eyes, from the time-worn, mysterious Pyramids to the modern casinos in Monte Carlo and Estoril. The Seven Wonders of the Ancient World listed below have become seven times seven wonders, most of which may be seen in the original on a two-months cruise or a six-weeks tour around the shores of the Mediterranean Sea today.

The Seven Wonders of the Ancient World Before Christ

1. *The Pyramids of Egypt* near Cairo, dating from around 3000 B.C., the only one of the Wonders left standing today.

2. *The Hanging Gardens* of Babylon, now in Iraq, constructed about 600 B.C. by King Nebuchadnezzar. World's earliest synthetic landscape.

3. *The Statue of Jupiter* at Olympia in western Greece, dating about 430 B.C. Built of marble, encrusted with ivory, with draperies of beaten gold.

4. *The Temple of Diana* at Ephesus, near Smyrna, Turkey, finished about 400 B.C., a masterpiece in pure marble.

5. *The Tomb of Mausolus* at Halicarnassus in modern Turkey. Built about 352 B.C.; so impressive that it has handed down to us the well-known word "mausoleum."

6. *The Colossus of Rhodes* on the island of Rhodes, built about 280 B.C. A bronze statue of Apollo 109 feet high, standing astride the entrance to the harbor.

7. *The Pharos of Alexandria,* Egypt. A lighthouse over 400 feet high completed in 247 B.C. that was a beacon for navigators for over 800 years, and probably the inspiration for the Moslem minarets we see today.

Predominant Phases in the Great Pageant

Because our treatment of each Mediterranean nation as it exists today is along the line of historical development rather than geographical convenience, we start with Egypt and finish with Morocco.

In the small part that each plays in the greater Mediterranean pageant, however, we shall keep uppermost in mind those phases in which the Mediterranean peoples played a concurrent part.

The Eastern peoples—Assyrians, Babylonians, Persians—first dominating the seas; the Greeks and the Macedonians from the west in turn driving to the south as far as Ethiopia and to the east beyond the Indus River; the rise and fall of the Roman Empire; the domination of the seas first by Christian and then by Moslem faiths; the romantic Crusades; the decline of the Mediterranean world after the discovery of America, and its resurgence with the construction of the Suez Canal; the effect of Turkish, Spanish, British, French and other modern cultures upon the life of the Mediterranean; the evolution of nationalism leading to the political freedom of the multiplicity of new African and Asiatic states—all these phases play a prominent part in the individual life story of each nation as we shall relate it.

The Mediterranean Type

It is often asked, "Is there a Mediterranean race?" A study of the Scenes which follow will answer that question. In no similar area of the world has the admixture of blood by infiltration and absorption been more thorough than in the Mediterranean. The white race from Asia and Europe, the brown and black races from the east and the south, even the yellow race at intervals—all have sooner or later passed over the Mediterranean stage.

Now, after 5000 years of fusion, we have not a race but a type of man, the *Homo Mediterraneus,* who could make his living in Tangier as easily as in Cairo, or Barcelona or Tunis. Racial experts say that the Mediterranean type is of only average height, with prominent features, dark hair, brownish-black eyes and swarthy skin. You will see a thousand variations of him in the seaports of the great Middle Sea, and you will hear him speaking six or seven languages in his daily routine, but all in all you will soon recognize him as a Mediterranean, neither European, African nor Asiatic.

The Mediterranean Today, One Geographic Unit, a Score of Political Divisions

Now we must ask how this Mediterranean type of man, evolving from the passing parade of peoples through the historic amphitheatre, with so much in common with his neighbor, finds himself living today in any one of a score of political units of different languages and customs. Only 1800 years ago, on the same physical stage, a Roman citizen could wander from Britannia to Arabia over a territory as large as our 50 states, under one flag, with one set of laws and speaking a common language. Today in that same setting he would pass through some 26 independent countries, each with its distinctive language, religion, local government and currency system. It is our purpose in the Scenes to follow to answer this interesting question as we trace the Pageant of the Mediterranean peoples from the time of Cheops 5000 years ago in ancient Egypt down to the formation of the new Libyan kingdom in 1951 and the subsequently-won independence of Tunisia and Morocco.

III. The Mediterranean Pageant of Twenty Scenes

A Continuous, Composite and Co-ordinated Story

We have observed the great Mediterranean physical stage with its limitations; we have identified the diverse cast of peoples who presently occupy this stage area; we are now ready to understand the events and scenes that took place in the Mediterranean Pageant over the past fifty centuries. The story of the Pageant must be continuous—it must be composite—to include all peoples simultaneously; it must be co-ordinated to show the part played by each group in the growth of Mediterranean civilization.

The Inspiration for This Book

For nearly thirty years I have been traveling about the Mediterranean and listening to the tales of hundreds of travelers returning from this great area. As a Director of Cruises in peacetime and as an intelligence officer in wartime, I have had an opportunity to crisscross the Mediterranean by sea and by air from the Azores to the Persian Gulf and from the Ethiopian source of the Nile to the Black Sea. In that time I have run across many fine books devoted to the description of a single country like Egypt or Italy, but few that carried the whole story of the Mediterranean in one correlated package. Here is one of the great stories of the world as yet untold.

The Man Behind the Pageant

When the ever-popular Mediterranean cruises were resumed after World War II, I was fortunate in my role of Cruise Director to persuade my long-time colleague, Mr. Sheridan H. Garth, to sail with my Cruise Staff as lecturer and editor. We had often discussed the merits of tying up the loose ends of Greek, Roman and Arab history in this area into one composite story, and now we had the opportunity to test our program. On this cruise Mr. Garth gave twenty-six lectures covering twenty-two countries but so relating the affairs of one country to the others that the effect was of a pageant making for real continuity. The interest of the guests on this cruise was instantaneous and sustained, and it was in the end at their insistence that we embarked upon the fifteen-month project of publishing *The Pageant of the Mediterranean*.

Only a man with Mr. Garth's wealth of practical information could write the Scenes in this Pageant. A graduate of Princeton, specializing in history, a competent linguist in Spanish, French,

Italian, and Portuguese, and familiar with the rudiments of other languages, a world traveler and lecturer, associated with one of the great international travel firms, Mr. Garth has here written a story that is authentic, colorful, and practical. To secure the material for these Scenes, Mr. Garth has collected over 3500 local folders and maps from every corner of the Mediterranean and digested them for your benefit and interest. He has indeed the equipment with which to present to you the "whole Mediterranean as a whole."

Colonel Kirk's "Famous Sights"

"One picture is worth ten thousand words" and a book on the Mediterranean would not be complete without some outstanding photographs. Based upon my experience as a Cruise Director on twenty-two extensive itineraries, I have prepared an all-Mediterranean album of "Characteristic Sights" to be found in the Picture Section of the Pageant. These photographs selected on the basis of antiquity, uniqueness, historical significance, and general popularity, are taken from a collection of 2000 art prints made by our cruise photographer, Mr. Charles D'Emery, during the past few years.

Before joining our post-war cruise staff, Mr. D'Emery had participated as photographer and lecturer in fifteen previous cruises to all parts of the Mediterranean. He had won five international awards for his pictures and has the distinction of photographing fifty-four foreign countries in the past twenty-four years. *Who's Who in Connecticut* lists Mr. D'Emery as a former member of the Underwood and Underwood staff, an assistant with Newman's Traveltalks and the originator of Publisher's Photo Service. All pictures presented in this book were made by Mr. Charles D'Emery and his staff, through the cooperation of the Manugian Studios, South Norwalk, Connecticut.

The Importance of Good Maps

No historical story can be thoroughly enjoyed without an adequate map for reference. For ready convenience we have inserted a map of the western Mediterranean in the front end-cover of the Pageant and a map of the eastern Mediterranean in the back end-cover. These two maps overlap at Italy in the center of the Mediterranean. They cover the territory from near the Tropic of Cancer on the twenty-third parallel on the South to the fiftieth parallel North, or about the northern boundary of the U.S.A. Longitudinal extremities are from the region of the "Lost Atlantis" in the Azores to the "Magic Carpet" area near Bagdad in Iraq. For the sake of clearness we have eliminated all political names except those having historical or popular interest today. Mr. Peter B. Andrews, a Professor on the staff of Syracuse University School of Architecture, in designing our maps, has inserted grids of 300 miles on a side for ready distance reckoning.

Twenty Books in One for Every Man's Library

Here then is your Pageant of the Mediterranean, an area offering more of educational interest than any other region in the world. In each of the twenty Scenes is the material for a complete book, and in the entire book forty-four separate countries and islands are discussed. (See The Cast of Mediterranean Peoples Today, page 369.)

The Pageant is not a guidebook to be used in Rome and then discarded; it is not a history book full of dates and statistics to be forgotten after college; it is the storybook of the Mediterranean world, explaining the romance behind the great historical events that took place there and the significance of the "Famous Sights" that are still in evidence today.

The Pageant of the Mediterranean is a book that will never go out of date; it is written for every man with a spark of adventure or a touch of curiosity in his soul. The younger generation will find "history come to life" in its pages; the Mediterranean traveler will find it "must" reading if he is to "know what he sees"; to every man it will be a challenge to "see what he knows" about this Mediterranean world where our culture and civilization were born.

LT. COL. JAMES W. KIRK

The Pageant of the Mediterranean

EGYPT

What the Pyramids Tell

CAIRO—modern metropolis on the ancient Nile—may seem to be a faraway city to Americans and an unexpected place from which to launch our Pageant of the Mediterranean.

But Cairo is the gateway to some of the most magnificent monuments of pioneer man. Since the story of our American culture can be traced back to Egypt, it is, after all, sensible to begin our story at the beginning.

Today's Cairo is the crossroads of the Middle East, and one of the most accessible of all crossroads cities. The growth of international air travel has made it a great junction spot. Travelers can drop into the ultramodern Cairo Airport from New York in nineteen hours, from London in eleven, from India in seven, and from South Africa in eighteen. People on cruises or arriving on other ships can reach Cairo by train in only three hours from the important ports of Port Said (on the Suez Canal) and Alexandria (on the Mediterranean).

Cairo is a bustling, colorful city of over two million people, thoroughly cosmopolitan. It is not only the largest city of Egypt, but of the whole continent of Africa. Yet it is not by any means African. Its basic culture is Arabic from Asia. Its people are the timeless blends of Egyptian, mixed with all Levantine races. Its culture and inspiration come from Arabia, while its rulers are steeped in the ways of Europe and in the fascination of all the modern world's inventions.

Cairo has grown up from a village founded only a thousand years ago. Egypt, on the other hand, has been an important segment on the world map for over five times as long. Through all of recorded history, Egypt has been roughly its present size and shape. From the shores of the Mediterranean up along the Nile to its Second Cataract; and from Sinai and the Red Sea to the wastes of Libya—these have always been the boundaries of Egypt, and so the map shows today.

Even though Cairo is "in" but not "of" Egypt, its builders placed it at the strategic site that has controlled Egypt through the ages. For only twenty-two miles farther upstream and across the Nile stands a palm grove that once was the proud city of Memphis, first capital of Egypt, and center of its great civilization. Directly across the river from Cairo today are the greatest relics of those faraway times—the three mystic-looking Pyramids, and the sardonic Sphinx.

Cairo has grown great as did Memphis because it is on the "throat" of Egypt. It sits firmly between Upper Egypt—that slender line of fertile green winding up the narrow Nile to the Second Cataract 650 miles to the south—and the rich delta of Lower Egypt, soil that has lost none of its magnificent fertility in five millenniums.

So today travelers can eat their cake and have it too. They can live in luxury hotels in a modern metropolis, yet fare forth in comfort to examine what ancient Egypt created and handed on to us. The finest things of ancient Egypt have lasted down through the centuries—the Pyramids, the treasures of the Pharaohs, and the life of the people of the Nile.

Before setting forth, however, everyone must get acquainted with his "dragoman." A dragoman is an important cog for touring Egypt—a wise, fatherly, and omnipotent individual dressed in fez and flowing robes, and employed by travel companies and hotels to conduct visitors around the city. These organizations will arrange the fee between dragoman and client per hour, and the dragoman will boss the chauffeurs, camel drivers, and other forms of feverish salesmen and enterprisers, with which Egypt is, alas, only too plentifully supplied.

The Pyramids Are Egypt

Seven miles out from busy modern Cairo lie the three great Pyramids. Every visitor to Cairo starts with them, as he should, since they were and are among the Seven Wonders of the World. The visitor travels by car across two arms of the Nile, then through the residential district abutting the town of Gizeh, and out along the wide, straight boulevard directly westward to the looming triangular piles.

This ride covers the width of the green Nile valley—the strip irrigated since time began by the Nile floods, and the inexhaustible source of Egypt's food supply. Beyond this narrow strip the land rises grandly up to a plateau, where stand the three Pyramids. Here begins the mystic desert, the rocky, sandy expanse that continues on with hardly a break for two thousand miles to the shores of the Atlantic Ocean.

Mystic is the word for the Pyramids. Numerous scholars have devoted their lives to reading their story, to interpreting the reasons why thousands of slaves should have toiled on them and the mystery of how engineers could build them. The story has been partially unraveled for our enthralment.

At this spot stands a famous hotel called the Mena House.[1] Rising in steps, following the mounting terrain from the "sown" to the desert, it is a place of fine taste, whose balconies give matchless views of the Pyramids, especially by moonlight. Here, in its verdant gardens, the arriving traveler should sit and drink in their story, gazing at their eminence from this enchanting distance before going any closer.

Egypt happens to be the place on the earth's surface where man got his most impelling start into a civilized state. Perhaps the men of ancient China and those who lived in the hot lands around the mouths of the Tigris and Euphrates rivers began to evolve out of the savage a trifle earlier, but nowhere do the actual accomplishments of the ancients compare with those of olden Egypt.

The Egyptians discovered, in their pioneer centuries, the very elements of architecture, of navigation, of engineering, of creative

---

[1] Here was held the international conference of Roosevelt, Churchill, and Chiang Kai-shek in 1943.

art, of boatbuilding, of economic and political science, of writing and reading, of sculpture, of astronomy, of erecting huge monuments and, incidentally, of the tricks of magic, back in the fourth and fifth millenniums before Christ.

This miracle happened because the setting was so propitious for it. Here was a river that flowed unfailingly through a warm desert land. The mild weather gave them ample time each year to devote to much more creative pursuits than just attending to their livelihood. The river ensured their food supply, but they had to show initiative and planning to lay in enough food for the long months when the river was low. They later had to devote their intelligence to invent methods of raising the water for irrigating extra crops. The surrounding desert, in the meantime, gave them protection from marauding enemies.

Thus these mysterious people showed an ability to build, fashion, and create while the rest of the world was still in a savage state. Who were they? Their reliefs show them to be a bronze-copper-colored race of erect, even tall, stature. The Bible considered them children of Ham, second son of Noah. Modern scientists thus classify them as a Hamitic people, a term that applies also to the original peoples of all North Africa, now snowed under by later stock.

A word similar to "Ham" exists in the vestigial Coptic language of present-day Egypt. It is *chem,* which means "black." The Copts, the Christian minority of Egypt today, proclaim themselves the descendants of the original Egyptians, and some ancient words remain in their religious liturgy. The very name "Copt" is supposed to be a modern rendition of the name that ancient Egyptians used for themselves, and which impelled the Greeks to coin the word "Egypt," which has spread over the world as the name for the country.

However, "Egypt" has never been used by the Arabs or other Semitic neighbors of the country. Today's official name for Egypt in prevailing Arabic is *Misr,* meaning "red mud." Compare this with the name used in the Old Testament—*Mizraim*—a plural form.

Returning to the ancestors living in this happy, sunny land, however, we see that in the early dawn of their career, religion played the motivating part of their culture. This was common in all early civilizations, but in Egypt the religious element gravitated into the hands of a powerful priesthood whose hold was never successfully challenged or overthrown by the Pharaohs, nobles, or serfs of Egypt.

With this in mind, the achievements of Moses at the court of Pharaoh become more easily understood. Since the ancient Egyptian priests early developed feats of magic through engineering to impress the people and the monarchs of their ability to control the supernatural, Moses confounded his adversaries by the type of steps he took to convince them at their own game, thus terrorizing Pharaoh into giving in to his determination.

However, the religion of early Egypt soon brought out two governing trends—the worship of the sun, and a preoccupation with life after death. This latter resulted from a conviction that the after-life was much the same as on earth, only so much more permanent that life here on earth was to be considered merely a preparation for the more lasting existence hereafter. Thus the tomb was glorified as an eternal home, and the homes built for the living were so simple that none have come down to us.

These two trends, intertwined, brought on the Pyramids.

After the primitive method of burying the dead in holes in the ground became outgrown, important Egyptians built flat-roofed tombs called by archaeologists *mastabas*. These were enclosures containing an antechamber for the living to present offerings; a few rooms for frescoes and reliefs portraying the servants, possessions, and occupations of the deceased to make him feel at home in his life after death; and, finally, a sealed-up room for the statue, or likeness, of the departed, done with great exactness, so that his spirit could easily find him after death.

This trend of belief brought on the art of mummification and painstaking embalming, a process that took as much as five months to complete. The mummies were then protected by being put into massive form-fitting cases, with the owners' exact features carved or painted on the various cases. Following along these lines of religious belief, many of the possessions, from the furniture down to the dishes, clothes, and toys of the departed, were enclosed in the tomb for future use. In early days, even slaves and horses were slaughtered and buried with their masters.

Since such a specialized form of theology brought permanent after-death peace to only a few, it evolved into an autocracy for Egypt. Obviously only the king and nobles could command the wealth and services of priests to embalm and preserve them, and of artists and handicraftsmen to furnish their tombs. The masses of common people soon fell behind in the race for salvation. No account has come down to us that they were ever mummified or given beautiful tombs. They instead became slaves, people without heavenly hope, terrorized thus into labor gangs and a servile status.

The local rulers of segments of early Egypt soon claimed relationship with the sun, the supreme god of Egypt, and took the name of "Ra" or "Ammon" with their other names. They soon grew impressed with the mystic symbolism of the setting sun, and built their tombs on the western shore of the Nile, growing convinced that they would merge with the sun in after-life.

These beliefs would be only of academic interest if they did not lead to such great effects. They ended by stimulating the Egyptian people to develop primitive engineering, architecture, and navigation, later methods of writing and sculpting, metal-working, stone-cutting, all of which lie at the root of our own scientific methods today. The Egyptians learned lessons that thus have direct interest to us.

About the year 3500 B.C. Egypt was united into one kingdom. King Menes (we know him only by his Greek name) united Upper Egypt (the long, narrow shores of the Nile) with Lower Egypt (the wide delta at the river's mouth), and built a new capital on the border between them. It was called the city of Noph, and is mentioned four times in the Bible.[2] Its name has come down in history to us as Memphis (or "Menes-Nophis," as written by much later Greek historians).

---

[2] Isaiah 19:13; Ezekiel 30:13; Jeremiah 2:16; 46:14.

Later on, King Zoser, when planning his mastaba, or traditional tomb, made it bigger and more extensive, with temples and
subordinate tombs, designed by the skill of his engineer-architect
Imhotep. However, Imhotep made refinements by raising a recessed
second roof above the original top of the tomb, for a mysterious
reason, and later two more above that. The result was a step-shaped
pyramid, and in this Zoser was buried. It can still be seen today
on the desert plateau inland from Memphis.

This startling and thrilling edifice, which looked so much more
grand than anything erected before, started a new idea in tombs.
Succeeding Pharaohs adopted it immediately. Three successive
Kings—Cheops, Khefren, and Mycerinus (best known by their
later Greek names)—elevated the lofty ones at Gizeh. These are
the supreme efforts of Egypt to crystallize the beliefs of its kings
and priests. So magnificent was this result, that it has defied the
centuries of time and invasion, and come down for all of us to
see and admire.

The building of these Pyramids demanded monumental architectural planning, exacting cooperation of the priests to indicate
the location and approach to the Pharaoh's tomb, and unimaginable
perfection of engineering, plus recruitment of adequate labor
forces. Thus the Pyramids stand as eloquent evidence of the
civilization, wealth, and orderliness of government in Egypt far
back in the dawn of our history.

To see the Pyramids being built would have been a sight of
the ages. The story of how it was done has come down to us
partly from Herodotus, who probably picked up tales from
descendants of the Pharaohs, and partly from the studies of
modern archaeologists and students.

It is estimated that the big Pyramid of Cheops took thirty
years to build. Work could only go on when the Nile was in flood,
allowing the heavy stone blocks we all can see today to be floated
to the base of a ramp leading up the face of the plateau.

Rough limestone was cut in the Mokattam hills from quarries
still to be seen near the largest mosques of Cairo. Ferried across
the Nile after being cut to measure, they were dragged up the

ramps and into place. It is figured that over 2,400,000 different blocks, each weighing over twenty tons, were needed for the Great Pyramid alone.

The building was done with great care according to specifications set down by the priests. Each Pyramid sits exactly facing the four cardinal directions. The slopes of the faces vary from forty-five to fifty-one degrees. The outside slopes were not rugged, as they are today. Instead, they were faced with fine limestone to make them smooth and even. (Note some of the facing still clinging to the top of the middle Pyramid.) This fine limestone was also brought across the Nile from underground quarries near Helwan.

When finished at last, the Pyramid stood as the culmination of all of Egypt's learning. As the eternal home of the monarch, it was considered indestructible and impregnable. The Pharaoh's mummy was placed in a stone sarcophagus and hidden in the heart of the Pyramid, with the access passages blocked by heavy granite plugs. A temple on the eastern face, connected by a sloping causeway with a landing on the floodstages of the Nile, allowed priests and slaves to attend to the dead king's rites.

However, the Pyramid symbolized the apogee of life to the entombed Pharaoh—it identified him with the sun. The degree of the slope of the Pyramid is conjectured to be equal to the slant of the sun's rays in midafternoon, with the idea that the monarch could mount up on these to Ra, his sun-father.

This close identification with life in the sun probably explains why the Pyramids do not possess the inscriptions, furnishings, and earthly belongings as was the custom in lesser, later tombs.

That is the story of the Pyramids. Now, leave your cool gardens, mount your camels, and follow up the road to the base of the Great Pyramid to admire from even closer range its size and agelessness for yourselves. And then—the Sphinx!

The Sphinx

The Sphinx crouches in the shadow of the second Pyramid, that of Khefren. It is the largest sphinx "in captivity" compared to all its smaller brothers in the land of Egypt, but it is dwarfed by the soaring Pyramids behind it.

The Sphinx is an animal with a semireligious symbolism. With the body of a lion, denoting courage and strength, and the head of a man[3] to represent wisdom and dominion, it was early identified with protecting the holy places of the Pharaohs.

Yet the Sphinx[4] of Gizeh has taken pre-eminence not only because of its size but because it later became venerated religiously. A tablet found between the paws records that King Thothmes dreamed in that very spot that the Sphinx complained of neglect in the face of the encroaching desert sands and asked Thothmes to venerate and protect it as the soul of his ancestors. The King immediately had the statue repaired, and the priests built a temple in front of it.

Today, when you dismount from your camels, you will walk into this temple to see the faultlessly cut granite blocks, each fitting together without mortar, forming all that is left of the temple. Floors of golden alabaster, a typically Egyptian stone from far up-river, give additional evidence of the ancient structure's workmanship.

Then, a walk up the sloping causeway leading to Khefren's Pyramid gives an excellent profile view of the recumbent, lime-stone Sphinx. It has now been entirely excavated, so that the outstretched paws stand free of the sand. Like all sphinxes, its tail curves gracefully up to the small of its back, and a little queue, or braid, spreads down the backbone from beneath the royal cap.

The eroding work of centuries of sandstorms on the body and breast of the Sphinx has left the surface rough and uneven. The sardonic expression on its face still exists, although it was badly disfigured from the days when the Moslem Mamelukes used it for target practice, since such a figure was idolatrous in their eyes. The expression, which looks as if indeed it had just posed its ancient riddle,[5] is matchless and brings on that feeling of mysticism which still lurks in the air of Egypt, especially when you watch the evening shadows creep over the face of the desert.

---

[3] Some maintain that this beardless Sphinx has a woman's head.

[4] A Greek word, Cairo dragomans pronounce it "Sphing-gis."

[5] The riddle: "What creature walks on four legs in the morning, two at noon, and three in the evening?" Evident answer: man.

Up to Luxor

That was quite a lesson for half a day, most travelers will agree, on returning to modern, busy Cairo, a city almost oblivious of the great stone storytellers out there on the desert.

Cairo's modern attractions are varied enough to be enjoyed by all, and its shops and clubs likewise. Sporting events out on Gezirah Island; an opera in the modern opera house; and diplomatic doings of various sorts will bring everyone back to the twentieth century, as will also the sight of a celebrity or two lingering over in Cairo between planes.

While driving around the city, one should make a detour to include the Nilometer, an ancient invention that enabled Egyptian agronomists to gauge the size of the year's grain crop.

However, before long a trip to Luxor should be planned. Luxor is the modern resort city 650 miles south of Cairo, far "up" the Nile, located on the site of ancient Thebes. Regular air services run up daily in three hours, and a train makes the journey overnight, with sleeper and diner service.

The main reason the tourist should visit Luxor is to see the wondrous remnants of Egypt's "Middle Kingdom." That is the term given to the Fifteenth, Sixteenth, and Seventeenth dynasties, whose reigns succeeded the Fourteen dynasties of the first age of Memphis. About 1800 B.C. a group of mysterious invaders overran the delta of Egypt, and this made the Pharaohs turn to Thebes, far up the Nile in Upper Egypt, as their independent capital.

Most famous of the Middle Kingdom[6] rulers was Akh-naton, who led a crusade against the all-powerful priests, and overthrew their supremacy and rituals. However, during the short reign of his youthful successor, Tut-ankh-amen, the priests managed to reinstall themselves; and when the young King died at the age of eighteen, they gave him a funeral and a tomb of such consummate

---

[6] "Old Kingdom" is the earliest period of independent ancient Egypt (First–Fourteenth dynasties); "Middle Kingdom" of Thebes (Fifteenth–Seventeenth dynasties); "New Kingdom" at Memphis (Eighteenth–Thirty-third dynasties). This division was made by Manetho, a historian of the third century B.C.

richness as to stun the whole modern world thirty-seven centuries
later. Such a pompous funeral is evident proof of their gratitude
to the young ruler. The next pharaoh was Hatshepshut, a woman,
who dressed like a man; had herself portrayed with a beard in
statues and hieroglyphs; and, incidentally, tried to eradicate
Akh-naton's memory from history by defacing many of his signa-
tures and portraits, replacing them with her own.

The most notable contrast of Luxor with Memphis in the eyes
of the traveler is the absence of pyramids. The Middle Kingdom's
rulers were buried in deep tombs carved into the rugged sides of
a dead, rocky valley far across the Nile. The reason probably is
that pyramids had "gone out of fashion," possibly because of the
superhuman labor involved in building them. During the dynasties
of the Old Kingdom, Pharaohs had built as many as twenty-two
pyramids in slavish imitation of their predecessors at Gizeh. But
these were so inferior in construction that they have been eroded
away into mounds and irregular-shaped piles.

Consequently, the rulers of Thebes chose their inaccessible
valley and ignored the pyramidal type of tomb. Yet their pious
regard for the symbolism of the pyramid lived on throughout
Egyptian history in the form of the obelisk, a tall column with
a "pyramidion" on the top, which raised the holy tribute to the
sun to a higher altitude, but by means of a cheaper and more
easily built method. Obelisks were later set up all over Egypt,
with elaborate hieroglyphs on them portraying the story of the
Pharaoh whom they honored.[7]

Visitors to Luxor should prepare to go sight-seeing as soon
as they have checked into the Winter Palace or the Luxor Hotel,
both built there specially for their comfort (though open in the
winter only; in the summer, things are more "ancient" in Luxor).
Crossing the Nile by launch, the visitor proceeds, traveling by
carriage or car, for an hour into the desert to the Valley of the
Kings. In this deep desert vale over fifty tombs were dug—at least
that many that we know of—into the stony side walls.

---

[7] Obelisks enchanted the Romans, and several of them were taken to
Rome and Constantinople. Today, there are more genuine obelisks outside
Egypt than in.

These tombs consist of long, sloping galleries (whose walls are heavily inscribed) which end with a high-ceilinged chamber. Here the royal mummy was interred in its sarcophagus and shut up with the most priceless royal possessions in a series of housings, put inside of each other within this restricted area. Smaller anterooms contained the royal furnishings, chariots, and the whole range of the ruler's possessions down to grain and seeds for his future crops.

Despite all these precautions, and the very remoteness of these tombs, robbers soon plundered them of their riches. Only Tut-ankh-amen's hidden resting place—and some others that are thought to be still missing from the list of buried kings—have escaped their depredations. Even the Holy Pyramids had been broken into as early as these historic days. Such human cupidity alarmed the priests of yore so much that they opened some of the tombs themselves to rebury more securely many mummies whose concealment was endangered by the rumors concerning the location of their resting places. One tomb yielded over eleven royal mummies when discovered over a century ago.

A side visit to the Valley of the Queens will show the remains of Hatshepshut's three-tiered temple outside her tomb; and then back to Luxor on the Nile, whose narrow green band of verdure is the only contrast to the gray desert on every side.

Luxor is equally famous for its great temples—Karnak and Luxor—erected in the second millennium before Christ. Mammoth lines of soaring columns, exotically carved, avenues of sphinxes, and mysterious courtyards doing honor to Egypt's religion and culture must be seen here—and on foot—to be admired as the inspiration of many later races, including the Greeks, who modified this architecture into a form that is used all over America today.

Gateway to Africa

The Nile, which flows past Luxor, comes from the heart of Africa. The actual source of the great river was never discovered by the ancients, and it therefore became a god very early in their religious development. However, to us today, its valley is the gateway to the whole heart of Africa, a travel field that has grown deservedly popular with overseas travelers.

Those who have more time than the usual cruise passenger or average vacationist can head south from Luxor. One hundred and fifty miles up-river lies Assuan, site of the immense British-built dam which has ended the cycle of Nile floods, and supplies water proportionally to modern Egypt all year round. Partially submerged above the dam is the Greco-Egyptian temple of Philae.

At near-by Shellal, regular Nile steamer services proceed southward into the Nubian desert. Along the way the boats pass the enormous seated images of Abu-Simbel, erected by Pharaohs who pushed their frontiers this far up the god-river. These majestic temples, existing over 3,000 years, are now threatened with flooding when the Nile's waters rise behind the new High Assuan Dam a-building far to the north. International engineering and financing have been called into a campaign to hoist the massive complex of these rock-temples on hydraulic jacks up to the new elevation of the Nile, transformed into a lake, to give them a new spell of eternity.

Treasures on Display

When you get back to Cairo, the first thing you will want to do is to see for yourself the treasures that were taken out of Tut-ankh-amen's tomb. These are the principal attractions today of the Egyptian Museum of Antiquities, a noble building in the heart of Cairo.

Voluble dragomans take all tourists, with manifest pride, down the long line of glass cases exhibiting the art and furniture of Tut's time. You will see statues of the King in hunting or court style. His chairs, his necklaces, his beds, his weapons, his royal boat, statues of his overseers, his toilet articles and costumes, are here displayed as if made yesterday. But the supreme thrill is still ahead.

A steel-barred inner room contains the mummy cases and jewels of the pampered youth. Each case, designed to match the contours of his body and to fit faultlessly inside an outer case of the same shape, is made out of beaten gold and adorned with lapis lazuli, carnelian, and turquoises, inset into exquisite designs. Gold was a metal used by Egyptians from earliest times in honor of its sunshine-color and its quality of reflecting the sun's rays so gloriously.

In the King's hands are held the emblems of his office—the hook and the flail—symbolizing power of life and death over his subjects. The wide-eyed expression of authority makes us pause to imagine a conception of how the King must really have looked. On his forehead is the double insignia representing lordship over Upper and Lower Egypt. From his chin extends the gold case containing his ceremonial beard.

The necklace of pink carnelian and blue turquoise lying on the King's chest is still so gorgeous to our eyes that modern-day ladies go out and buy expensive copies of it in Cairo's bazaars to wear with their evening dresses and formal gowns.

Tut's mummy is not on display, as the present government feels that this would be disrespectful. Its hiding place is not commonly known. Other mummies have also been taken from the Museum for more careful protection, but the rich sarcophagi, the countless jeweled ornaments, combs, necklaces, bracelets, earrings, articles of adornment and costume accessories can be seen in the Museum on every hand. This is truly a supreme show, and no one can ever dedicate too much time to it.

While in Cairo, there is one more "must" trip to take, and that is an afternoon drive to Memphis, or rather to the site of ancient Memphis.[8] This will prove to be of matchless interest.

It is necessary that a dragoman accompany you in order to hire the camels or donkeys, and to instruct the chauffeur thoroughly. Drive across the Nile and down through Gizeh, past the verdant grounds of Cairo University, and soon you find yourself back in ancient Egypt. The peasants, or *fellahin,* who crowd the road have changed their ways of doing things hardly at all since the days of the Pharaohs. Their blood is a little more mixed, and their religion has shifted to Islam, but their life has altered hardly a whit.

---

[8] Memphis, Tennessee, took its name from ancient Memphis, because it, too, was built at the head of a great, navigable delta.

Canals lead in from the great river. Peasants raise the water to their irrigated patches by the methods of their ancestors—a wooden barrel-screw which they turn by hand; or a wooden water wheel revolved by a plodding, blindfolded bullock. Their houses are flat-roofed and covered with straw. Our thoughts go immediately back to the Bible, where the children of Israel were made slaves to build "bricks" for their masters' homes. Bricks in Egypt still consist of slabs of mud "reinforced" by sticks of "straw," or by the long-dead shocks of grain that are kept piled up on the roofs to be seasoned, at the same time affording the occupants a little insulation from the hot sun.

The peasants pile heavy loads on their donkeys, and wear cotton covers on their heads, even as the ancient Pharaohs did (even the Sphinx wore one—made of stone), for the sun is remorseless all year round out in the open. Thick groves of palms show us that we are indeed in Africa. Bulrushes on the muddy shores of the Nile remind us of Moses and Pharaoh's daughter. Papyrus, the ancestor of paper (even of the word), was a riverside plant that the Egyptians learned to beat into a surface on which to paint their hieroglyph messages.

At last you will reach Memphis—or rather where Memphis used to be. Its site today is merely a sandy plain dotted with palms. The great temples and tombs have all tumbled into decay; the half-million inhabitants have vanished. Like its great empire, it is a tomb.

The Egyptians were the first to learn that their ostentatious riches only led to their downfall. The magnificent wealth created by their indefatigable craftsmen in their constant race to furnish the tombs and pyramids only served eventually to attract waves of invaders to the land of the Nile through the centuries, grinding its cities to powder. The curses in the Old Testament on the materialistic city of Noph have come true.

All that could be found here were two giant statues of Rameses the Great, and an alabaster sphinx. Rameses was the founder of the New Kingdom that followed the era of Luxor. He brought the capital back to Memphis, where it remained for nineteen dynasties. One of Rameses' statues now stands erect in front of Cairo's railroad station. There we can look up to his smiling countenance, his granite figure that is twenty-seven feet long, his neat vestments. This statue tried in stone to symbolize the greatness of Rameses. So vainglorious was he that he embarked on invasions of near-by Asia, conquering Syria and Mesopotamia. Rameses is considered to be the Pharaoh who "let Moses' people go" and then changed his mind disastrously.

Before leaving Memphis, stop to view the stately Step-Pyramid of King Zoser,[9] the ancestor of the true Pyramids, and take a ride by donkey out behind it into the desert to see the beautifully preserved tomb of Tyi, a typical mastaba of a royal overseer, complete with false door, colored reliefs, and vivid pictures of the life that was ancient Egypt.

Near-by is the underground Serapeum, a tunnel-tomb containing the burial chambers of twenty-four royal sacred bulls. This will remind us that, as Egypt grew old and weak, her religion grew decadent and chaotic, so that veneration was paid to bulls, to turtles and falcons, and eventually even to beetles. The "Apis" bull of Memphis, who after death joined the god Osiris in eternity, became the later Greek deity Serapis,[10] patron of the last personal sepulchral tombs of pre-Christian Egypt.

As you motor back in the late afternoon, the desert escarpment rises above you. Your road follows the line where "the desert meets the sown." A mile away you will see the Great Pyramids outlined against the setting sun. This enchanting vista will bring home to you the mystery, the power and the skill of the ancient Egyptians, the most remarkable trail-blazers of world culture, who laid the foundations for much of the civilization that we take so much for granted today.

End of Ancient Egypt

In the year 528 B.C. Egypt was conquered by Cambyses the Persian, son of the empire-builder Cyrus. Thereby ended the existence of independent, creative Egypt. The great and glorious

---

[9] Also called the Pyramid of Sakkara.

[10] This was the name borne by the British man-of-war defeated by John Paul Jones in 1779.

sweep of three thousand years was over. The Persians sacked and burned Memphis, ending the New Kingdom's last dynasty.

Almost two hundred years later came a still mightier conqueror—Alexander the Great—who made Egypt a province of his own as he in turn swallowed up all of Persia.

Alexander fell heavily under the sway of Egypt's mystic past. He plunged into the desert to the remote temple of Ammon-Ra to investigate the religion of the Pharaohs. In the year 334 B.C. he founded the new city of Alexandria in his own honor. When he died in Babylon a year later, he left Egypt under the control of his General Ptolemy, a Macedonian Greek who founded a dynasty of petty "Greekified" rulers.

Under the Ptolemies, Egypt turned away from Africa and, for the first time, out toward Europe. As Memphis decayed into oblivion, multipillared Alexandria grew into the flourishing capital of the country. Located on the Mediterranean at the farthermost western edge of the Nile delta, beckoning the ships of the world by the light of its magnificent lighthouse, it was free of the incubus of Egyptian traditionalism. It stood for the pre-eminence of Greek culture over the remnants of the old. Egypt's dynasties, kings, and even place names have thus come down to us in their Greek forms. ("Egypt," "Memphis," "Thebes," "Heliopolis," "pyramid," "obelisk," "sphinx," and "Apis" are all Greek words.)

The last of the Ptolemies was the storied Cleopatra. This irresistible and irresponsible young woman was mostly Greek by blood, yet she has symbolized the lure of Egypt in the pages of history. Using the glamorous cosmetics developed by the ancient mistresses of the Nile, adopting various ways of life inherited from the Pharaohs, she struck the fancy of the European historians of her day. By playing fast and loose with her wiles, she brought about a crisis in the affairs of the Roman Empire.

But she lost her dangerous game. In the battle of Actium off the coast of Greece in 31 B.C., she abandoned her lover Mark Antony to defeat and fled back home to commit suicide.

With her death Egypt became a Roman province, the granary of Rome, the home of the valuable grain fleets that plied grandly across the Mediterranean to the hungry city on the Tiber.

The Copts

That peaceful, prosperous Roman period of Egypt's history would be imperceptible to travelers in present-day Egypt, except for the Copts, a sect of Christians descended from the early believers of Alexandria. The Copts of today, who have survived centuries of the Moslem flood, pride themselves in being the direct heirs of the independent thought of ancient Egypt as well as of primitive Christianity.

A small minority, they nevertheless participate heavily in the business community of the country. The mid-Nile city of Assiut is their stronghold. Their bishops until recently held suzerainty over the official Coptic church of Ethiopia. This is the result of the activities of fourth century Coptic missionaries who worked their way up the Nile to one of its sources in Ethiopia and converted those distant tribes to the Christian faith. Monasteries and ruined churches in Egypt's desert wilds attest to the hold that Christianity had in Roman Egypt. St. Mark himself lived in Alexandria.

Alexandria, being the most cosmopolitan city of the eastern Mediterranean during Roman days, sheltered a large colony of Jews and Christians. Later on, rival sects of Christians often turned the great port city into a rioting shambles. Today, a solitary pillar in the slums of that city, misnamed Pompey's Pillar, stands as a monument of gratitude from the decimated citizens of the city to Diocletian, Roman Emperor, for sending them food and protection after a destructive wave of commotion in the beginning of the fourth century.

The Moslems

Cairo today is an eloquent story of what happened to Egypt after the prosperous days of the Romans and the brief reign of the Christians ended. From across the near-by Red Sea, from the wild deserts of Arabia, in A.D. 650, came fanatical tribes recently converted to a new religion called Islam. They overran Egypt with no difficulty and captured the great city of Alexandria. To the flames went the massive library filled with priceless documents; and the lofty Pharos lighthouse, wonder of the ancient world, sank beneath this hostile onslaught and lost its position of eminence in the world.

Cairo is the largest city of the Mohammedan world. Founded as the City of Victory in the tenth century by the Arabs, it has taken over the mantle of Damascus and Bagdad as Islam's most active religious center. The fellahin of Egypt became Moslems, their blood mixed with Arabs', their Hamitic language turned into a Semitic-Arabic dialect over the centuries. Look around you in Cairo, and you see a proud Moslem capital.

Upon the desert plateau rising to the east side of Cairo stand the great mosques of Hassan and Mohammed Ali. The Mosque of Hassan is a huge structure of the fourteenth century, plain, bare, but venerated. The latter, however, is particularly beautiful. Erected only a century ago in honor of modern Egypt's founding monarch, Mohammed Ali,[11] its walls are of alabaster, its carpets priceless, and its chandeliers most breathtaking when lighted. A third mosque, El Azhar, is today a theological university whose fanatical students irritate the sensitive nerves of the Moslem world into a flaming mood.

This part of Cairo is typical of the Moslem world. The veiled women, the befezzed men, the all-masculine cafés, the minarets and bazaars, are samples of the way of life found everywhere in the Near East. Brought in from Persia and Arabia are the cabarets where the insinuating music of an Oriental trio is accompanied by buxom girls whose sinuous "dancing" movements have been ecstatic to centuries of blasé Moslem men, but scandalized super-modern Americans at the Chicago World's Fair in 1893.

Most intriguing in Cairo are the extensive bazaars of the Mousky district. Here small shops fronting on winding narrow streets contain treasures fascinating to Western shoppers. On display are brocades from India or Damascus; perfume essences from Arabia; jewelry and bracelets from Syria; ivories and ebonies from Africa; silks from China; leather slippers from Morocco; beautiful alabaster and scarabs from ancient Egyptian soil, together with skillfully made brassware and leather goods

---

[11] An Albanian guerrilla leader under the Sultan. Reigned from 1810–48.

turned out by present-day Cairene artisans. Cleopatra's eye-darkener, mysterious *kohl* from ancient Arabian formulas, can be obtained on every hand.

Shopping in Cairo is a fascinating experience, but you need to have your wits about you. Remember that Oriental procedure through the years has been a matter of "haggling" over prices. If you shop for something that might be quite expensive, i.e., a carpet, urn, or necklace, the proprietor will serve you with Turkish coffee or Persian tea, during which time no talk of prices is entertained. However, when the negotiating duly begins, the price quoted is purely a nominal starting point; your own counteroffer should be less than you expect to pay. From then on the gap narrows. However, if the proprietor refuses to accept your price, start bargaining on something else, and often he will combine the two into a satisfactory total. Otherwise, leave the store politely, and you will see if your price would obviously mean a loss to him.

Such a process for shopping sounds devious and irksome to Westerners, but it often leads to excellent bargains. However, there is a move now under way to abolish "haggling" in favor of fixed prices. The newly created Tourist Police Force, which watches over the safety and contentment of foreign travelers in the country, is studying such a step, although it would be sanguine to say that they could very quickly overcome the tradition of the centuries.

The Touch of Europe

Yet Cairo is not entirely a pure Moslem city like many towns in Arabia, Iraq, and Syria. A heavy influx of European ways has insinuated itself into the life and outlook of this ten-century-old city. This European influence began a century and a half ago.

In 1798 Napoleon Bonaparte landed in Egypt and at the Battle of the Pyramids smashed the ruling clique of Mameluke freebooters. Even though Napoleon fled shortly afterwards by sloop when Lord Nelson sank his fleet in Aboukir Bay, Mohammed Ali's subsequent regime turned gradually toward Europe. Once the guerrilla-chieftain-turned-administrator unified Egypt under his strong government in the name of the Turkish Sultan, he brought in engineers, scholars, traders, and diplomats from infidel lands to the northwest. During his reign, Champollion, Mariette Pasha, and other archaeologists began sifting the sands of Egypt's deserts to unlock the tombs—the secrets of the lost civilization that had sunk back into the sands following Cambyses' successful invasion.

These scholars were able to complete their work enthusiastically due to a stone plaque[12] that was unwittingly unearthed by one of Napoleon's soldiers in 1799. This plaque contained an unofficial proclamation of Ptolemaic days written in three languages—Greek; Nilotic, or semi-Egyptian, Greek; and the hieroglyphs of ancient Egypt. Through careful study, this unexpected find turned out to be the invaluable key with which were unlocked all the secrets of hieroglyphic writing—thus giving vivid, exact meaning to the inscriptions on temple walls, obelisks, cartouches, statues, and sarcophagi throughout Egypt.

But Europe really descended on Egypt when the Suez Canal was completed by a French company in 1869. Almost overnight world commerce returned to the Mediterranean after five hundred years of seeking out more roundabout ocean routes. Steamships, unrecognizable progeny of Egypt's ancient reed barks, began calling regularly at the new ports of Port Said and Suez. Alexandria awoke suddenly from its long lethargy and sprang from a sleepy village into an international port. Italians, Greeks, Britishers and Frenchmen flocked to Cairo to operate the booming business of the new era. In 1882 a British army followed suit when Egypt went bankrupt. For thirty years afterwards Lord Cromer and Lord Kitchener made Egypt the anchor-stone for Britain's expanding African empire. In 1914 the British detached Egypt from her allegiance to Turkey and followed this by granting her independence in 1922. Its former King, Farouk, is the descendant of the line of Mohammed Ali, and was an aspirant for the position of leader of the Moslem world.

Egypt is still in the mainstream of world ideas. Its ruling classes wear Western clothes, spend their vacations in Europe,

---

[12] Known as the Rosetta Stone because of its discovery near the Rosetta mouth of the Nile. It now can be seen in the British Museum in London.

speak English and French, and their women doff their veils.
Cairo, albeit a Moslem city to the core, has great boulevards,
elegant hotels, luxurious suburbs like Heliopolis and Helwan,
and, most recently, a needle-like observation tower, with a restaurant revolving at its top.

Alexandria

Travelers who leave Egypt by plane usually "take off" from
Cairo after coming this far in their excursion program. But those
who depart by ship have a little more to see—since they must
needs travel down to Alexandria on the shores of the Mediterranean, reached either aboard a white train that steams across the
Nile delta, or by car over the Desert Highway.

The route passes through scenes that are fascinating. Here
is the delta—the flat expanse of land fertilized by the spreading
arms of the Nile, whose waters have flowed over three thousand
miles from Africa's heart to bring life and richness to these distant
fields. Towns of flat-roofed, straw-covered houses, unchanged by
the centuries, fly by. Lazy-angled masts of sailboats float along
invisible canals in the distance. The road that follows the rail
line bears a pageant of peasants on bicycles, on donkeys, in busses,
on camels, on foot. In the fields plows are often pulled by an ox
hitched up beside a donkey. The flat, green fields raise three
crops of grain and cotton a year. Figs, dates, and oranges galore
grow on the stately lines of trees.

As we get ready to leave Egypt, we think back on some of the
paradoxes we have noticed in this mystic land. For instance, why
are camels never portrayed on the reliefs and frescoes of ancient
days? Plenty of ducks, geese, bullocks, snakes, beetles, birds and
hawks feature Egyptian art, but no camels, or horses, for that
matter. Evidently this is a sign that those speedier animals only
came in centuries later with the Arabs, who brought them from
Persia, which had received them from Bactria in the heart of Asia.

Also, it becomes clear to us that Egypt's ancient heritage was
handed on to us in the West. Ancient Egypt fought its wars with
Assyria, Babylonia, Syria, Nubia, Libya, and Persia, yet those
lands show little lasting effect from their contact with Egypt.

Likewise, the patriarchs of the Old Testament showed contempt for the customs of the Egypt they had regarded as the "house of bondage."

Yet through Greece and Rome and the Crusades, and the western Arabs of Spain, our America has received, and cherished, the architectural, navigational, engineering, artistic, astronomic, cartographic, and inscriptional discoveries that grew up in this faraway land at the hands of the vanished bronze-skinned Hamitic tribes on the banks of Father Nile.

These great discoveries were expanded for us by the Greeks, but the Greeks would not have benefited from them or even absorbed them but for a curious group of middlemen known as the Phoenicians, for whose land we are now bound.

A Last Look

Alexandria is today a modern port city with a large Oriental section, and an ultra-European *corniche* of villas, bathing resorts, and hotels facing the blue Mediterranean breakers, cooled by the northern breezes into favor as official Egypt's summer capital.

Going aboard ship here, it is a solemn occasion in which to pack away just one more memory. Only sixty miles west of "Alex," on the seashore lies a patch of desert known as El Alamein. This reminds us that Egypt's history comes down to as recently as October 23, 1942. At El Alamein the British Tommies who had come to Egypt over six thousand miles of sea lanes from Britain and Australia, from New Zealand and South Africa, turned back the latest challenge to our own principles of life, while Egypt, which did not engender those principles, looked on with detachment.

Egypt did not give us our principles of democracy, nor our system of religion. We have rejected her cult of the dead and her rigid autocracy, but we have made our own the living discoveries she handed down to us through her conquerors.

THE LEVANT AND SYRIA

The Cedars of Lebanon

WHERE THE VIOLET-BLUE waters of the Mediterranean first meet the rising sun, there lies one of the world's garden spots. This lovely region is known generally as the Levant, or the "Rising Sun," from the name given it by the Venetian and Genoese sea merchants of the Middle Ages.

Today this pretty land is coming into its own. Located on one of the oldest battlegrounds of world civilization, it is yet one of the youngest United Nations and bears the name of Lebanon. On its flag flies the image of a cedar tree. The best harbor on this stretch of coast is its fast-growing, polyglot city of Beirut.

If you sail from New York on a gala Mediterranean Cruise, or on any of the regular ships in the trade, and travel as far into the Middle Sea as you can go, you will drop anchor in the harbor of Beirut, and see rising up before you the peaks of the Lebanons, which mark *finis* to the deep penetration of the Mediterranean into the land mass of the Old World. These mountains are real beauties. Direct from the blue sea they rise like a wall to eight thousand feet; and except in the dry months of summer, they bear crisp white snow in full view of the banana trees and orange groves of Beirut far below.

Small wonder that the Lebanon range struck awe into the minds of Old Testament writers. Ten times is it mentioned in the Bible, and its surroundings are mentioned even oftener. Cool and wooded, the Lebanons have stood for relief, high aspiration, and a source of water supply to the ancients.

Beirut—Heart of the Levant

Beirut is the haven of peace in the Near East. Located in the fertile region of oranges, dates, and bananas, protected from the desert heat and cold by the Lebanons, and tempered by the sea, it is a twentieth century Eden. It exists for doing business with all comers, and as the gateway to the finest pleasure-resort country of the Levant. In the winter, it remains warm and semitropical. In the summer its citizens have only to mount the mountain backdrop to a series of hotels and resorts, all ventilated by cool sea breezes.

Beirut's harbor is formed by a sharp bend in the eastern end of the Mediterranean Sea known as St. George's Bay, named for the saint who slew the famous dragon in this vicinity. A modern port allows most ships to dock almost in the center of town. The city itself has no historic, Oriental or Levantine appearance, but is semi-French, continental in its broad avenues and imposing buildings, European in the swift tempo of its traffic, its well-dressed crowds, its ultramodern movie theatres, bathing beaches, cabarets, cafés and shops.

As befits such a cosmopolitan metropolis, modern hotels dispense comfort and up-to-date hospitality from their advantageous locations on the sea front. The world's newest airport has just been completed on the seashore five miles south of the city's beaches, into which world-renowned airlines fly passengers from New York in only sixteen hours. Beirut is fast becoming the modern age's most flourishing foothold in a troubled Near Eastern world.

Yet, despite this encouraging show of modernity, you need only take a short walk from your hotel to observe that beneath the surface this land is indeed the Levant, or even the Orient.[1]

The faces of the people to be seen on every hand are Arabian, with an olive texture to the skin that we are used to calling

---

[1] Both words, from different Latin roots, mean the same thing: "rising."

Levantine. The street signs are written for the greater part in Arabic characters. The language spoken everywhere is definitely Arabic. On several streets there are the typical bazaars that show us we are in the Near East.[2] In them will be found wonderful things to buy, made here or in Damascus. Articles of gleaming silk brocades, such as bathrobes, dinner jackets; brassware in the form of big, Arabian-style trays, or lamps, or bowls; Oriental rugs in all varieties; cigarette boxes of inlaid wood—these are samples of what these fascinating bazaars have to offer.

An air of bustle unusual to the East characterizes Beirut, and well it might, for Beirut is located on very historic ground. It is the chief Mediterranean outlet for a host of peoples living inland on the desert—the Syrians, Iraqi, Arabians, Jordanians, and Persians. Oil-rich lands located on the barren inland regions pipe their production across the sands to ports on the coast near Beirut for shipment to Europe, thus saving the long and expensive tanker haul through the Suez Canal.

Beirut is the capital of an independent state—Lebanon. The people are Arabs by race; Lebanese by nationality; and predominantly Christian by religion—Christians in a huge Moslem sea that stretches out beyond the Lebanons as far as India and China. They are people who face the sea, and their tradition harks back through many centuries to their ancestors who created the first maritime traditions of history. These ancestors were the Phoenicians.

First Men of the Sea

The Phoenicians were the world's first middlemen. Like the modern Norwegians and Dutchmen, they lived close against the sea and took to it for a livelihood. Crowded on a narrow plain between the Mediterranean and the mountains, they had little other choice. By blood they were Semites of the same stock as the Syrians behind the mountains, and cousins of the Hebrews living to the south in Palestine. But being close to the sea brought out differences

---

[2] Near East is the traditional term for the Levant, Asia Minor, Egypt. During the war it was replaced by Middle East, a term more properly denoting Persia (Iran).

in aptitudes and customs that soon distinguished them from the Syrians in the same way that the Dutch differ now from the Germans, and the Portuguese from the Spaniards.

The Phoenicians may have developed boats of their own as soon as the necessity for survival impelled them to try the sea. But they were early given more expert lessons in navigation by none other than the Egyptians, who, during the second millennium before Christ, sent boats out of the Nile delta over to this coast to procure lumber from the groves of cedars on the Lebanon slopes. The Egyptians later came to depend heavily on the resin from these forests for the meticulous art of embalming demanded by their religion. During the years of these interchanges, the Phoenicians learned valuable lessons in navigation, commerce, and hieroglyphs, which they combined with other versions of the same skills that they imported across the mountains from their kinsmen in Mesopotamia.

Soon the chief harbors of the Phoenician coast began to vie with each other in sending out ships into the boundless sea. Four of these became predominant—Sidon, Tyre, Beirut (Beryta), and Jebeil (Byblos). Tyre and Sidon later far outdistanced the others in wealth and fame.

From the Lebanon Mountains, on a clear day the heights of the island of Cyprus can easily be sighted. Thus, early navigators had an objective for their frail craft. From Cyprus again, the peaks of Asia Minor are easily discerned; and once there, other islands and promontories lead gradually westward. In no time the Phoenicians had taken advantage of these land-sentinels to head far afield.

The Mediterranean is ideally designed for learning the art of sailing. Manageable distances, soaring mountains to guide helmsmen correctly, plentiful harbors for small craft, no fogs, and a mild average temperature were perfect conditions for primitive mariners. In addition, when heavy winds blew small ships out of sight of land, a few days of rowing or sailing in any direction would bring them against some coast, whence they could trace their way home. And steering by the stars was already worked out into a science for them by the exact observations of the astronomers of Babylon and of Egypt.

The Phoenicians really "covered the waterfront." By the year 1000 B.C. they had become familiar with the eastern Mediterranean. During the next two centuries they ventured still farther into the western basin of the Middle Sea. They founded colonies for trading with the tribes they met. Malta's strategically located harbor was so much home for them that their language and blood still predominate there. On the African shore opposite, they planted the trading post of Carthage. They even are credited with founding Marseilles at the mouth of the Rhone for trading with the Gauls. Soon they reached the Strait of Gibraltar, and despite all superstitious fears about its being the end of the world, they ventured outside of it and founded Gadir, now known as Cadiz, in southern Spain.

In later years their mariners, emboldened by their discoveries, sailed northward into the stormy Atlantic to the far promontory of Cornwall in southern England, where they traded Eastern luxuries for tin mined by the blue-tinted Britons. In the other direction they sailed far down the African coast. Tradition even maintains that they sailed completely around Africa on an assignment for the Egyptians, looking for the source of the Nile.

The result of these centuries of maritime monopoly brought great wealth to the cities of Tyre and Sidon. The lovely purple dyes made from seashells found in remote waters became so much in demand by the nobles and kings of the ancient world that "Tyrian purple" poured wealth into Phoenician coffers and founded the tradition of purple as the proper priceless color fit for a king. By carrying trade from Babylonia and Assyria across the sea to the civilized Mediterranean kingdom of Crete, and thence to Egypt, they soon found extra profits in reselling the luxurious fabrics, metals, and ornaments created by those artistic peoples. Their reputation for wealth came to the attention of the Old Testament prophets, resulting in much criticism. The lure of Tyre's luxuries was an ever-present temptation to the more austere Hebrew farmers living such a short distance to the south.[3]

---

[3] Culmination of this came with the marriage of Ahab, King of Israel, who married Jezebel, a Tyrian Princess. Jezebel brought in the worship of Baal, leading to the rebellion of Elijah, and his defeating the priests of Baal on the seashore at Mount Carmel.

Like many commercial peoples who followed them in history, the Phoenicians were not strong in creative arts or literature. No culture, temples, or architectural wonders grew up in their land. Their wealth eventually invited invasions from their relatives living in the less hospitable regions to the east. By 700 B.C. the coast of Phoenicia had been overrun by the Syrians and the Assyrians. The mariners of Tyre and Sidon then had to hire out to their new masters, and their explorations and golden era came to an end.

The Cedars of Lebanon

Time has been hard on a race of trees whose magnificence filled all the ancients with awe. The very word "Lebanon" in our ears almost conjures up "cedars" along with it. Many towns named Lebanon exist in the United States, because of the veneration associated with the word and its fragrant cedars throughout the Old Testament.

In Solomon's time cedars were so plentiful that Hiram, King of Tyre, not only contracted to supply all that were needed for the Temple then a-building in Jerusalem, but he engaged his Phoenician mariners to bind them into rafts and float them down to Joppa, the nearest port to the holy city.

Wars, wars, wars, invasions, and neglect have depleted all the cedars down to one lone grove that remains. A consistent enemy of the trees, since they lost their old grounds, are goats, which graze the hillsides so closely that cedar seedlings never get a chance to send up strong shoots.

The last grove is sixty miles from Beirut, and is so far up in the Lebanon range that the trees are snowbound for much of the year. The Cedars are thus Lebanon's favorite skiing resort. Located at the end of a very steep, winding road leading up from the coastal port of Tripoli, this grove rewards the quest of all visitors who take the time and don't mind the serpentine ride.

The cedars of Lebanon are not tall and graceful in silhouette, but are stocky, with thick foliage, and seldom exceed eighty feet in height. But in their cool greenness and ruggedness they stand for refreshment, invigoration and inspiration to the dwellers of a "dry and thirsty land" for hundreds and hundreds of miles all around their mountaintop retreat.

Lebanon Faces the World

The Lebanese, today's Phoenicians, are still citizens of the world as were their progenitors three thousand years ago. The breadth of vision engendered by the sea, and the easy access to the world's currents of thought, have preserved the distinctness of this narrow, verdant country through the ages.

After Phoenicia of old fell under the heel of the Assyrians, and then of their successors, the Persians, there followed master after master across the stage. Alexander the Great annihilated Persia's empire, and in the process proud Tyre "offered up the ghost." To capture the city, Alexander built a causeway out to its island walls; then starved it out and sacked it. Tyre today is therefore merely an Arab-type fishing town on a sandy peninsula south of Beirut. Sidon has likewise retreated into insignificance. After Alexander, came his General Seleucus, whose dynasty held on to the Levant until Rome took over in the last century before Christ. When Rome's Empire split in two, the Byzantine, or Eastern, half held on to the Lebanese coast until the Moslem incursions from Arabia overwhelmed it.

After the Moslems came the Crusaders, who landed here from bases on near-by Cyprus.

During the centuries of captivity, the people of the Phoenician coast were "hewers of wood" and "drawers of water"—and professional sailors—for whoever was in power. However, they dared to stand up alone, when the Arabs came, for Christianity. The rite of St. Maron had taken firm root in their affections. When all of the Christians of the Near East (except the distant Armenians) relapsed into Islam, the Maronites, or Lebanese of the coast, held out.

Thus the Crusaders, coming from all Europe to rescue Jerusalem in the eleventh century, landed on this hospitable coast and held it for a century and a half. The most striking remnant of their rule is to be seen in the rugged medieval castle known locally as the Krak des Chevaliers—high up in the northern Lebanons. A fortress in European style, with keeps, thick walls, dungeons, court halls, watchtowers, and gloomy passageways, its construction was so thoroughgoing that it has survived the centuries in its location high up on inaccessible crags. It can be visited on a day's automobile drive that can also include a stop at the cedars on the way back to Beirut.

After the Crusaders had been expelled by Saladin's Saracens, the lot of the Maronites was very precarious. The Ottoman Turks later conquered the Near East, and massacres were launched at various intervals. These became severer as time went on.

France, as the heir to the Crusaders and the power with the closest diplomatic contacts with Turkey, took special interest in the Maronites. In the year 1860, after a Lebanese uprising had been cruelly repressed by the Turks, the French secured concessions and special self-government for the harassed land.

This concession was so tenuous, however, and covered such a small extent of the Lebanon, that many of the inhabitants abandoned their beautiful land and sought a better life overseas. By now, over half of the Maronites have emigrated to Europe, North Africa, and the United States (where they are called Syrians). In all those countries, they have become well-to-do merchants and artisans.

World War I almost exterminated the Christian Lebanese. Turkey's declaration of war against France in 1914 ultimately unleashed a series of massacres as devastating as the ones inflicted on the Armenians a few years previously. Turkey's European ally, Germany, did nothing to stop this ordeal. Consequently, when the war ended, French forces lost no time landing at Beirut and proclaiming a protectorate over the whole region, including the bulk of Syria in the interior. The French were welcomed in Beirut, but had to bombard Damascus and expel an Arab dynasty before establishing their control there.

The peace treaties gave Syria and Lebanon over to France as a Mandate. For the first time Lebanon, in its original and natural frontiers, was separated from its Moslem neighbors. Full freedom of religion was enjoyed at last.

The French Mandate was terminated in the year 1943 during World War II, and the independence of both Syria and Lebanon was proclaimed by General de Gaulle and the British army of occupation which had rescued the region from the Vichy regime.

However, the massacres and the emigration have left Lebanon only half-Christian. This has made the modern republic resort to a unique experiment to balance the religious stresses in order to create internal stability. The constitution requires that if a Maronite Christian be president, the prime minister must be a Moslem, or vice versa. Seats in Parliament are parceled out on a strict, unchanging basis among the religious groupings—Maronites, two groups of Moslems, Greek Orthodox, Armenians, Greek Catholics, Jebel Druse Moslems, and Protestants.

America in the Levant

The cultural influence of the United States has become markedly strong in the Lebanon, thanks to the foresight of the Presbyterian Missionary authorities in organizing an American University in Beirut back in 1869. Visitors to Beirut should lose no time in motoring out to its lovely campus overlooking St. George's Bay.

Here American-style buildings, dormitories, playing fields, and laboratories are educating boys and girls from all Near Eastern races in the advantages of twentieth century humanistic, scientific, and medical achievements. The graduates of this institution have risen to important posts of power in many Near Eastern countries. Strongly oriented toward the West, yet conscious of their Arab nationhood and its place in the world, these graduates are most alert to the standards of American thought thanks to the breadth of their education.

Modern Lebanon has thus become a center of learning for its sister countries in its hinterland. The University of Beirut is on a par with Robert College at Istanbul in its influence in the Levant.

Across the Lebanons

No one should pay a visit to Beirut without going on to Damascus, only ninety-four miles inland from the sea. The route lies across the wall of the Lebanon Mountains.

Before saying good-bye to the warm Mediterranean coast,

however, let us make a beautiful detour of only twenty-five miles to see two vestiges of Phoenician days.

Motoring up along the blue sea, it is only eight miles to a narrow defile at the mouth of the Dog River. Here is the place where a custom grew up long ago for conquering generals to leave their "autographs." Rameses the Great testified to his greatness high up on a lofty rock. So did Sennacherib the Assyrian, and Pompey the Roman, and lesser lights of more recent invasions.

Continuing north the road passes some beautiful bays and promontories until it reaches Byblos, once a Phoenician city of prominence; now a quiet, half-Christian, half-Moslem town called Jebeil.

Standing amid the ruins of Byblos, one can be visibly impressed with the weight of history in this land. On one side are scattered pit-graves dating back to the earliest days of this site. Along the sea are two graceful pillars dating from Greek days, and a tiny harbor that served the Phoenician fleet. Inland stands a thick-walled Crusaders' castle. In between is uneven, rough land made up of the crumbled remnants of several successive cities. The town's name still stands for something important. It gave us the word "Bible" through the Greek word for "book," which was derived from this city, although history is unable to tell us what connection Byblos had with the evolution of books.

Now it is time to leave Beirut. A modern automobile will speed you effortlessly up a wide French military road from sea level to the pass over the Lebanons, 4,300 feet high. Stop for one last view. Down below there is the blue Mediterranean, beckoning the viewer westward, ever westward, toward Europe and America. There, with one sweep of the eye, one can view the coast of Phoenicia, whose mariners gave ancient cartographers a complete panorama of all the world that their limited means could comprehend. That narrow stage has been a lighthouse, a cultural beacon linking the knowledge of the West with the barren, turbulent desert lands we are now going to glimpse. Ports on that coast today are pumping oil from the Arabian deserts into stubby tankers—oil for the survival and the quickening of life in Europe.

Baalbek, the Inimitable

Across the Lebanon range there unfolds a fertile valley called the Bekaa, on the other side of which rise the Anti-Lebanon Mountains. The floor of the Bekaa is three thousand feet above the sea. It is good agricultural land. It originates two important rivers, the Litani, which flows south around the Lebanons into the Mediterranean; and the Orontes, which goes northward to the site of ancient Antioch and empties into the sea inside Turkey.

The people of the Bekaa, despite repeated massacres, are Maronite Christians, and their villages have the clean look of peasant towns in central Europe. Their women are unveiled, and their farms are well tended.

Thirty miles up this valley, on the far side, we come to a miracle. Rising up high above a small village are golden-brown columns of a lofty Roman temple. The village is called Baalbek.

There is something majestic in these ruins that attracts all travelers bound for Damascus to detour and linger here awhile.

This is a spot that has been sacred to the worship of the sun for countless centuries. Baalim, or the images of the sun that were the enemy of the prophets of the invisible God of Israel, were here honored by throngs of the faithful. There is no indication that this one spot was the only center of Baal-worship, but by a series of coincidences it has become the site of the loftiest temples in his honor.

Here at Baalbek—a site "sacred to the sun"—a copious spring bursts forth from a foothill of the Anti-Lebanons and flows into the Bekaa. The spring naturally became a crossroads supporting an important religious and trading traffic during ancient Syrian days. After Alexander the Great's time, the Hellenized inhabitants renamed the place Heliopolis, or "City of the Sun," and continued its holy rites. However, the Romans are responsible for the temples. Their motives were simple. Excellent golden stone was available here, and a lofty temple at this spot would serve to point up the glory of their Empire in building this overpowering edifice in such a remote spot.

Accordingly, 120 years after the birth of Christ, the Romans got around to elevating a temple that still is a wonder to us moderns. Heavy blocks of stone, massive in their weight, were piled up to form a platform sixty feet off the ground. On this were erected the loftiest columns of antiquity, eighty-five feet high, supporting a temple to Jupiter, their supreme deity equivalent to the Baal of the Syrians. A lesser temple to Bacchus was built close by. In front of the main temple was a huge courtyard, in the middle of which was erected the hugest altar in history—large enough to sacrifice a hecatomb of bulls. Beyond that is an octagonal forecourt.

A total restoration of this majestic pile has been done in miniature and can be viewed on the grounds. However, what is left is thrilling. Excavations carried out by the Germans fifty years ago have presented a site of rare beauty to our eyes.

Today, six lofty columns of the Temple of Jupiter rise high into the clear Mediterranean sky, a soft golden-yellow. Half the year the snowy tops of the Lebanon range furnish a striking backdrop to this combination. The labor of the ancients in erecting this temple to the glory of the highest religious concept they understood has outlived all the houses of commerce and pleasure that once filled this same humble village.

Entering the Baalbek enclosure, the traveler needs a good guide to show him clearly the many architectural features that made the temple so sumptuous. Fragments of a purplish stone called rose granite lie about, broken off shattered columns. This unusually tinted material was quarried a thousand miles away—in Assuan of Upper Egypt—then ferried down the Nile, across the sea, and up into these mountains. That huge altar was the supreme offering to Jupiter. A hundred bulls sacrificed in one day represented the epitome of human submission to the gods.

Many more of the stupendous columns would be standing today but for some Turkish governors. They found that iron rods bound the constituent blocks of each column together. Iron was precious for the art of war. Down came the columns for the bits of iron within.

The smaller Temple of Bacchus has many more columns upright, although one stands awry, leaning against the temple walls, as if to symbolize the vileness of medieval man in wrecking such

noble architectural work. However, the decorations of the lintels
of the temple door, and the proportions of the cella, or inner room,
once containing the statue of the god, are still complete enough
to be admired. This basic form of temple is the same one adopted
in Greece and Italy, and it should be advantageously viewed at
this spot for apt comparison.

Outside the temple a lively bazaar is carried on at all times.
Baalbek's enterprising inhabitants will sell everything, from
knitted skullcaps with matching pocketbooks, to an Oriental carpet,
while camels stand by to be photographed—for baksheesh,[4] of
course.

Baalbek must be seen for the thrilling combination of its
tradition and its matchless situation.

On leaving town, pause for a moment at the quarries where
Baalbek's golden rock was prepared for the builders. Here a
large base block, carved out for use in the temple, has lain abandoned in its place for eighteen centuries.

Damascus, Port of the Desert

Seventy-eight miles from Baalbek, by French military road
up and over the Anti-Lebanon range, an automobile brings the
traveler to Damascus, the oldest inhabited city of the world.

On the way, notice to the right the lofty snow-capped eminence.
That is Mount Hermon, which will be seen again from Galilee
to the south. Mount Hermon, snowy-peaked all the year round
amid a parched and dry land, rises over 11,000 feet into the skies,
a beacon to the desert peoples below. Here in Lebanon its name
is simply Jebel-es-Sheikh, or "Big Chief Mountain."

On its course through the Anti-Lebanons, the road crosses
the boundary from Lebanon into Syria. Until 1949 this line was
a formality. Now, because of differing financial policies of the
two states, and because of Syria's deep suspicion of foreigners
since the war with Israel, it means a stop, an inspection of pass-
ports, a checking of an important visa, and a search of the car
for arms. Then off one goes again, toward the desert.

---

[4] "Baksheesh" is the universal word for tip used all over the Near East
and in some of the Balkan countries.

Syria is the age-old name for this corner of the earth. It extends from the Mediterranean and the Anti-Lebanon Mountains down into the Arabian Desert and across those dry sands for four hundred miles to the Euphrates River. To the north lies Turkey; to the south the Arab Kingdom of Jordan and the sands of Arabia. And to the southwest, along the Sea of Galilee, lies Israel, the troubled, unsteady frontier line that is still shaken by occasional diplomatic earthquakes.

The capital of Syria is Damascus.

How this city has been able to survive the invasions and raids of the millenniums is a miracle. Its rivals of yesteryear—Babylon, Nineveh, Ur, old Bagdad—have disappeared beneath the sands. Empires that have captured Damascus have themselves crumbled into nothingness.

Perhaps this city has been too valuable to destroy. It is the port of the desert. Camel caravans plodding from Mesopotamia, Arabia, from Persia, head for this busy city on the edge of the sown. The lofty Lebanon ranges, which shut out the sea breezes and thus make a desert out of Arabia, give birth to two small rivers' that flow down through Damascus and then disappear into the desert. Sheltered by these mountains, and nurtured by this water, the city lives and works, and stands as the world's oldest crossroads.

It is a hard-working city. Its artisans, seated in their little, open-front shops, hammer out brasswork, cobble shoes, inlay tables with mother-of-pearl, carve ivory and rare woods. Out of sight, busy men, trained in age-old skills, interweave fabrics with golden thread that never tarnishes, and temper fine steel blades for priceless Damascus swords. Lively markets are stocked with the oranges of the oasis, and buy and sell everything from everywhere. The words "damask" and "damascene" were given by the world to products of fine workmanship that originated in the workshops of this city.

This preoccupation with the useful things to support life is what has undoubtedly saved Damascus from destruction. It never

---

' Named the Abana and the Pharpar in the Old Testament. "Are not [these] better than all the rivers of Israel?" said Naaman (II Kings 5:12).

was a proud imperial capital with rich temples and luxurious palaces to be looted. Its own Syrian kings never waxed powerful, but instead bent the knee to the Assyrian, the Chaldean, the Persian. Damascus lived for commerce, not politics.

In the time of Jesus, Damascus was no more important than Antioch, or Caesarea Philippi, or Philadelphia, or Palmyra—cities that lived in the style of Athens and grew rich as frontier emporiums of the Roman Empire. However, the whirlwind of the coming of Islam gave the city renewed pre-eminence, for it made the city the capital of the Moslem world for four centuries. Only the founding of Bagdad took this supremacy in religious matters away from Damascus, and just in time. For in the twelfth century, when the fury of the Mongols of Genghis Khan swept down upon the Moslem world, it leveled Bagdad to the ground. Damascus, however, opened its doors to the invader and was spared.

Motoring into Damascus after crossing the bare plains sloping down to the desert, one is impressed with the busy activities of this unusual city. The road leads into the city's heart, which now boasts a modern quarter built by the French, with fine hotels and several business and office buildings. Travelers will find the Orient Palace, the Omayyad, and the new Semiramis hotels equipped to serve them well, in the style of the capital of a new-old country. The Abana River flows underneath the main square, center of life for the industrious natives.

Visitors to Damascus lose no time in repairing to the old shopping quarter, where runs the "Street-called-Straight," probably the main bazaar thoroughfare for Damascus since the days of Nebuchadnezzar. Despite its name, it is a slightly winding narrow street as in all Near Eastern towns, protected from the sun by lattice work spread across it from roof to roof. On each side the small, open-front shops open out, with their proprietors squatting on carpets amid their wares. Some more elegant shops have glass fronts to entice the Western tourists who like more comfort and privacy. There is always a passing parade of veiled women, laden donkeys, bearded Bedouins, bare-legged men vending water from whole goatskins, and important men of the city dressed in faultless burnooses. This is a fascinating show to us, but our Western dress and mannerisms are many times more entrancing to the passing throngs who never miss a thing a foreigner does.

Shopping is irresistible here. The silk cloth and the brocades made gleaming by the golden or silver threads are woven into jackets, robes, and gowns. The expertly wrought silver daggers, brass trays, bowls of tinlike metal, lamps of brass, and ancient weapons of burnished steel can be bought at bargain prices after suitable haggling. Leather, in the form of deflated hassocks with bright geometrical designs, or shopping bags, or colored slippers, or portfolios, or suitcases, fills every shop. Damascene inlay, ivory articles, miniature camels of porcelain and wood, and, naturally, Arab-style robes and burnooses of all colors and qualities—these are part of the display in this port city of the desert.

While strolling down this Street-called-Straight, we can recall that St. Paul also came this way two thousand years before us; only he was led here by the hand, temporarily blinded by the brightness of his vision, to find peace and inspiration at the house of Ananias. There is a house on the edge of the busy bazaar section that is shown to foreigners as this very house, from whose windows Paul was lowered later in a basket to escape from the ire of his co-religionists who were discomfited at his conversion. Even if the original Ananias never lived in this house, its style could certainly not have been very different.

While still browsing through the bazaars, one suddenly comes out on Damascus' most resplendent building—the Omayyad Mosque. This edifice, with its long line of arched arabesque colonnades, and its wide-open courtyard to enable all the faithful to pray together on holy days, was constructed in the late Middle Ages. This was during a period of Arab resurgence after the defeat of the Crusades and the retreat of the fierce Mongols. Damascus' last golden age was put to an end when the Turks swept in in the fifteenth century and settled down to remain until the arrival of the French in our own times.

The great Omayyad Mosque shelters the tomb of Saladin,[6] victor over Richard the Lion-Hearted and conqueror of Jerusalem.

---

[6] His full name was Salah-ed-Din, or "Light of Religion."

There is also buried here one of the arms of John the Baptist, who ranks, like Jesus, as a lesser prophet in the Moslem tradition.

This mosque is sacred to the new Republic of Syria, for the Moslem populace here is very sensitive, and no Arab rulers resent the presence of nearby Israel more than those of Syria.

This unsettled atmosphere has prevented Syria from evolving into a stable state like the smaller Lebanon. The government was subject to violent overturns and assassinations.[7] Rather than develop a remunerative trade with Israel, or accept economic support from the United States, the Syrian regime followed a policy of strong opposition and hostility toward anyone who was an ally of Israel.

This culminated in 1951 with the placing of her army under Egyptian leadership with the purpose of evoking a spectre of united pressure against Israel. Syria even tried the experiment of establishing a political merger with Egypt in 1958 under the grandiose name of "the United Arab Republic." However, the union proved unworkable in the long run and Syria resumed her independent status in 1961.

---

[7] The word "assassin" originated in northern Syria. During the Crusades a band of Moslem fanatics was organized to prey on the invaders by killing them. Their name came from the fact that they were addicts of hashish to increase their ferocity.

HOLY LAND

Divided Land

THE HOLY LAND is triply holy. It is the stage for the storied events of the Bible—the cradle of Christianity—and the place where Islam's great Prophet Mohammed was last seen on earth.

Approaching this hallowed land from the sea, the first view one gets of it is not altogether prepossessing. The sea beats up on a narrow beach; the land stretches back in the form of a dry plain for an average of twenty miles before it slopes up into a range of low, barren hills. Behind those hills lies the arid depression of the Great Rift, here known as the Jordan Valley, beyond which begins the rocky Arabian Desert.

The green coastal belt here is only sixty miles wide, from Mediterranean Sea to Dead Sea. Its fertility is somewhat limited, as the land is green only after the winter rains. Patchy crops are raised then before the long unbroken months of summer sun come to dry up the landscape and to leave the land looking anything but fertile.

This strip of coastline was given the name of the Holy Land by generations of Christian pilgrims. To the peoples of the Near East it is known as Palestine, a name bestowed on it by the Greeks and derived from the Philistines, who were the first denizens of the coastlands. And, nowadays, the map shows a new-old name for most of this land—Israel, the official title for world Jewry to employ in place of the outdated Gentile name of Palestine favored by the Arabs.

Palestine's frontage on the Mediterranean covers 132 miles in all. This modest "window" on the Middle Sea fits in between the Isthmus of Sinai (which belongs to Egypt) and the Tyre-Sidon land of Phoenicia (belonging to Lebanon). It is broken by only two visible places of ingress. The first is the pocket harbor occupied by the ancient city of Joppa, now almost engulfed by the metropolis of Tel-Aviv and dotted with verdant orange groves. The other is fifty miles north. Here a headland known as Mount Carmel throws itself boldly across the plain to the very edge of the sea, and in its shelter lies the modern port of Haifa. There the coast bends around Carmel, forming the Bay of Acre, and makes room for the only first-rate harbor of the Holy Land.

The Holy Land is not beautiful, but it is holy—and to three great religions. It must be seen if only for that seeming paradox —a poor and barren segment of territory in which were shaped the thought-forces which have molded the modern world. As the Bible would phrase it—"the stone which the builders rejected has become the head of the corner."

The fact that these three religions are all monotheistic— honoring and worshiping the same one God—and that they have evolved closely from similar causes and been closely interconnected for many centuries has not brought harmony or concord to this harassed bit of semidesert land. But we in distant America have our institutions and history so impermeated with the ethics and the vital religion incubated in this land that we can never stay away from it when we are traveling in the Near East. Our very lessons taken from the Bible, from Sunday school, from sermons and catechisms, and our rules of morality and ethics come brilliantly to life as we trace the steps taken by the prophets and by Jesus and look on the hills and valleys where they wrought so mightily to show the power of God over material empires and conquering armies.

Divided Land

Palestine is today a land divided in two by an uncrossable wall —an Armistice Line drawn by United Nations mediators after the Israeli War of Independence in 1948. Since this is a military line and not an official boundary, travelers may not cross it, at least not until the countries concerned have entered into diplomatic relations with each other.

As the result of this partition, Palestine's historical sites fall into these respective sections of the country:

ISRAEL	JORDAN (ARAB PALESTINE)
Nazareth	Jerusalem (ancient section)
Mount Carmel	Jericho
Jerusalem (modern section)	Bethlehem
Sea of Galilee region	The Mount of Olives
Joppa	Garden of Gethsemane
Mount Tabor	Samaria
Armageddon	Bethel
Cana of Galilee	Hebron

Consequently, the traveler of today must decide beforehand which places in the Holy Land he wants most to see—for this decision determines the avenue of approach he makes from the outside world.

For instance, if you are in Damascus (as described at the end of the preceding chapter), and you want to see the historical places that are in Arab-held Palestine, then you should fly directly to Kalandia Airport north of Jerusalem, and motor into the Holy City. If, on the other hand, you prefer to see the Sea of Galilee and Nazareth, and also the many modern activities of the new Republic of Israel, then you board any of several air services and speed to the British island of Cyprus off the coast of Lebanon, a flight of only an hour and a half. Here you change to a connecting plane of the same airline and continue to Israel's great modern airport of Lydda, twenty miles from Tel-Aviv.

If you are in America, or western Europe, and are traveling by steamer to the Near East, your ship will take you either to an Arab port or an Israeli port, but *not to both*. You either are bound for Israel and steam into the port of Haifa directly; or you are bound for Egypt or Lebanon, and disembark at Alexandria, or Beirut, respectively.

If you are flying from America or Europe, several airlines will bring you to Lydda Airport, and others will come to Beirut or Damascus. But the airlines cannot serve both Arab and Israeli airports on the same flight.

Thus, if you want to see both sections of Palestine, you have to go to one first and then fly around by Cyprus to the other. But there are many difficulties regarding visas in this connection, so have your travel agency work out your routing carefully.

This division of Palestine is purely a political tie-up of a temporary nature. Israel is eager for friendly relations with its Arab neighbors and allows visitors to come in from any direction they choose. But the Arab lands, bound together in the Arab League, refuse to accept the idea of an independent Israel in their midst and thus are delaying the diplomatic relations that would open up the easy and direct routes of travel that were worked out in the Near East during the pre-war years. Travelers can cross the embattled Israel frontier therefore at only one point, the so-called "Mandelbaum Gate," a narrow crossroads in the northern outskirts of Jerusalem.

This political imbroglio is the result of the rivalry of races based on centuries of struggle and disagreements. History lies heavily on the Near East. That is why travelers must take a heady draught of history before going there. The inhabitants of those lands have been brought up on it—usually on the prejudices that come with too fervent a diet of it. Peoples are classified as to their religions, not their blood or ancestry, as we have seen in the case of the Lebanon. The paradox is that the Moslems and Jews, who in the main have existed on friendly and tolerant terms since the days of Mohammed, are now in sharp disagreement over Israel; while the Moslems and Christians, who have waged ceaseless wars through the centuries, now have no religious quarrel at all in the lands of the Fertile Crescent.

It is a further anomaly that the Jews and the Arabs are both descendants of the same Semitic race, and their official languages —Arabic and Hebrew—are closely related in sound and structure. The issue is thus, basically, not entirely a religious disagreement, but one based on differing ways of life. For Israel is definitely a state with a European orientation, working out a Western-style democracy and a socialized economy inside its religious refuge, while the Arabs hang on stubbornly to their ways of life based on the Koran and on the climatic influences in their methods of being.

The Face of Israel

Israel is definitely a twentieth century state and is employing all the inventions of the modern age of technology to make the barren land blossom as the rose. Travelers thus feel very much at home there; and because Israel occupies almost the entire coastline of former Palestine, it is more accessible. Consequently, the greater proportion of present-day travelers from America to the Holy Land come to Israel first.

The very bustle and energy of the new settlers in this ancient land captivates the foreigner. Comfort, luxury, and ease have taken a back seat while everybody pitches in to build. With a population that has soared from 650,000 to 1,900,000 in twelve years, and in a land with not many natural resources, this has been a necessity. And since the population comes from many different countries, speaking variegated languages, a strong hand from above assigning tasks to all has been essential to organize the citizenry into self-sufficiency, and even to furnish the bare essentials of shelter and alimentation for immigrants who arrived with no possessions except determination and courage.

This atmosphere is evident the minute you land on Israeli soil at Haifa, Israel's booming modern port. Haifa is an artificial harbor built by the British Mandate during the period between 1927 and 1933, complete with modern docks, warehouses, and railroad yards. In the days before the British rule, Haifa was a small Turkish settlement that had taken on importance from Jewish immigration in the nineteenth century, and from German Protestant missions. Before that, the important harbor in this curve of the coast was ancient Acre, a cluster of Arab mud houses that can be seen as a smudge across the bay. Acre existed in ancient days, and was the Crusaders' last hold on this coast, and was likewise the fortress that marked Napoleon's first defeat, back in 1799.

The beauty of Haifa's setting is that it has imposing Mount Carmel as a backdrop. Mount Carmel[1] is a long level ridge, whose highest point rises to 1,740 feet, extending for twelve miles from the plateau in the interior to the very edge of the Mediterranean. Today, Carmel is an up-and-coming residential district and summer resort, where every home basks in the unfailing sea breeze. Its inhabitants commute down into town aboard a handsome funicular subway.

But in Biblical days Carmel was the scene of one of the great events of history. Here came Elijah to challenge Queen Jezebel's priests of Baal, whom she had brought in from her native Phoenicia to subvert the God of Israel.[2] This is one of the few times that Hebrew history and associations came so close to the sea. Elijah's defeat of the sun-worshiping priests by calling down fire from heaven when their pleas to Baal failed and then by following up with his prophecy of a drought-breaking rain that would extinguish the flames re-established the pure religion in Israel on a firm basis.

Coming into Haifa, however, those days seem far away. Israel's new merchant ships and many foreign vessels and cruise liners await their turn to tie up at the overcrowded docks. Tankers are always in evidence, ferrying crude oil from faraway Venezuela to the huge refinery built by the British on the plain east of Haifa. That refinery marks the terminus of a long pipeline coming 354 miles across the desert from the Kirkuk oilfields of Iraq, a pipeline that is now bereft of oil since Iraq shut off the supply when Israel became an independent state.

Tourists are welcome in Israel. The latest types of buses and taxis are readily available. Prices are on the high side, since most of the products needed by this modern republic must be imported and paid for with a depreciated currency. However, compensating for the prices, the traveler will be met with proud courtesy. English-speaking young students and workers, either boys or girls, welcome the chance to show off their new homeland

---

[1] "Carmel" means "park" or "gardenland" and has inspired many towns in America to take its name.

[2] This graphic challenge is told in I Kings 18:19 ff.

to everyone coming from abroad. Sometimes these young people are *sabras*,[3] born in Palestine and moved by strong views about the hostility of their Arab neighbors; other times they are later arrivals from Europe, free and happy, but bitter over what they suffered in Hitler's camps.

Haifa is thoroughly modern and utilitarian. Shops and cafés, small hotels and businesses line the bustling streets. Restaurants and corner snack bars now proliferate in Haifa, most of them leaning toward the German style and taste. Haifa is caught up with the business of handling over seventy per cent of Israel's foreign trade and manufacturing articles of utility for the country. The refusal of the neighboring agricultural Arab states to trade with Israel cuts off many commercial opportunities, and has engendered more bitterness in the minds of the people of the land.

Shopping is becoming a more worthwhile activity every year. Ceremonial candlesticks, furs, leather goods, Yemenite filigree ornaments and olivewood souvenirs are some of the items to be obtained for friends at home.

Let us leave Haifa by car and follow the coast road down to Tel-Aviv sixty miles south. This will take us down the spine of modern Israel. Taking our last views of the gold-domed Baha'i Temple high above the city, rounding the headland of Mount Carmel, we motor through the fertile plain of Sharon.[4] Our young guide will tell us much as we go along. On one side he will point out grainfields that were swamps before the first Jewish immigrants came to drain them. On another, he will point out an Arab village whose people carry on life almost in the old-time ways. A detour into the hills will bring one to visit an abandoned Arab village which now has been converted into an artist colony called Ein Hod. You will enjoy the contemporary canvases hanging in their gallery, and take advantage of attractive bargains in ceramics, jewelry, paintings and other artistic creations turned out by Israel's most individualistic craftsmen.

Resuming our southward drive, we enter the districts where groves of the luscious Joppa oranges cover the landscape. From

---

[3] A Hebrew word for "cactus" (=) "tough on the outside, sweet on the inside."

[4] Pronounced on the last syllable in Hebrew.

these long-established orchards Israel collects its most valuable export cash crop.

This is the most fertile part of Israel, but it is also the narrowest. Those hills rising up within sixteen miles of the seacoast belong to Arab Palestine and have no commerce at present with the Israel lands at their feet. It probably forms an ironic thought for many of the immigrants that here at this point the Jewish National Homeland occupies the fertile seacoast that in ancient times belonged to Philistines and Canaanites, while the rocky hills of the interior, which formed the Hebrew kingdoms of Old Testament days, belong to the Arabs today.

Thus, associations with the Bible are few in our drive toward Tel-Aviv. The guide will point out a ruin on the seacoast a mile or so away, which is all that is left of Athlit, a castle built by the Crusaders. A few miles farther south is the site of Caesarea on a silted-up harbor. Caesarea in the time of Jesus was the Roman capital of Palestine, the place where Pilate and Agrippa had their palaces and legions. Today, excavations are unearthing Roman and Crusaders' relics of great value. Only two miles away, we reach Israel's pride—the Rothschild golf course painstakingly laid on top of what once were barren sand hills.

New towns, however, captivate our attention. Binyamina and Hadera are centers of the citrus industry. Next comes Nathanya, built on the sand dunes close to the sea. Named after Nathan Strauss, and founded as late as 1929, it is now the diamond-cutting center of the whole Near East, employing expert workers who came here from Antwerp and other European diamond centers. The inhabitants of Nathanya, comprising several nationalities, entertain people from the interior by running a bathing beach and several amusement festivals.

Farther down the coast, lies Herzliya, a garden town near the seashore. Named in honor of the founder of world Zionism, Theodor Herzl, it is a beach resort whose startlingly modern new hotels proclaim it to be the core of Israel's coming Riviera of the future, lying scarcely eight miles north of the busy avenues of Tel-Aviv.

Tel-Aviv

Largest city of Israel, though no census can keep up with the figures, is Tel-Aviv, the world's pioneer all-Jewish city. Beautifully situated on the open sea, it is fast expanding back into the low, semiforested hills of the central Israel coast.

Tel-Aviv is only a half-century "young." Founded in 1909, and named the Hill of Spring, it was first the home of Jews moving out of ancient, nearby Joppa. But during the British Mandate it became the center of many new industries and soon transformed itself into the modernistic wonderland of apartments, sea-view restaurants, tree-lined avenues, and fountains that the world soon recognized as a budding cultural center.

Walking through the crowds who live in this city of hope, one can readily see that Tel-Aviv is indeed that kind of center. The Habimah dramatic theatre, the Israel Philharmonic Orchestra and the Israel Opera all proclaim their programs on every hand. Libraries, art exhibits, auditoriums, a museum, a zoo, and occasional ballets also intrigue the visitor.

The throngs are all busy with the enterprises that make this city Israel's economic center. Not only is it headquarters for the banking system, the citrus industry, and insurance companies, but it is also the location of half of the country's factories. Textiles, clothes-making, food manufacturing, leather, and light-metal industries are the leading activities. Half of the country's foreign trade originates in this city and its surroundings.

Small wonder that the traffic was so heavy as we came down from Haifa. The original British military road is so taxed by this truck and bus circulation that it has of necessity been widened, while a secondary side-road and a new railroad line were being hurriedly completed. A fine diesel streamlined train now connects Israel's two metropoles in little more than an hour.

Busses of all vintages crowd this city, running not only to the suburbs, but to every corner of the country. No camels or overloaded donkeys in this corner of the Near East! In the city's fast growth, apartments and factories are thrown up even before their streets can be extended to serve them, while in the outskirts, trees, fountains, and curbs were installed after families had moved into the blocks of apartments.

As the central effort of Zionism, Tel-Aviv's short history has been turbulent. The Turks in World War I forced the evacuation of the five thousand inhabitants. It was bombed in World War II by the Italians. And when the British evacuated Palestine on May 15, 1948, Egyptian planes bombed it for several days.

Hotels have not kept pace with industries and theatres as yet. Tel-Aviv's hotels are small and by no means cosmopolitan, but several large international-style luxury hotels have now been erected on the seaside to cater to the swelling tourist tide.

Tel-Aviv is surrounded by several interesting suburbs. The best known is, of course, Joppa, or Jaffa as the modern maps show it. This tiny peninsula sheltering a dime-sized harbor was Palestine's chief port in Turkish days. Its crooked streets and imposing mosques make it of great interest today, but its Arab population is there no more. They fled almost en masse when the departure of the British brought on the short Israel-Arab war. Today forty thousand Jewish immigrants from abroad have moved into this vacant area, and it is now swallowed up by its swollen daughter-city, under the combined Israeli name of "Tel-Aviv-Yafo."

On the other side of the city is the separate town of Ramat Gan, or "Garden Hill," a town of gardens and cool parks, with open-air cafés and restaurants. Founded in 1921, Ramat Gan has maintained the easy way of life despite its busy factories that make chocolate candy, preserves, silk articles, and fountain pens.

Petah Tiqva, only four miles farther inland, is another show-place of modern Israel. Its name means "the Door of Hope," for it is one of the first Jewish settlements in Palestine, dating back to 1878. Once an orange-growing center, it is now a bustling city that manufactures pharmaceuticals, metals, pumps, soap, paper, and rubber materials.

Within a radius of fifteen more miles are three other important towns—Rehoboth, a garden town and resort, with a scientific institute and a glass industry; Ramleh, military center, and Lydda, site of an important school and of the big, modern international airport.

To the south are many small settlements and agricultural villages, as far as Beersheba, historic southern limit of Palestine and a center of life-giving wells on the edge of the vast southern desert.

Yet beyond Beersheba the state of Israel is making energetic plans for redeeming its segment of desert, the Negev. This territory squeezes like a wedge between Egypt and Trans-Jordan, tapering down to its frontier port of Elath at the north tip of the Red Sea. In future years, if water brought in from the north is sufficient, this redeemed barrenness will be a showplace of Asia.

Jerusalem "The Golden"

Jerusalem is only thirty-two miles inland from the Mediterranean, yet it is 2,400 feet high. By road from Tel-Aviv it is fifty-four miles. This includes the detour over the thoroughly modernized "Courage Road," which was staked out originally around an Arab strongpoint that cuts off the direct route. Up this now-permanent "temporary" route the Israel soldiers fought their way to break the siege of Jerusalem during the Arab attack in 1948.

Away from the warm coastal land of oranges and palms, we climb through rocky valleys to the heights of Judah, chilly and stern in winter, on which the Holy City lies.

Most travelers stay at Israel's celebrated hotel, the King David, built by the British twenty years ago on an imposing site south of the walled city. Across from it stands the stately International Y.M.C.A., a beautiful building erected mainly by American funds during the 1920's. Its architecture was carefully designed to offend none of the racial groups of Palestine. Its work of bringing peace and friendship to the Holy City through mutual understanding and athletics was cut short by the Arab uprising of 1936, World War II, and the Israel-Arab war of 1948. But it is still operating, with its lofty tower a conspicuous landmark.

While in Jerusalem we are free to explore only the modern city, the metropolitan Jewish settlement outside the historic walled city. This "New Jerusalem" is the official capital of Israel, the site of cultural and religious installations, the new Hebrew University, the Parliament and government offices.

So near—and yet so far—lies the walled, ancient town of Jerusalem, the goal of pilgrims and travelers, and site of all the remaining holy places. To reach its gates, however, requires a trip of over four hundred miles in the big circle via Lydda, Cyprus, and Damascus, for no traffic may cross over the Armistice Line between Israel and Jordan. Yonder walls of old Jerusalem are under the Arab flag of the late murdered King Abdullah.

However, nothing prevents us from going up to the roof of the King David Hotel and contemplating this quiet scene which has served as such a lodestone to most of the Western world.

Jerusalem stands for much. It is a holy site, a holy of holies, to the three religions that covet the Holy Land.

To the Jews, of course, Jerusalem is the site of their temple. Exiled and dispersed from it on two momentous occasions—by the Babylonians in 586 B.C. and by the Romans in A.D. 70— they still aspire to make it the center of their religious hope.

To the Christians of all sects, Jerusalem is holy as the scene of many of the notable acts of Christ Jesus, as the site of the Master's Crucifixion and Resurrection, and as the center of the activities of the early church.

Then the Moslems, whose religion sprang up in the near-by Arab lands, 632 years after Christ, rate Jerusalem with Mecca and Medina as their three holy cities. From Jerusalem the prophet Mohammed is supposed to have been lifted into heaven.

For three thousand years Jerusalem has been the "golden" home, the "scene of our solemnities," and the treasured possession of these three religions in their turn.

But for this deep significance, Jerusalem would be but another Arab-type city, whose attractions would not suffice to bring many world travelers over the seas and mountains to this plain, lofty site.

Yet so significant is the heritage of spiritual values and so vital the lessons worked out by the prophets and leaders of the people of this simple barren land, whose adherence to a pure religion has sparked the magnificent achievements of the Western world, that Jerusalem springs into life to all who come here.

With this impulsion, our thoughts go back to twenty centuries before Christ. In those days great civilizations existed in Egypt and in Babylonia. But these hills were the abode of primitive Semitic tribes living a pastoral existence. Then one day a sheep-herder whose name was Abram arrived with his flocks, coming from the rich city of Ur to the east in Babylonia. Perceiving a new concept of an invisible, all-powerful God, Abram—his name now changed to Abraham—settled down near Hebron.

Abraham's grandson Jacob progressed further in his contemplation of the nature of God, and he received the new name of Israel, or "striver with God." The Jews of today are some of the children of Israel, and have given his name to their revived homeland.

Israel and his sons went to Egypt to escape a famine, thanks to the invitation of Joseph, another son, whose story is one of the beautiful tales of the Old Testament. After centuries of enslavement under the Pharaohs, Moses led them forth as a numerous company and became their lawgiver. The Ten Commandments and the rest of the law form the Torah—or scrolls which are the holiest possessions of every synagogue and temple. Moses led his followers for forty years in wanderings through the Sinai deserts and at length arrived on the far side of the Jordan. His successor Joshua continued the pilgrimage into the Promised Land; and the twelve tribes, or the descendants of Israel's twelve sons,[5] divided up the land among themselves. It is significant that none of them took up territory along the coast of the Mediterranean, and three tribes remained beyond Jordan outside what is considered the Holy Land.

During two centuries the tribes struggled with their neighbors, all of which were Semitic tribes except for the Philistines, a powerful nation on the coast who are considered to have come there from Crete. Under various warriors and judges, the Israelites prevailed, and under King David established themselves firmly in the land.

David it was who chose the village of Jerusalem to be his capital. In wisdom he did this, for he knew that his people would be relatively undisturbed up in their barren mountains, whereas the people of the coastal plains would be forced to bend the knee to marching armies of powerful emperors. It was about 1000 B.C.

---

[5] Jacob (Israel) had twelve sons; but Levi's heirs were reserved for the priesthood. The tribe of Joseph was divided into two tribes (Manasseh and Ephraim).

when David set up this capital, naming it Jerusalem, or "Haven of Peace." His son Solomon erected the first great temple, whose glory is still a driving force in the religious life of the Jews.

After Solomon the twelve tribes split into two kingdoms. The northern ten tribes were called Israel, with Samaria as their capital. Its political life was stormy, with the unique monotheistic religion diluted now and then by the importation of Baals, so that the thunderings of the prophets Elijah, Elisha, Hosea, and Amos form some of the most moving passages of the Old Testament. At length the hosts of Assyria captured Samaria and drove the ten tribes into captivity, whence they have disappeared from the pages of history, to the mystery of world historians.

In the meantime, the remaining two tribes composing the more solemn and conservative Kingdom of Judah centering about Jerusalem continued to exist in their more rugged terrain. By its own courage Jerusalem repulsed an Assyrian siege by Sennacherib, but at length it was brought low and destroyed by Nebuchadnezzar, King of a revived Babylonia. The majority of the Jews of Judah were moved to Babylon, where they endured a tolerant captivity, preaching their religion to their children and enjoying the privileges of carrying on trade in the big emporium on the Euphrates.

However, when Cyrus the Persian overran Babylonia in 538 B.C., he permitted those Jews who so desired to return to the Holy Land. A detachment did so during the following years, and the walls and Temple of Jerusalem were rebuilt. Through the years the restored Jewish independence took on strength and virility. The coming of Alexander the Great and the Ptolemies made little impact; but when Syria annexed Palestine, the religious revolt led by the Maccabees repulsed the Syrian armies and saved the temple from further desecration and profanation by heathen practices. Finally in 63 B.C. Rome became the master of the Holy Land, but even then special autonomy under a native king was permitted.

Palestine was at its most prosperous period when Jesus was born in Bethlehem. He preached in Galilee in a rich area of pseudo-Greek civilization, and also in Jerusalem, where his adversaries were the Jewish sects of the Pharisees and the Sadducees.

After his Crucifixion on the hill of Calvary close to the walls of Jerusalem, his followers clashed with the Jewish leaders and many took refuge in Syria, Asia Minor, and Greece to bear the gospel to the Gentiles. However, after a bloody struggle, the Jews themselves were vanquished by the Romans in the year A.D. 70, and Jerusalem was again destroyed. All except a fraction of the Jewish people were expelled—dispersed—throughout the Roman world, although a tiny fraction remained and took refuge in Tiberias to carry out their studies and worship in one corner of their Holy Land.

The Romans built a city called Aelia Capitolina on the hill of Jerusalem, but when Christianity became the state religion of the Empire, the official attention of the new church turned to Jerusalem. Helena, mother of the Emperor Constantine, came to search out relics of Jesus' life, and the site of the holy places. She and her followers built the first Church of the Holy Sepulchre on the presumed place of Jesus' tomb. They also visited Bethlehem and Nazareth and marked out other sites for pilgrimage and worship.

Yet Jerusalem, the walled city we are now contemplating from our rooftop spot, is still not the city of Rome nor of the Jews. Too many invasions have intervened. First the Persians came to oust the Eastern Roman authorities; then the Arab incursions from the south, bringing the new creed of Mohammed, took over in the year A.D. 636. Jerusalem sank into the position of a forgotten town, unnoticed except by a few pilgrims from Europe, until in 1070 a race of Turks swept in from Asia, and in their fanaticism cut it off from Christendom. This brought on the First Crusade, which was led by Europe's most puissant knights. Godfrey of Bouillon, a chevalier from northern France, routed the Moslems from most of Palestine, while his colleague Baldwin of Flanders[6] became King of Jerusalem.

The century of flowering knighthood in the Holy Land brought new light, new tastes, new products, new materials, and new forces into play in Europe, then in the depths of the Dark Ages. Two

---

[6] The present King of the Belgians, Baudouin, carries this knight's name nine centuries after.

great orders of knighthood had their birth in the Holy Land—the Knights Templars and the Knights Hospitalers[7]—whose wealth and power in later years brought crises into the history of their countries.

However, a mightier warrior named Saladin swept out of Egypt and recaptured Jerusalem for the Crescent in 1187. Not even the prowess of Richard the Lion-Hearted or the King of France could undo that deed. The last of the Crusaders made their forced exit from Palestine when the fortress of Acre fell to the Moslems in 1244, but they left their imprint behind. A minority of Christian Arabs retained their entity in Bethlehem and in Galilee, and the Maronites of the Lebanon were enabled to keep their foothold from then on. A profitable trade with Europe took root, carried on by Venetian and Genoese fleets treating with astute Arab middlemen who had contacts with India and the Orient.

At length the Mongols out of the depths of Asia ruined the last remnants of the walls and churches of Jerusalem. Then came the Ottoman Turks, the militant warriors for Islam, who conquered Palestine in 1517. Solyman the Magnificent, their empire-building Sultan, paid honor to the holy nature of Jerusalem as a Moslem shrine by ordering the present walls to be built at that time. He allotted districts within to Christians and Jews. This is the city of Jerusalem that was discovered by Europeans again in the nineteenth century when they came to build churches and establish new footholds in the Holy City.

Missionaries of all sects of Christendom were sent in from Europe, while Jewish settlements came likewise from Russia and Germany. The Turks were powerless to resist this pressure from the outside world, except to create nuisances and annoyances, and to prevent the travel from abroad from increasing much beyond a trickle.

The really modern era came to Palestine in the year 1917, when two great events shook the world. First was the Balfour Declaration of the British Foreign Minister, Arthur Balfour, stating that British policy would henceforth include a national Jewish

---

[7] This Order lived on as the Order of the Knights of Malta.

home in Palestine.[8] The other was the actual conquest of the country by the British under General Allenby, who led an army across the desert of Sinai from Egypt and entered Jerusalem on foot. His victories, coupled with the legendary feats of Lawrence of Arabia, rolled up the Turks into total defeat and completely changed the political picture in the whole Near East.

By the peace treaties, Palestine was detached from Turkey and transformed into a League of Nations Mandate under the administration of Britain. Inside the next fifteen years miracles were performed. Roads and railroads were built; Jewish immigration soared to great heights; cities and farms were staked out; pilgrimage and travel brought visitors from the outside world in streams.

The Jews and the Christians of the world applauded this state of affairs, but not so the Moslems. The Arabs, or natives, of the country grew restive as they saw these wonders take place about them and realized that they were in no way capable of resisting the economic and political onrush of these energetic newcomers. Consequently the Arab world rose in revolt in 1936, bringing bloodshed to the Holy Land once more. The British army was forced to rule with an iron hand, while the British Government put a limit on the immigration of Jews, one of the points about which the Arabs were most determined.

As a result of this troubled era, the Jews organized a secret army of their own; and also a terrorist gang made its appearance. However, all warfare came to an end with World War II, in which the Jewish element supported the British against the Nazis. Peace reigned in Palestine until 1946, when the terrorist bands went on the rampage again.

At length the British determined to pull out of the tempestuous country and ended their Mandate on May 15, 1948, by putting it in the hands of the United Nations.

With the British gone, the Arabs and Jews raced to win the land by military campaigns. The best-organized army was the

---

[8] Partly as a result of efforts of Chaim Weizmann, the first President of Israel.

Arab Legion of King Abdullah of the Trans-Jordan, a force organized by the British along the lines commenced by Lawrence
of Arabia. This excellent army crossed the Jordan over the Allenby
Bridge, occupied the walled city of Jerusalem, and cut the Jewish
sections off from the rest of the country. Their Iraqi and Egyptian
allies occupied the whole central region of Palestine. The Jewish
settlers in the country, in the meantime, proclaimed the independent
state of Israel and managed to halt the Arab forces in the center,
while actually repulsing a Syrian army in the north. Gathering
strength, the Israel army occupied all of Galilee; seized the strategic road center of Beersheba; surrounded an Egyptian force;
annexed the Negev desert, and even raided far inside the Sinai
desert, threatening the Suez Canal itself.

The United Nations, through the efforts of Count Folke
Bernadotte, strove for the end of open warfare and finally forced
both sides to agree to an armistice. When the final line had been
drawn and a cease-fire had been respected, the State of Israel
occupied over three-fifths of Palestine, including almost all of the
coastline and coastal plains, plus the whole of Galilee, and the
Negev desert. The Arabs held central Palestine, with part of the
Jordan valley, and the walled city of Jerusalem. Egypt held on to
the strip of land around Gaza in the far south near Sinai.

And thus have matters stood to this day still. Israel has organized itself into a parliamentary republic and thrown open its
doors to full and unlimited immigration of Jews from anywhere
in the world. Several hundred thousand have come in from Arab
lands alone, filling the farms and homes left vacant by Palestine
Arabs who fled panic-stricken at the beginning of the war. These
latter are now a world problem, living in destitution outside their
old homeland. In the meantime, Arab-held Palestine was annexed
to the Jordan Kingdom of the assassinated King Abdullah.

Despite this turmoil, travel goes on freely in the Holy Land,
both Arabs and Jews welcoming tourists, provided they don't
try to cross illegally the Armistice Line, which, like the Chinese
Wall, snakes itself across the land like an impassable curtain.

Let us now leave new Jerusalem, having seen how it has filled
a niche in history similar to that of no other holy city. Having

gazed at it from the outside, we will later get into it and see what it has inside that has attracted pilgrims through the ages.

A Visit to Galilee

No one can leave Israel without making the drive by automobile through Galilee, the fertile northern province that extends for twenty-seven miles from Haifa on the Mediterranean westward past Nazareth to the Sea of Galilee.

A day gives plenty of time for this trip, as the distances are short. The Israel Tourist Bureau has laid out the route, and excellent guides well versed in the Bible are obtainable to show some historic sites. The scenery throughout is attractive.

Only twenty-three miles separates Haifa from Nazareth. The road between them crosses the Plain of Jezreel, Israel's most fertile agricultural belt, where grain takes the place of the malarial swamps that plagued this spot from time immemorial. Climbing out of this valley into the hills of Galilee, you pass through the refreshing green of the Balfour Forest[9] and then enter Nazareth.

Nazareth, the hillside town where Jesus spent his boyhood and returned many times during his ministry, is a pleasant place. It is almost entirely an Arab town untouched by the hustle of Israel cities. Bazaars, narrow streets, camels and donkeys pushing pedestrians out of the way make for an atmosphere little changed from the days the Saviour lived here.

A mere stopover in this place is sufficient to capture the atmosphere of Jesus' home district, but most visitors are taken to see the "sights" of Nazareth. These consist of the Church of the Annunciation, now being completely reconstructed over the ruins of the earliest church that covered the grotto where the Virgin Mary received the annunciation; the Church of St. Joseph, a modern Renaissance-style church on top of a series of caves supposed to be the home of Joseph and the Holy Family; and a nearby hall which is shown as the type of synagogue where Jesus did his preaching when in his home city.

A fountain on the edge of the city is still called Mary's Well, and here the Arab women come to carry away water in urns on

---

9 Israel is doing a thorough job of reforesting the denuded hills of Galilee.

their heads, in much the same way that the Virgin Mary must have done two thousand years ago. While old-style guides all over the Near East will swear that the shrines they point out to travelers are the actual ones in which great events took place, it must be remembered that the wastage of the centuries has torn away the original buildings. The guides think they are doing their job most efficiently when they tell a tourist what the tourist obviously wants to hear. The modern-day young guides of Nazareth are not entirely of this variety, but grains of salt must be taken along on all such trips to be shaken liberally on tales that sound too fanciful without proof. At Nazareth, the scene and the locale and the well and the unchanging Arab ways of its people are satisfactory proof enough that one has indeed walked in the steps of the Master.

From Nazareth the road eastward follows without doubt the route taken many times by Jesus as he and his disciples passed from town to town preaching to the multitudes. Only five miles along the way is Cana of Galilee, now known as Kfar Kana, a closely clustered Arab village on a rocky hillside. This is where Jesus turned the water into wine, the first of the many achievements he performed during his ministry.

Nine miles farther and the plateau of Galilee drops away from the road, revealing the enchanting scene of the Sea of Galilee, a bowl of limpid blue, lying far below in a desert basin. This pure lake of fresh water beneath parched, arid cliffs on the edge of the Arabian Desert is unruffled now by the fleets of fishermen of ancient days or the cannonades of the religious wars of a few short years ago. But in Jesus' time it was the center of a Hellenized Jewish Kingdom, and its waters washed the coasts of several Greeklike cities, whose citizens were Jesus' most attentive audiences.

The Sea of Galilee has two other names—the Lake of Kinnereth, or the harp-shaped lake; and the Lake of Tiberias, named after the main city on its banks. It is thirteen miles long and six miles wide. It is only twenty-seven miles from the Mediterranean and sixty miles northeast of Jerusalem. Even though lying seven hundred feet *below* sea level, it is fresh water, for it is drained by the Jordan River, which flows on down to the Dead Sea sixty-five miles south and five hundred feet farther below the level of the oceans. The Jordan valley is the northern end of the Great Rift, a geological gash in the earth's surface that extends almost all the way to South Africa.

The road winds sharply down the slope, past sea level, and down into Tiberias town. Tiberias was founded during Jesus' own boyhood by King Herod and named in honor of the reigning Roman Emperor.[10] During all the Middle Ages it was a center of Jewish learning and one of their last footholds in Palestine. Today the city re-echoes to construction work. Its ancient hovels are being demolished, making way for parks and smart new hotels, since Tiberias, with its superb view over the lake from inside its basalt walls, is intended to serve Israel as its principal winter resort.

The Sea of Galilee is indeed perfect for winter vacations. Its low level and dry atmosphere beside the desert give it a balminess welcome when Jerusalem and Haifa are chilled by the rains. And it has bluer skies all winter than the rest of the country.

At Tiberias one should turn left and follow the very shore of the lake northward. For the road goes through El Majdal, supposedly Magdala, ancient home town of Mary Magdalene, crosses the fertile little plain of Gennesaret, and passes many sites reminiscent of New Testament scenes. One can easily picture a multitude listening to Jesus so crowding the narrow shores of the blue lake that Jesus had to step into a boat and talk to them from out in the water. His great achievement of feeding them with the few loaves and fishes took place in this very locality.

Farther along is a beautiful hill known as the Mount of the Beatitudes, since tradition awards it the honor of being the site of the Sermon on the Mount. On its summit is an Italian hospice where pilgrims have been sheltered for many years. Its attractive gardens and a modern shrine are the usual place for a picnic on this day's outing. While munching lunch, the traveler can gaze down at the placid lake and its matchless associations. Here one should recall the story of Jesus walking on the surface; and of his calming the storm when the disciples feared their boat would

---

[10] Tiberius, A.D. 14–37. Same Emperor who lived on Capri.

sink. Farther up the lake shore lies the site of Capernaum, an important city where excavations show the synagogue Jesus visited many times.

Dominating the scene far to the north is snowy Mount Hermon, the white monarch whose eternal snows yield some of the waters for this lake at our feet, waters that flow down by the Jordan River. The Jordan is narrow and muddy where it enters the lake near Capernaum, but it leaves the lake a clear, placid blue.

Across the lake from our picnic spot on the Mount of the Beatitudes rise the steep cliffs of Syria. Damascus is not far distant. In fact, the road that passes our hill crosses the Jordan a few miles north and continues to Damascus. This was an important highway in ancient times. Paul, when traveling over it to organize a persecution of the Christians in Damascus, was struck with that blinding light, which was accompanied by the voice saying, "Saul, Saul, why persecutest thou me?"

Those cliffs across the Sea of Galilee belong to hostile Syria, except for the shoreline at their feet, which is the farthest-flung extension of Israel. A town hidden in the green trees at the end of Israel's territory is Ein Gev, a center of annual music festivals. It is connected with Tiberias by a regular motorboat service across the "sea."

The return trip to Haifa follows a slightly different route from the one by which we came. It goes down the shore of the sapphire lake, past Tiberias, to its southern tip, where the Jordan emerges. It is still the custom to fill bottles with Jordan water to take home. Here the water is clear and pure, and doesn't "ferment" after long storage. Nearby lies Israel's model *kibbutz,* or collective farm, of Deganya, which travelers are welcome to inspect.

The Jordan River is only fifty feet wide where it enters the Sea of Galilee and eighty feet wide when it leaves. Its onward course forms a serpentine band of green down the wide desert valley, all below sea level. It reaches its end in the world's saltiest sea—the Dead Sea—sixty-five miles farther south.

The Jordan signified holiness to the Hebrews of old. They entered the Promised Land by crossing it "on dry-shod feet" after their forty-year wanderings in the desert. Elisha, in his instructions to the haughty Syrian Captain Naaman, told him to wash in the Jordan seven times to be healed of his leprosy, a lesson of strong spiritual symbolism. John the Baptist baptized Jesus in this same river. With such a tradition of holiness behind it, small wonder that Jordan water is greatly desired by churches in Europe and America for christenings and baptisms.

Leaving the shores of the holy river, the road climbs up out of the deep valley to the plateau, and our journey continues past new agricultural collective camps to Mount Tabor, a conical-shaped mountain rising 1,843 feet, which had great importance in Old Testament days as a place of battle and as a landmark for the twelve tribes.

The plateau is barren and unsettled, but this land has echoed to the comings and goings of the ages, for the direct road from Galilee to Jerusalem passed this way. A crossroads we pass by with hardly any notice is the site of the ancient city of Nain, before whose gates Jesus restored to life a dead man being carried out to his burial. The range of hills off to the south, which forms the present boundary between Israel and Arab Palestine in this region, is called Mount Gilboa, where Saul, first king of the Hebrews, perished in a bloody battle with the Philistines, losing his son Jonathan and all his warriors. A hamlet off the road in that direction is called Indor to this day. Saul, the night before the battle, came to a cave there to consult "the witch of Endor," forgetting his prayers in order to have an incantation and a prophecy sung for his success.

Before returning to Haifa the road passes through the Valley of Jezreel again, this time in sight of the mount of Megiddo, or "place of crowds" in old Hebrew. A battle fought here about 1200 B.C. preserved the independence of the Israelite tribes against the Canaanite Sisera. In its Greek form of Armageddon, it is singled out in the Book of Revelation as the final place where those who "battle for the Lord" will be victorious over their adversaries.[11]

All of these Biblical sites can be seen on this one day's drive from Haifa in a wide circle, and should not be missed by any visitors to the Holy Land.

Back in Haifa, one can leave by ship for Europe or America

---

[11] Correct pronunciation is "Ar-*mah*-ged-*don*."

by many regular sailings. Or, at Lydda airport seventy-five miles south, he can board an international plane almost any day of the week to wing westward to Greece, Italy, and Paris, or to head eastward toward India.

"Jordan Jerusalem"

Suppose that you have decided to see old Jerusalem first instead of going to Israel, and that you left Damascus by plane and have arrived at Kalandia Airport in Arab Palestine. Taxi service has by now brought you into the vicinity of the thick walls of Jerusalem, and you have taken up lodging in one of the modest new hotels serving visitors who come to what is now called "Jordan Jerusalem," since you are now officially in the Hashimite Kingdom of Jordan.[12]

One of the first objects of your visit will be to see the Church of the Holy Sepulchre. This is located in the northwest corner inside the walls and is reputed to stand over the sepulchre in which Jesus was laid after the Crucifixion. The church of today is a restored building resting on pillars and walls of an edifice built in Helena's time—a Crusaders' church. The church is shared by Greek Orthodox, Roman Catholic, Armenian, and Coptic ecclesiastics, with chapels built over tombs and relics. A two-chambered chapel in the middle of the rotunda marks the supposed site of the sepulchre itself. On Easter and the holy days preceding, colorful processions of these different sects can be seen.

Always traveled by visitors is the Via Dolorosa, a long, slightly curving street, over which Jesus trod while carrying his cross to his Crucifixion on the Hill of Calvary.[13] The road is surrounded by high walls, behind which are chapels and medieval churches and monasteries. The "stations of the cross" are marked on the walls by plaques.

One of the most interesting things inside Jerusalem is the Pool of Bethesda. Today this appears as a group of basins hewn

---

[12] Once called Trans-Jordan, a British Mandate, it is now an independent kingdom, whose first King, Abdullah, was of the family of Hashim.

[13] Calvary, or in Hebrew "Golgotha," "the place of a skull," has not been identified positively as to location.

of rock, thirty feet below a courtyard belonging to the Church of St. Anne above. The story of the pool is printed in countless languages for the benefit of pilgrims. The pool was called Bethesda because it had "five porches," and the waters had healing properties in ancient days whenever some subterranean impulse agitated them. Here came Jesus and restored a man who had been lying for thirty-eight years waiting for someone to put him into the pool. The Bible states that this pool was close to the sheep market of the ancient city.

Continuing through the narrow winding streets of this typically Arab city of Jerusalem, we approach the center of its holy midst— the temple area. The Wailing Wall, once such a familiar sight to travelers, has no more wailers, for no Jews are allowed inside the holy city by the Arab rulers. The wall thus remains what it always was—a remnant of the foundation of the massive temple that Solomon built in 958 B.C.

The great temple is no more. Babylonians, Romans, and Persians smashed to bits the center of resistance of the Hebrews. Instead the triumphant Moslem faith has taken its foundations and its site to erect its own shrine—the Dome of the Rock. This is an octagonal structure of moderate size, with the interior of the dome filled by Byzantine mosaics. Protected by the dome is the bare rock of Moriah, which has been used for prayer and commemoration since the earliest days of Jerusalem in one way or another.[14] In a smaller domelike structure near by is commemorated the nocturnal ride of Mohammed on his donkey, El-Borak, from Mecca to Jerusalem, whence he ascended to paradise.

South of the Dome of the Rock, across a paved open space and an outdoor basin of water, stands the Mosque El-Aksa, second only to Mecca as a Moslem shrine of veneration. It stands on the site of a sixth century church built by Justinian of Constantinople. Its pillars date from the seventh century. The mosaics inside the dome were brought from Constantinople during Saladin's time. Many entrancing tales of miracles performed here for Moslem

---

[14] Among the legends connected with the rock is that it is where Melchizedek offered sacrifice, and likewise Abraham. When Mohammed and El-Borak ascended to heaven, the rock attempted to follow until restrained by the angel Gabriel, whose fingerprints are pointed out.

pilgrims, and of associations with ancient traditions, will be told by obliging guides.

Underneath the high platform on which these buildings stand are the underground vaults known as King Solomon's Stables. Eighty-eight square pillars hold aloft the rock ceilings. The Knights Templars of the Crusaders used these as stables, but how far back beyond those times these massive vaults existed is not known for sure.

Standing on the edge of the great mosque platform, which bears the name of Haram-esh-Sherif ("The Noble Sanctuary"), you can have a splendid view over the narrow valley outside the east walls of Jerusalem. Called the valley of the brook Kidron and also the vale of Jehoshaphat, it is a mass of graves and memorial stones. During the centuries all devout Jews have desired to be buried here, for this valley is expected to be the scene of the Last Judgment.[15] The Moslems, as well as the Jews, hold this belief.

These are the main sites to be visited inside the walls of Jerusalem. The next thing to do is to go out St. Stephen's gate, take a car, and motor up to the Mount of Olives, a ridge on the other side of the brook Kidron that rises to 2,680 feet above the sea, one of the highest points in the Holy Land. A fine view can be had here of the city of Jerusalem, which lies lower down in the west; and off to the east the valley of the Jordan and the Dead Sea can be seen. Winding off to the east is the road to Jericho, which Jesus used in his parable of the Good Samaritan. The first village at your feet is Bethany, where Jesus often went for rest and prayer.

The Mount of Olives is intimately associated with the last days on earth of Jesus Christ. From its summit the Master lamented over the faithlessness of Jerusalem and announced its eventual destruction. From here he rode into the city, mounted on an ass, to receive the temporary applause of the people, who welcomed him as an earthly Messiah.[16] On its slopes down toward the city is the secluded Garden of Gethsemane, where Christ Jesus came

[15] Joel 3:2.
[16] *Cf.* Matthew 21; Mark 11; Luke 19; John 12.

with his disciples the night before the Crucifixion, and where he was arrested during the night.[17]

The slopes of Gethsemane are now occupied by two gardens—a Latin—or Franciscan—monastery with olive trees of great age; and a Russian-Greek Orthodox garden. Both gardens have churches with paintings and reliefs.

Bethlehem

The other place of devotion in Jordan Jerusalem is the "little town of Bethlehem" where Christ Jesus was born.

Only five and a half miles south of the Holy City, this historic town is reached nowadays by a more circuitous, rough road to avoid a tongue of Israeli territory that intervenes between the two cities.

While covering this distance, one passes along the gentle hillsides on which "the shepherds watched their flocks by night" on the day of the Saviour's birth. Even now these hills are used for pasturage. Bethlehem lies on these hills, on a spot that has been so fertile throughout the ages that its name means "House of Bread," and its other name of Ephrata is Hebrew for "fruitful." Here lived Ruth and David of the Old Testament. Seven hundred and fifty years before the Holy Family came here from Nazareth to obey the Roman census, the prophet Micah prophesied the event.[18]

The people of Bethlehem today are mainly Arab Christians, and the women wear a headdress that has come down with few modifications from the days of the Crusaders.

However, all paths lead to the door of the Church of the Nativity, built on a site that has been venerated for 1800 years as the actual cave where Jesus was born and where the Three Wise Men came to pay tribute.

The church has been enlarged and modified after its various sackings since Constantine put up the original basilica here in the

---

[17] *Cf.* Matthew 26:36–56; Mark 14:43; Luke 19:29 and 22:39; and John 18:1.
[18] *Cf.* Micah 5:2.

year A.D. 330. Three convents—Latin, Orthodox, and Armenian—
partially conceal it from view. The small courtyard leading to it
can be reached only by stooping under a low entry way, made
purposely low to keep out camels, donkeys, and Moslem crowds.
Inside, the church is very simple, having red stone columns,
Byzantine mosaics, and some crests of long-departed Crusaders.
Twenty feet below the choir of the church is the Chapel of the
Nativity, thirty-three feet long, whose walls have now been lined
with masonry and marble. A silver star in the pavement represents the spot where Jesus was born. Fifteen ever burning lamps
hang above this spot, six tended by Orthodox priests, four by
Latin ecclesiastics, and five by Armenians. An altar in the chapel
can be used for any one of the three rites during special festivals.

Guides will point out many other churches, shrines, and grottoes
associated with sacred events in Bethlehem's religious history.
The native inhabitants offer for sale carved mother-of-pearl shells
and trinkets made out of shale.

Returning to Jerusalem, the average traveler will now have
seen the principal points of authentic value in Jordan's part of
the Holy Land. Naturally, Bible students will enjoy going down
to Jericho, or even to Hebron on the edge of the desert, and to
the sites of Samaria and Bethel. However, time has dealt harshly
with this land and cleared its surface of most of the elegance that
marked its cities in the time of the Romans, and of the primitive
dwellings that existed here back in the times of the Old Testament prophets.

Consequently, today's visitor to the Holy Land should content
himself with touring the sites of the most important events that
concern his particular faith, and read carefully what the Bible says
about them. Then these sites will have penetrating importance
for him, whether the particular places are now marked by Arab
hovels, bustling Israeli farms, remodeled shrines, or absolutely
nothing at all.

But one thing is certain—the Holy Land will make the Bible
scenes come startlingly to life. The rocky hills, the fertile places
and the time-honored ways of life that can easiest be seen on the
Arab side of the line make the Bible atmosphere stand out in

three dimensions of reality. The settings of the parables of Christ Jesus—treating of now-familiar places, and of simple ways of life, mentioning the flat housetops, the oxen and asses led away to watering, the tree that bringeth not forth good fruit being hewn down, the tares and the wheat, and the lilies of the field in all their glory—are here to be seen just as they were beheld by Jesus and held up as examples to illustrate his teachings, the very same teachings that he meant to have value and usefulness not only in his own simple homeland but in all other lands and climes as well.

Farewell to the Holy Land

From Jordan's Jerusalem, some experienced travelers might desire to motor across the Jordan to Amman, the mushrooming capital of the Jordan Kingdom, and thence down to Petra, the rose-red city of the desert carved out here in Hellenistic times for holiness and protection.

Otherwise, it is best to take wing and fly away—first to Damascus and Beirut, and thence to the next land of our interest— Greece—where lived the race whose culture and language was as familiar to the early Christians as their own Aramaic-Hebrew.

GREECE

Home of the Gods

ATHENS, THE PRIDE OF GREECE, is unique in a peculiar respect. It is a modern city trying desperately to live up to its glorious past.

Athens *is* Greece. That is what makes it so enchanting to visit. That is why it was chosen for modern Greece's capital. The achievements of this city in one single century of ancient history were so superb that the world has been in debt to it ever since.

There is vitality and bustle in the very air. When your steamer sails into Piraeus, the seaport section of the capital, this exuberance permeates the atmosphere. Piraeus is so small for the bulging trade of the Greek metropolis that ships have to grope their way carefully and then tie up end-to, moored to floating, narrow wharves. Every single inch of Piraeus' narrow peninsula is crowded with homes—dazzling white, flat-roofed, squeezed together.

Excellent new automobiles are on tap for immediate hire, and off goes the new arrival to Athens the moment he comes down the gangplank. Formerly, the road to Athens led prosaically across the six-mile plain. But now the approach is more scenic. Your taxi speeds through Piraeus to the open Bay of Phaleron, whose shore it then follows. The water is stunningly blue, like the Mediterranean everywhere; and in the bay, riding off at anchor, almost as a backdrop, invariably you will discern an American warship.

After three miles of hugging the bay, the new road to Athens turns inland and, in the form of a tree-lined dual boulevard, strikes straight toward the Acropolis, on which you immediately perceive the stately Parthenon standing up almost luminously, extending a gracious welcome that entrances you and hardly lets you take your eyes away.

The Parthenon is one of those glorious creations in the world that never disappoint. No matter how many pictures or movies of it the traveler may have seen, he watches eagerly for it as soon as he comes to Greece. And when he first sights it, it holds him spellbound. It is an object of simplicity as well as of beauty, and it symbolizes the glory that was Greece.

In no time you have passed below the Acropolis and find yourself in the middle of busy Athens. The very heart of the capital is tree-lined, table-filled Constitution Square facing the House of Parliament, in front of which can be seen—and photographed—the colorful Evzones, or soldiers who wear the close-fitting white tights and the flaring skirt.[1]

Strolling around the city is a gay experience. Coming from the Near East, the traveler rejoices at feeling himself in Europe. Here is a city after our own hearts. No veiled women, minarets, beseeching dragomans, insistent beggars, Oriental paradoxes. Athens is definitely European. The people are all friendly, very busy, thoroughly modern, and part of our world. Besides, Greece feels as close to America as do such countries as Ireland and Italy. Almost every Greek has a relative in America; and one out of every ten Greeks, it seems, has been to America and come home to live in royal style.

Before the war it was said that Athens was the only city in Europe where you could get a decent ice cream soda. And why not? An ice-cream-parlor magnate of Cincinnati came back home to show them how! The Greeks of Greece are poor because they have so few natural resources to build fortunes with. But they struggle; they took advantage of the great economic lift the Marshall Plan bestowed on them, and they dream. For, always overshadowing them is the soaring Acropolis with the Parthenon,

---

[1] This costume, with pointed cap and pointed slippers, originated in medieval Greek Albania.

standing almost as a model for their efforts and as an ideal for their aspirations.

It won't be long before the spell of the Acropolis will tell on you, and you will head for it in a comfortable automobile for the travel experience of your life.

The Acropolis

This small plateau standing up above the Athenian plain was the original site of the earliest city of Athens. Upon its rocky tabletop was the king's palace, the temple to Athena, and the houses of all the citzenry. The Acropolis means simply "the upper city," or "the city on top."[2]

The people who first settled down in this part of Greece, which is known as Attica, were tribes that came from the north. They were Indo-Europeans—in contrast to the people of the Near East, who were Semites or Hamites—and even different from the early inhabitants of Crete, who were of a Mediterranean stock that has since been swallowed up by later comers. The Greeks, in the Bible classification must have been "children of Japheth," Noah's youngest son, whereas the Hebrews and Babylonians, Phoenicians and Syrians, were children of Shem, his oldest heir.

Coming down from the Balkans to the north, these mysterious people were classed as Dorians or Ionians according to the time of their arrival. The Ionians were the first wave, arriving before 1000 B.C. and settling the Aegean Islands, the coasts of Asia Minor, and the southern peninsula of Greece, which is called the Peloponnesus. The Dorians came shortly after the year 1000 and infiltrated among the Ionians, while also settling the land north of them.

The early history of Greece is almost impossible to trace, since it is so intertwined with legend and with the activities of the gods. The Greeks so intimately lived with their gods and made them so human that the gods were always intervening, influencing, seducing, and interrupting the affairs of the humans below. They didn't have far to come, for they were supposed to live together on Mount Olympus in northern Greece, but the discord must have

---

[2] Note Akron (Ohio), whose name means "summit."

been unbearable up there, judging by the way they kept calling in human aid to redress the balance of their feuds. Thus the legendary Trojan campaign, which must have been based on some actual human warfare, is so intertwined with deific projects by Homer in his *Iliad* that it is hard to deduce what the fight was all about. Perhaps it was just an attack by an Ionian tribe on the Doric city of Troy, with the gods naturally brought in as a justification. Whether Helen,[3] whose face also is blamed for launching the thousand ships, was a free agent or not is glossed over by Homer, so that from human reckoning it is difficult to point out the aggressor.

In the years from 1000 to 500 B.C., the peninsula of Greece was being prepared for its immense flowering forth into the first civilization of mainland Europe. Instead of one big kingdom, it was developing into a collection of city-states, cut off from each other by mountains and inlets of the sea. Those cities close to the sea, or located on the Aegean Islands, were visited regularly by the Phoenicians. Greece was thus bathed in the learning of the Near East during her formative years. The alphabet devised by the Phoenicians from the hieroglyphs of the Egyptians and the cuneiforms of the Babylonians was gradually adopted by the Greeks and evolved into an alphabet of their own. The forms of architecture worked out by the Egyptians were likewise used as examples for Greek temples. The methods of fashioning tools and ornaments out of bronze and brass, of cutting stone into blocks and pillars, and of shaping it into statues—all were acquired by the meeting of Greek city-dwellers with the worldly merchant-sailors from Phoenicia, who arrived in their many-oared boats, well equipped with tales and samples.

The Greeks also adopted from these visitors the art of boatbuilding and boat-handling. Having originally been a land-bound people, they learned the art of living on the sea from the master mariners of ancient times—the traders and sailors from Tyre and Sidon, from Beirut and Byblos.

And so, when Phoenicia's homeland was submerged by invaders from Syria, and their merchantmen arrived in Greek waters

---

[3] Her name means simply "Greek."

much less frequently, their Greek pupils began to launch out for themselves. In the days when the Persians and the Babylonians were fighting it out for the mastery of the East, Greek sailors were penetrating along all the near-by shores. They not only went through the Hellespont, founded Byzantium, and continued to the farthest reaches of the Black Sea, but in the other direction they began settling in Sicily, in southern Italy, and even on the Riviera.[4] The epics of Jason and the Golden Fleece, and of the Odyssey, tell of the far-flung explorations of the Greeks in those early days.

As a result of this influence from overseas, the maritime cities of Greece began acquiring culture and wealth faster than those remote from contact with the foreigner. Athens, Corinth, and Rhodes began to develop fleets, found colonies, build walls and temples, and grow into miniature empires, while Sparta, a crude city in the heart of the Peloponnesus hills, remained an isolated, militaristic society.

Most important of all, however, was the system of government evolved by these industrious little Greek communities. Their equalitarian background, from being simple tribal immigrants with no authoritarian tradition, led them to water down the system of kingship. The early Greek "kings" remained elders and judges, rather than taking on the trappings of divine autocrats, like the Pharaohs, or the monarchs of Babylon. At the same time the citizens asserted some control over their kings and participated in the business of governing. They did not degenerate into serfs who slaved for exalted rulers, as happened in the Near East.

The gods of Greece were so human and so mixed in with everyday affairs that no exalted ruling class of humans could develop. Everything had to be subordinated to the patron god. Athens paid special homage to the goddess of wisdom, Athena; while Rhodes, perhaps because it was so much closer to the Oriental lands, adopted Apollo, god of the sun.

While the deities of Greece were thus more benevolent and human, so that the Greek people could mold them into the relationship that filled their needs best, their religious development was severely hampered. For while human systems of philosophy

---

[4] Nice, founded by them, is named after their word for "victory."

and education developed to their very highest under the ancient Greeks, the searching for the truths of religion bogged down in the morass of ramified mythology and anthropomorphic gods. It was in this particular field that Greek civilization fell short, and eventually it had to adopt what had been discovered by the more primitive and unsophisticated people of the Holy Land.

The peoples of Greece pioneered the art of government by eschewing monarchy and developing the oligarchy, or rule of an elected few over a select band of citizens. This was not democracy, but it established the foundation on which democracy could be built. It *was* republican, and semi-elective. It did not include all citizens, or full representative government, nor equality of the sexes, nor abolition of slavery. What they did in the line of government was to light the torch for us.

In this ebullient period of Greek development, by far the most progressive group of Greeks were the Athenians. That is why Athens is the capital of modern Greece. And that is why we are climbing the Acropolis today.

A period of trial eventually came to this robust peninsula. Persia, whose autocratic kings had overturned the independence of Babylon and of Egypt, soon took umbrage at the proud Greek tribes. It is a tribute to the Greeks that by their commercial and exploratory achievements rather than by their prowess at war or empire-building, they drew down the jealousy of the world's mightiest land power and autocracy.

Perhaps the energetic forms of Greek government, as shown to Persia by the many successful Greek colonies established in Asia Minor, or else their ingenuity as fighters as evidenced by a band of free-thinking soldiers of the Anabasis on the very edges of Persia, most alarmed the imperial court of Persepolis. At any rate Darius the Great, with his whole fleet and army, assaulted Marathon in Attica in 490 B.C., only to be humiliatingly defeated by the small band of free men mustered by Athens.[5]

Darius' successor Xerxes,[6] now more thoroughly aroused, decided to use method and planning to clean out the hornets' nest

---

[5] "Marathon" now means a "foot-race," since Pheidippides brought the news of victory to Athens, twenty-two miles away, without a rest.

[6] Xerxes is considered to be the King Ahasuerus of the Book of Esther.

across the Aegean. In 480, ten years later, he sent a much larger army into Europe over a bridge of boats spanning the Hellespont and marched them the long land way around. The Greek cities, uniting for the first time, went to meet them at the Pass of Thermopylae. Their heroic stand still awes the world, but numbers told, and the Persians swept ahead with their magnificent land army.[7]

Nothing could stop them. They entered Athens, smashed its walls; burned the city, and cleared the Acropolis of all its buildings. The inhabitants sought refuge offshore on the island of Salamis, and there they played their last remaining trump—their united Greek fleet.

King Xerxes set his throne on top of the Acropolis to watch this last gasp of Greece as an independent people. But the battle on the sea went to the craftier[8] and the Persian fleet was destroyed. Cut off from his homeland, Xerxes soon had to beat a hasty retreat back the way he came, and Persia started on her long decline.

The exultation of the victory over this massive empire is what inspired the building of the Acropolis all over again as a tribute to gracious Athena. Only sacred buildings were now to adorn its summit; the city was rebuilt on the plains below; and strong walls, extending all the way to Piraeus, were set up to guard the city.

Thus begins Athens' golden century, which historians measure from 480 to 404 B.C. In that short time the genius of this city burst forth, and we today can still stand in awe of what it created.

As you leave your car and walk up the steep steps to the top of the Acropolis, you pass through the pillared portals called the Propylaea, the sacred entrance to the hilltop, under which passed the animals to be sacrificed, and the garlanded processions to do honor to Athena. You will find the top of the hill still cluttered with blocks of stone, awaiting the time that the archaeologists can find their former places to fit them in again.

---

[7] History repeated itself in April, 1941, when a Nazi army thrust through Thermopylae against a small British detachment.

[8] History again repeated: the Spanish Armada was worsted by the English in 1588 with a similar decisive conclusion to the war.

The Parthenon is the glory of the Acropolis, and even in ruins, it stands serene and masterful. One can hardly dare to describe it. To us, its value lies in the lesson it tells, namely, that a simple structure of this kind can be so utterly magnificent. No gaudy decorations or novel architectural inventions were used to make it so unique. Its Greek architects merely took the simple elements of an oblong box with a row of uprights to hold up a temple containing treasures dedicated to a goddess. Yet they so molded these simple elements with their concepts of pure beauty that the Parthenon emerged as the model for everything classic.

The columns are made up of drums hewn out of marble from near-by Mount Pentelicus. The drums are so carefully mounted atop each other, without mortar, that needles cannot be thrust into their joints. To make the edifice look perfectly straight, there are no straight lines in the Parthenon! All are carefully bent or curved. The slopes of the roof were set at the angle of gentle Mount Pentelicus in plain view to the north.

Inside this building was the cella, or throne room, of the goddess Athena, whose statue was made of ivory and gold and plaster on a wooden core. A small chamber used by the priestesses called the Parthenon ("maidens' chamber") later came to be used as the title for the whole temple.

Around the outside of the building ran Phidias' matchless frieze showing many scenes from the life of Athens, in which the acts of the gods were generously mingled.

The Parthenon was recognized as a gem of beauty by all the later peoples who asserted mastery over Athens. While its costly interior and its great statue were pillaged during the centuries, its faultless exterior, so excellently constructed, lasted on without change. Here came Alexander the Great to exhibit his booty won from the Persians. Later Cleopatra chose the Parthenon as the place to be acclaimed as a goddess by the admiring Athenians. When Christianity triumphed, it was made into a church. After the Turks came it was easily transformed into a mosque. However, this exquisite edifice was smashed by an unnecessary incident in the year 1685. A Venetian army besieging the Turks atop the

Acropolis bombarded the Parthenon because it was a Turkish arms dump. In one instant its arsenal exploded, scattering the marble columns and breaking down the roof. Only in the last twenty years has the exterior portico of columns been reconstructed for our admiration.[9]

The other building of beauty atop the Acropolis is the Erechtheum, a temple likewise dedicated to Athena, but built a century later. Its name is mysterious, but it was holier as a shrine because the ground it stood on had been specially blessed by Athena ages before when contesting with Poseidon (Neptune) for the honor of serving as patroness to the city. Most distinctive feature of this Erechtheum is the Porch of the Maidens, an ornament erected only for beauty, having caryatids, or maidens, to support the roof instead of pillars. The Erechtheum is considered the classic example of Ionic style.

Before leaving the summit of the Acropolis, pause to enjoy the view of Athens and its "fruited plain." Southward is the Aegean Sea, with the shapes of Salamis and Aegina looming up from its purplish-blue surface. To the east is the long ridge of Mount Hymettus, famed in ancient times for its honey.

To the north, beginning at the very foot of the Acropolis, extends modern Athens. Now a city of a million, it was only a Turkish provincial town 130 years ago. Chosen as capital of independent Greece in 1830 purely on the strength of its classical reputation, it was beautified and laid out anew by the kings of modern Greece. Then, in 1924, it received a great upsurge of population, accepting thousands of penniless refugees expelled by Turkey—Greeks who had lived in Asia Minor in the towns of their ancestors and had never seen Greece.

The most striking feature of the landscape beyond the modern city is Mount Lycabettus, a sharp, cone-shaped peak rising to 1,775 feet, with a monastery on top. Off far beyond it, at the northern edge of the plain of Attica, is Mount Pentelicus, a solid block of marble, rising in the center to a gentle peak, the angles of which inspired the slopes of the roof of most Greek temples.

---

[9] Many fragments of the frieze, the Elgin Marbles, are in London.

Mars' Hill

Coming down from the Acropolis, passing again through the remaining pillars of the Propylaea, you descend by foot to a horn of the holy hill, which is called the Areopagus, or Mars' Hill. On this rocky platform the early kings of Athens heard cases and dispensed justice. Its name comes from a celebrated trial when Ares, god of war, defended himself against a murder charge brought by Poseidon, god of the sea.

However, our thoughts go back to the year A.D. 55 when St. Paul came to Athens and was asked to give a speech on this hill to "certain Epicureans and Stoics" who were curious about the new doctrine he was preaching as the true religion.[10] Today Paul's speech has been carved on a bronze plate and set into the virgin rock on Mars' Hill. All who remember this wonderful exposition from their Bible readings will want to have the guide read it off to them in the original Greek, following it from memory in English.

The Theseum

Just below Mars' Hill, and easily seen from it, is a perfectly preserved temple that looks like a miniature Parthenon. Any other city but Athens would have made this temple into an attraction of the first order. But here, this beautiful colonnaded structure, called the Theseum, is too close to the Parthenon to be noticeable.

Originally a temple to Hephaestus, god of fire, it later became a Christian church; then a mosque; and now a tomb for foreign fighters for Greece. It is called the Theseum because some of its frescoes depicted the hero Theseus. It is beautiful in its simplicity and lovely to study as an aid to help our imaginations picture the nobler Parthenon as it must have looked in the days of its glory.

Below the Acropolis

On the slopes of the Acropolis, as it levels off to the south, are several interesting ruins.

---

[10] Related in Acts 17.

Coming down from Mars' Hill, you first see the remains of the Odeon, a small open-air theatre built by a wealthy Athenian in the second century after Christ, but now battered by being robbed of its marble and used as a dye factory in the Middle Ages.

Next to it is the spring of Aesculapius, a shrine sacred to the god of medicine. Here wealthy Athenians came to leave their offerings to the priests and to lie in a portico while incantations and movements of mascot snakes brought about healings. Votive offerings of parts of the body healed in this rite can now be viewed in the museum at Athens.

To the east of this site stands the Theatre of Dionysus, and here we can sit for many an hour and re-enact for ourselves the romance of how our drama evolved from the customs of the Athenians. Dionysus, god of wine and joy, was also patron of the drama; and in this theatre, which "grew like Topsy" during the years of Athens' ascendancy, tragedies of Aeschylus and Euripides and many forgotten dramatists were staged for the tripod prize awarded by a jury. Comedies by Aristophanes were then put on for "relief." The evolution of the Greek chorus from a set of dialogists explaining some primitive dances in honor of Dionysus, and the gradual changing of the chorus in Roman days into individual actors reciting parts, are the pioneer path traced by the ancients for our first playwrights.

The Romans later "gilded the lily" by turning this theatre into marble and staging gladiatorial contests in it. Thus the ruins of today are Roman, but the site and the lessons it tells us are ours to absorb as we sit in the seats on the slopes of the Acropolis rising behind us.

Hadrian's Temple of Zeus

The most spectacular ruin in Athens today that is not on the Acropolis lies just below it and is situated in a park that borders the great highway over which we entered Athens from Piraeus.

Zeus, the chief of all the gods, had no imposing temple in Athens to match the ones put up to Athena and many others of the exclusive club of Mount Olympus. However, this site had been marked off for such a temple by an early tyrant named Peisistratus, and a temple half-finished was robbed of its columns by a Roman general named Sulla.

Consequently, when the Roman Emperor Hadrian[11] decided to shower munificence on Athens, his favorite city, he determined to complete this temple to Zeus, honoring at the same time the god's Roman equivalent of Jupiter. Lofty golden-yellow columns held up the roof, and a triumphal arch marked the entrance. The Middle Ages were hard on this temple, for it was used as a quarry of ready-made columns to embellish Italian churches. But the dozen that remain standing today on their lofty stone platform are eloquent witnesses of the beauty and elegance of Roman Athens.

This takes us back to our story of Athens' Golden Century—the fifth century before Christ. The tally of philosophers, dramatists, architects, artists, sculptors, and lawgivers who worked together in this city in that one age includes the greatest of the centuries. Under the rule of Pericles, Athens was indeed the "hub of the universe" in producing things of beauty for sheer beauty's sake; discussing new doctrines for the pure love of investigating intellectual solutions to ethical problems, and composing literature that soon became the standard for all ancient writers.

Athens also was busy at politics and empire-building and, because of her haughty diplomacy, became involved in that bloody civil struggle known as the Peloponnesian Wars. Despite her fleet, her allies, and her wealth, she lost some disastrous campaigns, and her arch-enemy Sparta won the conflict in the year 404 B.C., taking over the primacy of Greece.

Athens was weakened and devastated, but her reputation was so great that her university attracted students from all over the world and set the styles for later and lesser artists and philosophers. Consequently, as Biblical language would put it, Athens "led captivity captive," setting the cultural pace for her successors. In 360 B.C. all of Greece was overrun by the crude pastoral state of Macedon to the north. The Macedon court adopted Greek ways, and the heir to the throne, Alexander the Great, studied and worshiped at the shrines of Athens.

---

[11] Hadrian reigned from A.D. 117–138. His circular tomb in Rome is now called the Castel St. Angelo. The Adriatic Sea was named for him.

When Alexander later conquered the entire known world, he established the Greek language and Greek learning as the official and only culture of his entire empire. Under his successors this policy was rigorously pursued, and from Greece to the boundaries of India, Hellenistic culture, architecture, and religion were adopted and honored. Alexandria, Babylon, Antioch, and the larger towns of Palestine looked like small-sized Athenses with their colonnades, temples, and agoras.

Athens also won over her next conquerors—the Romans. Rome established her supremacy in Greece by 146 B.C. However, everywhere the Roman legions marched, they found Hellenistic culture in their path. In annexing these conquered regions of the East to their city-state on the Tiber, they scrupulously respected the Greek culture that reigned in those lands. Thus, during the years following the life of Christ Jesus, the eastern Mediterranean world lived through a wonderful era, ruled by a universal Roman law and uniform Roman armies, and sharing a common culture and language that was Greek.[12]

Athens, under Rome, was a university and artistic center that even if it did not produce any more culture of its own was the gathering place for students who did, and its fame reached greater heights than ever before.

Other Sights in Athens

A stroll around the center of Athens is never tiring, because it is so interesting. Ancient sites are mingled with lively centers of today's life, and the mixture of all periods of Athens' history makes for a refreshing variety.

Setting out from your hotel and ambling up Stadium Street— the wide, straight thoroughfare that is the main axis of modern Athens—you pass many stores, sidewalk cafés, the University, various public buildings, and a few small parks. The people, in their active ways, in their discussions, and eager friendliness, contribute most of the attractiveness of the scene.

---

[12] The New Testament was written in Greek. St. Paul, born a Pharisee of the strictest sect of the Hebrew religion, spoke and wrote in Greek, and was a Roman citizen.

When you reach the Ommonia Square, the busy crossroads of the modern city, you feel that Athens is indeed a twentieth century city. Bustling traffic, newspaper stands, restaurants, and hurrying pedestrians dodging the clanging streetcars almost obliterate your memories of Athens' ancient wonders. However, you need only walk a few more blocks to reach the magnificent new Classics Museum, in which statues and sculptures excavated from Athens' lost monuments can be admired at leisure.

In the Ommonia Square you can also board Athens' modern subway line and ride the eight miles down suburban row to the port of Piraeus. This ride is greatly recommended if you would like to mingle with the Greek people, watching to see how many of them look as if they stepped off a Grecian urn or belong in a statuesque setting enhancing some famous temple.

However, there is more to see of Athens if you turn to the left and start walking toward the Acropolis, whose now-familiar profile stands only a half mile to the south.

In passing through the modern market place, where gesticulating Athenians are trading foodstuffs and furnishings with each other, you quickly reach the Tower of the Winds. Here you will discover a well-preserved eight-sided building of late Roman style that houses a water-clock of mysterious mechanism. Everyone who examines it is entitled to a guess as to how it worked! It is considered to have been a gift of some rich business men to the ancient market place of the city.

A few steps farther and you come out into the wide area of the excavated *agora*, or business center—market place of the heart of ancient Athens. For over twenty years a group of archaeologists directed by a Princeton professor and financed by the Rockefeller Foundation have been sifting through the accumulated debris of the centuries. Every important find has been put into the Museum, so that the area is empty of buildings or monuments. Rather ironically, the modern subway skirts the agora at its far side, with trains passing this ancient scene every few minutes. While in the agora, you can look up and see above you the modest Theseum, and then you realize that you have gone completely around the Acropolis. In short, you have now "done" Athens' most outstanding remains. Only profound students of Greek history or mythology need comb the city any farther, for the rest of Athens' history is buried, and one needs a more detailed study of Greek culture than this book can hint at, to evoke the scenes into suitable life.

Marathon and Sunium

However, before leaving Athens, a day's drive by automobile over modern roads will be an enjoyable feature, especially since two important spots form such pleasant objectives.

It is only twenty-two miles from Athens across Attica to the field of Marathon. The route climbs over the pass between Pentelicon and Hymettus and skirts many olive groves until it reaches the quiet spot where "the mountains look on Marathon and Marathon looks on the sea."

Standing on a pyramidal mound that still contains the Athenian dead, one can absorb the view over the whole marshy plain, hemmed in by hills and the Aegean Sea, where the Persians of Darius were met and dispersed by an Athenian band under Miltiades. In that year—490 B.C.—the event was earth-shaking, for the unmilitary Greeks had actually inflicted the first defeat on the omnipotent Persian forces.

But the most popular short drive from Athens is the one that follows the seashore road past the smart beaches and bathing clubs to Sunium, where there stands a temple built to Athena and Poseidon. The view is superb. The temple is classically simple and of a later period than the Parthenon. The poet Byron was the first of the moderns to come here and write about its beauty. Near-by shafts of ancient Athenian silver mines gave importance to this corner of Attica. The temple of Sunium is dazzling white instead of the more muted golden tinge of the Parthenon. This makes it visible to every ship that rounds the promontory when sailing from Athens toward Constantinople.

Eleusis and Corinth

Another pleasant day's drive which also "treads on history" leads off in the opposite direction, westward, from Athens. It includes Greece's holiest city of antiquity, Eleusis, and Athens' closest rival power, Corinth.

From Athens the route follows the Sacred Way, a road to Eleusis over which candidates for admission to the famed Eleusinian Mysteries had to walk on foot. These Mysteries were a rite of entering into the secrets of the goddess Demeter with a chance to understand the mystery of immortality, something that intrigued those pagans whose gods failed to give any satisfactory explanation. The ceremonies were outgrowths of primitive agricultural rites[13] that, over the course of centuries, became fashionable and respected. At first limited to Athenians, they later were extended to all Greek-speakers, and eight Roman emperors went through the Mysteries. The priests at Eleusis, however, had the courage to refuse Nero's application, since he was a murderer.

Today only the marble floors and fragments of walls of the majestic halls built for the Mysteries remain, but the site still possesses the enchantment of what it meant for so select a band of initiates, beginning with great Athenian times before Aeschylus and Aristophanes and coming down past the age of Cicero to the very twilight of Rome itself. Most graphic of the remains are the semicircular grooves scraped in the solid marble where the great gates of the inner Mysteries were rolled open every year.

From here you continue on along the Gulf of Salamis to the narrow Isthmus of Corinth, only four miles wide, from which the Peloponnesus hangs from the rest of Greece. Today the Isthmus is cut through by an arrow-straight canal completed in 1890. Alexander the Great, Caesar, and Nero all tried to dig this valued short-cut for the frail triremes of their times, but none could master the task.

The canal is over one hundred feet below the land level. Crossing it by a new bridge, the road continues to Corinth, only fifty miles from Athens. Corinth's site is well suited for commerce, and as an ancient Greek city it existed for commerce and intrigue rather than for the creative arts. It was dedicated to the

---

[13] The most thorough modern explanation of the full rites of the Mysteries can be found in a book *Hellenic Travel* by W. A. Wigram, published in London by Faber & Faber Ltd., 1946, pp. 74 ff.

Phoenician-Syrian goddess Ishtar, patroness of both love and war. As an ally of Sparta, it was saved from destruction at the hands of her rival Athens, but its less crafty leaders two hundred years later drew upon themselves the ire of Rome, and the city was destroyed and sacked in 140 B.C.

The ruins now to be seen are of the later Roman commercial city, and have been excavated by American archaeologists. Its site on the inner tip of the narrow, blue Gulf of Corinth where it cuts into the heart of Greece is the main attraction for visitors of today.

St. Paul dwelt in Roman Corinth and later wrote two letters to the Corinthians here. However, today's city is on a modern site five miles away from the ruins of the ancient towns. It is the jumping-off point for tours into the Peloponnesus. Students of Greek art who have sufficient time can motor down to Mycenae, Greece's earliest civilized town, which reflects the Cretan tradition in its walls, beehive tomb, citadel and much-praised Lions Gate. Only a few miles farther south lies the smiling sea, washing the historic port of Nauplia, which now has become a gay tourist center. A new hotel on the waterfront; a smaller one offshore in an old Venetian fort; a backdrop of soaring fortified hills; and the nearness of Epidaurus, whose majestic open-air ancient theatre still serves as an arena for classical Greek dramas—all combine to make Nauplia one of Greece's most appealing resort centers. Travelers with more time can go on to Sparta's ruins seventy miles south. Or, they can follow the beautiful Gulf of Corinth to the modern port of Patras and to the site of Olympia, with all its grand and significant traditions.

On returning to Athens, many travelers can't resist the interesting daylight sail by excursion steamer down to the historic island of Aegina, the old-time resort of Poros, and the unusual island of Hydra, whose artists, gay festivals, and massive mansions dating from heroic times two centuries ago, provide a pleasant atmosphere for its new Montmartre-type of insouciant living.

Athens Today

Are the Greeks of today the same people who created such a civilization of old? Europeans and Americans, who owe so much to Athens for the exquisite worship of beauty and the art of government, their style of literature and drama and poetry, and for the countless Greek words that have enriched our languages, never tire of asking that question.

History would say yes, they are. There is no record of any overwhelming barbarian invasion that could have changed the type of the populace. The arts that were Greek disappeared under the heel of the invasions and wars of so many centuries, but the people have received little foreign influx of blood.

After Rome started on the wane, Constantine divided his empire in two. The eastern half was ruled from Constantinople, which, thenceforward became the dominating cultural force of the Greek world in place of decadent Athens. Modified Greek art, called Byzantine, then reigned supreme until the Western world's freebooters, in the Fourth Crusade, conquered Constantinople, upset its empire, and ruled Greece as an Italian province. Later the Turks overturned the Christian powers, and Greek sites suffered during futile campaigns launched by the Venetians to embarrass and annoy the Turks.

However, the grandeur that was Greece sprang to life in the hearts of the growing commercial powers of western Europe, and when the Greeks struck a weak blow for their independence in 1821, Britain, France, and Russia took to the diplomatic hustings, while writers and poets sang loud songs of praise at the rebirth of Greece. Thanks to this help from abroad, the Sultan of Turkey was obliged to recognize an independent, but weak, Greek state. The British stood as guardians during the nineteenth century and protected the small kingdom from Turkish encroachments during several dangerous periods.

Under the guidance of Greece's greatest modern statesman, Eleutherios Venizelos, the little country achieved all its territorial claims against Turkey during the two Balkan wars and World War I, with Greece becoming mistress of the Aegean, of part of Asia Minor, and one side of the straits. She held part of Alexander's Macedonia and Thrace, and was an ally of the victorious powers of the world.

The sad events since that time—1920—are well-known and read almost like fiction. When the young King died in that year from a monkey bite, his exiled father, Constantine, came back and fired Venizelos. Then the Turks struck and rolled up the overextended Greek armies in Asia Minor. In the national revulsion over this catastrophe, Constantine abdicated, and his son a year later. This time Greece established a republic, and the exiled Venizelos returned to lend some leadership to the unhappy country. Then Turkey expelled over 350,000 Greeks from her Asiatic dominions, and Greece had to make room for them as best she could.

As the tension in Europe increased during the 1930's, the weak republic was ended in favor of a return of King George, who inaugurated a drum-tight dictatorship under General Metaxas. However, Greece was stronger in spirit than her setbacks and her volatile changes in government would indicate. For when Italy invaded the little country on October 28, 1940, expecting an easy expedition, the Greek army not only stopped the Fascist legions but actually expelled them from Greek soil. The whole world took courage from this first defeat administered to an Axis army. Only the German invasion of the next year plunged Greece into an occupation that brought on famine and disorder.

After the end of the war, in which Greece won honor and laurels, and a place in the United Nations, the Communist states of the Balkans tried to foment a revolution that would bring Greece supinely into their number. But ready aid from the United States in the form of munitions, military guidance, and strong diplomatic support threw back that challenge.

Greece today is a confident and united country of eight million homogeneous people, struggling with economic challenges, but more prosperous than ever before in modern history, thanks to the vital transfusions of the Marshall Plan and the support of prosperous Greek citizens in many parts of the world.

It is with admiration for the role played in history by this race so few in numbers and resources—yet so valiant in spirit—that we leave Athens in gratitude. Swinging toward the west, we are bound for the mystic island of Sicily, which played such a role in history as one of the fairest daughters of Greece.

SICILY

Fateful Land Bridge

WHO WOULD EVER THINK that Sicily, now somewhat off the beaten path, was once a battleground between two great civilizations? So quiet and almost forgotten now; yet so significant during the tug-of-war between the Greeks and the Carthaginians.

That contest (only twenty-three centuries ago!) had such a great effect on Sicily and its people that its invisible load still weighs on their bent backs in the form of a constant struggle for existence. In the United States we can see palpable evidence of this, for sizable colonies of transplanted Sicilians can be found in almost all American cities and towns.

Yet to arriving travelers Sicily is one of the loveliest islands imaginable. As one of the farthest-south lands in Europe, Sicily lies in a gentle latitude. It is surrounded by the bluest of seas. It is the first corner of Europe to bask in the arrival of spring. Its prime money products are lush products of balmy springtide— lemons, almonds, tangerines, oranges, and grapes.

Sicilian spring! The very words bring thrills to winterbound travelers up north. The sound of the words symbolizes romance. And all around the civilized world Sicilian spring is identified inseparably with the charming little town of Taormina, finest of the island's resorts for outsiders.

Around the semitropical coastlines of this triangular island are other beckoning centers of charm. Palermo, Sicily's capital, is a city of fine hotels and imposing buildings, cradled in an amphitheatre of jumbled peaks. Syracuse, only a shadow of its majestic self of Greek days, breathes the sunladen breezes from Africa. Messina is a hospitable city beside its narrow strait, surrounded by orange groves and cypress-dotted hills. Catania, a modern-style metropolis, boasts a first-rate opera and gives unfailing views of Sicily's imposing tyrant and master—Mount Etna.

Off on remote hilltops there still stand chaste and classic temples erected by pupils of Greece's finest architects of old. Medieval towns whose names have never been heard by Americans boast enormous cathedrals containing art and architecture second only to the richer endowments of Italy. And on the quiet southern shores of the land are the gentle sandy beaches of Gela and Licata where America's own G.I.'s suddenly swooped ashore no longer ago than the summer of 1943.

On that beautiful tricorn island life can be gentle. An opera has been written about its "rustic chivalry."[1] Its farm carts are painted with an extravaganza of bright colors that never fail to enchant every tourist landing at a Sicilian port. Its horses sport towering plumes. The people are full of friendliness for visitors. They sing and play their guitars whenever they can find a chance. They are masters at tuning up street organs. They are heroic in getting along with so little.

Is it any wonder that Sicily is a land beloved by travelers?

Reaching Sicily

It isn't always easy to go to Sicily directly. However, several sailings of transatlantic steamers from New York call at Palermo, arriving there on about the twelfth day out. The simplest way is to go to Sicily after being in Rome or Naples. An overnight train runs from both cities, reaching the Strait of Messina after fourteen hours from Naples. Through cars, carried across by train ferry, serve Messina, Catania, and Palermo. There is also an overnight steamer from Naples to Palermo on certain days of the week, and, of course, air service by Italian planes from Rome.

Between the various cities of Sicily there is an excellent service by luxury busses on various days of the week, and diesel-type train units occasionally, too, over the main rail circuits. Distances

---

[1] A more widespread name is the original *Cavalleria Rusticana.*

are not great, but the contrasts between provinces and scenic regions are.

Mediterranean cruise liners call at either Palermo or at Messina, with excursions running inland to the important scenic points adjacent to those ports. Travelers who arrive from the Near East, coming along the route we have been following, can voyage by Italian steamer from Alexandria, Haifa, Beirut, or Athens direct to Syracuse or Catania.

So, while it is not always possible to reach Sicily on the exact day you may wish, you can get there conveniently. While she is no longer on the economic map of the Mediterranean, she is too squarely placed athwart all travel lanes in that sea to be entirely avoided except by those determined to do so.

Sicily Spans the Mediterranean

Sicily's turbulent story can partly be blamed on the fact that the island is a land bridge across the Mediterranean Sea. As viewed by a glance at the map, it is a triangular football lying in perpetual jeopardy of being kicked clear out of the Middle Sea by the boot of Italy.

It is separated from Italy only by the two-mile-wide Strait of Messina. And it extends westward to within a mere eighty miles of the shores of Africa. Its era of greatest magnificence came when its nearest neighbors in both Europe and Africa created lofty civilizations. And its frustration and downfall came when those civilizations, clashing, used Sicily as their battlefield.

The Phoenicians "discovered" Sicily, of course. Its southern shores they used as a bearing in their headings westward toward their daughter city of Carthage on the nearest part of Africa. And from Sicily's beaches they could descry the presence of Malta, whose magnificent harbor they soon made good use of.

The Phoenicians found a native tribe on Sicily who called themselves the variant of Siculi.[2] They may have been an isolated group of Celts, but it is most likely that they were of the same Mediterranean stock as the Cretans and the Philistines. The Siculi, however, were too primitive to compete when the Cartha-

---

[2] Also spelled "Sikels," which is pronounced much like "Celts."

ginians and the Greeks began to settle down on their island, and they were swallowed up by the newcomers during the ensuing centuries.

The Phoenicians made no permanent settlements on Sicily. The first people who did so were the Greeks. Colonists from Corinth, feeling their way along the southern coasts of Italy, began arriving in the seventh century before Christ, and soon settled down thickly along the eastern shore of the island, to which they gave the name of Trinacria, the "Three-Cornered Land," for Sicily is a definite-shaped triangle.

Chief of the Greek cities was Syracuse, which soon outgrew its mother city of Corinth, and began building an empire of its own. It sent out colonists to the western end of Sicily, who found themselves challenged by newcomers from another city with imperial ambitions—Carthage. A battle fought at Himera in 480 B.C. between these two strangers led to a truce in Sicily, giving the Greeks mastery over the south and east coasts, with Carthage holding on to the western tip and the rugged north shore.

Just on the Greek side of that line of demarcation are to be found the finest set of Greek classical ruins anywhere in the world —Agrigento.[3] This city built temples that are still exquisitely well preserved, standing on a long ridge nobly aloof from the unpretentious medieval city cowering on the higher hills inland. Philosophers like Empedocles[4] and many poets flourished here.

How superb the cities in western Sicily would have become had they not been located in what became a no man's land! Certainly the long line of temples at Agrigento and the relics of Solinunte and Segesta are sumptuous enough to make this a fertile line of thought.

No one who finds himself in Palermo should fail to motor out to Segesta fifty-seven miles away. For there, standing in a bucolic setting, is the lonely, abandoned, never finished, simple temple built by the busy people of a Greek city that has long ago

---

[3] Known in ancient days as Akragas.
[4] The port town for Agrigento was renamed by Mussolini Porto Empedocle. American G.I.'s, landing here, irreverently rechristened it "Okle-Dokle."

vanished completely. The temple, still without its roof as it was when Carthage's soldiers swaggered in, now sits in a quiet but often windy dell. Thirty-six Doric columns, on a platform two hundred feet long, create a scene of beauteous charm. Near-by is a Greek-style amphitheatre, carved out of a slope, with the distant sea furnishing the superb backdrop that the Greeks always preferred for their theatres. Not many miles away are the tumbled blocks that once formed the huge temple of Solinunte, a temple more massive than anything in Greece itself, yet located here in what was never more than a frontier provincial town.

Poor Sicily became a football for four hundred years, never able to germinate her own civilization. Yet in her turbulent years she shared an epic age of glory with Greece, the motherland. Syracuse, a city of almost a million, rivaled Athens so brilliantly that an Athenian fleet led by Alcibiades came to humble the proud upstart town. The genius of the city's rulers' and the greater zeal of the Syracusan fleet demolished this assault, but at a frightful cost. Greek met Greek and thousands perished. Athens was so weakened by this disaster that she soon lost her independence to Sparta.

No Man's Land

The difficult as well as the glorious years of Sicily's history all combine to teach a historical fact. Whenever the Mediterranean was contested by hostile naval powers, Sicily was on the front battle line of the belligerents. But when one maritime empire ruled the Inland Sea, Sicily was in a backwash. History may not repeat itself in detail, but its trends always recur when various factors fall into place.

Thus, when Greeks and Carthaginians became irreconcilable racial and cultural enemies, Sicily became their battleground. This happened again a thousand years later when Moslem and Christian fought for supremacy in the Mediterranean world. And once again, two thousand years later, when Mussolini's Fascist pretensions clashed with the democratic defenders of the free world, Sicily was the bridge for the victors.

' The word "tyrant" was the Syracusan word for its governing magistrate.

Greece and Carthage were too evenly matched to defeat each other. Then came Rome on the scene. Jealousy between Syracuse and upstart Rome involved Sicily in those mighty convulsions among the ancient warmakers—the three Punic Wars. Syracuse called in the ancient enemy, Carthage, to hold off the rising one. For over a hundred years the opposite shores of the Mediterranean were locked in mighty combat. Rome, the heir of Greek-European civilization, was pitted against Carthage, the daughter of Phoenicia and thus of the Asiatic world. Rome called these wars "Punic" —i.e., Phoenician—as a sign of this racial aspect of the struggle.

When at length total victory was achieved by Rome, a thousand years of peace came to Sicily. Rome was supreme, and the *Pax Romana* governed the whole Mediterranean. No enemies were left to ravage Sicily's shores and despoil her temples. But what a costly peace! Plundered by rapacious governors, neglected by distant rulers, the island sank into a backwater. Its polyglot people lost their verve. Its riches went to its masters. Sicily disappeared from the ancient map of important places.

Palermo and the "Sunny Period"

But the cycle of history had some exciting chapters to unroll as soon as roving freebooters returned to the vivid blue waters of the Middle Sea. The Roman fleet vanished, and pirates began to infest the scene. Vandals and Goths marauded in defiance of the nearest keeper of the peace in distant Constantinople, whose splendid emperors finally sent a fleet to occupy Sicily and protect it. But they were no match for the pirates of the Prophet—those descendants of Sinbad crusading for Mohammed. In A.D. 827 they were strong enough to land in force, and in a few years had annexed the whole island. The balance of power was tipped back in favor of the hosts from the East, the heirs of Carthage.

Yet the Arabs of Sicily were considerably more advanced in science and art than were the vanquished Christians, whose kinsmen of Italy and Europe were wallowing in the stagnation of the Dark Ages. Pretty mosques and palaces were set up, tiled and tinted with the art of the Oriental homeland. One of these former mosques now forms the center of the Church of the Hermits in Palermo.

The dawn of the Middle Ages in Europe brought another turn of the wheel to forgotten Sicily. It so happened that Norman knights, unemployed warriors who had become Christian gentlemen, were chafing at the insufficient room in their little duchy of Normandy to live as befitted such swashbuckling ex-Vikings. Very little inducement was needed to bring them to the warm and beckoning Mediterranean. At the service of their new faith, they readily took up the Pope's hint that the infidels closest to the Holy City of Rome should be evicted. Accordingly, in 1061 a Norman detachment led by Count Roger d'Hauteville landed in northern Sicily.[6] After ten years they had the strength to evict the Saracens from the capital city of Palermo, and Sicily was once more made a part of Europe.

The Normans liked their new conquest and, by permission of the Pope, settled down to run it. Their energy soon had turned it into a prosperous kingdom. Further conquests by the Normans in Italy and the Holy Land brought wealth and many skilled artisans to the neglected island.

Palermo under the Normans became the fairest and freest of all the cities of Italy. A royal palace was built, whose chapel is still one of the artistic jewels of the whole world. Called the Palatine Chapel, it was decorated by Arab and Greek workmen in the styles they knew best. Scalloped arches and tiled walls were done by Arabs, while the Greeks used mosaic motifs to portray the hierarchy of heaven after the style of Constantinople.

However, the finest monument left by the Normans is the imposing cathedral and cloister at Monreale, a suburb high in the hills overlooking Palermo's fruited valley and majestic bay. All visitors to the city lose no time in driving up the five miles to this little town to see the massive church whose walls are lined with exquisite mosaics illustrating the whole story of the Bible and portraying a Greek-style figure of the Christ at the head of the apse. These mosaics, all laid down with infinite care on the walls of this cheerful church during the years between 1174 and 1198, have given inspiration to thousands of Italian artists.

The Norman Kings are buried in sarcophagi here, and some of them are perpetuated in less conspicuous mosaic figures.

---

[6] Only five years before other Normans subjugated another island—Britain.

Palermo in the thirteenth century was at its happiest period. The successor to the Norman dynasty was Frederick Hohenstaufen, Emperor of Germany, though born in Sicily. He invited Italian poets and artists to his court in such numbers that even Dante admits that modern Italian literature got its start from Frederick's patronage. Frederick made Sicily the headstone of his mid-European empire, but because he incurred the hostility of the Pope, his empire was torn apart at his death in 1250. Sicily was turned over to a French count from faraway Anjou who happened to be a knight chevalier for the Church. Yet this proved a mistake—for inside of twenty-two years, on the sad night of the "Sicilian Vespers," the people of Palermo rose in desperation and slaughtered every single Frenchman within reach. They then invited the King of Aragon, to propose a ruler. When this new dynasty died out in turn during the early 1500's the Kings of Spain carried on, sending ineffectual and corrupt viceroys to rule the island in their name. Sicily again sank into a period of decline and slept a sleep of stagnation during the exciting years when Europe woke up in the full light of the Renaissance and began to move into the world of empire-building.

Before the G.I.'s Came

Thus the traveler to Sicily is like the American soldiers and sailors who came to the island in such numbers in 1943—he looks at it with mixed rapture and bewilderment. The beauty of this mountainous land bridge is at first overwhelming. The fertile valleys with their almond and orange trees, lemon orchards and exquisite temple ruins; and the attractive people, who are of differing types—Norman-blonde, Arab-dark, Greek-classic, noble-Roman—are appealing. But then the stark poverty of the towns and villages, the bareness of the landscape, and the untutored ignorance of the people hit them. The contrast is impressive.

Only history has the ultimate answer, and that is why the fascinating story spun by the centuries must be unraveled to us travelers of today, for its weight crushes down on the dispirited islanders. Added to the anguish of being ruled by alien conquerors is the harshness of economic deprivation. For the ordinary

Sicilian peasant is a sharecropper and near-serf to distant wealthy landlords, who won their privileges under feudal Spanish rule.

After four and a half centuries of association with Spain, Sicily was swapped in 1720 like a bag of marbles to the Bourbon Kings of Naples. More years of depression and neglect set in. Napoleon's wars brought no change except a temporary British occupation of the northeast tip of the island.

However, breezes signaling a kinder fate for Sicily's oppressed multitudes came along a little later. In the spring of the year 1860, Giuseppe Garibaldi with his red-coated "Thousand" landed at the western tip of the island, declared Sicily's freedom in the name of a united Italy, and on the field of Calatafimi routed the comic-opera army of the Bourbons. Today an obelisk honoring this skirmish rises high in proximity to the lovely Temple of Segesta.

Garibaldi captured Palermo and swept on to southern Italy. The same year a Kingdom of Italy was proclaimed, and a few years later Sicily found an economic good wind blowing with the opening of the Suez Canal. Sicily's ports of Catania and Syracuse became jumping-off places for Italy's share in the new trade currents of the Middle Sea.

However, independent Italy did very little for Sicily. The only "break" that came along was the chance to emigrate overseas, and thousands of Sicilians gave up the unequal fight to move to Argentina and the United States. In Buenos Aires today the largest and finest city park is named after Palermo. In the United States hardly a single town is without its Sicilian family. But in their great numbers, a few came along who brought a less constructive heritage with them, in the form of a knack at brigandage that later blossomed into techniques adopted by American gangsters. For, at the time of the emigration, a mysterious secret society known as the Mafia, a gang without a purpose or a publicly known leader, terrorized the island at will with its assassinations and robbings. The Sicilians paid it tribute and did not resist it.

The world turned its sympathies to Sicily in the year 1908, when a shattering earthquake hit the Strait of Messina, killing over 200,000 persons in the debris of the large cities of Messina and Reggio. Relief funds poured in to reconstruct the towns in their original style.

Fascism, so flamboyant and extravagant, neglected Sicily woefully, except for building some new air bases from which the Germans later sallied forth to devastate helpless Malta to the south.

New Paths Around an Old Island

A natural travel route leads around Sicily from Palermo. One can follow the ancient line separating Carthage's domains from Greek, marveling at the ruins of Solinunte and Agrigento. Near-by are the crescent beaches of Gela and Licata, from which the G.I.'s swept inland to quick victory after their landings in 1943. Pompous baroque towns like Ragusa and Modica, built under the Spanish viceroys, give pause before warm Syracuse is reached.

Now a minor port of 68,000 in a corner of the metropolis of ancient times, Syracuse has much to show today. Here the traveler can see the cave where St. Paul preached on his way to Rome, and wander through the tree-festooned quarries where thousands of Athenian prisoners were left to languish. In the Roman stadium acanthus plants grew wild,[7] as they did when Greek artisans lived on this very spot. The Greek amphitheatre is larger than any in Greece, another sign that Sicily was the "wild west" in Greek days, the daughterland where "things came big." The diameter of this theatre is 483 feet, and from its seats the spectators can look down on the whole city and its harbor.

On leaving Syracuse, the traveler quickly reaches Catania, the second city of Sicily, and its musical center. Catania of today was built after an earthquake disaster in 1693, and up its straight main street today's pedestrian can have a superb view of towering Mount Etna, 10,742 feet high, covered with snow all year, and the most active volcano in Europe.

---

[7] These common plants were used as the inspiration for Corinthian capitals in ancient architecture.

Taormina

From Catania the main road along the coast passes over the sloping contours of Etna to reach Sicily's most famous and beautiful resort—Taormina. Here travelers come from all Europe to spend Sicilian spring in rustic simplicity, in small hotels amid semitropic beauty, on a mountainous shelf 672 feet above the vivid-blue Ionian Sea. Its Greek amphitheatre is the most beautiful of all, for from its stone rows can be enjoyed a majestic combined view of the entire slope of Mount Etna and the surrounding expanse of sea.

All should sit in that eternal theatre and muse on the meaning of Sicily. Here is an island that tells us of the glory that was Greece. For the achievements of that near-by Hellenic land—without kings, without natural wealth, without pomp—stand out for us to admire humbly. The worship of beauty, the idealization of its concepts in the forms of its gods, the ineffable skill at designing arts and architecture that we today lean on heavily in our own forms of self-expression, its first concepts of equality of man and freedom of government, form a legacy that cannot be tarnished by the passage of centuries. The Ionian Sea, lying at the foot of Taormina, binds Sicily to Greece and gives the downtrodden island a glory that some day will bring its crestfallen people to a position of happiness when they awake to claim it.

Messina

Near Taormina is Sicily's great entry point—Messina, the tip of the island where it almost touches the toe of Italy, facing the strait where Ulysses slipped between the rockbound siren of Scylla and the windy whirlpool of Charybdis.

Only two miles of blue water separates Sicily from the mainland here, and both sides of the strait rise up sharply from the water. Yet there is room for the city of Messina on a narrow "shelf," opposite which a narrow spit of land bends around like a perfect sickle, almost as if the gods of old had shaped this site for a city.

Across this strait in late August of 1943 the German army

escaped after it had failed to push the Allied armies off Sicily. The result of their effort was a Messina once again in ashes, bombed into rubble by American planes trying to block the retreat. Yet today it has industrially arisen to its former size and elegance.

Stromboli

Hardly twenty miles out in the sea north of Messina rises Stromboli, a safety valve for the mysterious volcanic disturbances below. Out of the cone of this isolated island, 3,037 feet above the sea, pour sparks and fiery lava at almost any minute of the day and night, a volcano in constant display, lighting the sea highway from Sicily to Naples, where we will now follow, heading along the most traveled seaway of the ancient mariners.

THE BAY OF NAPLES

Playground of the Centuries

STEAMING INTO THE BAY OF NAPLES is an experience of such beauty and languor that for centuries the world has marveled at the famous slogan *Vedi Napoli e poi mori.* ("See Naples and [then] die.") This means, of course, that no one must be allowed to die until he has seen Naples.

Naples dominates the whole bay, which makes a scintillating backdrop to the big port city. As the traveler comes in by ship (and it can't be admired in any better way), the beauteous scene unfolds before him in a sweep of welcome. All ships must steer around the guardian islands of Capri or Ischia, and then sail right in. On the right are the cliffs of lovely Sorrento; on the left are hills covered with villas, leading into the city of Naples. Straight ahead is the monarch surveying all—passive, graceful, soot-blackened Vesuvius, the four thousand feet of its height giving elegance to the scene.

This panorama has been the same since the dawn of time, and has been admired by all comers. The same view met the earliest Phoenicians as they rowed their trading barks in from the Levant. It opened up likewise for the Greek colonists who were following the leadings of Neptune from Trinacria to the south. And in Roman days, Naples became the center of a string of pleasure resorts as gay and sun-bathed as the very towns we see rising up on all sides today. The city and its satellite towns were stately ports, into which noble triremes swept from the rich shorelands of the Middle Sea. Their cargoes and passengers, once landed, were conveyed up the Appian Way only 127 more miles into Rome itself.

Today Naples is again the chief port of Rome and the largest city of south Italy. Its 1,100,000 people live simply and frugally, working around the docks, fashioning articles of coral, cameo, leather, and silk; catering to tourists, and doing a lot of the gentle loafing and merrymaking that is symbolized so well in its "theme" songs like "O Sole Mio," "Funicoli, Funicola," "Ciribiribin," and "Santa Lucia."

Its harbor is nature-made, and a blessing, for even the most primitive mariners could appreciate its fog-free, warm-water, spacious Bay. Today the biggest ocean liners can come up and dock, using for that purpose an elegant pier that is called the Maritime Station. This is a massive area of marble and concrete built by the Fascists as their proud showplace, then bombed into dilapidation, and now restored by Marshall Plan aid to its former lavishness.

As all the Allied soldiers who slogged their way through Italy can testify, Naples is distinct from the rest of Italy. Its architecture is as different from that of Florence or Venice as it is from that of Paris. Its people are of a southern type strange to the Milanese or Venetians. Neapolitans are shorter, darker, more Greek in cast, semi-Arabic in complexion, more loyal to their own dramatic, semi-operatic southern ways than to those of their cousins of the north. And small wonder, for Naples has followed a separate course in history from the rest of Italy since late Roman days.

Ashore in Naples

Let us leave our ships and go ashore into welcoming Naples, just as thousands and thousands of our own soldiers and sailors did. Its buildings look almost Sicilian—stucco or stone, with lacy balconies for every single window on all floors, windows that are heavily shuttered almost all day and night. The streets are narrow except for some main avenues. There are hundreds of stores selling attractive things. A heavy traffic of streetcars and trucks provides animation all the time. There are lots of urchins; also individualists who contact foreign travelers and offer to show them everything and to guide them anywhere. The main shopping street is the straight and narrow Via Roma,[1] built only a few decades ago. Any G.I. "graduate" of the Italian campaign remembers exciting moments on the Via Roma, dodging its whizzing truck convoys by clinging to the crowded, narrow sidewalks.

The center of Naples is only a few steps from the Maritime Station, revolving around the intersection of the Via Roma with the big Square of the Plebiscite. Here is the massive, baroque King's Palace, built in the seventeenth century by the Bourbons. Adjoining is one of Europe's most famous opera houses—the San Carlo. And opposite that rises the glass-domed Galleria Umberto, an arcade in the shape of the cross, where shops, cafés, and crowds all throng together.

As a city, Naples has much of the distinctive. It has broad avenues along its bay front, with big hotels and office buildings staring across the blue water at Vesuvius. It has colonnades, and tree-lined esplanades, arches, funicular cars rising steeply up to residential districts atop the Vomero, and several frowning, medieval fortresses. It has supermodernistic government buildings bequeathed by the Fascists, tunnels for traffic under obstructive hills, pretty restaurants with the much-desired views, seaside cafés, and of course countless churches of baroque and rococo. And it has two museums that should never be missed—the San Martino, high up in an old monastery attached to a fort, containing exhibits of majolica and porcelain, and paintings of the Neapolitan Renaissance, and another museum down in the city on the Via Roma. Called simply the National Museum, it is filled with the priceless relics of Pompeii and Herculaneum, and with rich artistic collections from historic Italian palaces.

The city merges into a suburb of grace called Posillipo, and then into Bagnoli, a town of villas, beaches, and hot springs. Next comes Pozzuoli, a congested port on a side bay of its own, where most of the Roman commerce was handled in ancient days. St. Paul, coming from his shipwreck at Malta and heading for his trial at Rome, landed here. The bay at Pozzuoli was also the

---

[1] By rigid custom (or ordinance) the main business street of every city and town in Italy (except in Rome itself) is named the Via Roma.

staging point for the hundreds of landing craft and naval ships
that convoyed the invasion troops to southern France in the
summer of 1944. Pozzuoli today has an imposing Roman amphitheatre, and sites of ancient temples on which many churches have
been built.

Roman Playground

The name of Naples is ironic. In Greek, it means "the New
City"—but it is at least 2,400 years old. Originally a suburb to an
older town, it eventually swallowed up its neighbor. It served as
the farthest-flung outpost of Greek civilization, and even after
being subjugated to Rome, it was a self-governing, Greek-speaking
city almost down to the time of Christ.

Its history is entrancing, for the ancients loved this bay and
its natural wonders. Deep volcanic fires burn beneath, as evidenced by Vesuvius' eruptions, the fuming sulphur holes of
Solfatara, the many craters and boiling springs. Thus the ancients
regarded this region as a gateway to the underworld and a point
under close attention of the gods. This made it a center of contact
between such familiar races as the Phoenicians and Greeks, and
the Iron Age Latin tribes of the Samnites and the Etruscans.
Naples occupies a site hallowed by ancient reverence.

In a series of caves beyond Pozzuoli there dwelled in bygone
centuries the sibyl of Cumae, a divine prophetess who could read
oracles. Virgil tells of Aeneas stopping to see the sibyl to hear her
prophecy about the founding of Rome. Near-by is the crater
lake of Avernus, whose name means "without birds," for winged
creatures avoided this air. It thus came to be considered the
gateway to Hades, and Dante so honored it when he was conducted by Virgil by this route down into inferno.

The people of ancient Neapolis grew to outstrip their rival
settlements on the Bay of Naples generally by siding with the
right parties in the tribal and cultural wars of old. Thus, when
Rome became the mistress of the world, Naples was prosperous
and the shores of its scintillating bay were thronged with villas
and resorts. Augustus and Nero spent much time here, and Tiberius
lived almost his whole reign on Capri. Lavish temples lined the

shores also, and the richness of life in that opulent age is vividly attested by the artistic exquisiteness of the objects found in Pompeii's storehouse of treasures.

Pompeii, Libidinous and Carefree

Let us enjoy the beauties of past and present together and travel around this amphitheatrical bay. Every vista pleases, and almost every little town is known for glamor, music, or history.

The Fascists bowed to the tourist trade by building an *autostrada*, or express highway, between Naples and Pompeii, a distance of seventeen miles. On the way a stop should be made at Herculaneum, a small residential Roman town dedicated to Hercules. This town was solidly buried by volcanic mud, which hardened and piled up to a depth of eighty feet. It has been only partially excavated, because of a modern town covering its site, but the richness of the homes and baths, and the artistic treasures recovered from them, make it worth visiting, especially as a contrast with Pompeii.

Continuing onward, we ride over the slopes of Vesuvius that reach down to the bay. The rich lava soil supports many orchards of olive and orange trees, and almost one continuous town hugs the shoreline.

Vesuvius was asleep in primeval days. Its single summit was covered with vines and grasses, and farming towns grew up on its fertile flanks. Not until the sixty-third year of the Christian era did it get a good shaking up from an earthquake, and only sixteen years later it "blew its top." August 24 of the year 79 was the date of this terrible event. With a roar and a quake the summit opened, and clouds of ashes and little stones rained into the air. Then came clouds of a poisonous gas, which rolled down the slopes into Pompeii and nameless other towns. This, rather than the eruption, marked the end of Pompeii. The Latin poet Pliny, observing this frightful eruption from the far side of the bay, tells how ships trying to approach and rescue the frantic multitudes couldn't penetrate the heat and the fumes.

Then after the gases came bombardments of pumice and ashes, which cascaded on Pompeii until the surface lay twenty-five feet above the old rooftops. Wet ashes and mud followed after, deluging Herculaneum, and lava streams slogged partway down after it was all over. Vesuvius, the volcanic culprit, was then found to have two summits, with a smoking, blackened crater in between.

Other eruptions have come in the centuries since then, and the height and shape of the mountain have been changed by each outbreak. Until the year 1944, tourists could ride a cogwheel railroad up to the edge of the crater and watch the red flames and smoke pillars belching forth from the central cone. But in that year, inconveniently during the war when the Allies were holding a battle line only forty miles to the north, the villain came to life and rained black dust all over the landscape. This time the cone blocked itself up, and the crater has henceforth remained cold. No fiery plume now makes Vesuvius the unfailing beacon which it was before. The cog railway was demolished by the eruption.

Arriving at Pompeii, we find ourselves on the threshold of a travel experience without parallel. For since the year 1748, when canal-diggers came across its buried houses, three-fifths of a complete Roman imperial city has been laid open to our view. In all the world there is only one Pompeii. It is a sample city of Rome's golden age, miraculously preserved for our eyes to see and enjoy.

So lifelike is Pompeii today that anyone's imagination can picture the colorful crowds of Roman days; the chariots and horsemen clattering down the narrow streets. He can hear the voices of the athletes, mixed with the bustle of shoppers, reverberating from brick walls.

Pompeii was an unusual city in its heyday. Not only was it an important commercial town, but it harbored the elegant homes of many rich Roman business men. In short, it was a city of pleasure, of easy and opulent living.

The heyday of Pompeii, the happiest years of its life, were its last twenty years, the time when the Emperor Nero fiddled. Perched on a sloping plain overlooking the beauteous Bay of Naples, it had its own corps of gladiators, and every one of its homes had a lovely view of the sleeping mountain, Vesuvius.

Yet only ten years after Nero, and only forty-eight years after the Crucifixion of Christ, the life of the city was brought to a sudden, frightful stop. The whole city disappeared from sight. The world went on its way forgetful of the pleasure resort that had paid such a heavy price—extinction—for its gay days.

You enter uncovered Pompeii today through its Sea Gate the same way as travelers who had come across the sea in olden times entered the town. This leads you into the forum, where the crowds gathered in ancient days to do business, to worship, and to exchange the news of the day.

Here stand the pillars and foundations of temples dedicated to many gods, as it was the fashion in Rome's golden days to "play it safe" and adopt the deities of many nations. Here is a graceful statue of Apollo and stately columns in Greek style.

But the narrow, straight streets that run out of the forum are more interesting to us nowadays. And narrow indeed are the streets—as it is still the custom to plan them in Latin cities of Italy, Spain, and also in Mexico and South America. Pause and gaze at the deep ruts cut in the hard stone paving by countless speeding chariots. Note how the width of the chariot tracks so approximates the width of our railroad tracks of today.[2]

A cheerful Pompeiian sight is formed by the high stepping-stones laid across the narrow streets—ideal for avoiding puddles after heavy winter rains.

Along each street there is something to see: here a baker's shop, with heavy grindstones, and the big sockets to hold fat urns of grain; next door an oil shop, with excellently carved channels in the stone to carry off the olive oil into the proper vessels.

The people of Pompeii loved pleasure. Many of them were rich, and their homes were enlivened by beautiful murals and frescoes on the walls. These murals all showed gods of plenty, artistic poets, and scenes of games, done with a delicate hand and painted in a rich shade of red that has been equaled nowhere else. We moderns call it Pompeian red and use it to decorate stylish gathering places and swimming pools.

[2] This is not just a coincidence. Wooden rails laid for carts in England's coal mine districts determined the width of standard railway gauge today. English carts must have been copied by many generations of farmers after their Roman counterparts.

Other ancient homes had mosaic floors put together with great skill. Several portray fierce-looking dogs, all done in multi-colored pieces, chained in mosaics, and bearing the familiar warning *Cave canem*—or to put it modernly, "Beware of the dog."

Pompeii's elegant homes had gardens open to the sky, where flowers, ancestors of the ones growing there today, gave fragrance to the center of the living quarters. These gardens were the origin of the modern patios so customary in Spanish and Latin American homes of today. Wealthy home-owners decorated their gardens with artistic bronze statues and fountains, and we can admire these today by visiting the National Museum at Naples where they have been put on display.

Romans of Pompeii liked their baths, and now travelers can visit the excavated baths, with the cold room, hot room, and the bathing rooms. More interesting yet is the vast amphitheatre. Pompeii was an excitable city during gladiatorial combats, and once the Roman Senate outlawed games there for ten whole years as a penalty for riots that had broken out after a tumultuous spectacle. Alongside the theatre is an open field, or palestra, where sportsmen used to train while citizens walked around the porticoes and cooled themselves under fountains. Today a swimming pool has been built in the middle of the palestra.

Life in Pompeii was not chaste. Its statues are mostly erotic and sensuous, as are many of the paintings on the walls of the houses. Life was also strident. Many walls, when scraped free of the ash and lava, still bore bold scrawls touting political candidates or proclaiming next week's schedule of events in the amphitheatre.

Leaving Pompeii, visitors stop at the museum to see some of the household articles retrieved from the excavations. But then, we must visit again the museum in Naples and see with more appreciation the exquisite mosaics, reddish frescoes, and statues, the latter of which all show the effect of being showered with hot gaseous ash, for they have oxidized into a uniform green. The most poignant memories anyone can take away from this museum in Pompeii are those of the plaster casts of the chained dog and of the prostrate refugees, made from cavities inside the solidified ashes.

Amalfi

Beyond Pompeii, it is only a short distance over the spur of the mountains which enclose the south side of the Bay of Naples to the smiling, wide-open Gulf of Salerno, whose chief attraction is the charming medieval port city of Amalfi.

This little fishing town, hemmed in between mountains and sea, sprang to fame in the ninth and tenth centuries as a nest of bold and daring mariners fighting against the Moslem pirates who had turned the Mediterranean into an Arab lake. For, with the smothering of Pompeii and the fall of the Caesars, there had set in a slow decline in the fortunes of Italy resulting in the end of the Pax Romana. Grass sprouted in the streets of imperial Rome, and the long reign of classic Roman-Greek culture was snuffed out. Goths and Vandals, rude bearded warriors from northern Europe, roamed the land, sacking, burning, pillaging. When Belisarius, Christian General sent by Constantinople's emperors, arrived in 536 to restore the Empire to Rome, his battles of liberation only added to the destruction and wastage. Belisarius' hosts marched on to Rome, the only army before the Anglo-American array of 1944 to have taken the city from the south. Yet Goths and Lombards returned, and for several centuries southern Italy was in their weak and barbarian grasp. During this time corsairs from Africa raided the shores at will. They even captured the Isle of Capri and sailed away with its entire population to be sold into slavery.

Yet little Amalfi took heart and began to do something about things. Its ships freed southern Italy from Saracen incursions. Trade began to stir again, and the little city was able to build a semi-Byzantine cathedral and striking edifices which stun the eyes of today's visitors. Amalfi's sailors helped convoy chivalric warriors to the Holy Land for the Crusades, and it was in an Amalfi-supported refuge for wounded knights in Palestine that was born the Holy Order of the Hospitalers, the Knights of St. John of

Jerusalem, which later bloomed into the Knights of Malta, a historic international order which still exists.

Amalfi's pioneer struggle in this region was taken up by the Norman rulers of Sicily after their conquest of that island, and when the Normans came over to conquer southern Italy, Amalfitan fleets furnished valuable aid.

Today Amalfi has only slightly changed from those valiant days of almost a thousand years ago. The steep slopes that rise up behind the town furnish perches for palm-surrounded villas, lemon groves, and delightful small hotels. High up on the heights is the old town of Ravello, famous as a retreat for modern-day celebrities who want to rusticate for a short while in utter peace and bliss. Down in Amalfi, two fine hotels give grand views from their rooms and balconies. One of these hotels is located in the structure of a deserted Capuchin convent.

All of the seaward windows in Amalfi look across the water at Salerno, an industrial city distinguished only by its strategic location, which figured in the first Allied landing on the mainland of Europe in World War II. After the fall of Mussolini, following the conquest of Sicily, an armada of Anglo-American warships and landing craft assaulted the magnificent beaches curving south from Salerno and, after a month of bitter struggle, secured possession of this commanding entrance into Italy. From here the armies swept on to Naples and began the agonizingly slow push up the boot of Italy against Germany's evasive "underbelly."

At the far tip of those beaches lie the beautiful old Greek temples of Paestum, deserted near the shoreline. Liberated by the first American landings of September 1943, they were un-harmed in the fighting, although irreverent G.I.'s joked that Italian towns fell into ruins even before the bombing started. However, Paestum was once the richest of the cities of southern Italy, founded by Greek colonists six hundred years before Christ. In those days the whole south of Italy was dotted with Greek settlements and was called Magna Graecia. However, unsubdued Italian tribes destroyed many of the coastal towns before the Romans came, and one of these was Paestum. Yet today the three temples of Paestum are well preserved; are pure samples of classic

Greek art; and are worthy of their past glory. Their marbles and columns have been stripped for the churches of all the towns round about. Only twenty-five miles south of Salerno, it should be visited and admired as a sample of Greece's far-ranging fingers of culture and beautification.

The Amalfi Drive

Leaving Amalfi by the road that has been cut along the slopes high above the sea is one of the most thrilling drives in the world. No visitor to Naples dares deprive himself of the feast of beauty that is rightly ascribed to the Amalfi Drive. For fifteen miles each bend of this winding road unfolds startling new panoramas of exquisiteness. The mountains crowd down to the turquoise sea. Terraces supporting lemon or orange trees, and little villas and homes dot the coast here and there. The sea changes hue with every vagary of the sun and clouds. Almost every day of the year there is sun and warmth in this lovely scene, which faces the south and the warm sun of Africa. Along the way is the charming village of Positano, now popular with artists and writers, who live in the same charming old houses built by the original settlers, who were refugees from Paestum a thousand years ago.

The drive at length crosses the spine of the mountains and comes into Sorrento, another beauty spot and world-famed resort town, perched on cliffs high above the southern reaches of the Bay of Naples, looking across twenty miles of blue water at the city itself. Vesuvius, inscrutable and commanding, is always seen over one's right shoulder.

Sorrento

Sorrento is famed for its holiday air, its lemon groves, its cliffs and bathing, its luxurious hotels, and for its haunting song that captivates the world. "Take Me Back to Sorrento" symbolizes the carefree atmosphere of this corner of Europe. It can be played in countless accents and arrangements, and there is no Neapolitan orchestra that will not strike up its melody at the slightest encouragement.

Sorrento is also a shoppers' paradise, offering particularly excellent embroidered linens and silks. Dining on the hotel terraces in the gloaming, with the lights of Naples flickering far across the water, is a romantic experience dear to all travelers. This is also the place to witness a performance of the tarantella, Naples' most sparkling dance. Originating in Sardinia as an exercise to drive away the poison of a tarantula bite, it is now a whirling, lively dance to stirring tambourines and guitars. The costumes of the men are seventeenth century Bourbon style, complete with red cap and white stockings, while the women wear the broad skirts of the peasant workers. Because of the way it captivates foreigners, the tarantella has outdistanced all its rivals to win the reputation of the typical Italian folk dance.

Lazing the hours away at Sorrento, nothing can be further from the thought than turbulent moments of history. Yet Sorrento has seen these, although managing to escape their fury. As a village, Sorrento saw Vesuvius overpower Pompeii. It witnessed the Saracens under ferocious Red Beard, or Barbarossa, raid helpless towns along the near-by coast. Sorrento heard the clashing of arms when Amalfi was conquered by energetic Pisan invaders. It heard the furore across the water when loyal troops of Frederick Hohenstaufen, the deceased German Emperor who loved Palermo and Naples more than all his other dominions, were crushed by the French supporters of Charles of Anjou, sent by the Pope in 1250 to demolish Frederick's empire. The Frenchmen stayed to rule Naples for two centuries. They then gave way to Spanish kings of Aragon, who owned Naples for almost three more centuries until the Austrian Hapsburgs elbowed them aside in 1707. Finally, by a shift in the balance of power, the Bourbons of Spain came back and put a younger son on the throne as "King of the Two Sicilies." Under these changes, the people of southern Italy languished in a backwater, insulated from the tide of history, the cultural and religious movements, and the social changes going on to the northward in Europe under the impulse of world exploration and scientific discoveries.

The Isle of Capri

Almost as if created for the pleasure of world fugitives from cold and harsh climates is the little Isle of Capri, which sits off the end of Sorrento's peninsula like the dot of an exclamation point. It is only two hours by the regular boat from Naples, which calls at Sorrento, and anyone can step ashore at its little harbor, the Marina Grande, and ride by leisurely funicular to its chief town 450 feet up in the hills.

Capri, whose name means "island of goats," is a group of hills, tablelands, and peaks shaped like an old galleon. It sits on the horizon nobly when viewed from Paestum or Naples or from its larger island neighbor of Ischia.

Although only four and one-half square miles in size, Capri is known around the world as an international meeting spot. Its Hotel Quisisana is skilled in providing all the luxuries of great *métropoles,* and the smart Caesar Augustus, perched atop a cliff which drops a sheer 800 feet into the sea, is as recherché in elegance as any small hotel could possibly be. Many others of medium size specialize in hospitality, for over a third of Capri's population exist and labor to serve the needs of the tourists. (The rest of the inhabitants cultivate olive trees, go fishing, or engage in weaving).

There is nothing to do in Capri except loaf and have a good time. Amid such gorgeous scenery, and with a warming sun all year, who could ask for anything more? The little town has a picture-book main square, too small for cars, and set out with café tables every evening. Enticing shops, pretty walks, and panoramic spots are on every hand. Paths lead down to the Marina Piccola, on the south shore of the island, where the swimming is superb. The three sheer islands, or Faraglioni,[3] give lovely perspective to the picnic-swimmer.

Highest village of all is Anacapri, 950 feet in the air, and a center for more villas and homes, including the renowned Villa of San Michele, which is shown with pride to all visitors. This villa

---

[3] Compare with the loftier Farallones off San Francisco harbor.

is the tasteful home built by a Swedish doctor, Axel Munthe.
It incorporates countless artistic fragments of a departed Roman
home into its own walls and columns.

Capri is the proud possessor of the Blue Grotto, known to all
travelers and situated almost directly underneath the towering
heights of Anacapri. The grotto can be reached only by small boat
from Capri harbor, with the traveler changing outside its entrance
into one of the rowboats hovering around the spot. A well-timed
dash through a low-bridge opening, and the rowboat is inside a
bowl of the fairest blue light. Coasting on the placid water, one
can quickly see that all this light is coming in through the water,
reflected from outside, and thus the very air is like a bath in
sapphire. Capri's charm in having good weather almost every
day in the year means that not many people are disappointed at
the Blue Grotto, for the rowboats can only get into it on a
dead-calm day.

Naples' New Day

Steaming back in the comfortable boat from Capri to Naples,
amid the surrounding serenity of the scenery on all sides, one can
easily appreciate the passing of the centuries that have brought
so many different actors onto such a stage, of which we are
the latest.

Naples at last awoke out of its dreamy slumber of neglect
when Napoleon overturned the whole map of Europe. As he began
to threaten the Bourbon dynasty of Naples, his British adversaries
tried to buoy up this last remaining outpost of unrevolutionary
Europe. Britain's naval forces were led by Lord Nelson, the
tiger of the Mediterranean. In Naples, Nelson's duty was to stiffen
the will of the Bourbon king, and in this he was assisted by the
British ambassador, whose wife, Emma Hamilton, led Nelson to
dally on his duty for some time. The scene of his romance with
Lady Hamilton was the magnificent royal palace of Caserta, whose
imitation of Versailles is striking. This rich structure of 1200
rooms and 30 grand staircases, filled with marbles and frescoed
ceilings, is twenty-seven miles north of Naples. Its stately park
and avenues of trees made the assignment to the court of the

kings of Naples much sought after by diplomats. When the cascades were turned on, water splashed over many steps into limpid pools for the glorification of parties on hot nights and the admiration of the distinguished company.

Caserta was not often visited by travelers until the recent war, when it housed the whole Allied Force Headquarters for the Italian campaign. King George of Britain, Marshal Tito, and other wartime callers put Caserta on the map again, and hardly a G.I. in all Italy did not hear of its sumptuous rooms and salons.

The tryst of Lord Nelson and Lady Hamilton was brought to a gradual end by the advance of Napoleon, who eventually overturned the Bourbons and put his own brother Joseph on the Neapolitan throne. But the episodes at Caserta had almost shaken the British Empire, as Nelson persevered with his romance until his death at Trafalgar. Napoleon's Neapolitan dynasty was in turn ended by his defeat at Waterloo. The Bourbon kings returned, but their tenuous rule lasted only until Garibaldi swept it away in the year 1860, after his march up from the conquest of Sicily. In that year Naples for the first time in modern history joined with the rest of Italy under a common government. Its heritage made it at first a drain on the rest of Italy, for its economic and social system had been retarded by its centuries of neglect. But today, all over the south of Italy, a government-inspired economic campaign is regenerating the life of the *Mezzogiorno,* or "Land of Noon," with new public works, hotels and industries.

In Italy, all roads lead to Rome. And so it is with the most celebrated of them, the Appian Way, the master road of ancient times. Over this colorful route moved the heavy traffic from the Levant and Greece, coming up from Brindisi on the Adriatic heel of Italy, then rolling from Naples on up to Rome. Over it passed the great men of Roman days—Cicero, Caesar, St. Paul, Augustus, and later Belisarius with his army. The Allied armies during the war required seven months to cover the distance, being stopped at Cassino and Anzio for agonizing weeks on the way. This victory, however, has paved the way for us, and in a luxurious electric train, we make the distance with fleetness in less than three hours.

ROME

"Urbi et Orbi"

"URBI ET ORBI" shouted out the heralds of ancient Rome. "To the city, and therefore to the world" was the prefix of all the decisions of the Roman Senate. Rome was a city used to giving orders.

To the city, and therefore to the world. There is a thrill that comes from the ring of this pompous, yet significant motto. Travelers, as soon as they reach Rome, should waste no time in hastening to the top of the Janiculum Hill to gaze down at this clustered city, which is heir to such imperial traditions.

From atop this gentle slope, there is unveiled a sweep across the fertile plains beyond Rome to the graceful Alban Hills rising fifteen miles away. Running straight out to those hills—and beyond—is the Appian Way. In this fertile valley rose the imperial center of the world, the ruler of all the civilizations of the Mediterranean. Events decreed in this cluster of dwellings contained by the ancient walls shook the world. Down in those streets and squares echoed the voices of the *populus Romanus* and rose the huzzas as captive kings were dragged in chains to the Capitol. Around those sturdy walls have sounded the roars of attacking armies and wails of citizens whose homes were wrecked by the triumphant ones. This city below has etched quite a record on the tablets of the world's story. Its emperor ruled the whole Western world at the time the "Bethlehem babe" was born at the far corner of the Mediterranean Sea. Something in this site has kept it alive through ups and downs, so that we still call it today the Eternal City.

This city beside the swift-flowing river which is called the Tiber rose from nothing to become the boss of the civilized lands around the Middle Sea.

Rome the Modern

Despite such aged traditions, our first views of Rome are thoroughly up-to-date. As the capital of a modern Italian nation, the city has been embellished and greatly extended in recent times. It is packed with good hotels, beautiful wide avenues, excellent shops, graceful public buildings, fast-flowing traffic, and a smart-looking population made up of all elements and types of this land of Italy.

The hotels favored by Americans are grouped either along the curving Via Vittorio Veneto,[1] on which is also to be found the majestic American Embassy, or over by the railroad station. They are modern enough for the most demanding nabob, with excellent plumbing, fine dining, cheerful and meticulous service, and lush furnishings. Strolling is a pleasure, what with the illuminated fountains, exquisite façades, hospitable people, shaded squares, lovely gardens right in the heart of town, and ornate palaces.

There is plenty to do in Rome. Theatres, movies, parties, a super-gorgeous and comfortable opera house, concerts, and diplomatic goings-on make Rome an oasis of gayety.

But the uniqueness of Rome to the most modern-minded of visitors is the acute presence of Rome's imperial past, the cheek-by-jowlishness of the ancient with the sophisticated modern. The Via Vittorio Veneto, for example, leads into the solid buttresses of the ancient walls of Rome. The arriving traveler at the ultra-modernistic railroad station first sees before anything else the much-patched-up Baths of Diocletian. The bright glare down in the distance comes from modern floodlights lighting up the old Colosseum. Musical symphonic concerts are given among the shapeless ruins of the Baths of Caracalla. The mid-Victorian,

---

[1] Named after Italy's final victory over Austria in World War I.

styleless Law Courts buildings rise only a block or two from the papal Castle of Sant' Angelo, which was originally the Tomb of the Emperor Hadrian. And scattered about the city, to be encountered on even the most minor promenades, are clumps of flat-bricked wall, or excavated foundations, marking the survival of some nameless ancient home.

Our feet, as we walk about the city, are passing over hallowed ground, for on this very site lived uncounted thousands of people whose vanishing changed the even course of the world's story.

Sightseeing in Rome is very enjoyable. There are automobiles a-plenty of all vintages, also horse carriages, and now supermodern busses, with all the new refinements of loud-speakers, concert radios, reclining seats, and glass roofs.

It doesn't take long to notice that Rome has more hills than its fabled seven. There are at least ten of them, and many smaller knolls. The "seven" is probably a mystical number symbolizing completeness. Some of the original seven seem much more insignificant than the others when you find yourself walking up one of them.

The approach into Rome is more symbolic and awe-inspiring than into almost any other city of Europe. Travelers arriving by train see the tracks following one of the ancient aqueducts over the last miles. Those coming by plane motor in from the airport over the new Appian Way, entering through the old walls by narrow openings, pierced inadequately for modern traffic, opposite the original home of the papacy, the Lateran Palace. Coming down from Florence and the north, the road crosses the Milvian Bridge, which spans the Tiber at the same spot where Horatius defended a primitive bridge against the Etruscans. Motoring down the coastal road from Genoa, the traveler enters by means of a tunnel under the Vatican, while the route up from the ancient seaport of Ostia reaches the city at the massive Cathedral of St. Paul's-outside-the-Walls, where tradition holds that St. Paul was beheaded in A.D. 67.

Rome today covers only a little more ground than its ancient imperial ancestor. Seven-eighths of it lies on the eastern side of the Tiber. The remainder across the river is almost entirely residential and abuts on the Vatican, which is at the western extreme of the modern city. Around the walls and the modern villas are clusters of modernistic apartment houses built in Fascist days, which reach out into the countryside and then come to an abrupt stop. Rome has no suburbs. Its inhabitants now, as of yore, prefer to live either inside the *urbs* or far out in the *orbis*.

Because there are no large industries or sizable population centers about modern Rome, it would seem strange to find modern Italy's capital here, so far from the wealthy and progressive centers to the north. But that is where the imperial tradition of Rome comes in. Because in ancient times the metered phrase "the plain of the Tiber, the seat of the world" held good, modern Italians agreed that the capital should be set up nowhere else than in Rome. That they did not succeed in this until as recently as the year 1870 was due to the protests and vetoes of the Popes. Thus, the exciting story right under our footsteps is the solid substance on which the present importance of this city has been erected.

Rome Once a Village

Almost every big city in the world has had a humble start from some small village, and so it was with Rome. Originally, Italy was a land of local tribes, of a mixture of Celtic and other Indo-European blood, descendants of unknown ancestors who had come down from the north, as was the case in Greece. The tribes were restless and were led by minor "kings"—a situation similar to that of the Indians in America at the time the Pilgrims came. They were always in a state of a temporary truce among themselves. The Italian tribes were called "Latin" tribes in their dialect, as spelled by Greek writers, and their language was related to Greek in its Indo-European origin.

The Latin tribe that first built the village of Rome soon began gathering more strength than its neighbors. This was because of their happy choice of a location. The original Rome grew up on an island at a bend in the Tiber River, which became a natural crossing place and a safe sanctuary from ordinary attack. Rude bridges were built, over which the trade of this fertile plain began to flow.[2] As the little settlement grew more important, it spread to the eastern bank of the Tiber, and this spot today is still the richest in antique ruins of a devotional nature. The Temple of Vesta and the Temple of Fortune are later buildings remaining for our sight. The town, in expanding further, grew over a prominent hill known as the Palatine. From earliest time this hill has been associated with the governing heads of the city, and today it is a mass of ruined palaces,[3] houses, corridors, and stables. A smaller near-by hill, later called the Capitol, early took on religious stature and became the divine nucleus of the city's solemnities.

As this settlement on the Tiber assumed size and importance, it became the center of the tribe's interests. Their name of "Romans," from which their town took its name, is mysterious but is thought to have been derived from their chief deity, the tribal goddess Roma, who, from her later portrayals, must have been concerned chiefly with fertility, and protection in war. With their new-found wealth and strategic importance, the Romans were able to dominate the neighboring tribes either by commercial superiority or by successful war.

Then Rome's location began to take on additional advantages. The little island in the Tiber was only eleven miles from where the river flowed into the Mediterranean. Its mouth formed a harbor of sorts,[4] and the keen Phoenicians, always looking for trade possibilities, put into this easily found mooring-place and set up contacts with the Latin tribe, which appreciated the values of good bargains. Through these interchanges, the Roman town took on wares for its markets, and valuable ideas on arms, armament, and rudimentary culture and writing. The Greeks, who came along later, continued this growing trade. The Romans fashioned a crude alphabet from the Greek, and began importing new gods and "advanced ideas" with their merchandise.

As Rome grew, it drew upon itself much hostility from a progressive nation to the north—the Etruscans,[5] who had already

---

[2] This whole region of Italy is still called Latium from the Latin tribes.

[3] Our word "palace" has descended from "Palatine."

[4] Ruins of the later, greater port of Ostia on this site can still be visited. They are well excavated.

[5] The province of Tuscany (surrounding Florence) still carries on their name.

evolved a noteworthy civilization from their own contacts with the Phoenicians. A series of wars with Rome took place, as the result of which their culture and their independence were lost, and the Romans achieved a prowess at the military art that completed their supremacy over any other tribe in all Italy that might try to challenge them. The Etruscans had no writing that has survived to tell their whole story, but their handicrafts, their mastery at the art of painting and coloring, and their general character have come down to us in the well-preserved circular tombs of Tarquinia, only forty miles to the north of Rome, as well as in several other places.[6]

Naturally, after Rome had become an imperial-minded city, legends were trotted out to ascribe importance to the divine auguries of the city's birth. Virgil's *Aeneid* leads to the mighty climax of Aeneas, refugee from defeated Troy, being divinely directed to settle on the Tiber. His own progeny later founded the city, which grew to swallow up the Greek states that had conquered Troy—a dramatic tale. A more pertinent legend is that the city was founded by Romulus and Remus, twin brothers who had been suckled by a wild wolf, and thus developed their prowess and military valor early in life. The names of these brothers, both directly derived from the goddess Roma, would show that they were semi-divine characters and thus suitable for the nucleus of a legend, since nothing else is known about them. The result of this divine soul-searching of later historians was the decision that Rome had been founded in the year 753 B.C. This was contemporary with the last gasping days of independent Egypt; was subsequent to the days of the Phoenicians, was contemporary with the dominance of the Assyrians and the Babylonian kingdom, and with the early days of the rising Greek city-states.

Such semilegendary history goes on to tell that early Rome, after its founding, was ruled by seven successive kings of the family of Tarquin, who conducted the long struggles against the Etruscans, but that they were later ousted to make way for a republican government in the fifth century B.C. This latter de-

---

[6] The Romans adopted this custom of building circular tombs, but gave up the practice of stuffing them with wealth and art.

velopment is indisputably correct, for Rome's great rise to glory took place under her republican institutions. And these institutions sprang from the fact that commercial interests and the powerful mercantile class of the city were so important that they took over control of the government.[7]

Under this republican system, the city was ruled by two consuls, elected each year for a one-year term. The word "consul" means "a stander-together." The years of all of Rome's history were reckoned according to who were the consuls. Caesar, Cicero, and all Roman leaders served as consuls at one time or another, and even after the rise of the emperors, the legal governors of the city—after whom the years were named—were still consuls, puppets of the emperor though they became.

This novel development of government was far and away more progressive than any other system in Italy, whose tribes were still ruled by "kings" and warriors. It gave Rome a powerful head start in the development of the traditions of law and government that she later codified and handed down to modern times.

Serving with the consuls were police and legal officials, the *quaestores* and *aediles*. The concept of citizenship was perfected into a status of those who were entitled to take part in the government of the city. (Our words "citizen" and "city" come from the Latin *civitas*—or a collective unit for governing.) The citizens later developed into a superior class of patricians, or "fathers," who conducted the government, but the plebes, or "lower classes," who were considered to be originally transients, slaves, and undependable persons, were never entirely frozen out, and plebes were able to get into governing positions by their organizing talent or by their influence with the people. The office of "tribune" later grew up to care for the needs of the people and

---

[7] Many of our common terms of trade have been handed down from the Romans: "speculation" and "pecuniary" come from *pecora*, or "flocks of sheep," which were important items of measuring wealth; "market," "commerce," and "merchant" all come from *merx*, or "the place of trade"; "trade" itself means "handing across"; "salary" means "salt payment," from the custom of paying Roman soldiers in Spain in salt; monetary terms and denominations have also been handed down from the Roman—*solidus, denarius, libra,* etc.

their interests, and the two Gracchi brothers became immortal in history for the zealous way they carried out their task.

At the same time, a legislative body took form called the "senate" (or "old men," in the sense of being wise and experienced citizens. Our word "senior" has the same origin). Peopled almost entirely by patricians, the senate became a tight little club, but it did its job so well that it lasted all the way down through Roman history, even under the emperors, and became a debating society in which Cato and Cicero achieved their greatest fame and influence. The mystic symbol of SPQR (*Senatus Populusque Romanus*), which later became venerated as the divine essence of Rome as the lawgiving city, meant simply "the Senate and the Roman People," who were the source of the law that later ruled the world with an equality and a forcefulness that no other ancient people had been able to develop.

And that is the great significance of Rome in the pageant of world history. It grew in stature because of its concept of equality that was born of its basis of commerce and trade. This very commerce gave it the wealth and power to be superior in methods of defense to its neighbors. As the needs of trade and defense against envious tribes expanded, Rome's territory expanded. Its military victories brought on the supremacy of the military caste, which led to much aggressive warfare and empire-building. This process was helped immeasurably by the disordered state of the Mediterranean world—its division into hostile kingdoms and empires that could be devoured piecemeal. Always, however, the higher concepts of government and progress by commerce were important, so that Rome's enemies were quickly absorbed. The conquered peoples, once their rulers had been defeated by a Roman army, quickly responded to the new, advanced system of living brought in. (This was the same method of penetration adopted so many centuries later by the French Revolutionary armies, who combatted dynastic rulers but were welcomed by their oppressed and weary subjects.)

The only enemy too strong for piecemeal conquest was Carthage, and Rome's struggle in the three Punic Wars was exhausting and perilous to the extreme. Hannibal's invasion could very easily have meant the extinction of Rome and her budding civilization, had it not been for Rome's recourse to more masterful strategy and wily infiltration tactics. (See Scene X.) The victory over Carthage led to three important developments: (1) the beating back of African-Oriental expansion, with its ideas of absolute monarchy, cruel forms of idolatry, and the enslaved status of the populace, thus giving European civilization a chance to develop and take on strength; (2) the birth of Roman sea power, which gave great furtherance to Rome's cardinal motives—an efficient method of carrying on commerce—ever wider-spreading—and efficient ways of maintaining the peace by enforcing a world-wide equalitarian law; and (3) the drawing of Roman power into the vast maritime lands once dominated by Carthage, to fill the vacuum—in Spain, Gaul, and western Africa, lands still primitive in every way. Rome thus had to learn the art of administration; and the needs of these undeveloped, uncultured areas brought about Rome's interpreting and molding the civilized arts of the Eastern world for their benefit.

Thus Rome was launched into the orbit of expansion, and she soon occupied all the shores of the Mediterranean, overrunning the lands of the ancient empires and religions and bringing into those war-weary lands her concepts of a common trade and law, under which the Middle Sea became the center of a well-ordered, well-governed, and peaceful domain, ruling unchallenged for two hundred years in what is still affectionately called the *Pax Romana*. Jesus was born into this prosperous and idolatrous age. St. Paul was saved from priestly violence and given trial in the city of Rome itself because he was one of the many non-Italians who had taken on the privilege of Roman citizenship extended by expanding Rome decades before—the first time such a thing had ever been done by an empire. Ancient empires and city-states had been too exclusive and jealous to have ever made such a gesture. The Jews were dispersed as a nation and their temple destroyed during this *Pax Romana* because they dared to be different; to hold on to their religion and traditions; to be a religious dissenting entity; and thus to fight for their heritage. For this they had to be crushed, as Carthage had been, as a menace to the Roman concepts of uniform law and government.

Naturally, during this victorious and significant expansion of the Romans, they had to fill vacuums in their civilization with what they learned from more advanced neighbors. In the arts of government, administration, justice, commerce, and civilian equality, as well as that of war, they were supreme. But they were lacking at the same time in the "finer things of life." They were no match for the Greeks in the fields of art and aesthetics, of philosophy and drama, and they adopted the learning of the Greeks wholesale. Roman art is so thoroughly Greek-inspired that Roman culture is known in world history as Greco-Roman, being the later manifestations of what the Greeks developed. Roman literature, music, and refinements all were taken from the Greeks, so that Greece, while conquered by Rome and added to its empire, took her conquerors captive, as if in a Greek drama itself.

In the handicrafts and skills of the artisan, Rome was deficient and copied what she discovered in Egypt, the Levant, and Asia Minor. In architecture and engineering, the Romans were keen students of what the Egyptians and Babylonians had developed, particularly in the idea of the arch, and in military machines, and they carried them to great sizes and new uses. But in one department the Romans were most of all lacking—and that was in the field of religion. They had created no concepts at all on this subject, and thus were fair game for everything they picked up in the lands they annexed. Greek gods, with new Latin names, formed the core of their worship, but deities from Syria and the Levant, as well as from Assyria and Egypt[8] were imported wholesale to honor special new temples and rites of worship. One especially backward idea they brought home from the Near East —the idea of making human rulers divine, of endowing emperors with the title and holiness of gods. This idea was what brought the greatest sorrows to the sincere-minded early Christians in the imperial city.

Thus, Rome was a great administrative, commercial, legal, and judicial center of empire. But it was not a religious holy city. The great victory of Christianity in winning over the Roman Emperor in A.D. 323 was not due to the fact that the new faith was setting up its standard on a consecrated spot. The victory

---

[8] A temple to Serapis has been unearthed at Pompeii.

was that it secured control over the government and over the Empire because it conquered the heart—Rome.

The Pax Romana—Two Centuries of World Peace

The birth of Jesus the Christ and the rise of Rome to its highest pinnacle of power took place almost at the same time. During the century before the Saviour's advent, Rome had gone through some troublesome civil wars and changes in government due to the imperial strength of the city, which had brought too many ambitious men to power at the same time. Back in 80 B.C. a civil war between Marius and Sulla had split most of Italy and caused some dangerous blood-letting among the vanquished cities that had championed Sulla. Then strode that monumental character onto history's central stage—Julius Caesar. An admirer of Marius, a courageous aristocrat who had cleaned the Mediterranean of pirates and had risen through all the honors of the republican government, he was hounded by lesser men of great ambition, particularly Pompey. Caesar's immortal *Commentaries* on his eight-year campaign to annex Gaul—a victory that extended the Empire up into cold northern regions for the first time—were inspired by the need of the political arena.

Caesar's and Pompey's private civil war ranged all over the Mediterranean world, and again helpless provincial towns had to take sides. Caesar's reportorial style of Latin reached a new height in this war. His terse *Veni, vidi, vici* was his entire report on a battle fought in Asia Minor.

In the year 46 B.C. Caesar vanquished Pompey and then lingered in prosperous Egypt to settle a palace revolution, in which Cleopatra had seized absolute power. He dallied almost two years in Alexandria before hurrying to Rome to smash another plot of ambitious men. His assassination on the Ides of March in the Forum followed, and then came a period of political chaos. Brutus, Cassius, and Mark Antony, the triumvirs who had banded together to "wipe out" the dictator, fell out themselves, and another civil war dragged itself out. However, retribution followed when Caesar's adopted son Octavian gathered together all the war-weary elements of the government and the legions and won supremacy over the beaten triumvirs. Mark Antony went down in the most dramatic fashion, being whipped in a sea battle at Actium, off the western capes of Greece, after the Egyptian fleet deserted him and bore Cleopatra back to suicide in her native, mystic land.

Octavian then was left the unchallenged dictator, and "some great changes were made." Deciding that Rome's republican institutions had grown too stylized and stiff to govern a sprawling empire of so many divergent races, he invented the position of emperor, or *imperator,* a military title meaning "he who gives orders," and took the job himself, in order to establish his power over the legions. He then took on the additional cloak of religious stature by assuming the title of *Pontifex Maximus,*[9] or supreme priest, and instituted worship of his person as divine. Finally, he changed his own name from Octavian to Augustus, or "he who is favored by the divine auguries." With the grateful applause of opulent, prosperous, and war-tired Romans, he launched out on a rule of peaceful government that became the exalted Pax Romana.

Augustus paid no attention to such a petty event as the childhood of Jesus in the faraway, semi-Greek market town of Nazareth. Paradoxically, his imperial-divine command for an Empire-wide census had caused the natal hour to take place in the strange town of Bethlehem, a place so crowded by the census-taking that the Holy Family had to be housed in a stable.[10] Instead, Augustus was busy at that very time embellishing the lovely city of Rome. "Lo," he said on his deathbed, "I found Rome a city of brick and have left it a city of marble."

We are very indebted to Augustus for lavishing his semi-divine attention on glorifying his capital, for most of the ruins of his city that have lasted down to our day date from his time or later, thanks to the durability of marble and the size of the works of his successors. Of early republican Rome we can find very little, alas, to feast our eyes on. The oldest structures are the temples of two centuries before Christ, lying in what is known today as

---

[9] The title, taken from pagan priestly prerogatives, literally means "Chief Bridge-Builder."

[10] This account is given in the Book of Luke, chapter 2.

Argentina Square. Only their stone platforms and front steps
are there today, but their size and expert construction can give
rise to long contemplation from the parapets above.

The best section of Rome to give an impression of the city in
late republican days is the San Sebastian Gate, where the old
Appian Way passes into the city through the encircling walls.
Here the gate and its supports are all made of the flat, wide bricks
so characteristic of ancient Italy; and the historic road, penetrating
the city, follows between high walls like those that must have
stood there then, and are still the fashion of all Italian towns today.
Going out the Appian Way in the other direction, the road is no
wider and no different than it was in imperial days, and many of
the walled enclosures that hem it in have probably stood through
the twenty centuries. But the imposing circular tombs of the
patricians that by some rule of fashion all lined this one route
have mostly all vanished into nothing.

Probably the most inspiring relic of Augustus' age is the
Pantheon, the oldest building still intact in Rome. Built in the
year 27, restored a century later, it was dedicated to the gods
represented by the planets. It is admired by travelers because of
its big dome with the hole in the top, through which the only
light enters the great edifice. The Pantheon has endured to our
day because of its having been made into a church. It stands now as
a would-be burial place of Italy's modern kings, the two first of
whom are buried inside.

The Pantheon today stands lower than the streets that pass
by it, giving us silent evidence of the centuries through which Rome
has survived. In the golden age of Augustus the Pantheon stood
on an eminence; today Rome has risen above it, built on the rubble
and dust deposited by countless troubled decades.

Augustus' circular tomb, known as the Augusteo, has also endured, and can be seen on the edge of the Tiber partly disintegrated
and overgrown, but cleaned away of its encroaching buildings.

The justice of the Pax Romana was hideously stained by the
persecutions of the tyrant Nero. This lazy prince, such a typical
product of the golden plush period of the classic age, a cruel

despot who could also delight in performing on the stage and in writing poems, unwittingly laid the foundations for the Christian age.

It is a tribute to the revolutionary teachings of Jesus Christ that his few and untitled followers could have carried his gospel into the heart of Rome inside of thirty short years after the Crucifixion of Christ, which took place in the year 31. St. Paul arrived in Rome for his trial in about 65, and already there were "brethren" who came out to an inn on the Appian Way to meet him. Paul evidently was acquitted of his accusation of stirring up disorders in Palestine, but the Christians' first trial by fire placed him again in jeopardy in 68. Nero would probably never have thought twice about the Christian sect except for one startling fact—the Christians refused to respect the dogma of divinity of the Emperor.

It obviously was impossible for converts to the new religion to bow before the Emperor's effigy on holy days, when such idolatry was explicitly denounced by the teachings of the Nazarene and his most erudite apostle Paul. This sect thus struck at the very heart of the institution of the Emperor, whose position outside the traditional republican system of Rome may not have been entirely accepted by Nero's time. Thus the frivolous Nero could easily have done what the story says—set fire to a part of the city to clear it for new monuments—celebrated by festivities—and then raked in the Christians to pay the penalty when the citizens criticized him instead of praising him for his deed.

Nero's persecution, which took place in the circus across the Tiber on a hill known as the Vatican, must have killed most of the Christian population of Rome, since only tradition relating to this event has come down to us and it does not tell us who the victims were and how they ranked. However, there is little doubt that tradition is right in dating the martyrdom of Peter and Paul, the foremost apostles, to this frivolous and scandalous outrage. Paul writes of his forebodings of the ordeal in his Epistle to the Philippians. Peter had only just arrived from Palestine. Tradition tells of a crossroads outside the walls on the Appian

Way, where the apostle, fleeing from Rome, was met by Christ. As they parted, Peter is said to have asked, "Quo vadis, domine?" —"Where art thou going, Lord?"—to which Christ answered that he was going to Rome to be crucified again. Peter was then overcome with shame, and he reversed his steps. An old church built at this spot shows a footprint in a stone, said to have been left by Christ as he ascended back into heaven.

At any rate, Peter is considered to have been crucified, upside down on the Cross, in Nero's Circus, and buried later by the survivors outside the edifice, where the Cathedral of St. Peter now stands. Paul, on the other hand, was beheaded outside the walls, and a massive cathedral commemorates the spot of that dreadful deed.

When Nero had committed suicide in the year 68, and the Emperor Titus had built his arch in the Forum to commemorate his destruction of the Jewish Temple in Jerusalem a few years later, the peace of the Roman era returned. The "five good emperors" reigned over a hundred years, during which time the massive monuments of Rome rose one after another. The Colosseum, the Forum of Trajan, newer walls, baths, and temples; the fanciful country villa of energetic Emperor Hadrian, basilicas and palaces were all brought into being for the embellishment and pleasure of the city. Obelisks, which fascinated the Romans beyond measure, were brought over from Egypt to decorate squares, and Emperor Marcus Aurelius erected his own column, on which he inscribed the details of his victories over the wild Germans on the Danube.

This great philosopher, Marcus Aurelius, charitable and public-spirited, was yet able to stain his name by unleashing persecutions of Christians. By this time, however (A.D. 171), the faithful were much more numerous. Many survived this time by retreating into their cemeteries, now called Catacombs, and hiding out among their dead. Others were in positions of prominence and warded off the blow.

The death of Marcus Aurelius in 180 marked the end of Rome's silver age. Palace revolts, army rebellions, assassinations of emperors, incursions of enemies on the far reaches of the

Empire, and the decadence of the population itself blew out the candle of the glorious era of the classics.

Christianity Comes to the Fore

One of the great turning points in the even flow of history up to this point was the rise of Christianity to supremacy. The teachings of Jesus Christ produced a revolution in world thought and world government.

During the first two centuries of the Christian era, the doctrines of this radical new faith spread like wildfire to all corners of the great unitary Roman Empire. Paganism had no rationalism with which to oppose it. Only inertia, apathy, and the power of the emperors in Rome hampered its growth.

Two features of its teachings undoubtedly exerted the most powerful draw. The first was its promise of eternal life, of salvation, through the lessons proved by Christ in the Resurrection and Ascension. This hopeful element shattered pagan devotions at their emptiest point. The colorful, semi-human gods of Olympus made no provision for an after-life. They themselves gloried in the deeds of earth. Intelligent and thoughtful people were captivated by this new departure in religion, and they turned to the new faith at first more rapidly than any other social class. Pudens, a Roman senator, gave the first refuge to persecuted Christians. The site of his home is covered by a church of old vintage. Three centuries later, a Pope persuaded a wealthy patrician to build the magnificent Basilica of Santa Maria Maggiore, the best-preserved of the four holy basilicas.

However, another teaching of Christianity was also potent. This was its equalitarian, untraditional preaching that all men are equal, the plebes as well as the patricians. Jesus had inveighed against entrenched privilege in religion, and the early Christian congregations were sincere people assembling to discuss and worship in untrammeled ways. They elected or chose their "overseers," or bishops, and practiced the healing works taught by Jesus. Thus the poorer classes felt at home in such a religion.

In addition, the sacrifices and processions in the pagan temples had become stilted and old-fashioned in the eyes of people everywhere. A thousand years of devotions had made their purpose meaningless. Centuries of peace and learning made many people long for progress in religion. Christianity supplied that need to the full.

When the Emperor Diocletian, worn out by wars and by his frenzied persecution of Christians, abdicated the imperial purple and retired across the Adriatic to his palace in Dalmatia, he divided the Empire between two co-emperors, hoping to restore some peace and order through their efforts.

Yet only ten years later the Empire was reunited by the last of the powerful emperors—Constantine the Great. This man had been a leader of imperial troops in Britain and along the German border; the army, which made and unmade emperors by this time, obeyed him and propelled him into the top position. And once there, he had no opposition. Diocletian had swept away the last remnants of the republican institutions of consuls and senators, and only the emperor counted from then on.

Constantine came to power in 313. Five years later he issued the edict which shook the world. Christianity was not only to be legal, but it was to be the official state religion. This rebound from persecution under Diocletian to supreme victory only twenty years later not only rocked the shell of the Roman Empire, but it had profound and significant effects on the structure of Christianity itself.

Constantine, however, did not stop there. In 323 he enacted an even more startling official act. He decreed that a new city was to be built far to the east and named after him Constantinople. And, what was more, it was to be the capital of the Roman Empire.

From that day Rome saw the beginning of a steady decline. No longer the capital, nor even the center of the weakened Empire, it lost thousands of its population and almost all of its importance. To be sure, after Constantine's death in 336, the Empire was divided and emperors returned to rule the western half, but they were weak prisoners of arrogant legions; and besides, they lived mostly to the north in Milan, a city of greater importance because it was on the main routes between the western, military provinces of the Empire, and the rich eastern sections in the Levant. Rome was in a backwater, down on the Italian peninsula, on a road that led to nowhere.

After a temporary reunion under the powerful eastern Emperor Theodosius, the Roman Empire split in two for good at his death in 396. Then followed a spate of barbarian invasions. The uncouth Western Goths, under their leader Alaric, sacked Rome from top to bottom in the year 410, prying the gold and marble off the Colosseum, robbing the churches and temples, carting away precious metals and smashing works of art. Later on, in 455, the even more barbaric Vandals, coming across the sea unchecked, landed at the mouth of the undefended Tiber and ransacked Rome a second time. In 476 the last of the weakling legitimate emperors was pushed off his throne by the Eastern Goths, and all civil rule deteriorated. For three centuries Rome and all Italy were ruled by a succession of rough warrior tribes from across the Alps.

Such prolonged chaos coming after the glorious memories of the Pax Romana dumped Europe into the Dark Ages. In this stagnation, the Christian continent was almost conquered by triumphant Moslems, who were stopped only by the desperate Battle of Tours in the heart of France in the year 732. Thus there was a desperate need for some return to law and order, some establishment of a recognized and powerful ruler.

The bishops of European cities, the only men of authority in that black period, still recognized the drawing power of Rome as the only traditional binding source of government. They recognized the Bishop of Rome as the leading authority of government and eventually of church administration because of his control of the once imperial city. This latter official, later on called by the title of Pope,[11] also longed for some way out of the vacuum, and the only solution seemed to be to re-create the Roman Empire.

A God-given candidate for the position of emperor soon appeared in the person of Charlemagne, King of the Teutonic tribe known as the Franks, and undisputed ruler of most of France, the Low Countries, and northern Italy. He was a Christian and was busy converting the defeated German tribes to the new faith. Thus

---

[11] A Greek term meaning "father." In Orthodox Church lands, it is the title of a priest.

the man and the hour were joined together. On Christmas Day in the year 800, Charlemagne was crowned Holy Roman Emperor at Rome by the vigorous Pope Leo III.

That act was highly symbolic and the effects of it split Europe into civil wars and religious struggles through all the centuries of the artificial new Empire. For the Pope, remembering that an Emperor, Constantine, had given honors and authority to the earlier Popes, determined to change the balance and to crown the Emperor himself as a symbol that the church now dominated secular power.[12] Charlemagne himself did not foresee the consequences of this act on future European history, but instead rewarded Gregory with a large slice of territory that he had conquered from the vanquished Lombards. This made the Pope for the first time a temporal ruler, an administrator not only of shrunken Rome but of a large territory of his own. This act itself had consequences that affected Italy's whole political history for a thousand years.

The Transformation of Rome

The exalting of Christianity into a state religion by Constantine the Great transformed the city of Rome into a different, almost opposite, type of capital. The Christians, emerging from their catacombs and their humble, hidden places of worship, found themselves overnight teachers of multitudes and faced with the responsibility of making their simple, un-formal faith accommodate whole thousands of skeptical converts.

Outward forms of service, and spectacles to rivet the attention of these fickle throngs, were absolute necessities. The pagan temples were now unsuitable for worship, not only because of their profane traditions, but because they were too small. Pagan devotions had almost always taken place outside the temples, around the raised altars where sacrifices were made and the auguries read.

---

[12] This precedent rankled so much that the Norman conquerors of Sicily in 1141 crowned themselves, as did Napoleon in 1804, with the Pope present.

Thus the Christian leaders turned to the basilicas—the massive market buildings located in the several forums of Rome, impressive edifices donated by emperors (their name is Greek for "royal houses") for purposes of trade, public meetings, and special assemblies. Here crowds could be and were herded in to hear the teachings of the new Christian doctrine. To meet their need for visible devotions, various forms of ritual, later including music and prayers, were devised.

At the same time, idol-smashing and other similar acts were perpetrated by Christian leaders as another visible move to impress and shape the thinking of worldly-minded populations. Temples were broken down, their works of art dispersed, and heathen celebrations ridiculed if they could not be adopted as neo-Christian observances. More important still, massive processions were organized, in which effigies of lowly martyrs, killed in past persecutions and tumults, were raised on high and paraded into the basilicas in the same manner in which statues of gods had been carried into temples in olden days. All these activities became forerunners of actual rites of Christian worship, which later grew more formal as the centuries went by.

Any traveler in Rome today can have a thrilling view of what a Roman basilica looked like on the inside, and how it evolved into a Christian cathedral,[13] by visiting the magnificent Santa Maria Maggiore, one of the four holy pilgrimage churches of Rome.[14] Built in 352, it has been altered and restored but little. Sitting atop the Esquiline Hill, it is a lesson in architecture all by itself. Its interior is lined with rows of lofty columns holding up a high ceiling with clerestory windows. Fine medallions, marble, and art work covering its interior walls are of course Christian-inspired versions of the gorgeous decorations of early Roman-style basilicas. Like its ancient forerunners, this one has no seats, as indeed few churches or cathedrals do today in all Italy. Today's

---

[13] The four pilgrimage churches of Rome are still called basilicas to this day.

[14] The other three are St. Peter's, St. John Lateran, and St. Paul's-Outside-the-Walls.

visitor in Rome can see the polished marble floor of this and other basilicas, unobstructed by pews or seats, as they were in ancient times. For services and religious holidays today, portable wooden chairs are set out, only to be removed immediately afterwards.

During the centuries that followed, Rome continued to change under its Christian tutelage. Churches were built in endless number to commemorate sacred scenes of suffering and triumph all over the city. Some temples were converted into parish churches. The others were stripped of their columns for the benefit of embellishing churches. The glittering circuses where the fiendish persecutions had been perpetrated were the first to disappear, stripped of their ornaments and marble, and then allowed to sink beneath rubble. The Forum and palaces, strongholds of pagan tradition, likewise disintegrated, and were used as quarries for fine building materials. Rome shrank, until in the Middle Ages it had become an unimportant provincial capital, crowded into one bend of the Tiber. Only the churches and basilicas took on elegance, and the only large building to be completed was the Palace and Basilica of St. John Lateran, constructed as the cathedral church of Rome and the residence of the Popes. To this day the Lateran is the official church of Rome. The Eternal City had lost its economic and civil being. It was a shell of its mighty past. At last even the Popes deserted it, leaving it in the year 1305 for the more pleasant city of Avignon in southern France.

Rome's Return to Greatness

From that absolute nadir of the fourteenth century, Rome has slowly won its way back from rags to its resplendent present position of a city of beauty and life.

The pulsations of a new life and a new culture, the first breaths of the Renaissance, came in time to save it from extinction. Leading families of aristocrats began to vie with themselves to draw down powerful allies from the north. The Great Schism, by which a rival series of Popes came to power in abandoned Rome, eventually started the city on its way up, for the Avignon capital was closed down and the Popes returned in 1377.

The city's ruling families then decided to brush up their faded city and to give it the elegance of Italy's rich northern cities. They plundered ancient forums and temples for the remainder of their marble and pillars, and erected palaces for themselves. One family even turned the small amphitheatre of Marcellus into a palace by erecting apartments atop its arches—and the result is today one of Rome's most incongruous buildings.

The Popes, on their return, settled down on the Vatican Hill across the Tiber and soon decided to erect an imposing basilica on the ruins of the small church honoring St. Peter on that spot. As the full fires of the golden Renaissance illuminated all Italy, various Popes, many of them members of the Medici and other northern families, began to plan sumptuous buildings in Rome. Great artists were engaged for the work. The new basilica of St. Peter's was laid out in the new Renaissance classical style of a Greek cross with a dome. St. Peter's was over a century and a half in the building and was completed in the present form of a Latin cross.

But before it was completed, Rome was no longer the center of a united Christendom. The vast sums of money needed for building St. Peter's and the other new edifices had led to difficulties. Some Popes, like Julius II, extended their temporal rule to take in new territory, wealth, and prestige. Another Pope, Leo X, authorized the sale of indulgences to bring in revenue. The exactions of the indulgence-sellers in northern Europe were one of the factors that brought the monk, Martin Luther, out of his cloister to protest.

During the sixteenth and seventeenth centuries, Rome took on new beauty, as churches, palaces, and fountains were finished. The inspired architect and sculptor Bernini is responsible for many baroque statues and fountains, and for the immense piazza in front of St. Peter's.

Secular Rome

After centuries of papal rule, Rome was abruptly drawn into new adventures when the French Revolution broke out in 1789, interfering with the reign of divine rights of kings, established churches, extralegal rights of nobles and churchmen, and ancient privileges left over from feudalism. Propelled by the doctrines that promised to wipe the slate clean of historical injustices and abuses, revolutionary armies swept over the whole of western Europe, producing a ready-made leader in the person of Napoleon Bonaparte.

Napoleon gloried in the prestige and honors of the Roman emperors. He had himself portrayed in a toga, wearing the laurel crown. Rome was irresistible to him. His armies captured the city in 1798 and brought the Pope a prisoner to Fontainebleau. After Napoleon crowned himself Emperor, he annexed Rome to his dominions as the "second capital of France." His only son and heir was awarded the title of "King of Rome" while in his cradle.

The fact that all this neo-imperial façade soon crumbled into dust did not change the altered spirit that came to bloom in Italy. The Pope returned to his large state in central Italy as absolute ruler, but Italian patriots now dared to plan for a united Italy, in which Rome—yes, the papal city of Rome—would be the secular, temporal capital.

When idealistic new revolutions broke out in waves all over Europe in 1848, Italy became a hotbed of civic agitation. The popular leader Mazzini went to Rome and organized an uprising that created a Roman Republic, which the Pope Pius IX condemned from his refuge in the fortress at Gaeta. Garibaldi, another popular leader, or agitator, depending on what angle people viewed him, also went to Rome, and his cohorts drew down a baptism of fire when Austrian and French troops finally extinguished their republic in 1849.

A united Kingdom of Italy was at last set up in 1860, but the Pope would not surrender Rome. Most of the rest of his domains, including the important city of Bologna, had gone over to the new King Victor Emmanuel. But nothing could be done to annex Rome so long as the Holy City was garrisoned by French troops sent by Napoleon III to keep revolutionists out.

Rome did not stay out of the Italian kingdom for very long. When the Franco-Prussian War engulfed Napoleon III in 1870, he withdrew his troops from Italy, and the King's army marched in. The date of his entry—September 20, 1870—is marked by an important street of that name today.

Pope Pius IX condemned this act. He withdrew into the Vatican, proclaimed himself a prisoner, and forbade all Catholics to have anything to do with the new government.

Rome, however, entered into a period of new elegance as the capital of an important European kingdom. It began to spread outside its walls. Hotels, government buildings and fine avenues sprang into being. Lovely hillside retreats like Tivoli and Frascati once more became centers of villas. The ancient roads were rebuilt to connect all Italy with its capital. And when King Victor Emmanuel II died in 1878, the largest monument of the whole city was built in his honor.

Rising in tiers of classic marble in the very heart of Rome, adjoining the Forum and the Capitol, this massive memorial stands over modern Rome in startling whiteness. Appropriately dubbed by the American G.I.'s of 1944 "the wedding cake," it is Rome's landmark, seen from almost all districts of the capital. And it is practically the only white building in all Rome—the typical color of the palaces and homes of the city being a mellowed brownish-orange. Ironically, this memorial honoring the King is not his burial place; instead it includes the tomb of Italy's Unknown Soldier of World War I.

Fascism gloried in Rome. Mussolini took the *fasces*, or the faggots and axe symbolic of consular authority in ancient Rome, as his emblem and determined to make Rome once again a center of the ancient imperial solemnities. He cut the straight avenue through the excavated Forum from the "wedding cake" to the Colosseum. He ordered every excavated relic, however rudimentary and insignificant, to remain untouched wherever it was, even if on a crowded business street. He drained near-by Lake Nemi to raise the imperial pleasure barges of the Emperor Caligula.[15] He sanctioned the illumination of fountains and ruins, the restoration of some temples, the spotless cleaning of the city. He even

---

[15] These are well described as they were in their heyday in the novel *Quo Vadis?*

designed a new railroad station in imperial style, with sweeping arches made out of travertine marble, the same rock used in the Colosseum of old.[16]

Fascism transformed Rome by cutting new business streets through jumbled blocks, erecting modernistic piles of government offices, and countless apartment houses for the bureaucracy brought in from all over Italy. It held expositions honoring Augustus and other emperors.

And it came to terms with the Pope. By the Lateran pacts of 1929, it gave the Pope sovereignty over the Vatican city, the other three pilgrimage basilicas, and various additional properties. The Pope then recognized the unification of Italy.

Fascism, despite its worship of the past glory of Rome, brought the city once again down to starvation and misery by its alliance with Nazi Germany, which led to a cruel German occupation in 1943 and 1944, ended only by the heroically enthusiastic days of the American liberation of the city. When the war ended, party politics and a democratic constitution came at last to a rejuvenated Italy. The kingdom turned into a republic. American flags became commonplace in Rome, as economic aid from the youngest heir of old Roman culture poured in to establish the fledgling republic on the firmest basis of popular government it had managed to achieve since the days of the Gracchi.

Envoi

There are plenty of excellent guidebooks to Rome. Every visitor should use one and wander around the city for as many days as he can, for the art treasures, the monumental architecture, the fountains and ruins, the sites of exciting history, the beautiful palaces and gardens, the fountains and avenues, are almost endless in their number.

In addition to the many places mentioned in this chapter as playing such a great part in Rome's ageless story, many other places must be seen. The Vatican Galleries, with the matchless Sistine Chapel and collections of exquisite art; the Venice Palace used by Mussolini as his office, complete with balcony, and a mag

---

[16] This station was completed by Marshall Plan funds.

nificent Renaissance edifice; the little Protestant cemetery where Shelley and Keats lie buried; the fascinating walls with their gates of all periods; the countless churches, including the one called St. Peter-in-Chains, where Michelangelo's heroic statue of Moses is located—all these and many others too numerous to mention cannot be missed. Even the ironic, self-glorifying forum of Mussolini is interesting. Far in the north of the city, the Duce built his own "forum," stadium, and marble buildings to do honor to the "sawdust Caesar." It has proved very useful as a rest and recreation center for the American army's troops during the four years of their presence in Italy.

Thus this chapter can only be a portrayal of the stage and the backdrop, and of some exciting scenes of the epochal drama of unperishable Rome. Everyone who goes there must bear in mind that Rome's energetic leaders unwittingly gave us our finest heritage. They wove together all the learning of the ancient empires and handed it down in a form easily assimilated to our forebears in northern Europe, who mingled it with their own ways to create what is known now as modern Western civilization. In America, three-quarters of our language, and great proportions of our mass of learning, come directly down from the culture nobly bequeathed by Rome, *urbi et orbi.*

CONSTANTINOPLE

Byzantium—The Second Rome—Istanbul

A CITY THAT BEARS four illustrious names must indeed be an important place in the annals of mankind.

This city has meant so much, in peace as well as in recurrent war, that its sonorous titles have resounded with either fear or glory in the hearts of all Europeans. Its history is exciting. Its existence has influenced world affairs for over a thousand years. Its fall led to the discovery of America. And its location is superb, so much so that its site can be said to rest on solid layers of history.

Founded as a classical Greek town with the name of Byzantium, known to modern man as an Oriental-type capital of a once-antique Turkish Empire, when its name was Istanbul (or more colloquially, Stamboul), it has always been most significantly known by its pompous given name of Constantinople.

Constantinople has had some hard times because it sits astride the world's most heavily invaded land bridge. Just as Sicily forms a bridge between Europe and Africa, Constantinople rests upon the very center of the mightier land bridge between Europe and Asia. The city stands at the far tip of a European land mass known as the Balkan Peninsula and looks across a narrow strait of water at Asia Minor flung out from the Middle East mass of Asia. The narrow strait between these continents has always been known as the Bosporus—a Greek word meaning "Ox Ford"—since the waterway was so narrow that an ox was supposed to have no difficulty swimming across it.

The Modern City

There is hardly any city more intriguing for an American to visit than this one, which as the metropolis of modern-day Turkey bears its alias of Istanbul. The easiest way of reaching it is by sea. Ships coming in from the Mediterranean arrive, seven hours beforehand, at the narrow entrance to the strait called the Dardanelles. For forty miles they steam up between the bare, silent hills of this narrow watercourse. The southern shore is noted as the seat of ancient Troy and as the place where King Xerxes flung his bridge of boats across to speed his army bound for the battle of Greece.

Leaving the Dardanelles the approaching ship passes across an inland sea called Marmora, in honor of marble deposits known to the ancients along its shores. Three hours more and the bluff-like Acropolis of Constantinople rises on the horizon. On the approach, passengers can study this super-strategic site with great ease. The Acropolis of Constantinople was a site well-selected for defense. Surrounded by deep water on three sides and standing up boldly in a commanding position—no wonder this plot of land on the earth's surface has been such a decisive center for globe-shaking events.

Three sides of the city face deep water. The first fronts on the Sea of Marmora. The second lines the Bosporus itself, the city lying at its juncture with the third, the Golden Horn. Where the city faces the Bosporus there is a narrow point, known by the Turks as the Grand Seraglio. On the hilltop can be seen the rambling *seraglio,* or official palace of the sultans, marked for our wonderment with a line of ten high, cone-shaped chimneys over what was once the imperial kitchen.

Once inside the Bosporus, the city retreats again, making way for the real blessing of its existence—the Golden Horn. This body of water is the real harbor of the city. The Sea of Marmora is subject to sudden storms; the Bosporus has a heavy, steady current. But the Golden Horn is calm and wide and, as its name indicates, runs inland in a gentle curve for several miles.[1]

---

[1] Fremont, who early surveyed the Bay of San Francisco in California, visualized the Golden Horn from tales of its wealth. Inspired by its Greek name, Chrysokeras, he made up the name Chrysopylae, or "Golden Gate," with which he honored California's entrance strait.

Ships run up the Bosporus across the mouth of the Golden Horn to the modern section of the city, where they can either anchor or tie up. This section of the city is known as Galata and is European in style and pace. It boasts of business streets, shipping offices, modern shops, and the best hotels, two of which are up-to-date Western luxury hostels.

On every hand this city shows its appeal. Its Oriental touch is felt in the leisurely air and in the Persian-influenced architecture of the homes and parks. The people, despite their drab Western-style dress, are a little more inscrutable and fenced-off in their manners than they would be farther west. But the grandeur of the views over the Bosporus and the Golden Horn, with the district of Scutari over in Asia looking only a stone's throw away (an ox could swim it, we are reminded by the ancients), makes this city distinctive and captivating.

As befits a city straddling two continents, the narrow gash that separates them is the paramount attraction. A drive by modern auto along the shore of the Bosporus passes the Yildiz Kiosk, a semi-Persianate, semi-baroque palace of the once royal family; the Dolma Bagche Palace, which is used by the Turkish president on state occasions; and then many villas and little towns. The Bosporus looks like a river, with its current and narrowness, but it is salt water and is deep enough to have an abundance of fish. Each little town is always busied with readying its nets for the next catch.

Three miles up and we reach the magnificent site known as Roumeli Hissar. Here the Bosporus tapers down to a mere three-quarters of a mile in width, both sides hilly and covered with attractive "homes with a view." At this point the waterway makes a curve, and here we can see the frowning, medieval walls of a powerful fortress winding down from a citadel to the very edge of the waters. This marks the farthest outpost of independent Constantinople for the last two hundred years of its life. The Turks built this fortress at record speed to choke off all military threats to their control of the Bosporus. A smaller fort stands on the Asiatic shore.

Yet Roumeli Hissar's crenellated walls are promenades now for students of a new era, young Levantine and Turkish people who come to learn of a world freed of the heavy incubus of these century-old hatreds. This is Robert College, an American-founded-and-operated institution, whose buildings stand at this scenic point. Its campus runs up to the very walls of the fortress. Robert College has stood since 1855, performing an incalculable assignment of introducing new, secular learning into this Moslem corner of the world. For many decades its students came from the oppressed nationalities of the Turkish Empire. Now, the Turks themselves are eager to learn, and their serious young people crowd this unique institution of American philanthropy. Visitors should go through the college to see its library and classrooms, all filled with students eager to learn and not lose any time doing it. Schooling is still a luxury to these people, whose fathers never had such an opportunity.

Taking it easy high above the Bosporus, it is satisfying to let our thoughts spin backward beyond all the bloodshed that has marred this exquisite site. If our thoughts go back 2,500 years, we can see this stretch of scenery in a state of nature, which must have delighted the ancient pioneers, for exciting legends about it have enriched mythology. First came the role of the flying ram bearing Helle and her brother in full flight from Thessaly. An accident happened, for she fell off, leaving her name to mark the Hellespont, now called the Dardanelles.

Then came Jason and his Argonauts, pointing their tiny ship into the mysterious Black Sea to hunt for the golden fleece of the vanished ram, which was stored at the far side of that sea. His adventures on the way back with frightful Medea thrilled the children of ancient Greece as they still do ours today in school.

Equally famed is the tale of Leander, who swam the Hellespont every night to visit his beloved Hero. While the Hellespont is the same as the Dardanelles, Leander's fame has made him more honored in Istanbul, and a castle in mid-Bosporus is today named in his honor.

As time dawned into the historical era, Greek mariners came plodding against this sharp current, and some of them settled down at Scutari on the Asiatic side, founding a village called Chalcedon. However, in the year 652 B.C., a small ship hove in sight in the Sea of Marmora, on a trading and scouting voyage for the little town of Megara in Greece, a "weak sister" between the overshadowing rivals of Athens and Corinth. The skipper was named Byzas, and he was perturbed because the Oracle at Delphi had told him he would prosper only if he founded a city "across from some blind men." Yet, when entering the Ox Ford, he was thrilled, for he knew he had found his site. Certainly, anybody living at Chalcedon instead of atop the natural hill across the strait must be blind, he decided, and he forthwith founded the town of Byzantium on the Acropolis surrounded by the deep water on three sides.

Byzantium became a famous town because Greek colonists heading for the Crimea and the Caucasus regions must have stopped there for rest and provisions before breasting the Bosporus. However, it never became rich in ancient times because of the Persians, who swallowed up the Assyrian and Babylonian Empires and thus won title to this region. After the Persians had been humbled by Alexander in 335 B.C., Byzantium remained a point of minor importance because the land to the north was uninhabited and its commerce was only a trickle.

Constantine Founds His City

It was the twilight of the Roman Empire when the spotlight of world attention was suddenly focused on little Byzantium's majestic site. The year was A.D. 313. The Empire was now officially a Christian state, but its center of gravity had shifted far from Rome.

Constantine was a rough warrior and a good politician, and a steady traveler, who had crisscrossed the Empire on many expeditions to put down revolts and invasions. With half the Empire in Europe, and the other half in Asia, it seemed logical to him to plant the administrative center of the straggling realm at the one strong spot where the twain could meet. Accordingly he decreed Byzantium as the capital of his dominions, and he rechristened it the City of Constantine, or Constantinople.

That his move was successful was borne out during the very first century of the new city's life. A population of over a million crowded into it, Greek-speaking, Greek-styled people of many races, coming up from impoverished Syria and Asia Minor to share in the glitter of the new capital. Emperor Theodosius had to rebuild the walls to make room for this horde. The walls he built, shutting off the open land between the Golden Horn and the Sea of Marmora, still stand today, breached only once by hostile invaders—even though that one time was fateful.

The death of Theodosius split the Empire finally and for good. He gave his elder son Arcadius the throne of Constantinople and left to Honorius the insignificant, poorer western end of the realm. The dividing line between them was very easy to draw, for just as in our own days, geography separates eastern Europe from western quite perceptibly, and this split has made for struggles that have retarded the border regions through the centuries.

Arcadius inherited by far the wealthier and richer half of Rome's ancient Empire. He had Greece, Asia Minor, Syria and Mesopotamia, and Egypt. The isles of the Aegean, the granary of Africa, the gold and purple of Phoenicia were his. His boundaries touched the exotic land of Persia and the gulf that led to India.

Separating him from the west were the Adriatic Sea and the easternmost Alps. Thus the Balkan Peninsula, very thinly populated, was his buffer against the west, while the cold and distant Danube River was his northern boundary.

During the next century the Eastern Roman Empire, as it was called, climbed even higher in the firmament of success. The acme of its glory came in the reign of the Emperor Justinian, the golden ruler who reigned from A.D. 527 to 565. This was, it must be remembered, the same period in which Rome had sunk into the position of an East Gothic provincial town, and the Western Roman Empire was no more. Saxons were landing on the deserted eastern coasts of Britain; Gaul was divided into many more than three parts; and Vandals were trampling down the fair Roman cities of Africa.

To appreciate the glory of Constantinople at its height, let us leave our hotels and go to the heart of Byzantium. Motoring down through Galata, we cross the floating bridge across the Golden Horn, which serves double duty as a mooring-place for steamers and fishing boats. Reaching the far side, we are in

Stamboul, historic Byzantium, and our cars quickly mount the slope leading to the Acropolis. Disregard all the mosques and their minarets, for they were not here in Justinian's reign.

Crowning the Acropolis, enjoying a splendid view over the three bodies of water, and far into Asia, was the center of Justinian's capital. Most resplendent is St. Sophia, his magnificent cathedral, still awe-inspiring after standing for 1,415 years, and noble in appearance despite the incongruous note of its four minarets contributed by the Turks. A little farther on is the Hippodrome, or open race course, which was the central gathering place of the city.[2] We can well pause here to gaze at the remnants of what was once a gorgeously monumented site. Columns still upright once bore priceless statues of Byzas, of Constantine, and of deities that decorated pagan temples. The rich-green serpentine column brought here from the pagan Oracle of Delphi by Constantine still rises from its pit in the heart of the one-time race course. This bronze work of art, representing three entwining serpents holding up an offering to Apollo, had been contributed to Delphi by several Greek cities in gratitude to the sun god for their victory over Persia at Salamis in 480 B.C. Near-by stands an obelisk of rose granite, brought from Heliopolis on the Nile by Theodosius.

A riot that took place here in the year A.D. 532 is responsible for the glorious Cathedral of St. Sophia. The carefree mobs had divided into "blues" and "greens" for several years, depending on which side they supported in the chariot races. When this furore reached a frenzy at a race in that year, the two sides fought so fiercely for two days that much of Constantinople was burned down, despite the entreaties of Justinian and his forceful wife Theodora. Among the buildings destroyed was a church named St. Sophia, or "Holy Wisdom." In anger and shame, Justinian swore to erect the most magnificent church to God that had ever been built in honor of the new Christian religion. Architects, workers, and materials were devoted to this vow so solemnly that in five years an exquisite cathedral was completed.

---

[2] The Romans and Byzantines were fond of spectacles. Three of the places where they went to see such shows—Hippodrome, Circus, and Colosseum—still have their counterparts in the show world.

St. Sophia

This glory of the Byzantine world has given its style of architecture the name of "Byzantine." Its great arches and its dome show how the Roman scheme of massive construction prevailed in that century, but the decorations, mosaics, marbles, and art work show the full Greek influence.

High on the Acropolis above the Bosporus, this cathedral quickly became the pride of Constantinople. To embellish its interior, lovely and stately columns were plundered from ancient temples, such as that of Diana at Ephesus, one of the seven ancient wonders of the world. Marbles of most unique colorations were brought from other shrines and buildings, while skilled artisans were put to work setting the masterful golden mosaics doing honor to Christ and the historic scenes of the Bible.

Justinian inaugurated St. Sophia on December 27, 537. Throughout the remaining nine hundred years of his Empire, it was the center for all great occasions of Constantinople's stormy history. Under its soaring arches were held solemn ceremonies, processions, councils, thanksgiving services for victories, prayers of invocation in times of trial. Relics and icons were bestowed on it by emperor after emperor.

Then in 1453, when the Turks had finally conquered this noble city, they turned the building into their chief mosque. The icons and statues were hauled away. The mosaics and frescoes, with their images abhorrent to Islam, were covered over with coats of plaster. The spacious marble floors were covered with rich rugs from wall to wall. Massive medallions bearing Arabic proverbs from the Koran were hoisted up to the ceiling. A steep stairway and high platform were built in one corner for the mullah's Friday sermons. A niche was hollowed out on the southeastern wall to stand for Mecca, toward which the multitudes kneeled on the call of the mullah. On the outside, four slender minarets were raised.

For four and a half centuries St. Sophia served, in this unplanned way, the conquerors of the Cross on this forgotten Oriental hilltop. Only its name and its fame reminded faraway Europe of its one-time glory as the largest and finest church in Christendom.

Then times changed again. Turkey became a republic and freed itself from Moslem clerical rule. Western-minded President Atatürk decreed St. Sophia's new status—that of a museum in honor of the city of Istanbul. Archaeological experts headed by a Princeton professor came to perform the delicate operation of freeing the masterly art works from countless heavy coats of rough plaster.

They succeeded. Today the glorious building is restored to its original beauty, a testimony to the magnificence of this one-time center of the Byzantine faith.

The Second Rome

Justinian's reign marked the height of the glory of the Second Rome. He created a code of laws that comprised the most up-to-date collection of legal principles then known. He then dispatched his General Belisarius to the rescue of the First Rome.

This able general scored great successes in expelling barbarian chieftains from Sicily, North Africa, and most of Italy, including Rome itself. At Ravenna, in the Italian marshes near the mouth of the Po River, a Byzantine capital was built, and to this day the mosaics depicting Justinian and Theodora are still as brilliant and gorgeous as they were when first cemented into the cruciform church of Ravenna.

However, the passing of the strong man Justinian led to intestine strife in Constantinople, and from that day on the Empire began to wane. Yet it lasted another eight hundred years and performed many valuable services to our Western civilization. During the long years when Western Europe wallowed in the Dark Ages, Constantinople preserved much of the Christian tradition, many works of art, and shreds of classical learning. It held high the tradition of a strong empire and a strong priesthood as the twin pillars of Christianity. Its emperor was the only authentic Roman emperor, heir of the powers of the Caesars and the theological donations of Constantine. It was the protector of the holy shrines of Jerusalem and Nazareth. Under its reign Christian churches and monasteries thrived mightily in Egypt and Syria, with the remains of the vicious idols of ancient empires cast to the earth.

It was during this long succession of years that differences grew up between the Christian rulers of Constantinople and the Christian leaders of the West. The patriarchs of Constantinople, with their wealth, their connections with the Holy Land, and their closeness to the emperors, acknowledged no superior authority in ecclesiastical matters, but observed strict equality with the Bishop of Rome, whom they honored because of their veneration of the sanctity of the First Rome.

As wars and invasions came along during the later years, the differences between the two wings of Christian power grew wider, mainly due to complete separation and the many difficulties of communication. Liturgical costumes and observances varied more noticeably. Church councils struck snags in the hair-splitting between the "Latin rite" and the "Greek rite." The cultural chasm between Rome and Constantinople became reflected in the official religion.

In Rome, the church language was Latin, and the cultural background of the church leaders Roman. In the Eastern Empire, however, Latin had never supplanted the use of Greek during the entire Pax Romana. The people of the eastern Mediterranean, whatever their racial origins, still considered themselves "Greeks" because of their common culture and language, introduced by Alexander the Great's conquests. Thus, when Constantine built his new capital in the east, its language was Greek, and its church liturgy, customs, and traditions were entirely Greek.

The Pope, as has been noted in another chapter, crowned a Western Holy Roman Emperor in the year 800 and determined to restore the imperial pillar of the twin sources of government, whose sagging had brought so many disasters on Rome's western provinces. This only accentuated the differences with Constantinople, and at length the two rites drifted completely apart. In coming years the Roman church took on the name "catholic," meaning "universal," in its claim for pre-eminence over the schismatic Greeks; while the Greek church of Constantinople adopted the title of "orthodox," or "faithful to original teachings."

Both wings of Christianity were subjected to trials by hot fanatical fire during this period. The mighty rush of Mohammedanism changed the entire face of the cultural and religious world only a hundred years after Justinian had completed the Cathedral of St. Sophia.

Mohammedanism dates from 622, Mohammed's famous Hegira from Mecca to Medina. The Prophet died in 632. Almost instantaneously his new simple religion called Islam galvanized the forgotten and scorned desert tribes of Arabia. Rising to life, they rushed into the Byzantine Empire's southern reaches. Conquering all before them, they seized the rich city of Damascus and the magnificent classical port of Alexandria. Inside of twenty years the new creed had stripped Syria, Palestine, Mesopotamia, Egypt, and all of North Africa away from the Eastern Empire. With one stroke the richest provinces, wealthiest cities, and holiest lands of church history were lost forever, leaving the emperors of Constantinople only with Asia Minor, the Balkan Peninsula, and a few islands.

The Slavs

To replace these lost treasures in the south, the Eastern Empire began turning its eyes northward to virgin territories, hoping to redress its commerce and power in uncontested new areas.

Winter is often penetratingly cold in Constantinople. Unlike the rest of the Mediterranean lands, which have relatively balmy and rainy winters, the city on the straits has freezing temperatures and snow at frequent intervals. Wild winds swooping down from the endless plains of Russia are only slightly tempered by the Black Sea before they blow into the unsheltered streets of the imperial city.

These northern lands, too inhospitable for Greeks or Romans, became the homeland of the Slav race. Beginning with the fourth century, these strangers began crossing the Danube into the vacant hinterland of the Byzantine Empire. Missionaries from Constantinople gradually converted them from heathenism to Christianity. Later on, two learned pioneer missionaries, Cyril and Methodius, devised an alphabet for the new Slavonic liturgy which is the basis for the present-day Russian system of writing.

At the same time, trade currents took shape from the north. Swedish Vikings, making their way down the ramified river systems of Russia, began appearing at the back doors of Constantinople, bringing furs, amber, grain, and lumber—articles of the greatest value. This commerce resulted in a spreading of Western culture across the Black Sea into the southern regions of Russia. In the tenth century the Ukrainian King Vladimir adopted Orthodox Christianity as his official creed. Later, after centuries of invasions by Tartars and Huns, the faraway Duchy of Muscovy took over the leadership of the Slavs of Russia. As the great empire of Russia strode onto the world stage, its Orthodox patriarchs gave the kings of Moscow the title of Czar, or Caesar, in the Roman tradition of Constantinople. In their further zeal to spread the faith, they christened Moscow the Third Rome. The lure of avenging the fall of Constantinople—the Second Rome —into the hands of the Turks thus launched the series of wars and crises that stirred up the diplomats of Europe through the years down to our own times.

The Rise of the Crescent

The religious mission of the Byzantine Empire and its impregnable strategic position held the forces of Islam at bay for eight hundred years. After the conquest of Damascus in 639 by the Arabs, that much time elapsed before the final victory of the Turks over Constantinople in 1453.

However, the hostility and closeness of warlike infidel forces imposed a creeping paralysis on the Empire beside the Bosporus. Concern over their enemies' movements kept the emperors from trying any bold moves, or from developing a broad policy of action. For century after century the shrinking Empire's history is a sad account of palace revolts, cruel massacres, and military defeats.

Much of the time of the citizens was taken up with religious dissensions, particularly the centuries-long struggle of the iconoclasts versus iconodules. The former were proponents of removing icons from the churches; the latter class, which insisted that they be retained, finally won out.

As years went on, a new menace arose in the West, in fellow-Christian lands. The maritime republics of Venice and Genoa began to organize trade with the Arabs for the priceless goods of India and the East, such as silk, spices, jewels, textiles, and artistic handicrafts. In so doing, they drained away what should have been a source of strength to the Eastern Empire. Instead of Venice, Constantinople could have become the great emporium of this rich trade.

One other service performed by the Eastern Empire was an energetic patronage of the arts. Emperors and ecclesiastics manifested continued interest in mosaics, frescoes, reliefs, sculpture, and painting. Constantinople kept far ahead of any of the medieval cities of Europe in this regard. At the same time many of the classic Greek writings which had been taken from libraries and temples of the Hellenic world for safekeeping were preserved. This was "keeping the torch alight," which the world never appreciated until after the Turks had captured the city in 1453, when these treasures were lost, although skilled artisans and philosophers escaped to Italy in great numbers.

Worse times portended when in the eleventh century a new race of pagan horsemen appeared on the stage of history for the first time. These people were called the Seljuk Turks, a tribe from the inner fastnesses of central Asia, speaking an unknown tongue and hardly skilled in the barest elements of civilized living. Converted to Islam by Arab missionaries, they immediately went on the warpath, supplanting the Arab caliphs as chiefs of the Moslem movement. They closed off the holy places from Christian pilgrims and invaded Asia Minor, menacing Constantinople itself.

In panic, the Emperors called for aid from the West, and this led to the several Crusades. Wanderers, men of fortune, zealous princes, and adventurers bound for loot were among those responding to the papal echoing of the cry for a crusade; and soon these dangerous elements began to converge on Constantinople. The imperial authorities, out of fear of them, denied them hospitality and raised other annoyances, which created a bad state of feeling among the Western elements and in turn established a bad reputation for harassed Constantinople among the rulers back home.

In the year 1204 a thing that the emperors feared came upon them. A Venetian fleet bound for Egypt on the Fourth Crusade headed for the Bosporus instead when a deposed emperor's son implored them to come and restore his father to the throne. Willingly they accommodated by chasing the usurper from the city. However, the ransom they demanded for their aid was so high that they occupied Constantinople when it went unpaid. This brought about the Latin Empire on the Bosporus, which was a devastating blow to the hopes of maintaining the supremacy of the Cross in that beleaguered part of the world.

For the new rulers, led by Count Baldwin of Flanders—the new Emperor—decreed that the people of Constantinople were not Christians, but heretics, since they did not recognize the authority of the Pope. During the following years, the city was mercilessly pillaged. Golden icons, holy relics, illuminated books, and precious ornaments disappeared westward with the returning fleets. The many bronze statues were taken off their columns and melted down into coins. Among these lost works of art were a classical statue of Romulus and the she-wolf, a colossal Hercules whose thumb was as big as a man's torso, and a classic Helen of Troy, considered as perfection in feminine grace. The bronze plaques hanging on the obelisk in the Hippodrome were stripped off. The four golden horses of Lysippus, detached from the imperial palace, were shipped to Venice, where to this day they ornament the façade of the Cathedral of St. Mark.

At the same time the Venetians took over most of Greece, annexing its ports and islands and carrying away many of its classical remains to embellish Italian churches and palaces.

Even though the Byzantines rallied and, under Michael Palaeologus, retook their imperial city in 1261, this episode has been included here to relate one of the many events that brought about an unbridgeable abyss between the two wings of Christendom—the Latin and the Byzantine—which feud has existed down to the present day. The resentment of the Byzantine patriarchs against the overweening deeds of the Latins was later communicated to their successors, the Russian Orthodox patriarchs, whose zeal to occupy Constantinople became an irresistible prod to the Czars in later years.

The Seljuk Turks having been crushed by the Mongol hordes of Tamberlane, their bellicosity was inherited by another tribe of Turks who had rallied from a similar defeat more rapidly. These Turks called themselves Ottomans, after their first Sultan Osman, who led them into Asia Minor in the fourteenth century. These fierce Oriental fighters advanced up to the Bosporus and the Dardanelles, setting up their capital at Brusa, a rug-making town of ancient Greek origin lying across the Sea of Marmora. Later they crossed into Europe and crushed the rising Serbian and Bulgarian empires. For a hundred years they besieged isolated Constantinople, at length breaking through the stout walls of Theodosius and conquering the invincible city on May 29, 1453.

Turkish Constantinople

The conquest of Constantinople was one of those shocks heard round the world. It upset the Mediterranean balance of power. Its effects were immediate, as we will see in the next Scene of this Pageant.

Byzantium's loss was Italy's immediate gain, for a while. The richness of the Renaissance resulted from the "torch" of learning borne to Venice and Florence by escaping savants of Byzantium.

But the conquering Turks, in their fanaticism, only ended up by pushing Europe into its great age—the era of explorations and empire-building all over the world. The fall of Constantinople and the closing off of the East to European trade prepared Portugal and Spain for listening favorably to the plans of Vasco da Gama and Columbus. So, by losing the Mediterranean, Europe expanded into a new world.

Constantinople delighted the Turks. They made the city their capital; they adopted its crescent and star as their own emblem; and they beautified it in their own fashion for over four centuries. They lavished on it the wealth and trophies of the lands they overran.

The city that we visit today is thus a treasure-store, a Turkish-Oriental-styled city whose Greek-Western foundation shows through the veneer in various ways. The metropolis is enchanting as a combination of two completely different civilizations.

For over a hundred years after the Turkish conquest, it was sealed off from the Western world. The Ottoman sultans extended their realm in every direction. Under the irrepressible statesman-warrior Solyman the Magnificent, who reigned from 1520 to 1566, the Turkish Empire extended from Vienna to Mecca, from Algiers to the Caspian Sea. The Mediterranean Sea, from the medieval highway that the Venetians had made of it, was turned into a Turkish lake, a backwater of redoubtable corsairs and pirates under the banner of the Crescent. The shores of far Spain, the Italian islands, and even the Riviera became dangerous for their Christian inhabitants without watchtowers and protecting fleets on guard at all times.

Such imposing strength split the Christian forces in Europe, as the Moslems had succeeded in doing on a smaller scale during the Crusades. King Francis I of France signed an alliance with Solyman in an effort to unite their forces against their most dangerous mutual foe—the Holy Roman Emperor. Solyman, in reward, allowed the French to set up an embassy in Constantinople, to establish contact with the Christian minorities of the Holy Land, and to set up their own courts, or "capitulations," with jurisdiction over their own nationals. Thus the French funneled the only European influence into the courts of the Sultans for almost two hundred years, while they at the same time were the only reporters of Turkish affairs to the Western world. Through the French, the government of imperial Turkey came to be called "the Sublime Porte," the French translation of the imposing gateway that led to the Sultan's Palace of the Saray.[3]

The Turks built many mosques in their capital city, and two of them are gems of art and beauty. Visitors who go to see St. Sophia are taken immediately afterward to the adjoining mosque, which resembles it but is still bigger and, what is more, enjoys the distinction of having six, not four, minarets. Completed in 1610 by Sultan Ahmet, it was immediately named the "Blue Mosque" for its blue tiles which cover the entire interior. The

---

[3] This word was Europeanized in its Italian form *seraglio*.

six minarets caused much recrimination among the Moslem hierarchy, since only the mosque of the Kaaba in Mecca had this many. It is believed that a seventh minaret was later set up in Mecca to preserve its pre-eminence over Constantinople, the seat of the ambitious caliphs of Islam, who were at the same time warrior-sultans of the Ottoman dominions.

These thoughts give distinction to a visit to this Blue Mosque. Its most amazing architectural achievement is the fact that the many domes of the Byzantine-shaped building seem to rest on four single pillars, each one of which is almost twenty feet thick.

Solyman the Magnificent had also erected a stunning mosque, which is a short distance away toward the Golden Horn. This mosque is the largest in the city and the most sumptuous. Its courtyard of white marble is surrounded by pillars of rare colors collected from ancient ruins. Its lofty interior, rich carpets, exquisite candelabra, and carved arabesques make it a delight to every visitor. This mosque seems to attract more of the pious few than do the others. Almost at any time small groups of Moslem gentlemen can be found praying or reciting together on a few of the many carpets.

Surrounding this mosque are dependent buildings with cupolas and colonnades which once were used as poor asylums, hospitals, libraries, schools, and baths, and made the mosque the center of a charitable settlement, as is the case with mosques in Arabia, Persia, and sometimes Egypt.

There are many other attractions to be seen in old Stamboul before today's visitor returns to Galata and the modern city. Several mosques, each with historical and artistic significance, rise high above the low-lying homes, many of them weird-looking with their scores of cupolas. One of these mosques, the Kariye, was originally the Byzantine Church of the Holy Saviour. An unimportant mosque, it is worth visiting because of its ornate mosaics which still show scenes of the life of Christ. Only one minaret dignifies this out-of-the-way place of worship. Another ancient church, St. Irene, was made into a military museum, and here today there are on display all kinds of valuable medieval arms, military uniforms, and even the famous iron chain which the beleaguered Byzantine emperors had stretched across the Golden Horn to protect their harbor from the Turks.

However, there is still one climactic place to be seen on the Acropolis, and that is the Saray (Seraglio), or the Palace of the Sultans, whose gardens glide down the slopes to the point where the Bosporus meets the Golden Horn. This core of the Turkish Empire was a secret fastness until the modern Turkish Republic opened up its treasures for all to admire. The magnificent rooms of the sultan, of the vizier, of the harem; the assembly rooms with their official divans, on which the sultan received ambassadors; the beautiful rococo fireplaces and tiled walls; the balconies and domed kitchens—all are on display. What is most exciting, however, is the exhibit of treasures owned by the sultans. Unequaled except perhaps at Peiping is this display, with its room on room of porcelain objects of the most diverse designs. Here the rich Sèvres tea sets presented by the kings of France vie with magnificent Oriental vases sent by the emperors of China. So far did the political importance of the Ottoman sultans spread during the centuries of their glory.

"The Sick Man of Europe"

After the year 1700 the Turkish Empire began slowly to shrink. More up-to-date empires began to crowd it back onto its center on the Bosporus. The sultans, instead of being warriors, became experts in intrigue and diplomacy. They also became more fanatical in resisting the march of modernism, since such currents came from the hated *rayah*, or despised infidels of Christians.

As the Empire stagnated, Constantinople became more of a picturesque, fanatical Oriental capital. The first foreign visitors, who went there in the late nineteenth century, saw much to marvel at, little to admire. The Turks—warriors and not artisans; soldiers but not creators—imported their art forms from Persia; their religion and education from Arabia.

Strict seclusion was enforced on women. The men dressed in Persian style, with flowing garments and towering turbans. Oriental sweetmeats were sold by merchants on every corner. The bazaars, instead of being covered over by latticework as in the hot Arab countries, were roofed over with brick arches, so that they seem today like underground warrens.

The houses of Constantinople are unique even today. Unlike every other Mediterranean city, the city's houses are of wood. Flimsy firetraps they appear, as they tower up three and four stories in unpainted frames. Yet they add today an air of quaintness, and they point to the ever present geographic fact of the nearness of Russia. For such lumber could have come from hardly anywhere but the forests of southern Russia in greatest measure. The Turks dominated that area for four hundred years, and the lumber could easily have been floated down the Dnieper and across the Black Sea.

From this epoch came other Turkish styles to appeal to the bored royal salons of eighteenth century Europe. The kiosks, or Persian-style domed pavilions used for tea houses, palace roofs, or panoramic viewpoints, so caught the fancy of the French that newsstands in Paris have all been built in that style and are called kiosks still. The Janissaries, or elite corps of troops raised from kidnapped Christian infants stolen from their parents, were a fierce, unmanageable group of fanatics, until they were massacred by the Sultan's orders in the year 1826. Their word survives as a terror in all the Balkans.

Before leaving the Seraglio Palace, visitors are shown the underground galleries, or cisterns, which date from Byzantine days as sources of water for the multitudes. This water was brought over the lordly Roman-style aqueduct built by the Emperor Valens in the fourth century. Its arches still run across half the city.

However, the Turkish Empire, "The Sick Man of Europe," was a long time a-dying. The weak sultans became pawns in the hands of the powers of Europe. Defeated in several wars with Russia, the Turks were nevertheless rescued by Britain and France, who distrusted the megalomania of the expanding czarist empire. The one war in which Turkey was victorious was the Crimean War of 1853-1856, in which the British and French took the offensive. That was an international episode in the story of Constantinople, for the city became a military center; and, also, its large military hospital, set up on the Asiatic shore in a barnlike barracks, exhibited to the world for the first time the barbaric lack of care suffered by wounded soldiers. Florence Nightingale, one of the British nurses in that hospital, exposed these atrocious facts from the experiences she went through in this faraway Oriental-style city.

Europe's balance of power was shaken later in the century when the Sultans fell in with the Kaiser of Germany, whose own megalomania made him take over this bankrupt but strategic property. The Kaiser sent a military mission to build up the antique Turkish army. He sent economic and banking experts to run its primeval economy. He declared himself the Protector of Islam, and donated a ponderous fountain to be placed in the Hippodrome with the remains of classical wonders. But what torpedoed the complacency of the world was his plan for a Berlin-to-Bagdad railway, which would run through Constantinople almost to the gateway of India.

The Sultan at this time was Abdul "the Damned," a recluse who used poison and massacres as his method of maintaining order in his backward country and who flirted with the Kaiser to keep the Russians at bay. With the outbreak of World War I in 1914, Turkey sided with Germany against its old Russian enemy and its former British friends.

At first this seemed a brilliant stroke, for the new Turkish army gave a good account of itself. In 1915 a British-Australian-New Zealand force attacking the forts on the Dardanelles in order to capture Constantinople and to open the way to communication with Russia was defeated by Turkish heroism and the generalship of the German Liman von Sanders. However, the war proved disastrous. The Arab provinces, fired with nationalism and skillfully led by Lawrence "of Arabia," revolted. The British finally overran the strategic lands to the south.

In the heat of the conflict, Russia had demanded of her allies Britain and France the right to capture and annex the imperial city of Constantinople.[4] Hard-pressed London and Paris had to

---

[4] "Tsarigrad," the Russian word for the city, means "City of the Emperors."

agree, yet this strategic step, which would have reversed the course of Middle East history, was washed out when Russia went over into Bolshevik revolution.

When Turkey surrendered at the end of the war, the British, not the Russians, occupied Constantinople. In the interests of reversing history's long backslide from its original course, the Greeks were allowed to land an army in Asia Minor, and Italy and France were given spheres of influence along the Mediterranean shores of that peninsula.

At this time, however, one of those amazing breaks took place that always enliven history. Men and circumstances combine under such influences to wrench the course of affairs abruptly away into new channels. And this is what happened in Turkey, one of the fortunate developments for the twentieth century.

Turkey was reborn. A patriotic general named Mustapha Kemal Pasha proclaimed a Nationalist Government at the town of Sivas near the Black Sea and gathered other constructive leaders and forces about him. He cleverly manipulated the three powers occupying Asia Minor, expelling them all and then coming to terms with Britain for the evacuation of Constantinople.

To clear the ground for his new orientation of his country, he deposed the last Sultan in 1923, abolished the office of caliph, declared Turkey a republic, and renounced all non-Turkish territories by the new treaty of Lausanne.

Constantinople, now officially baptized Istanbul,[5] was deprived of its position as the capital, which was moved to the ancient city of Angora in the heart of Asia Minor.[6] In succeeding years Kemal instituted radical reforms to disestablish the Moslem religion, to adopt the European code of law, to abolish the Arabic script in favor of Latin letters in the spelling of Turkish, to emancipate women, to encourage modern ways of life in neglected, backward Turkey, and to participate in world affairs as a national, progressive state.

Such reforms have changed the scene inside Istanbul perceptibly. In lieu of fezzes and veils, men and women wear Western

---

[5] "Istanbul" is the medieval Turkish transliteration of the city's old name.
[6] "Angora" is now respelled in Turkish "Ankara."

clothes exclusively. Instead of Moslems prostrating themselves openly in the streets, traffic moves unchallenged. Many of the mosques are silent, with the voices of the muezzins muted. Instead of mystery and official obstruction of foreigners, the city is wide open, with every historical sight freely open for inspection. All the favorite spots once restricted to Moslem visitors, such as the lovely islands of the Princes[7] in the Sea of Marmora, or the Greek ruins of Asia Minor, or the retreats where veiled women used to go off by themselves, are now free to all.

Turkey has thus filled the bed of the "Sick Man" with a thriving, eager state and people. Naturally the many centuries of Eastern incubus have not worn off the people's conduct entirely. The men still congregate by themselves for entertainment in Arab fashion and listen to modern-dressed chanteuses wail some endless ditty in Oriental style. The people are still inscrutable even if polite and do not grasp the language of foreigners as fast as other European citizens, so that contacts in the streets of Istanbul are not easy. Turkish to an outsider is a language without clues.[8]

Istanbul is most changed, however, in the matter of statuary. Up in the Square of the Republic, adjacent to the Taksim Gardens, stands a large sculpted group of figures in modern dress gathered around the epochal image of Kemal, whose modern name is Atatürk.[9] Such a sight, abhorrent to the precepts of the Koran, is unknown in the great cities of Islam.

As the traveler sails away from his visit to this magnificent city on the place where Asia and Europe almost touch, he feels the wonderful lift that comes from a story with a happy ending. Heading toward the grim Dardanelles with their 30,000 buried Empire soldiers and the barren fields surrounding Troy of the wooden horse, he feels that a bright new light is shining where darkest clouds have reigned for centuries. All around him is Turkish soil, but a Turkey that is now an ally of America, that is opening up its resources to American engineers and strategists,

---

[7] Better known as Prinkipo.

[8] Turkish, a Turco-Iranian speech, is distantly related to Hungarian and Finnish.

[9] "Atatürk" means "Father of the Turks."

and that is standing as a bulwark of twentieth century stability on the edge of a welling sea of Near Eastern tumult. The traveler can take inspiration and pray that several other nations whose unhappy past has brought tribulation to the world will follow the same upward path to integration with the constructive forces of the century.

No longer the "terrible Turk" of past decades, the Turk of today represents the flowering of the epic tale spun by the long development of the city that sits beside the Golden Horn and the Bosporus.

ITALY

Dynamo of the Renaissance

ONE OF THE MOST LUSTY and vigorous periods of European history is that creative epoch called the Renaissance. For several short decades semi-stagnant, medievalized Europe caught fire with a new zest for learning and a welcome willingness to experiment with new forms and new arts. No wonder such a term—Renaissance—has come down to honor that reawakening to life, for "Rebirth" it surely was.

Even though this event signified rebirth to the Europeans, it was really only a new scene in our unfolding Pageant of the Mediterranean's story. For the impetus of culture, and an appreciation of what the world had created ages before, came to Western Europe; and there receptive hands and minds welcomed it, studied it, and reshaped it nobly after their own fashion.

The part of Europe that launched this Renaissance was the small but nature-blest region of northern Italy. Here several cities blossomed out with famous men who have left their names on history's records as leaders in their fields. Here were city-states competing so frantically with each other for survival that they welcomed every promising genius who would give them the lead.

The fact that northern Italy had progressed to this point of appreciating the arts and crafts by the middle of the fifteenth century was matched by the phenomenon of Constantinople's falling to the Turks at precisely the same instant. For into the eager and questing hands of the energetic Italians came a ready-made, proved form of learning and achievement called the classics, which they immediately accepted instead of painfully trying to evolve something new of their own.

Thus the Renaissance simply signifies that process whereby classic civilization was remolded and broadcast in line with the new times. In other words, ancient Rome and Greece had evolved the finest lessons out of all the inventions and wisdom of the old civilizations in the East. The Byzantine Empire preserved this synthesis through the long Dark Ages and handed it on to the Italian city-states, who in turn enriched it for us with their own skills. The result was the introduction of the modern age and modern civilization into Western Europe.

The Renaissance penetrated every field of a man's life. Even though some of its teachings met with resistance from ecclesiastical authorities, it swept through all barriers and revamped the whole European picture by the end of the sixteenth century. In art, it released painters and sculptors from charming but stylized religious motifs and allowed them to attempt what had been stigmatized as profane. In architecture, the age of the neoclassic, with columns and domes, niches and porticoes, began to supplant the Gothic and the heavy Romanesque. In literature and philosophy, classic learning poured into the field of the humanities. In study, medicine, the sciences, and history whole new fields opened up overnight for daring thinkers. In men's minds the willingness to question and explore led to their zealous pushing back of limiting horizons and to the concentrating of all their knowledge at hand to open up the outside world to Europe's ken. And in the field of religion, the desire to examine anew the basic origins of faith accompanied the most significant concomitant force of the Renaissance—the Protestant Reformation.

Let us look briefly into the factors that had been gradually leading northern Italy into playing the host and the father to the new learning, the Renaissance.

The people of the great plain of northern Italy were not in ancient times Italians or Latins. They were Celts. When this region was overrun and annexed by republican Rome, it was given the name of "Gaul this side of the Alps" (Gallia Cisalpina). Later mixings of blood with the Latins came as the result of military campaigns, migration of families, and close integration with the Roman heart of the Empire. But the northern Italians, by retaining traces of their Celtic beginnings, have an appearance distinctive from the Neapolitans. The Florentines south of the Apennines, however, were not Celts, but are considered to have been descendants of the Etruscans.

The present flourishing cities of northern Italy were at the beginning military camps, commercial centers, or resorts built in Roman times.

While the Roman Empire was still in its flower, incursions from beyond the mountains began to affect the population of north Italy. The Veneti who appeared in the lands about Venice are considered to be identical with the Wends, a Slavo-Teuton tribe that lived near the Baltic.[1] As the Empire weakened, the pressure from the north grew greater. Emperors had to spend almost their entire reigns fighting beyond the Alps. For this reason the military camp of Mediolanum (Milan) began to assume importance and size, and before the time of Diocletian it was more often the capital of the Empire than Rome itself. Another fortress city was Aquileia, off to the eastward at the very tip of the Adriatic, a wealthy town of classic beauty protecting Italy from hostile tribes to the east.

Germans from the north later poured into the Po Valley, followed by the East Goths and the West Goths—also Germanic tribes from some unknown homeland beyond the Alps. Worst of all by far were the savage Huns, a yellowish race of wild horsemen who somehow or other pierced sharply from central Asia into the heart of Europe. Led by the fierce-looking Attila, they poured into Italy; sacked Aquileia and burned it to the ground; and held all the cities of north Italy ransom until they finally were smashed at the field of Chalons in central Gaul. Later came the Lombards and the Burgundians.

By the eighth century after Christ these invasions died down, but Italian civilization was in shambles. The prosperous Roman

---

[1] Modern Kings of Sweden have the title "King of the Sveas, the Goths, and the Wends."

cities of the Po Valley had decayed into desolate shells. The people had fled to hilltop fortifications, grim, ugly castles, or poverty-stricken villages remote from streams of communication. The disheartened citizens of Aquileia, tired of rebuilding for the benefit of new invaders, had taken refuge in the impenetrable swamps of the Venetian lagoon at the head of the Adriatic. The land was filled with homeless refugees from destroyed Roman towns beyond the Alps. Farther south, refugees fleeing from across the Adriatic sought sanctuary on the impenetrable summits of the Abruzzi ("abruptnesses") or on peaks like San Marino. Port cities, river towns, or road centers were shunned.

Thus the road back to civilization was long and arduous for the northern Italian peoples. Yet out of such tribulation came an energetic race, a people accustomed to struggle and change, and more than willing to experiment.

As a result of their rebuilding of their shattered land, they worked out a form of life that has been a direct heritage for us moderns. Our everyday life has absorbed refinements that came from those peoples. For example, "millinery" is a word coined from Milan, once the leader in this field. Fine porcelains were for a long time known as *faiences* from Faenza. Pistols were forged the earliest in Pistoia. Hard money prized in northern Europe took the name of "florins" from Florence, or "ducats" from the ducal money of Venice. More humble and later importations were Leghorn poultry, Bologna sausages. Exciting court stories told in petty Italian palaces formed the basis for some of Shakespeare's plots in many cases, such as *The Merchant of Venice, Two Gentlemen of Verona, Othello, Romeo and Juliet.*

Ravenna

One single town that had escaped the tragic course of events was picturesque Ravenna. This place had been of no importance in Roman days, but Christian Emperors of the fourth century had turned to its swamps and its relative remoteness to build a castle and a small port for their use. When the last Emperor had been defeated by the East Goths in A.D. 476, Ravenna became the barbarians' capital until Emperor Justinian sent a fleet to evict them. The Byzantines then set up an Exarch, or sub-emperor, to rule Italy. The exarchs of Ravenna failed to extend their sway over all Italy, but for two hundred years they made of Ravenna a tiny light of civilized living amid the general holocaust.

Ravenna is only thirty miles below the mouth of the Po and is twenty miles north of the tiny stream known as the Rubicon, which in Caesar's day was the boundary between Cisalpine Gaul and Italy. Today the city lies several miles inland from the retreating seashore of the Adriatic and is little more than a sleepy provincial town. However, several above-average hotels exist to shelter the travelers who come to marvel at Ravenna's monuments.

Chief among the latter is the central church, a Greek-style square building, whose walls still bear exquisite golden mosaics showing Justinian and Theodora, and important people of the court of faraway Byzantium. More exciting still is a country church four miles south of town called San Giovanni in Classe Fuori (or "St. John's in the village of Classe outside the walls"). Mosaics abound there as well, but architecturally it is an epochal structure. For, off to a side of the church is a square tower containing once upon a time a bell. From this bell such a tower took the name of *campanile* in Italian. As later, Romanesque churches were built in Italy the campaniles gradually were brought close to the main buildings, and then they were made taller and taller. As an art form they became admired, and so were even attached to older classical buildings. Sometimes they were built so high that they began to lean. In the lands of northern Europe they were placed on top of the churches, and as "steeples" they have come down to our day as distinctive adornments to a church. In ancient days neither temples nor basilicas had such towers, and their origin was thus not religious but architectural.

In the seventh century the Exarchs weakened, and Ravenna was swallowed up by the Lombards, whose Kings and iron-crown resided at Pavia on the Po, until the Franks of Gaul, led by Charlemagne, crossed the Alps and demolished their vacuous rule in 771.

Pisa

After the year 800, when the Holy Roman Empire was set up by the Pope and Charlemagne, northern Italy once again came under a government and acquired a protector in the form of an emperor. However, these Emperors were forced to reside far to the north to fight the heathen tribes of Europe. Their capital was not at Rome, nor at Milan, but at Aix-la-Chapelle.[2] Besides, their rule was weak, for they followed the policy of dividing up their domains among many sons.

However, the imperial title was powerful. Thus the northern Italian cities, as they took on strength under the new relative stability, did not coalesce into the foundations of a national state. Their overlords were already established, and they had no title to become anything but segments of the empire that was holy and neo-Roman. Consequently, as the cities grew strong and began to govern themselves, their ambitions led only so far as self-determination, and not primacy over all Italy, since rulers for Italy were already determined. This factor is probably the single strongest influence that effectively kept Italy from progressing toward unity until our own modern times (1860).

One of the first cities to rise from obscurity and take on a new entity was Pisa. A city below the Apennines, on the Arno a few miles from its mouth in the Mediterranean, its people early took to the sea. As fishers, then as traders, they ranged far and wide. With great daring, they ousted Saracen-Arab rulers holding Corsica, and they made Elba, Monte Cristo, and other near-by islands their advance-warning points against hostile Moslem fleets. Later they defeated the rival mariners of Amalfi, and began sailing to the Levant for trade, crusading, and loot.

Pisa thus grew opulent and wealthy, and also receptive to art forms. The cathedral and baptistery, designed and built in the fourteenth century, represent the climax of their constructive genius. The Leaning Tower was originally merely a decorative campanile for the cathedral, but it began to lean while in con-

---

[2] Its present name is Aachen, located in Germany where Holland, Belgium, and Germany all meet.

struction, and was finished at an angle, with compensations that can be noticed by the onlooker.

In the fifteenth century Pisa was overrun and annexed by Florence, a "landlubber" city. Thus Pisa's overseas holdings were gobbled up by the near-by maritime republic of Genoa.

The Leaning Tower was only one of many leaning towers in medieval Italy. But it is the most ornate and beautiful. The other towers, made of brick without ornamentation, usually were run up by noble families whose homes were thick-walled "castles," and the towers were needed for vision as well as for prestige. Most of them collapsed. However, two of them, leaning, can still be seen in Bologna, and one church campanile that leans is visible in Venice. To see how a city looked with many tall towers of this kind, visit San Gimignano, just off the road between Florence and Siena.

Siena

Southward of Florence, almost halfway to the center of Italy, is this beautiful medieval city. Siena grew rich in the twelfth century from war, tolls, and agriculture. It is the first city for travelers coming up from Rome with a north Italian flavor. Its cathedral and tall campanile are elegant in bright-striped marble, an art brought back from the Levant by crusading Sienese.

However, the central square is distinctive of most north Italian cities. Large, paved, and surrounded by lovely buildings and palaces of burnt-orange color, with balconies and candy-stick-columned windows, the square also is faced by the vast municipal town hall with its sky-high tower. Even though Siena lost its independence to Florence long ago, it has held on to the elegant pageantry of medieval days in the form of its *palio,* a horse race around the main square held several times each summer.

Perugia and Assisi

In central Italy, two cities high on hilltops developed architects and sufficient wealth to design beautiful squares, churches, and fountains. Assisi is famous, however, for its St. Francis, whose fame brings admirers from many parts of the world. St. Francis was canonized in 1228, two years after his death, and the present "double church" was begun shortly afterwards. The town is quaint, with pretty, narrow streets, beautiful views, small friendly hotels, and a temple of Minerva that has been modified into a church.

In Perugia the museum has many examples of Etruscan art for those interested in this mysterious people. The city is the capital of the medieval county of Umbria, a region of pleasant valleys and hilltop towns. It reaches up in the high Apennines, and in it is located the source of the Tiber. Umbria came into the possession of the Popes in the sixteenth century and remained in their possession until the unification of Italy in 1860.

Padua

Up in northern Italy, north of the Po, and in the heart of the rich Venetian plains, there grew up a city in the early Middle Ages called Padua. Its prestige in medieval Italy stemmed from its university, which is often called "the Oxford of Italy." Visitors to Padua today can see the interesting courtyard of the university and can occasionally witness some of the student contests in which they wear their medieval-inspired caps.

Padua also possesses a town council hall of great interest architecturally. Called the Palace of Reason, it is a turtleback building surrounded by a later loggia. Its interior is a vast unobstructed hall 263 feet long and 88 feet high. Padua also is famed for being the place where St. Anthony died, and a lofty basilica has been built over his tomb. The basilica stands high above the city, as it has done since 1307. Smaller churches have beautiful frescoes done by Giotto and Mantegna in the fourteenth century.

Padua lost its independence to Venice shortly after this time, but it has retained its stately beauty and its important university. It is a road junction for routes coming from the rest of Italy to unite in the straight-as-an-arrow *autostrada* that covers the last twenty-two miles to Venice.

A Temple Courtyard in Luxor: One of Egypt's *gulla gulla* conjurors finds Egypt's most elaborate temple an ideal stage.

"The Divine Riviera" is the name given to the majestic Italian coast centering around the district of Amalfi south of Naples.

Tel Aviv Faces the Sea: Tel Aviv's modern buildings and apartments face the open Mediterraean across sub-tropical gardens.

On the Sea of Galilee: These fishermen's boats have changed hardly a whit from the type described in the New Testament.

Classic Perfection in Athens: The Parthenon, erected at the height of Athens' golden age five centuries before Christ, still stands as the perfect model of classic, symmetrical architecture.

Classic Costumes and Faces in Modern Greece: Here on the island of Corfu is a group of peasant dancers in a classic pose.

The Isles of Greece Again the Vogue: The Greek Islands in the Aegean Sea, playground of the gods, are now sought after by travelers as never before. This is a view of charming Hydra.

Pompeii Beneath Its Destroyer—Vesuvius: Its ancient forum, walls, arches, cast a spell over travelers.

Ancient Rome's Showplace—the Colosseum: Built in the year 80, once faced with marble, it provided spectacles for huge crowds.

Dazzling Scene at Siena: This cathedral of black and white marble stripes proclaims the dramatic era of the Renaissance in this creative Italian city.

Rhodes Harbor Once Boasted a Colossus: Gigantic statue of Apollo, the Colossus, probably straddled this Aegean harbor.

Glory of Constantinople: St. Sophia Cathedral is here viewed beyond later buildings in the historic heart of the old Byzantine capital, now known as Istanbul.

The "Ponte Vecchio" at Florence: Exquisite medieval bridge over the Arno, still crowded with shops.

"What's New Along the Rialto?" inquired medieval merchants in Venice. Here the Rialto Bridge crosses the narrowest point of the Grand Canal.

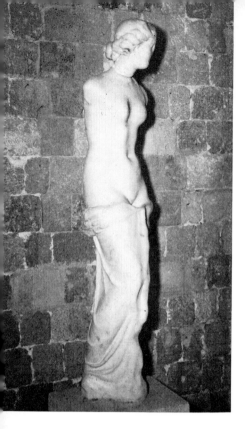

The Lovely Venus of Ancient Rhodes: Symbol of the aesthetic art of ancient Greece is this unearthed marble beauty.

A Portuguese Singing Windmill: The little jars on the connecting ropes provide a busy melody!

Monte Carlo's Casino and Gardens: Glamorous symbol of the Mediterranean's modern role as a luxury travel region.

The Belem Monastery Church Near Lisbon: Magnificent edifice in Manueline Gothic, honoring Vasco da Gama's voyage to India.

The Most Elegant Scene in a Spanish Bull Ring: The brightly capari-
soned toreadors march in to the strains of a martial tune.

Display of Royal Coaches in Lisbon: Made by the painstaking labor of
the most skilled artisans of all Europe.

"Delicate Fancy of the Moor" is a term often used to describe the artistry of columns and fountains in the Alhambra at Granada.

In the "Casbah" of Algiers: Unchanged through the centuries, this Arab quarter is still thoroughly Oriental in its way of life.

"Dancing Girl" of the Barbary Coast: **In Tunis an Arab entertainer shows her favorite costume and unfailing appeal.**

Yugoslavia's Scenic "Window" on the Mediterranean: **The sparkling-clear Adriatic here bathes the steep slopes and the tiny medieval villages of the magnificent Dalmatian Coast.**

Maid of Majorca: With artful coif and ingenious costume, she gives lustre to Spain's "garden island."

This Genuine Apartment House Has Long Stood in Beirut: Built of necessity on a shoestring lot, only five feet wide at one end, it is fully rented!

Gibraltar—Front Door of the Mediterranean: Crossroads of world sea lanes, the "Big Rock" faces nearby Spain.

Malta's Fantastic Display of Renaissance Weapons and Armor: Scimitars, shields, helmets and suits of armor belonging to both Europeans and Turks were collected after the great siege.

Madeira Is a Holiday Island: Old-time fishing village adds old-world charm to this flowery Portuguese isle.

A Young Moor: This young lad of Morocco descends from warrior races that conquered Spain and overran Western empires.

Milan

Largest city of Italy today—the most European-appearing of Italian cities, and industrial center of the country—is great Milan, the metropolis of all the Po Valley cities. Its heavy traffic, wide esplanades, modern buildings, and cosmopolitan crowds have a distinctly twentieth-century aspect, and seem to be in a different country than are the languorous cities south of Naples.

Milan's interests have always been more closely linked with surrounding European neighbors than with southern Italy. Its cathedral is famed for being the most perfect Gothic church in the country. Its long nave (486 feet) supports a richly ornamented roof, with room for 185 frets. Its grandeur impressed early travelers to proclaim its beauty similar to that of "frozen music." The cathedral was begun in 1386, but the last decorations of its great façade were not put in place until 1815.

Busy travelers should stop in Milan long enough to see the magnificent Teatro alla Scala, famed for its prestige among world opera-lovers. La Scala has inspired the architecture of most opera houses in the outside world as well as in Italy, and has been completely rebuilt since it was hit by a bomb during the war.

A small church, called Santa Maria delle Grazie, a few blocks west of the cathedral, contains a Dominican chapel on whose wall the genius Leonardo da Vinci painted "The Last Supper," an inspiration to the world. Bomb damage to the building, resulting in a great deal of moisture and rubble hitting the painting, has caused it to fade excessively and its glory is perhaps best admired in photographs and imitations of its original perfection.

Milan's history has been extraordinarily tempestuous because of its early rise to wealth and power in the Middle Ages. Medieval Italy was torn by an unending civil war because of its anomalous political situation. Owing allegiance to the Holy Roman Emperor, who almost always was out of the country, and after the tenth century almost invariably a German or Austrian, the Italian cities were faced with the alternate of supporting the Popes against these dissident absentee Emperors. Thus the ambitious cities were always taking and changing sides, being classed as Guelfs when they supported the Popes, or Ghibellines when they espoused the imperial cause. Famous men of science and letters were often fugitives from their own cities as the result of selecting the wrong side, and whole cities were besieged for months over such causes. Milan's ruling dukes of the Visconti family resorted to the ruse of hiring mercenaries to fight her battles. There were always many of these soldiers of fortune, called in Italian *condottieri,* and they were also used by foreign kings in their battles, often to their sorrow, since bribes were often raised in the heat of battle. However, Milan won notoriety when in 1499 the leader of the Milanese condottieri, named Sforza, ousted the dukes and took over himself. This led to a scramble among the powers of Europe to oust such a dangerous upstart.

Milan thus went under foreign domination for three centuries. The French, the Spaniards, and then the Austrians controlled the unruly city despite many uprisings and a Napoleonic interlude— that is, until 1859, when a Franco-Italian army finally liberated it from the Austrian troops.

In a graceful, large park in the center of the city stands an excellent specimen of a sixteenth-century Italian palace. Called the Castello Sforzesco, built in 1450 by a Sforza, it has parapets, towers, and the heavy walls of a medieval fort, modified by Renaissance artistic refinements, and it is now an excellent museum of art.

Milan is connected by autostradas with Turin, Brescia, and Bergamo, and also with near-by Lake Como and Lake Maggiore. The slopes of the Alps are only twenty miles to the north.

Genoa

Italy's largest port is the historic city of Genoa, whose location is so beautiful that it is called La Soperba by its recorders. Genoa sits between two segments of the Italian Riviera. The Apennines crowd so close to the sea at this point that the city rises like an amphitheatre around its bowl-shaped harbor.

Genoa outstripped its sister port cities centuries ago because a gentle pass leads from it back into the Po Valley. Today it acts as the gateway to the sea for Italy's most important industrial region. Genoa also handles much of Switzerland's overseas trade.

Americans sailing into the crowded port are amazed at its modern appearance. A real-life, full-sized skyscraper rises beside the crowded old medieval section of town and stately public buildings line busy, straight streets. Many tunnels, or *gallerias*, carry traffic under obstructing hills. Fine hotels, palaces, and churches are to be found in this thoroughly up-to-date metropolis of 700,000 people.

Genoa with its valuable harbor played a master role in the Middle Ages. It was a maritime republic, a city of ambitious merchants and seamen. It inherited the island possessions of Pisa; it carried on lucrative trade with the Arabs and Egyptians; and its stately fleet ruled the Mediterranean for much of the Middle Ages. It rivaled Venice for the trade of the Byzantine Empire and of the Crimea. A Genoese castle still rises at the Black Sea entrance of the Bosporus. In one sea fight with the Venetians, Genoese sailors captured a homing traveler named Marco Polo, who used his long sentence in a Genoese jail to good advantage by writing his exciting tale of medieval China. In 1380 the Genoese assaulted Venice in her home waters and almost won the battle.

This repulse at the hands of Venice marked the end of Genoa's great prestige. A period of civil wars followed, during which a young boy, discouraged at the lack of a future in such a decadent empire, left his home city and discovered an empire for another homeland—Spain. His name, of course, was Christopher Columbus.

When Constantinople fell to the Turks, Genoa's empire in the Levant disappeared, and the mother city had to call in Spanish and French rulers to restore peace to her own warring citizenry. The republic still owned Corsica, but after two hundred years of warfare with the patriots of that island, Genoa sold Corsica to the King of France in 1768, shortly before a famous child was born on the island who was to be named Napoleon Bonaparte.

When Italy became a united kingdom in 1860, partly due to the unending work of Genoa's own Giuseppe Mazzini, the city regained importance because of its harbor and its closeness to the big cities of Milan and Turin. Today it has grown to greater eminence than ever before.

Visitors of today see very little of ancient Genoa, but can marvel at the ornate palaces and the sumptuous home of the city's greatest Renaissance citizen, Admiral Andrea Doria, who led many European fleets against the embattled Turkish galleys of Barbarossa, not always victoriously, however. An insignificant, small wooden house is shown as Columbus' birthplace, and a small temple called Sant' Andrea is attractively placed amid an extensive development of modernistic government buildings. Travelers are also taken out to the ornate cemetery at Staglieno, very typical with its expensive tombs, excellent plantings, and flowery epitaphs complete with photographs of the departed.

Florence

Amid this multitude of wealthy and powerful cities, Florence stands pre-eminent and glorious, the pulsating center of Renaissance Italy, a never dying city of exquisite art and handicrafts. No one ever comes to Florence without feeling captivated by its mature atmosphere of achievement and brilliance.

Some of the greatest figures of the Renaissance were Florentines. Dante Alighieri, the founder of the modern written Italian language, poet and philosopher . . . Petrarch, of poetic repute second only to Dante . . . Boccaccio, the Italian Chaucer . . . Galileo, who studied astronomy and physics, propounded the startling discovery that the earth revolves around the sun, and was tried for blasphemy by the Church . . . Amerigo Vespucci the enterprising merchant, whose vivid reports of the lands he saw aboard a Spanish ship led European cartographers to bestow his name on the new "American" continent . . . Verrazzano, a mariner in the service of France who first sailed into New York harbor . . . and of course Lorenzo of the Medici, the Magnificent, whose patronage gave Florence the leadership in all fields of art during the Renaissance.

Florentine art is of the dramatic type, reaching a power and depth rarely achieved elsewhere. Florence gave opportunity to such renowned painters as Cimabue, Giotto, Ghirlandaio, Botticelli, Lippi, Andrea del Sarto, Michelangelo, and Leonardo da Vinci, to give just the best-known first-raters. It was the favorite home of great architects like Brunelleschi and Michelangelo; of sculptors such as Donatello, Ghiberti, Della Robbia. Its master goldsmith Benvenuto Cellini created unsurpassed utensils of intricate beauty. Florence also was the city of that cynical Renaissance political strategist Machiavelli. And it even boasted a reformer, the determined monk Savonarola, who made the whole city wear sackcloth and ashes to repent for the lavishness of the Medici, until he was overthrown and burned at the stake.

The Medici family were dynamos even for such a dynamic era. They achieved their wealth by money-lending. (Their family crest—the three pills[3]—is now the symbol of pawnshops everywhere.) They patronized artists and attracted them from all over Italy. Such pre-eminence coupled with such wealth enabled Florence to swallow up its sister cities of Pisa and Siena, and to become the grand ducal capital of Tuscany. It had its share of civil wars and struggles with other Italian cities, but Florence retained a measure of independence down to 1860, when it became the first capital of united Italy.

Such a city is replete with things to see. Everyone should sooner or later come to spend at least a whole week just enjoying the treasures of this unique city.

Florence sits astride the Arno River, and its greatest buildings were all standing in the age of the fabulous Renaissance. The Lungarno, or riverside promenade, the main squares and palaces all knew Dante and Galileo. The lofty tower of the municipal hall, known as the Palazzo Vecchio, or "Old Palace," still soars high over the red-tiled roofs of the center of the city. For an anguishing week in 1944 the Arno River became the front line between the advancing American Army and the Germans. When the latter pulled out, even they were unable to bring themselves to destroy the medieval Ponte Vecchio, or two-storied bridge with the medieval arches and the tiny silversmiths' shops crowding together on its narrow lane.

Dominating the city's skyline is the Cathedral of Florentine Gothic, which was completed in 1461. The striped exterior, made of white, green, and red marble, gives an exotic, brilliant appear-

---

[3] *Medici* means "doctors (of medicine)"—the original profession of the family.

ance. The cathedral is crowned by Brunelleschi's stately dome and adjoined by the richest-decorated campanile in all Italy. The baptistery in the same square possesses three famous doors of solid bronze portraying many scenes from the Bible in exquisite workmanship. The doors were cast by Vittorio Ghiberti in the mid-fifteenth century, and have been newly polished.

After the cathedral in fascination comes the Palazzo Vecchio, nearer to the river, facing a huge open square paved with blocks and lined with fine-type shops selling illuminated paper, art objects, and the unique tooled leather, stamped with the gold-leaf lilies of Florence, unmatched anywhere for style and taste.

The Palazzo Vecchio offers to the casual onlooker outside an illuminating example of how architectural styles changed from fortification to imposing castle proportions. Like the municipal buildings of the early Middle Ages, this building has high, thick walls, with small windows and crenellated parapets. The tower soaring high above the city is a leftover from the days when defense needs required lofty lookouts, yet its style here shows that the tower was also designed for proportion and dignity. The newer age of artistic embellishment is represented by the graceful Gothic windows, and decorative edgings. Naturally, this sober exterior gives no hint of the magnificent decorations in the big halls inside. In the square in front of Florence's palace stands a replica of Michelangelo's David, and across the square is the famous arched Loggia dei Lanzi, which is an emblem of Florence.

Two museums filled with artistic treasures unmatched elsewhere in the world are located on opposite sides of the Arno from each other. The famous Uffizi Gallery is part of a palace adjoining the Palazzo Vecchio, built in the sixteenth century. On each of the columns supporting the palace is sculpted a bust of one of the famous Tuscan characters of the Renaissance. The casual traveler is amazed at the numbers of world-famous men who lived and worked in this one segment of Italy during that land's days of glory.

A colonnade leads from the Uffizi Gallery to the Pitti Palace across the river. It crosses over the ancient Ponte Vecchio ("Old Bridge"), standing in its present form since 1345. The Pitti

Palace was the residence of the Grand Dukes of Tuscany, and the art gallery is located in its right wing.

The many other things of first-rate interest in Florence are catalogued in the numerous guidebooks obtainable in the city. But the marble-lined Medici Chapel, the Church of Santa Maria Novella, the Bargello Palace, and other churches, squares, gardens, and *palazzos* offer unending interest and wonderment. And no one should miss the gracious hill town of Fiesole looking down on the great city. Fiesole's villas and homes have long been favorites with English and American expatriates.

A few hours in Florence will give any observer an unforgettable idea of the impact of the New Learning on Italy and will show how this laboratory of art and culture developed an influence of beauty and skill that has moved the whole civilized world to emulate its example.

Venice

Unique in the world is this island city, which for over a thousand years was a republic with an empire and a fleet that made it a world power in its own right.

Venice today is a jewel of interest, since it has not changed outwardly in any important particular since its heyday in the fifteenth, sixteenth, and seventeenth centuries. The palaces that look down on the Grand Canal and the Square of St. Mark stood there when the great figures of Renaissance history, and their successors of all nationalities, lived and moved in this beautiful, original, semi-Levantine city-state.

Venice today is like an outdoor museum, but a very lively one. Coming into the city by train or by auto, travelers must needs forsake those outer-world conveyances at the edge of the city and take to boats. Venice offers three types of water conveyances, and all have their charms. The "taxis" are the gondolas, which can penetrate even the tiniest canals and deposit the wayfarer at the humblest doorstep. The boatman stands aft and sculls the craft silently ahead, sometimes singing a repertoire of Venetian songs if he senses his passengers are in the mood. Gondolas are always black, by a law over four hundred years old. Their prows rise gracefully to a crest whose origin is lost in history. They are built by tender, careful working and are slily bent on their frames so that the boatman, standing on one side at the stern, does not tip them.

However elegant, the gondolas are slow, so that many people travel by *vaporetto,* the Venetian streetcar, a specially designed steamboat with adjustable speeds and low freeboard. They ply up and down the Grand Canal, making regular stops at marked "stations." Since these are also too slow for hasty travelers, a third "vehicle" is available called a *motoscafo,* a rakish motorship that makes satisfactory speed in a beeline from the railroad station to St. Mark's—the axis of the modern city. Venice in addition operates larger, more glamorous steamboats between St. Mark's and the Lido. Otherwise, the only way to get around the city is by "shank's mare." There are three hundred bridges, all gracefully arched to let gondolas through, and countless little winding walks called *calli* or *ruge* or *calleselle.* It is fascinating to amble around Venice, admiring the life of a town that has hardly changed in centuries. Graceful old wellheads adorn the little courtyards; pretty windows and rococo palaces and stately churches with priceless art inside can be encountered at almost any step.

But the pride and boast of this remarkable city is St. Mark's Cathedral and St. Mark's Square, an ensemble of perfection and artistic precision that was completed practically in its present form back in the 1400's. Around three sides of the square run the porticoes in which famous shops and restaurants are tucked away. On the fourth side are Venice's magnificent buildings—the cathedral, and the Palace of the Doges. In front of the cathedral are three lofty flagpoles, on which the flamboyant banners of old medieval Venice are hoisted on gala occasions. These flags, maroon and gold, bearing the rampant Lion of St. Mark and trailing long streamers of maroon, once struck terror in the ranks of Moslem and Turkish fleets of long ago.

An exit from the square leads under an arched clock tower, whose Moorish figures have been striking the hour since 1497. The other exit is a smaller square that leads to the entrance to the Grand Canal. The water is there so deep that cruise liners and

warships can anchor to form a contrasting backdrop to this exquisite scene.

St. Mark's Cathedral is different from its counterparts in
northern Italy. It is pure Byzantine, built in the eleventh century
when Venice as a commercial nation received all its artistic
stimulus from regal Constantinople. It is a small cathedral as
cathedrals go, and can be admired at leisure. Five domes sit
astride its Greek-cross plan. Pillars of varied kinds of marble,
brought from ruined temples of the Levant, are fitted into the
walls. Graceful Byzantine arches mark the entrance, but most
magnificent of all are the gold mosaics of intricate design that
crown the entrances, all worked by forgotten Greek artisans with
consummate care and painstaking skill.

The Doges' Palace is equally striking, although very different.
For the palace is Gothic, albeit a Venetian-Eastern type of Gothic.
The best way to admire it is to relax in a gondola off in the Grand
Canal and gaze at its unique proportions. For it is a four-story
square palace that represents by its style the power and glory of
Venice at its height—the 1300's, when Venetian artists were
beginning to develop their own semi-European motifs and were
freeing themselves from the Byzantine. The upper stories are
solid, of striped pink-and-white marble, broken by a few large
arched windows. The second floor is a loggia, or open-air promenade, holding up the palace by small columns and Gothic arches.
However, this heavy building stands on still smaller and daintier
arched columns below, as if defying all the laws of structural
gravity.

Both inside and outside this palace is original and magnificent,
even to the eyes of the most outspoken of tyros in the fields of
art and architecture. The courtyard inside is marked by a massive
Staircase of the Giants, so-named from the sixteenth century
statues of Neptune and Mars. Atop this staircase the Venetian
doges, or "dukes," were crowned every year. The regal apartments of the doges, the hall of the Venetian Senate, and the
Council Chamber are all decorated with sumptuous art portraying
both scriptural and historical scenes. From the Doges' Palace a
short bridge called the Bridge of Sighs leads to the dungeons.

Yet only on the other side of the dungeon and prison buildings rise two of Venice's most luxurious hotels of today.

Venice, like Florence, takes at least a week to study, and the visitor must cast continual glances into his guidebook, for history and art are lying in glorious wait at every turn of a canal or passageway. Venice has a lofty campanile rising out of the St. Mark's Square, with a modern elevator to take admirers up for the view. It has a modern and sumptuous Opera House, called the Phoenix (Fenice). Many of its old palaces and villas on the Grand Canal are open for visiting. And then there is the Lido, a gentle beach of shallow sand on the Adriatic Sea, adorning the sandspit that fences Venice in from the open sea. Not to be overlooked is the Rialto Bridge, a world-renowned single-arched bridge built in 1592, and until recent years the only bridge across the Grand Canal.[4] Two rows of shops line the arched sidewalk that spans it.

Three hundred thousand people live in this congested but beautiful group of islands and houses called Venice, caring not at all for the anomalous fact that their homes are built on mudflats and marshes, supported by countless thousands of piles, noble trees stripped from the Dalmatian islands hundreds of years ago. The mainland is only four miles away, while the nearest of the Alpine foothills, only an hour's drive by automobile to the north, can easily be seen on clear days. Yet Venice's charm holds its population as if by a magnet, and it is powerful enough to attract thousands of visitors from across mountain and ocean.

This city built on sand and marsh has played a master role in European history. Its valuable commerce with the Levant, Constantinople, and Egypt brought cargoes of the utmost value and necessity to the rulers of medieval Europe, while its fleets for many years were the first line of defense against the encroaching Moslem empires.

This arrogant, overwealthy, autocratic "republic," which talked down to dukes, Popes, kings, and sultans, grew up on a lagoon

---

[4] "What's new along the Rialto?"—a question asked by travelers about business news from Venice—inspired the name's use by countless movie theatres in America, signifying a place where people come together.

where no city had ever existed in Roman days. The refugees in these marshes who had fled from Attila's Huns in the fifth century gradually made their new homeland a source of wealth. They traded valuable salt and fish to mainland communities; they built ships and floated in lumber and more fish for trading. In the ninth century their zealous citizens brought the mortal remains of the apostle Mark, having filched them from under the noses of the profaning Arabs of Alexandria. In the tenth century they bridged a channel between two bits of high ground called the Rialto (*rivo alto*), and the town took shape quickly. In no time Venice had grown into a powerful trading city, and to protect its wealth it conquered the whole northeastern corner of Italy to serve as a supporting pedestal to its empire.

The Brenner Pass, the lowest crossing of the high Alps and one that can be used all year round, was handy to Venetian merchants. The trade that began to course through it enriched not only Venice but all the German and Dutch cities that lay along the trade route northward. Augsburg in Germany and Rotterdam in Holland became cultural centers, handy to the new luxuries and latest ideas coming in through Venice.

The Crusades brought vast riches to this city, making it undisputed Queen of the Adriatic. Kings and princes paid solid gold for passage to the Holy Land and Asia Minor on Venetian galleys. But knights and pilgrims who had no money were put to other use. They were given free tickets if they would do a little fighting along the way, and this they were glad to do. Thus, while the Crusades were focusing attention on the wars against the infidels, Venice picked off rival Christian cities and towns thanks to the manpower of her distinguished passengers. Slavic sea fighters called the Uskoks were defeated and chased from the Adriatic; Dalmatian towns belonging to Austrian, Hungarian, or Bosnian overlords were snatched and annexed; and the best harbors of Greece, Crete, and Cyprus seized from their Byzantine owners. And, as we have seen, Constantinople itself was captured and pillaged by this process in the year 1204.

Despite her system of republican institutions, capped by a cloaked doge and a Senate and Council, Venice was an oligarchy

of imperial rulers, under the name of the "Most Serene Republic."
Its empire in the Levant, and its choice Italian lands, made it
wealthy beyond the dreams of all the kings of Europe, and
arrogant in the same measure. Yet the Venetians were good busi-
nessmen as well as imperialists. They originated the modern
concept of a diplomatic service among nations by assigning
shrewd observers of commercial possibilities to the important
cities of Europe and the Near East. These observers later became
ambassadors, and were given the status of superior and exalted
personages. The reports that they sent back from all over the
medieval world are the purest sources of historic value for
scholars. The style their ambassadors soon acquired is well illus-
trated by the mighty palace built in Rome for their envoys to the
Pope. Located at the edge of the Forum, its magnificence surpassed all other palazzos in the Eternal City. When Venice lost
her independence to Austria much later, the Austrian Government
took over the building as an Embassy, and after Austria lost to
Italy in World War I the building soon attracted the attention
of Mussolini. Its huge Map-of-the-World Hall became his "office,"
and its balcony his platform for swaying the world. The square
outside is still called the Piazza Venezia.

The rise of the Turks and the discovery of America cut the
ground out from under Venice's economic life. Her trade and her
empire both shrank away, but the city was too wealthy, and
cushioned by its glass industry for the effects to be felt immediately. In fact, the era of Venice's most talented artists came
the next century, when Titian and Tintoretto, Veronese and
Mantegna, and countless lesser lights produced a school of painting combining Venetian-Byzantine with the Renaissance streams
pouring out of Florence.

The Venetian Republic languished amid its dreams and faded
splendor until Napoleon Bonaparte's young army arrived in
its territory in the year 1797, when the republic gave up its
independence without a struggle. After the dust had settled
around Napoleon's many conquests, the city and its Adriatic possessions were annexed by Austria, whose Hapsburg archdukes
had been the republic's most jealous competitors during the three
hundred previous years. Venice's pride and majesty had much

to do with this long struggle, since cities that she had founded on the eastern side of the Adriatic, and others she had conquered, like Trieste, threw off her yoke and called in the Hapsburgs in order to have more power for themselves and a share in the rich trade of the sea.

Venice existed as an Austrian provincial town for fifty years despite its success in temporarily re-establishing its republic after a vigorous uprising in 1848. However, the Austrians finally had to give up the city despite a victorious war with Italy in 1866, when Bismarck, Italy's ally, demanded it as a price for peace.

Today Venice is a favorite with tourists. It is old and gracious, yet very modern in its ways. An international movie-judging competition takes place every summer, and the world-famous Lido at its front door is a first-rate resort for statesmen, social leaders, actors and royalty. The Lido's wide beach is decorated with bright-colored cabanas and has long led the world in the degree of luxury that can be designed for serving weary mortals on a hot strand. The shallow water is warm and beckoning to even the weakest heart. And the most daring of bathing suits are constantly modeled by the young international set that congregates here during the long hot months.

Venice is a gay town that stays up most of the night, singing in its "streets" and enjoying concerts on the canals. The music is furnished by floating orchestras, especially romantic under the irresistible Venetian moon. A midsummer festival called the Feast of the Redeemer is a "must" for everyone at least once in his life because of the water pageants, dancing, processions, and the bridge-of-boats that is set up across the Grand Canal.

Italy's proud cities burned themselves out in creating the masterpieces of the Renaissance. Their skills and their greatest artisans were drawn into France, where their art was remodeled into a form that has conquered northern Europe, including Britain, and been passed on to us through those channels.

Yet the results of this glorious age are always with us. Today Italy's cities are more full of monuments to human culture than any other collection of men's dwellings to be found in any comparable area of the world.

THE RIVIERA

Window on the Mediterranean

WHERE THE MEDITERRANEAN penetrates closest to Paris and other capitals of Western Europe, there lies one of the world's most glittering playgrounds. It is as if Nature, the atlas, and the gods of old had united all of their combined forces to create an ideal Eden for twentieth century fun-worshipers.

Through wars and depressions the resorts of the Riviera have operated unharmed. Once the rendezvous of the elite and of the aristocracy, this Coast of Blue now ministers largely to the more numerous vacationers of the surviving classes of society, yet still manages to retain a reputation of style and good taste.

The miracle that gives the Riviera such a geographical advantage is its proper juxtaposition of mountain and sea. The mountains are the Alps—the Maritime Alps—which tumble abruptly down into the blue Mediterranean. This range cuts off cold north winds and furnishes a slope well exposed to the sun even in the short winter days. In addition, the coastline slants in a general direction of southwest to northeast. The mountains thus cut off the west winds as well as the north, and the slopes catch the sun's warming rays from the early morning hours.

The mountains, as they fall steeply down to the sea, create many coves and valleys where resorts and villas can keep warm all winter. As if in proof of its mild winters, Nature gives easy survival to such tropical plants as orange trees, lemons, bananas, mimosa, and palms, together with varieties of exotic flowers. When it is considered that this stretch of fortunate seacoast is only overnight by train from Paris, and even less by plane from London and Scandinavia, its worldwide appeal can readily be understood.

On the old-time maps, this segment of the Mediterranean coast was always called the Riviera, or "the coast," in old Italian. No more sonorous name ever grew up, perhaps because the Italians had other Rivieras of their own. But to the French geographers, seconded by the hosts of winter refugees from the fogbound north, it is now officially known as La Côte d'Azur, or "the Coast of Blue."[1]

The fashionable, the world-famous international Riviera is that section of the coast belonging to France. It can be said to begin where the coast makes its turn to the northeast at a point thirty miles east of the great naval base of Toulon. For sixty curving, indented miles, the seacoast of the Riviera continues from here until it reaches the Italian border, beyond which it includes the Italian resorts of Bordighera and San Remo before losing its "glamor status."

Coming in from the sea by ship, either directly from America, or on a leisurely Mediterranean cruise, the arriving traveler is treated to a scenic panorama: irregular peaks, seascapes of many shades of blue and green, multicolored little towns clustered on the narrow footing between slope and sea, glittering cities along crescent strands, and pleasure boats, yachts, and cabin cruisers coming out in greeting. Two good landing places for liners exist— one, the perfect landlocked bay of Villefranche only three miles from Nice, and the other the protected anchorage off Cannes.

Once ashore, there is glamor and luxury without stint or limit, with prices to match, of course. However, amid all the opulence of the Riviera resorts and their flashier devotees, there are many places for those existing on the most limited budgets. And if in the latter places there should be a lack of the latest creature comforts, at least there is exquisite beauty of view to go with each room, and a balcony from which to admire it.

---

[1] This name distinguishes it from "the Coast of Silver" (Biarritz on the Bay of Biscay) ; and "the Coast of Emerald" surrounding Brittany.

Queen city of the Riviera is, of course, Nice, which now has risen to the fourth largest city in all France, boasting a permanent population of 300,000. This city has everything for its all-year-round procession of visitors—a casino, vaudevilles, a mardi gras, several battles of flowers, parades, and the celebrated bicycle race around France. It has a tiny, congested medieval town around a pocket-sized harbor. It has a pink-tinted central square built in late Renaissance days. It has shopping streets whose stores contain all the elegant perfumes and luxuries of their Parisian counterparts. It has restaurants famed far and wide among the great and near-great of the cosmopolitan world. And it has, as supreme façade for the whole ensemble, its promenade along the curving bay, the Promenade des Anglais, named for British expatriates who raised the first money to build this tree-lined boulevard. Many comfortable benches line the promenade, as the passing parade of visitors furnishes an unending treat of differing nationalities, classes, pocketbooks, and ancestries.

At Nice during the winter there are also daily excursions for skiing and tobogganing in the Maritime Alps, which rise up directly behind the city.

The only first-class feature lacking at Nice is a superior beach. But it is an odd fact that the Riviera is very badly supplied in this regard. At Nice the beach is narrow and stony. And except at Cannes, where a fine, but narrow, sand beach exists, most Riviera resorts have rocky seascapes, or gentle coves for swimming, and for the landing of their sailing craft.

Closest rival to Nice is the resort city of Cannes, twenty miles to the west. Here, there are more chic and exclusive meetings of "the set," but also there are almost fifty hotels and countless pensions for anybody else who likes the beach, the yacht harbor, the casino, the beautiful, palm-lined promenade called the Croisette, the interesting shops, night clubs and restaurants, and the narrow streets of the old original town. The view to seaward is more majestic at Cannes, for two islands lie offshore,[2] and the rugged

---

[2] Called the Iles de Lérins. On one of these, St. Patrick (whose name means "a nobleman" in Latin) served as a monk before making his successful trip to Ireland.

seashore range of the Esterel Mountains forms an impressive backdrop for the view.

Twelve miles inland from Cannes is the city of Grasse, a perfume center without equal in France, surrounded by fields of flowers grown intensively to produce the fragrances and essences. And between Grasse and Nice, along the inland road, there lie charming old towns like Vence and Gourdon and St. Paul, where history has stood still. Here handicrafts are painstaking, and the shopping for artistic goods entrancing. There is also a canyon called the Gorges du Loup, and renowned eating places in the many small villages.

The shoreline between Cannes and Nice is the heart of the Riviera. The popular resort of Antibes, and its seaside promontory Cap d'Antibes; the beaches of Juan-les-Pins and Golfe-Juan; and the artistic suburb of Nice called Cagnes-sur-Mer are dotted with villas of the most famous names, with unpretentious little pensions, and with terraced flowers and oranges galore.

Monte Carlo

On the other side of Nice, continuing northeastward to the Italian border, is another exclusive and exquisite stretch of seacoast.

Beyond Nice and its deep-water harbor of Villefranche, which is almost always host nowadays to American warships, is the resort of Beaulieu, so tucked away in its cove that no winds can harm its banana trees. Up above it is romantic Eze, a little hilltop town perched high above the magnificent seascape, a survival of the days when Moors and Turks ravaged the Coast of Blue, and wise people built their cities on hills. Then we arrive at what is surely the most amazing anomaly of this part of Europe—the independent Principality of Monaco.

A fief of the Grimaldi family since the feudal days of the thirteenth century when the coast belonged to Genoa, this little territory perched on the shore under towering mountains has kept separate from its mighty neighbor states. The recent Princes of Monaco have contributed to the distinctiveness of their domain by many means, maintaining a fine aquarium, a brightly dressed militia, red-and-white sentry boxes, and an atmosphere of quiet, scrubbed propriety. However, this little state of fifteen thousand people, of whom only two thousand are "Monegasque" citizens, is famed the world over for its great casino at Monte Carlo, a noble eminence over the sea separated from Monaco town by a picture-book little yacht harbor.

The gods of chance and of elegance have ruled Monte Carlo since 1861, when the first casino was built. Today it is still a dignified, well-dressed, quietly efficient center for testing one's favorite systems of luck at roulette, baccarat, *chemin de fer,* or crap shooting. Stories abound in and around Monte Carlo telling of fortunes won and lost, of intrigue and romance, and even of suicides that have taken place here.

From Monte Carlo it is six miles along the coast to Menton, a quiet and drowsy resort, where the air is so mild that lemon trees abound, even though the latitude here is farther north than New York. Beyond Menton lies the bridge to Italy, the "flowery Riviera" around San Remo.

One could write endlessly about the attractions of this exciting segment of the earth's surface, but many detailed guidebooks exist to bring out the appeal in more complete facets. Suffice it to say that the Riviera is now as well known and loved in America as Americans are well known and appreciated on the Riviera. No traveler from this country will feel alone when on the Côte d'Azur. Besides the expatriates and the movie set rubbing elbows with him, there will always be hundreds of bluejackets—young, avid-eyed sailors from Uncle Sam's war fleet, enjoying to the full the offerings of this unusual type of "naval base."

"Pipeline" from Italy to France

The modern Riviera is indeed a story by itself, yet how many guess at the exciting role it has played in the years gone by? Hardly any of the sunbathing thousands there today realize that the coastline here has been a pathway from Italy to France through the ages; and during two epochal periods of creative history—the Roman Pax Romana and again in the Renaissance—

it was the only "pipeline" bringing the advanced graces and learning of Italy to the hospitable but less privileged land of Gaul.

From earliest times men have lived on these hospitable shores, and they are known to archaeologists as Ligurians, a troublesome race who were quite martial and hard to conquer. The hardy Phoenician pioneers who founded Marseilles,[3] and their Greek successors who first came to Antibes and Nice,[4] were confined to the coast by these inhospitable natives. Only the later Romans were able to dominate the land, and then only after decades of intermittent war. The Romans so loved the Riviera that they had penetrated here fifty years before Caesar ever went to Gaul, and they turned it into the prosperous Province of Gaul. To this very day the inhabitants of the Provence, as it is now known, speak their own Latin patois and cling to their semi-Italian traits and customs.

The Emperor Augustus finally vanquished the Ligurians, about the time Jesus was born in faraway Judaea, and caused to have erected on an imposing crag above modern Monte Carlo a commemorative edifice bearing his statue and marking the frontier of Gaul with Italy. The columns and rounded stones of this memorial have recently been reassembled by an American lover of the Riviera, and the restored tower stands again in the village of La Turbie.

The finest collection of Roman monuments outside of Rome to be found today exist in southern France in this old Province. To the west of Cannes lies Fréjus, once known as Forum Julii, a naval port with remnants of its forum and temples. Farther west, beyond the big industrial port of Marseilles, are the towns of Arles, Nîmes, and Orange, clustering near the mouth of the Rhone River. They all have colosseums, temples, arches, cemeteries, and other Roman monuments. Between Arles and Nîmes stands the superb Roman aqueduct across the Gard River, three tiers of arches in height, and still spanning the wide valley. In Nîmes

---

[3] No one knows the original meaning of "Massalia," the Phoenician name for it.

[4] "Nice" means "victory," and "Antibes" "the city opposite" (Nice).

itself there is still, amazingly preserved, a Roman temple dating from Christ's time, which is now a museum of Roman antiquities. The design of this temple and its dignified columns make it superior to any surviving temple in Rome. Known prosaically to modern Frenchmen as the Maison Carrée, or "Square House," it so excited the wonderment of Thomas Jefferson that he sent back its plans to serve as the model for the State Capitol of his native Virginia in Richmond.

Later, when Caesar had conquered the "three parts of Gaul" and annexed them to Rome, the vanquished inhabitants derived their new education, customs, and learning from this Provence. From the Riviera the broad valley of the Rhone River leads northward from the Mediterranean, a natural "water-level" route into the heart of Gaul. The land became Romanized so speedily and thoroughly that very little is remembered of the original Celtic heritage of the Gallic tribes. When mother Rome was trampled under by the barbarians, Gaul remained loyal to the vanished shell of the Empire, until barbarians of a new stripe streamed into Gaul—the Lombards, Burgundians, the Visigoths and Alamanni, and the ferocious Franks. Down into chaos went this smiling land. Government disappeared. On top of the holocaust, unknown new enemies came from the sea—the Saracens, or Arabs, who ravaged the beautiful Riviera at will and even settled the southern edge of the region. To this day the hills southwest of the old town of Fréjus are called "the Mountains of the Moors."

However, so strong was the Roman tradition in converted Gaul that the Burgundians and the Franks gave up their Germanic speech and took to the Gallo-Roman tongue. As order returned, Provence once again took on life and relative grace. The pipeline from Italy functioned anew. Warlike lords and their ladies in grim castles in northern France listened to wandering singers, or troubadours, chanting stories of love and merriment from their homes in the land of the "language of Oc."[5] These love tales were always sung in that Roman dialect of Provence, which made the northern listeners come to call these stories "romances," a

---

[5] Early French word for "yes." It still survives in the Province of Languedoc.

colorful term still striking a chord in the heart of modern readers and movie-goers.

The open route down the Rhone from northern Gaul, or France, as it was coming to be known, brought the feudal lords and the early kings of France themselves. In the province of Dauphiny on the Rhone, those early kings found a heraldic crest for their heirs apparent—the dolphin of the Mediterranean borne by the rulers of that province—and from that day on the crown prince of France was known as the "Dauphin." Down this way came French kings and knights bound for the Crusades. Provence was the fairest province of the French kings during the age when knighthood was in flower. Only in one particular did some of these energetic people vary from the Roman line—and that was in the field of religion. Early reform and secessionist movements made great headway around Nimes and Montpellier until cruel wars and Crusades almost exterminated the communicants.

St. Louis, King of France,[6] came to Provence when bound for his Crusade and death in North Africa in 1270. At the same time the dukes of the Rhone-side city of Orange went north to inherit a duchy in Germany, from which their descendants continued to the throne of Holland centuries later. As defenders of the Protestant cause in Holland, and later as heirs to the crown of England, they inspired many towns in America to take the name of "Orange."

Avignon, too, on the Rhone, became the residence of the Popes of Rome from 1305 to 1377, where they were "guests" of the French kings. Their palace, a gem of medieval architecture, still stands in walled Avignon. And leading out into the river Rhone at this storied city stands the Pont d'Avignon beloved by children for its merry song. The bridge no longer extends all the way across, but gypsies sometimes can be found singing, and cooking their dinners under its shoreward arches.

When the Renaissance burst into flower in Italy, France was still in the feudal state of dynastic wars, rebellious ducal conflicts, and tattered knighthood. But in the year 1515 there came to the French throne a young Prince called Francis the First, who was

---

[6] Louis IX reigned from 1226–1270. St. Louis, Missouri, founded by the French in 1764, was dedicated to his honor.

so enthusiastic over the tales he had heard from the Italian cities that he invited, bribed, and enticed Italian men of art and letters to come to France for high pay and a clear field. Over the Riviera road flocked such men as da Vinci and Cellini. The châteaux of central France; the palaces of Paris and Touraine; the artistic decorations on many of the leading city squares of the country— all took form under the enthusiastic hand of these imported Italian maestros. Long after Italy had ceased breeding such geniuses, France studied under them; and in the following century, when France reached the peak of its glory under the Sun-King Louis XIV, the Renaissance had become Frenchified, extended, and raised to even higher levels of conception and elegance.

Francis the First also had designs on conquering Italy, but the warfare he took to that land brought ruin to the pipeline of the Riviera as well. Finding himself worsted by the superior armies of his rival, Charles V, ruler not only of Italy but also of Austria, Germany, Holland, and Spain, Francis had to call in the conquering Turks as his ally to smash at Charles from his rear. The Turks not only did so, but sent their unbeatable fleets under the unscrupulous Admiral Barbarossa to hit at the flanks—the coasts of Spain and Italy. For one winter Solyman the Magnificent prevailed on Francis to let them occupy Toulon and the Mountains of the Moors even though they had just burned Nice and sent its inhabitants off into captivity. The Oriental corsairs took such a fancy to this fertile land that they would only leave the next year when they could take some booty. The arrogant Turks then paraded past Genoa, the home city of their adversary Admiral Doria—so weak and divided had Christendom become.

During the succeeding centuries the land of the Riviera dozed off to sleep. The pipeline slacked off again; the towns vegetated and fell apart. As France grew rich and imperial, the Mediterranean coast was too poor in resources, crops, or other wealth to be given much attention.

Napoleon changed all this by making Marseilles, Toulon, and Nice his naval bases for attacking Egypt and Malta. He loved this coast dearly, for it is within sight on clear days of his native Corsica. When he landed here from his exile in Elba, the people of

Fréjus rose to welcome him, thus setting the style of spontaneous uprisings that took Napoleon to Paris in two weeks without a shot being fired.

A new day of glory dawned on the Riviera, however, when France took an interest in Mediterranean conquests. From this "window" on the Middle Sea, French colonists and armies went forth, under the impulse of the new industrial era, to found the proud empire in North Africa, the first time since Roman days that a Latin flag was successfully spread over that opposing coast. French engineers and investors went to Egypt to build the Suez Canal; to Turkey to control the interests of the oppressed Christians. They then went on to Madagascar; to Indo-China; to the Pacific. Thanks to this orientation, France's port of Marseilles rose to be the highest-ranking harbor of the land and the second city of the republic.

During all these centuries, French rule had extended along the Riviera only to the mouth of the Var River, between Cannes and Nice. However, the dilettante Bonapartist Emperor "Napoleon the Little" scored his chief tour de force on the diplomatic chessboard during his reign by securing Nice, Menton, and their hinterlands for France, winning them from the fledgling Kingdom of Italy in 1860 after a plebiscite.

Titled English travelers began "discovering" the lovely climate and unappreciated beaches of the Coast of Blue during the following years. Russian Grand Dukes, the Prince of Wales, British aristocrats, and rich men the world over soon flocked here to make the Riviera their playground and rallying point. Their taste and their style have set the standard ever since along this blessed stretch of earth. Instead of boardwalks, they designed avenues; and instead of cottages, they erected villas. Instead of fishing boats, they brought their yachts, and, since it was before the days of the cinema, they specialized in the amusements of the casino.

Thus the Riviera stands today as an unparalleled type of resort. All of us who go there can enjoy ourselves with extra gusto when we cast our minds over the three great functions it has played in history: the pipeline through which the great learning of Mediterranean culture was funneled into France; the window of

France on this great Middle Sea through which French influence
has spread over so many neglected parts of the Old World; and
the playground that today's vacationers enjoy because it has almost
the ideal in climate, scenery, amusement, quaintness—and budget-
fitting.

Northward the Torch

Here in France we take leave of that invisible but powerful
force—the Torch, or wave of culture and learning, that was generated and fed during the ages by the countries bordering on the
magnificent Mediterranean Sea.

The Torch has continued westward. France made it glow
brighter and more beckoningly, for northern Europe was at last
ready for it. Germany, Britain, Scandinavia, and faraway Russia
came to Versailles to see what secret Louis XIV was hiding to
make France the leader of Europe in art, literature, science, philosophy, thought and culture. Northern Europe then leavened its
own ways of life with the Torch, and today we have the twentieth
century—an American-British-French-German mixture of science,
engineering, industry, and newer letters—original, yet infinitely
refined and deepened by what the Mediterranean peoples had
passed on to them.

THE   BARBARY   COAST

Legacy of Carthage

THE NORTHERN RIM of the great African continent is as much a Mediterranean land as are the coasts of southern Europe. We took leave of Africa in our story when we told of the defeat and destruction of Carthage and then had to divert our attention to the development of the victor city of Rome and its type of civilization.

Yet Carthage still exerts a spell over travelers, and the descendants of the dispersed Carthaginians still inhabit the land. They have cultivated their own customs and turned to their own religion. Their progress, although much slower and more measured than Europe's, has had its effect on our Pageant and on some phases of our life in America.

The southern shore of the Mediterranean looks very much like a prolongation of the northern European topography: rolling mountains of the Atlas range, fertile valleys of olive and orange trees, steep seacoast with occasional beaches, the same blue water and fine clear atmosphere, the same pine and cypress trees, bright sun, and short rainy winters.

Yet there are significant changes and variations that the seasoned traveler quickly sees. The land seems drier and needs more irrigation than in Europe. The weather has greater extremes of heat, and longer summers. And there is an occasional uncomfortable wind called the khamseen, which brings heat and sand particles. Europe knows this same wind as the *sirocco*.

The khamseen comes from the great desert, the Sahara, nowhere very far from the southern edges of the Mediterranean. This great sea of sand, rather than the inland sea itself, has marked the southern limit of Mediterranean culture and history for so many thousands of years. For North Africa and Europe have shared the same history and vicissitudes over the centuries despite their endless wars and struggles. The parting of the ways came when the people of Africa were conquered by the influence of the desert—the heritage of Islam—and turned their way of life away from the Romano-European. In other words, their agriculture, their interests and their development are closer to the European heritage—far closer than they are to the pagan peoples of Africa beyond the great desert. Only, it can perhaps be said, the North Africans stopped developing the pattern of life several centuries ago, while the Europeans quickened their pace until they reached what is known as "modern times."

The Barbary Coast

The Barbary Coast is the age-old name given by Europeans to the long, straight stretch of African coast beginning with the Strait of Gibraltar and running to the gates of Egypt. The name came from the ancient Greek term "barbarous" applying to people who could not speak Greek. This word later came to apply to the nearest hostile neighbors of Greece, the Persians and Carthaginians, and was used as a term of reproach, since they resisted the advance of Hellenism.[1] The western half of this coastline, a distance of eight hundred miles, is mountainous and well watered, and separated from the Sahara by almost a hundred miles of the Atlas ranges. The shoreline is steep and beautiful, but contains no harbor of any natural size until it reaches its eastern edge at Bizerta. Here there is a beautiful harbor on the farthest northern tip of all Africa. And here is that famous land bridge—the close approach to Europe's outposts of Sardinia, Sicily, and Malta, all of which radiate around Bizerta no more than eighty miles away. Just twenty miles south of Bizerta is the strategic site of Carthage.

---

[1] This is the origin of two popular girls' names—"Helen," a Greek; and "Barbara," a non-Greek.

Beyond Carthage and its modern daughter city of Tunis near-by, the coast plunges due south away from Europe, around the flanks of the dying Atlas, and reaches the edge of the Sahara before turning east for a thousand more miles. This is now Libya, a barren coast of sea against sand, with here and there an oasis supporting a port city, and at one place a range of green mountains forming a semi-fertile region called Cyrenaica. But the shoreline goes on drearily until it approaches Egypt and the delta of the Nile.

This long stretch of coastline is relatively straight and even, in sharp contrast to the north side of the Middle Sea, which has many giant peninsulas, offshore islands, deep harbors, and many fertile plains.

This land of Barbary, so long drawn out east and west, and so narrow between sea and desert, has never taken on stature as a series of distinct states, as happened on the European shore. Names like Mauretania and Numidia covered part of it in ancient times, and the land of Libya today uses its old name, as restored by the neo-Roman Fascist conquerors. The coast is united only under the name of what was once just a part of it, a native name shortened by the Romans, and then through their successors gradually extended until it now covers the huge land mass of which Barbary is only the northernmost rim. That name is Africa.

The Modern Scene

Americans have never been strangers to this great North African shoreland since the days when their fledgling fleet whipped the impudent pirates of Barbary back in the time of Thomas Jefferson. And in their tens of thousands the lads from across the ocean came back in 1942, to cross Africa to the land bridge over the Mediterranean leading toward Italy and victory over the Nazi colossus.

American travelers of peacetime days have likewise come along this coast. Its greatest port of entry is Algiers, the pride of France's colonial achievement. Thanks to the energy of French rule, the fertile belt of North Africa became closely tied to European ways of life—with railroads, roads, important cities, olive groves, vineyards, wheatfields, orange and lemon orchards, mines

of phosphate and bauxite, power plants and airfields. The wealth
of North Africa reached its highest pitch of production, even ex-
ceeding that of Roman days, and it guided the influence of the
Western world far into this strategic region.

Yet the charm for the traveler lies mostly in the native scene.
The changeless ways of the Arabs, with their mosques and markets, veiled women, turbaned men riding spindly donkeys, and their
Arab-Persian homes, are on constant view here—and closely
mingling cheek-by-jowl with the modern European methods. And
never far away are the sand dunes; the oases with their date palms,
their camel caravans and bags of fried locusts for sale; the
mystic Ouled Nail dancing girls covered with bangles of coins;
the produce from beyond the Sahara; the Foreign Legion and
the Roman-type forts belonging to the epoch of *Beau Geste*.

North Africa is exquisite as a travel land, and there is no
better place to begin with than Algiers. To many American
travelers, Algiers is like a Miami-in-Africa—a white city of modern
houses, fronting a blue bay under a warm sun, with an air of
insouciance hovering over its busy streets. Bougainvillaea adorns
the rising walls of villas and apartments. Palms line the avenues,
and great palaces of modernized Arab motifs serve as government
buildings. On the central hill stands the Algerian Government
House, rising in tiers of smooth, shiny glass. And off to the seaward
side of this beautiful ensemble is the dazzling-white conglomera-
tion known as the Casbah, where life is still truly Oriental and one
can hide away forever from any pursuer. Bazaars offer for sale
the finest of Arab wares—rugs, leather articles from hassocks to
purses, delicate slippers, hammered brassware, hubble-bubble pipes,
carved tables and ornaments, fezzes and robes, and elaborate
daggers and knives. Only a few steps away are smart Parisian
shops staffed by modern French stylists and *parfumeurs*. Algiers
is a melding of East and West, but like a film of oil amid drops
of water, not a consolidating or a fusing of such opposed elements.

Algiers shudders at the reluctant slogan which now symbolizes
it to the outside world—"Come with me to the casbah!" For the
Algérois stay away from that congested and indubitably smelly
district, preferring their villas and hilltop homes, casino and

country club, beaches and balconied apartments. But every traveler must needs go to the Casbah. The usual practice is to drive to the top of that sloping mass of white. Up at the top is the Moorish palace in which the haughty Dey once disdainfully received American naval skippers coming to demand retribution for captured American ships. And in 1830, this Dey made the mistake of whisking the French consul's face with his fan—a gesture that brought a French fleet into the harbor and ended the independence of this semi-legal pirate's nest.

At the top of the Casbah there is also the ancient gateway, near which is a fascinating museum. Here all Americans will enjoy gazing at the trappings of the Foreign Legion, the costumes of the fighters and pioneers, and the arms with which these much-sung soldiers of fortune extended their rule into the Atlas ranges, to carve out this modern empire for France in lands that had been lost to Europe for fifteen centuries.

Then one begins his walk down the Casbah—there is no way to go except by foot. If you keep going downhill, you won't get lost, for you'll end up at the harbor sooner or later. The passageways are narrow and full of smells, for life takes place right out on the steps and pavement. Bargaining, begging, cooking, sewing, and haggling provoke scenes every so often. The whitewashed walls on each side are thick and high, having only tiny windows and narrow doors, but are beautified by narrow balconies propped up by straight, unadorned wooden braces as originally cut from trees and then whitewashed. These balconies are the originals from which the fancy and carved varieties have developed in Spain and Malta (and later in South America). In some places these balconies meet each other over the narrow alleyway, shutting out the light completely.

That is the Casbah as seen by the traveler. More inquisitive souls, who wish to pay for guards and guides, can come by night to secret rendezvous and doors bearing certain signs on their lintels, where night life, crude as in the days of the earliest Carthaginians, goes on.

In Algiers there are also a casino, two good hotels, many more modest ones, a colonial official life, and an opportunity to take excursions out into the Atlas Mountains, or down to picturesque villages by the sea. There are always sleek steamers coming in from the Mediterranean, and blue night trains for the outlying cities of the country.

The great hinterland of Algiers has been named Algeria after the city itself. Algeria contains other important cities. Second to Algiers in importance is Oran, a port rising on bluffs facing an artificial harbor entirely constructed by the French. Three miles westward is the bay called Mers-el-Kebir [2] which is France's greatest naval base in Algeria. Oran's harbor became one of the landing points of the Americans in the invasion of 1942 and served as a valuable base of supplies for over two years.

Other port cities of Algeria are small—Philippeville, Bougie, and Bône, artificial harbors with rail and road connections to the grain and vineyard regions inland. Largest city of the mountainous interior is Constantine, a strikingly strategic city of Arab ancestry, built on a height surrounded on three sides by a deep and impassable abyss. In western Algeria there can be visited Sidi-bel-Abbes, which served as the headquarters of the renowned Foreign Legion. And beyond that on the road to Morocco lies Tlemcen—a medieval Arab city that was the capital of an Arab dynasty—whose fortresses, citadels, and mosques create sights of impressive interest.

Farther inland, and over the mountains in the desert, are such oases towns as Bou Saada, Biskra, and Touggourt, almost Hollywood-like in their faithfulness to foreigners' ideas of frontier desert towns. Each of them possesses very comfortable hotels [3] built in Arab style, some with swimming pools, all with gorgeous tropical gardens, fine settings, and excellent cooking. Here, with no trouble, visitors can take those celebrated camel rides out into the sand dunes, or mix with throngs of Arabs watching the local magicians, snake charmers, and fakirs in action during a sunset fair. From here the more explorer-minded travelers can swing aboard French desert-cars for the long safari across the eternal sands and rocks

---

[2] The Arabic meaning is "Great Bay."

[3] Almost all are named, ironically, Transatlantic. They were built by the French Line (Compagnie Générale Transatlantique) to attract American vacationers.

of the wide Sahara, far southward to the Niger River, Timbuktu, and the heart of France's Sudan.

Tunisia

East of Algeria lies a smaller land, Tunisia, once a French protectorate clustered around the site of Carthage. Its capital city of Tunis is a combination of old, walled Arab town surrounded by a modern, tree-lined little Paris.

Tunisians are of the same mixed strains of blood as the Algerians, but they have developed a separate entity over the centuries because of their detached geographical situation. Tunis has also played the role of being dangerously exposed to attack from Europe, and has been more of a religious center than a lair of pirates and sea dogs, as was Algiers.

Modern Tunisia has expelled its hereditary bey and his French advisers. It has become an independent republic, no longer a dependency or protectorate of France. Most of its once-large minority of French and Italians, who settled in Tunisia during the 20th century, have fled. Tunis is closely bond to Europe by steamer and air.

The city of Tunis is very attractive to European travelers and is growing in favor as an all-winter resort. It lies only a few miles inland from the Bay of Carthage, the shores of which are lined with beautiful seaside resorts like La Marsa, Sidi-bou-Said, and Carthage itself. The mountains of the Cape Bon Peninsula, Africa's finger stretched out almost as if to touch Sicily eighty miles away, form a lovely backdorp for all views.

Many excursions can be made in this small country, the principal one of which is to Kairouan, sixty miles south of the capital. Here is a city so holy to Mohammedans that it is third only to Mecca and Medina as a place of pilgrimage. Built in the ninth century, it is a walled town with many mosques. The Grand Mosque in its center is a vision of grandeur, with its carpets and chandeliers and lofty ceiling. Even more impressive is its great courtyard, lined with marble columns brought from now-forgotten Roman cities in the African interior. The mosques with their clusters of small domes bob up over the rooftops of this city in all directions. The other principal thing to see in Kairouan is the rug-making industry, which goes on in every household. These rugs, with their uniform black-and-red design, are made with age-old care and are cherished possessions of homes all over the Moslem world.

The lowering slopes of the Atlas range are dotted with olive groves planted by the French, and the seacoast has small, efficient ports like Sfax and Sousse and Gabès. To the south is the Sahara Desert, and on the edge is an oasis resort called Tozeur, built by the French into an attractive sun-worshiping vacation center. Beyond Gabès, in the Libyan Desert, are towns of troglodytes, or cave-dwellers, people who from time immemorial have taken to caves and underground burrows as the most comfortable and secure homes they knew of in such a land of roasting heat and cold desert nights.

Off the coast of Tunisia is the round island of Djerba, claimed to be the land where the lotus-eaters of very ancient days lived— a paradise described by Greek writers as the place where ship-wrecked mariners would eat the lotus blossom and immediately forfeit their ambitions and their very wills.

Tunisia is also the scene of many battles of the late World War II. During the cold winter months of 1943, American forces coming in from Algeria made their triumphant junction with veteran British armies chasing Rommel from his wrecked lair of El Alamein in faraway Egypt. In the rolling hills of Tunisia the meeting of these two Allied armies marked what Churchill called "the end of the beginning" of the long, hard war. For it saw the last stand of the German-Italian Axis armies in Africa. Early in June 1943, they gave in as the Americans and British crowded them into Cape Bon. Over 350,000 of them surrendered in one great debacle outside the gates of Tunis. The equipment Hitler's men handed over made sweet retribution to the British for what they themselves had left behind on the beaches of Dunkirk just three years before.

Carthage

And now, at Tunis, let us look at Carthage, the fabulous imperial city whose existence menaced the Greeks and Romans for four centuries, and whose ruins today excite as lively an interest as they did in Roman tourists ages ago.

Carthage represented a Semitic civilization grown rich on the intelligent use of the native wealth of Africa. Founded by Phoenician fleets in the ninth century before Christ, the city took deep root.

When Phoenicia was swallowed up by the Assyrians, daughter Carthage followed where its motherland had paved the way. It built stout galleys that scoured the western Mediterranean for new trading goods and ideas. By the sixth century Carthage was a world power and a military state of the first rank.

The Greeks developed legends to explain this new rival's rise to power. They told of the city's being founded by a daughter of a Phoenician king of Tyre, who deceived the natives by bargaining for a spot of land that could be covered by an ox's hide, and then cutting the hide into such tiny strips that it encompassed a whole hill which became the center of Carthage. Romans carried on the legend by naming this Princess Dido, and having her commit suicide over love for Aeneas, the exiled Trojan Prince who sired the founders of Rome.[4]

Carthage's story would certainly be more fascinating if only a few more facts had survived to our day. But when the city was shattered by the Romans in 146 B.C., its entire memory was committed to oblivion. No documents, illustrations, paintings, histories, or descriptions were left for historians to use in reconstructing the proud city's glorious days. Even its language was lost.

But it is known that the city was governed by an oligarchy; that it worshiped the Phoenician sun god Baal[5] and also the more fierce Babylonian fire god Moloch, whose cult demanded infant sacrifice. The city was a naval power of imposing strength. But it was not a democracy or even a commercial republic. It was autocratic like its Levantine mother state. Its interests were trade, navigation, and the search for wealth and power.

Carthaginian navigators explored along the Barbary Coast as far as the Straits of Gibraltar. They had none of the dread of this

---

[4] This legend is told in detail by Virgil in the *Aeneid*.
[5] This god's name figures in Carthaginian names such as Hanni*bal* and Hasdru*bal*.

exit from the Mediterranean that so held back the Greeks and the Romans after them. They founded Tingir (Tangier) and expanded the Phoenician harbor of Gadir (Cadiz), both of which lie just outside the straits on the open Atlantic. They founded settlements in Spain—Malaga (probably originally named Malaca after Moloch) and Cartagena (New Carthage) and Barcelona (whose name suggests common origin with Hamilcar Barca's patron god). They subdued the wild islands of Sardinia and Corsica, and from the Balearic Islands they imported the famous native slingers[6] into their own army.

Their galleys swept out into the Atlantic and down along the coast of Africa to the Guinea coast. This is probably the origin of the use of elephants by Hannibal's army. The elephants must have been brought by ship from beyond the Sahara, as those heavy beasts could not ordinarily survive a trek across those hot sands.

The Carthaginians were not colonists and settlers, but inde-fatigable traders and improvisers. While they included the Barbary Coast and Spain in their empire, they never penetrated beyond the coasts of those lands; instead they traded with the natives for the iron, copper, gold and lumber that they paid well for. They may have followed the Phoenicians to Britain in search of tin.

At any rate, the city of Carthage began in the fifth century before Christ to impinge on the Greek world, whose sea power up till then had been a guarantee against the rising African state's attack. Carthaginian expansion overran western Sicily and put an abrupt stop to the growth of Greece's rich daughter cities on that island. The defeat of Athens by the Spartans cleared the seas for the Carthaginian, or Punic fleet, which had only contempt for its successor—the rival city of Rome—which was land-minded.

Both states thus entered the First Punic War rather light-heartedly, but soon found they were up against formidable antagonists and made an eventual truce. The Romans found Carthage too wealthy and loaded with imperial allies to be shrugged off easily. Carthage, on the other hand, shuddered from naval defeats

---

[6] "Slingers," in Latin, is translated "Baleares," the name for the islands of Majorca, Minorca, and Iviza.

caused by Roman improvisations in the form of boarding barges, a device enabling Roman foot soldiers to overwhelm a warship. So, while Rome hurriedly drummed up allies of her own and started building a fleet, Carthage decided to outdo and outclass Rome in its specialty of land fighting. She dispatched her leading citizen and general, Hannibal, to make his way to Rome's own backyard and extinguish the enemy before it got too powerful.

Hannibal's stirring saga is one of the most thrilling epics of ancient warfare and statecraft. It is well described by Rome's historical narrator Livy for schoolboys to follow in detail. Hannibal actually marched his soldiers and his elephants from Spain across the unknown land of Gaul, over the highest Alps and into Italy. Crossing the Apennines he chalked up his first victory on the shores of Lake Trasimenus in Tuscany, where the Roman foot soldiers panicked at the charge of the elephants. Rome then rose as a man to defend itself, but Hannibal, too wary for his own good, merely threatened the capital, before proceeding to far southern Italy, hoping first to entice the Roman army into his power. In this he succeeded brilliantly, for his trap set for them on the tragic field of Cannae has been studied as a classic in military science over all the centuries down to the days of the German Kaiser. Over 100,000 Roman soldiers were killed in one day when surrounded and cut off by Hannibal on that mournful field.[7]

However, even this victory in the year 216 B.C. did not bring the results Hannibal could have expected. Roman bluffs and threats held this hostile army at bay in Italy until a naval battle cut off Hannibal's reinforcements from home. Fearing a Roman invasion, Carthage recalled him to defend itself. And eventually a Roman army led by Scipio, protected by the new Roman sea power, landed in Africa and smashed Hannibal at Zama in 202 B.C.

Peace in the form of a truce ended the war and stripped Carthage of much of her empire. But the city was still so strong and wealthy that a final battle to the death followed in a few years. Rome then decided that Carthage "must be destroyed" as a standing menace, and in 146 B.C. the city was indeed leveled to the

---

[7] Cannae, near the American wartime airbase of Foggia, is still a desolate field with only a small marker containing Livy's dirge.

ground, its ruins sowed with salt, and its population dispersed.

This setback to Africa's strongest civilization since the ancient Egyptians changed the course of Mediterranean (and world) history, as we have already seen. The world became Roman-Greek instead of Carthaginian, or, to put it more topically, European instead of Afro-Asiatic. The development of Asia's type of thought and life was arrested for seven hundred years, until the Arab peoples, under the impulsion of the Mohammedan religion, began making up for lost time.

In the meantime Africa turned into a Roman province. When the rich trading opportunities of Carthage's situation on the northeast hump of Africa became appreciated by Rome, a new Carthage was built on the same site. But it was a little Rome, and its citizens were transplanted Romans. Later on, other stately, Roman-style cities rose up on the fertile soil of North Africa—Dougga and El Djem in Tunisia; Hippo (Bône), Thamugadi (Timgad), Theveste (Tebessa), Caesarea (Cherchel) and Pomaria (Tlemcen) in Algeria; and Volubilis in faraway Morocco; while in Libya the three cities, or the "Tripoli" of Leptis Magna, Sabratha, and Oëa, took on the glory of the motherland. The grain and luxury trade made Africa rich, and in the prosperous centuries, Christianity took a firm hold. St. Augustine of Hippo was honored as one of the most original Christian theorizers during the period of the Faith's triumph in imperial Rome.

The Heirs of Carthage

Rome's hold on Africa vanished rather quickly when the barbarian invasions of Italy summoned the Roman legions home. North Africa had never been converted thoroughly to Roman ways. The native peoples, called Berbers, a mixture of a non-Semitic race and the original Hamitic inhabitants, had been infiltrated with Negro blood during the centuries of commerce with mid-Africa. These people reasserted their independence as Rome weakened. However, in the fifth century there arrived a strange band of warriors called the Vandals, a small, destructive gang of Germanic people who had marched through Gaul and Spain and sailed to Africa. They smashed and looted the wealthy cities of

Africa and even sailed across to pillage Rome itself in the year A.D. 455. Their reputation so alarmed Europe that the Byzantine Emperors eventually landed at Carthage and overturned their ramshackle realm. The Vandals have disappeared completely without trace.

However, the foundation of Islam in Arabia changed the whole map of the Mediterranean in the seventh century. This irresistible wave of conquering Moslem tribesmen left Arabia in 651, conquered Egypt in 657, overran Libya by 670, and in 685 seized Carthage. By 711 they had reached the Atlantic and crossed into Spain. Africa was lost to Christianity and Europe. For over a thousand years the unity of the Mediterranean disappeared, while the inland sea became a barrier between the two hostile faiths of the Cross and the Crescent.

Tunis, the Islamic town that rose to power after Carthage became prostrated forever, turned into a cultural outpost of Egypt and a cultivated Arabic city while Europe was in the midst of her Dark Ages. The wellsprings of Semitic-Arab thought, now released by the Arab conquests, brought a wave of learning to all Moslem lands. Cities like Bagdad, Damascus, Cairo, Tunis, Fez, Granada, and Cordoba rose to wealth and became centers of study and art. The lost and neglected civilization of the Babylonians, the Egyptians, and the Syrians were revivified in an Islamic Renaissance. The studies in which the Asiatics had most excelled—astronomy, geography, mathematics, medicine, and navigation—came into their own. These fields had not been the favorites of the Greek and Roman savants, but they fascinated the professors of the Islamic centers of study. The wealth of this lore began percolating into benighted Europe during the Middle Ages, and today many of the most important doctrines and terms of those subjects came from Arabic words.[8]

The mixed Berber-Negro blood of North Africa became further adulterated as Arabs, Persians, and, later, Turks came to this land, where all races were equal and indistinguishable under the mantle of the faith of the Prophet.

---

[8] Names of stars ("Betelgeuze"); the words "algebra," "zero," "zenith," "nadir," "horizon," "alchemy," "chemistry"—even "admiral" are Arabic.

This Arabic world broke up into independent emirates that began to war upon each other as the medieval age developed. At this time, however, new dangers came from Europe in the train of the Crusades. Having been defeated in the Holy Land and in Egypt by Saladin, the Crusaders cast about for easier targets, and Tunis was easily the most exposed and the most tempting. Accordingly, the Seventh and last Crusade disembarked in Tunis in the year 1268, led by the King of France, St. Louis himself. Disease and disorganization helped defeat this first incursion of post-Roman Europe against the Barbary Coast, and St. Louis was killed in battle. His loss was so mourned in Europe that France regarded Tunis as its own holy ground, and in this century a large Roman Catholic basilica dedicated to St. Louis has arisen over the site of Carthage.

Two hundred years later European powers again began to menace Barbary, whose Arabic rulers took alarm at the new array of enemies looking avidly across from Europe. The Arabs were led by the Dey of Algiers, a town that had become powerful because of its harbor and the shelter it afforded from storms and hostile ships. On the site of Algiers there had been an ancient Roman town called Icosium, but its Arab successor took on the more practical name of Algiers, or Al-geirah, meaning "the Island,"[9] since a small offshore island gave it a modicum of protection from sea gales.

For an ally against Europe, the Algerines invoked the protection of Barbarossa, a swashbuckling mariner who had scourged the Venetians and Genoese by his magnificent navigation and leadership. Barbarossa quickly came, saw, and conquered the attractive city for himself.

Born on a Greek island, of Albanian parentage, Barbarossa was such a fierce battler for the crescent of Islam that a Turkish sultan later gave him the new name of Kheir-ed-Din, or "Benefits of Religion." His exploits made him Admiral of the Turkish fleet by the appointment of Sultan Solyman the Magnificent. With these new squadrons, he started to raid the Spanish and Italian coasts of the Mediterranean. Emperor Charles countered by seizing the

---

[9] Compare with El-Gezira, name for the sporty island in the Nile at Cairo.

city of Tunis after a battle of such savagery that the Moslems of North Africa were shocked into a thirst for revenge. The Turkish fleets soon converted the Mediterranean into a Turkish lake. At length, in 1544 the Emperor Charles, determined to smash Barbarossa by seizing his bailiwick of Algiers, landed with a mighty army of 40,000 men—Spaniards, Germans, and Italians. Even while battling at the gates of Algiers, the emperor had to beat a hasty retreat when his fleet was smashed by a sudden gale, losing most of his army and over three hundred grandees of Spain.

An uneasy peace returned to the coasts of Barbary after this fortunate victory. The death of Barbarossa, followed by Turkish defeats at the sea battle of Lepanto in Greece and at the siege of Malta, caused the Turks to give up their interest in the western Mediterranean. Thus the Barbary states of Algiers, Tunis, and Tripoli had to rely on their own cunning for protection. Using their small feluccas to good advantage in the changeable weather along their shores, they raided Christian merchant ships for loot and slaves, until the European powers were reduced to paying a yearly tribute for "protection." The slave markets of Algiers were the wealthiest institution in the swashbuckling town, and their galleys were manned by these slaves who once were brave knights and gentlemen of Christian Europe.

This practice of demanding tribute early became loathsome to the fledgling republic of the United States of America. Distaste for putting up with the insolent rulers of these pesky Barbary ports was the impelling cause for the creation of the American Navy in 1798, and its main task under President Jefferson was to clean out these nests of pirates. The new American warships began appearing in Algiers and Tripoli in the years 1804 and 1805, and they succeeded in lowering the tribute and releasing American seamen captives. However, the Sultan, or *Bashaw* (Pasha), of Tripoli went back on his word, and a full-fledged battle took place at the latter city after the American frigate *Philadelphia* got stuck on a sandbar. Stephen Decatur's exploit in burning the stranded ship is well-known to all schoolboy students of history. The result was that the "barbary pirates" were forced to leave American ships alone thereafter.

When the European powers had finished their preoccupation with Napoleon, in 1815, they turned to Barbary with their large fleets and concluded similar treaties ending the humiliating practice of ransom and tribute. The Dey of Algiers, anguished by his loss of revenue, became more hostile to all Europeans, with the result that his fit of anger with the French consul marked the end of independent Barbary. A French expedition seized his city in 1830, and inside of thirty years the French had completely overrun Algeria. Next they turned their attention to the weak and wobbly neighbor state of Tunis. In 1882 the French moved swiftly when word came that Italy was going to seize that area. They landed at Tunis, forced the Bey to agree to a protectorate, and soon turned Tunisia into a bastion of their African empire, as well as a prosperous colony for the exchequer.

The angry Italians, frustrated by France's action in Tunis, turned in dudgeon to the arms of Germany and Austria for solace and support, forming the Triple Alliance that dominated the European balance of power for the next twenty years. They had turned their attention to barren Libya as the only other spot in which to commence their share of trans-Mediterranean empire-building. This insensate imperialistic drive became an obsession with Italian politicians, inasmuch as they felt the old Roman urge toward dominating the opposite shore of the Middle Sea, or "Our Sea" (*Mare Nostrum*), as the Romans called it.

Their chance came in 1911, when they seized a trivial provocation to declare war on Turkey and quickly occupied Tripoli and Benghazi, the chief ports of Libya. Turkey surrendered and withdrew in 1912, giving Italy almost a thousand miles of African seacoast, and endless deserts, thus bringing her flag up to the border of Egypt.

After World War I Italian Fascism turned to Libya with great energy. Italian colonists crossed over to Africa in sizable numbers. New wells created new oases. Tripoli was turned into a modern Italian city of good hotels, big banks, imposing avenues, and a seafront promenade. Leptis Magna's and Sabratha's ruins were excavated. A paved road was built in the traditional Roman manner from Tunisia to Egypt. The tribes of the interior were suppressed with modern efficiency. Fascist military men like Balbo and Graziani made their reputations in this campaign.

World War II brought new armies to North Africa. Epics of the burning sands were created through two whole years of impassioned battling. New reputations were made for fighting men like Montgomery, Wavell, Rommel and Alexander. Skeletons of tanks, guns, jerricans, beached ships, and shells still line the endless sands of North Africa, disintegrating into the same oblivion as the arms of Caesar, Pompey, Hannibal, Alexander the Great, Belisarius, and Barbarossa.

Meanwhile, in Algeria, a political drama of great importance was being played. Eisenhower's successful landings on the Barbary Coast in 1942 created the first area of reclaimed French soil. Algiers served as the capital of the whole French Empire for over a year until the liberation of the home country, and it likewise was the center of the Allied Armies' General Staff. Those who visit the Hotel St. George in Algiers today will be courteously shown to rooms where Churchill, Eisenhower, and other leaders stayed, and the very spots where important conferences took place in those touch-and-go days of the war.

The end of the war brought new problems and a great need of reconstruction to Barbary. Libya, freed from Italian rule, emerged as a separate Arab monarchy. In the 1950's France withdrew from her protectorates of Morocco and Tunisia. Before the French flag came down over Morocco, the United States had built four strategic air bases, which she later evacuated completely at the King of Morocco's request. Tunisia expelled her hereditary bey and became a republic. As for Algeria, France determined to retain this jewel of her colonial crown, absorbing it with her into the North Atlantic defense alliance. But a rebellion that broke out in 1954 brought the world's attention to this linch-pin of the Barbary Coast, where guerrilla raids, terrorist attacks, severe repressions, and relocations of populations finally resulted in France's recognizing Algerian independence—once an unheard-of possibility. This solution has restored peace, even if not prosperity, to the center of the Barbary Coast.

Barbary, the land of unending drama, awaits the next scene.

PORTUGAL

A Story of Explorers

IS PORTUGAL A MEDITERRANEAN STATE or not? Is its impact on history connected with Mediterranean developments or not?

Paradoxically, the answer is yes. Portugal *is* a Mediterranean state, even though its entire coastline faces the open Atlantic. And its role in history, ironically, fits into the Mediterranean Pageant, even though that role helped launch the era of oceanic trade that wrecked the economy of many Mediterranean states and turned the Middle Sea into a stagnant backwater.

The reason that Portugal *is* Mediterranean is that it consists entirely of a segment of the Iberian Peninsula, which definitely borders the Mediterranean. The Portuguese people are a branch of the Iberian mixture to which the Spanish also belong. Portugal's racial heritage, its culture and its way of life are bound up with the Roman legacy. Its language, its religion, its architecture and ways of life are closely intertwined with the Mediterranean's heritage, and its climate is definitely that of the Middle Sea.

Portugal shares a common history with Spain down into the Middle Ages, at which time the influence of the Atlantic began to draw her off into a side orbit divergent from the rest of the Iberian peoples. Once separated, history carried the Portuguese trend of development into a path of original creativeness, until this small state evolved into the richest empire-builder of Renaissance times.

Portugal therefore played an individualistic part in the Mediterranean Pageant. Her people were the first in Europe to throw off the Moorish yoke. And yet they fused the learning of the Moors with their own advantageous position on the shores of the Atlantic to develop geography and navigation into a practical science never perfected by older maritime peoples. With this new instrument, they steered history into a new course.

The Portuguese played their lucky draw so thoroughly that they have retained down to our day their independence, built up a noticeable prosperity, and kept a large proportion of their empire. This is no mean achievement for such a small nation.

Lisbon—Pride of Portugal

One of the finest harbors in Europe has been the base on which the Portuguese state has built its eminence and wealth. The rough Atlantic coast here is cleft by the mouth of a deep river, the Tagus, which pours out a steady tide that it has brought down from the heart of inland Spain. Four miles up from its mouth, the river widens into a smooth inland bay, and on this natural harbor floats the commerce of Lisbon. Portugal's capital has over 800,000 people. It is one of the cleanest and most beautiful cities of Europe.

The charm of Lisbon lies in its self-contained and modest grandeur. It has large squares, stately shopping streets, gracious fountains, a large opera house, fine hotels, several palaces, many parks and boulevards, and steep hills climbed by dauntless little streetcars. It has blocks of modern new flats. Its houses are bright with glazed tiles or gaudy tints of stucco. It has an old Moorish fortress, a lofty Roman-style aqueduct, and an ultramodern marble sports stadium. Its streets are filled with the latest models of American cars. Most of its sidewalks are paved with mosaics of vivid patterns. It has miles of docks and basins, accommodating transatlantic liners as well as fishing fleets. It has its share of richly decorated churches. Fine restaurants are on every hand. Its night life is varied and copious. In short, Lisbon is a cosmopolitan and thoroughly modern European capital kept spotlessly clean and shining.

Lisbon is also a crossroads of the world. Air services from the United States, from South America, and from all Europe congregate here at a modern air terminal to interchange their freight and passengers. It also is a port of call for express steamers running between Europe and South America, as well as an important stop for all Mediterranean cruises. By train it is easily reached—the Sud Express makes it only thirty-six hours away from Paris.

Once arrived in Portugal, the visitor can travel about by modern car over very good roads to all corners of the small republic. Touring Portugal is a never ending experience of delight, for it is a compact-sized country of fertile valleys, picturesque towns, and a bold coast. The most astounding feature, however, is the survival of so many cloisters, castles, abbeys, and palaces. Portugal has been spared the invasions, lootings, and wars that were so hard on such structures in the rest of Europe. Thus the little country is a treasure house of medieval architecture, with large and magnificent cathedrals and forts existing to tell of the days of its glory.

In motoring around the country, it is a simple thing to grasp the source of its economic wealth. In the south and along the Spanish frontier are forests of oak trees whose cork bark is a staple in the world markets. Portugal vies with Spain and North Africa (Barbary) as the chief supplier of this vital material. Up in the north, along the sloping valley of the Douro River, are terraced vineyards whose tender grapes produce the rich red wine known the world over as port.[1] The seacoast, which borders Portugal on the west, is indented with tiny bays where fishing fleets land their rich catch of herring, cod, and sardines. At the town of Nazaré, only ninety-seven miles north of Lisbon, is the most colorful of these fishing harbors. The boats are Oriental in style, with high curved prows decorated with symbols that must have come from the early Phoenician galleys, and the boats are painted with bright Oriental colors.

-----

[1] Port wine was so named by medieval English traders who imported it from the port of Oporto at the mouth of the Douro.

This smiling land of Portugal differs in appearance so strikingly from higher, dryer Spain that it is no wonder that its people took on different traits from their neighbors in the rest of the Iberian Peninsula. It is a rolling, green land of hills and moderate climate, no part of it being very far from the open Atlantic's winds and waves. Its impetus comes directly from the sea—ever since Carthaginian traders first sailed up the coast—from the need of going down to the sea for fish, and from the effect of the moist winds that bring rain and moderate weather to the land. These forces were stronger in molding Portuguese life than the weaker influences that came across the long, barren miles from the rest of Spain—or from Rome beyond.

The people of the Iberian Peninsula were originally a mysterious vanished race called Iberians by anthropologists. They may have been the same people as the Basques, who, like other primitive tribes when hard pressed by alien invasions, took to the mountain fastnesses they knew so well but which the invaders feared and passed by.[2] No one can really know. Celts are presumed to have mixed with the Iberians, and both peoples were affected by their contacts with the Carthaginians along the shores.

When Rome supplanted Carthage as ruler over the Spanish coasts, the interior of the great peninsula submitted surprisingly promptly to the new overlords. During the first century before Christ, the whole land became Romanized. The Latin language was adopted by the inhabitants. Stately Roman cities were built, aqueducts raised, stadiums erected, roads laid out. Spain, or, to use its original Latin name, Hispania, constituted a firm western pillar of Rome's European Empire.

The farthest-flung portion of Hispania was called by the Romans Lusitania, a mysterious term that has been exalted by Portuguese epic writers to glorify an ancient separateness of their country that had to be recognized by the Roman legions. However, Lusitania did not correspond with present-day Portugal; it included the southern half of the country but comprised as

---

[2] Like the Welsh (Britons) retreating before the Saxons; the Albanians from the Slavs; the Rumanians from the Bulgars and Tartars; the Montenegrin Serbs from the Turks.

much again of what is now Spain. Be that as it may, Portugal has clasped Lusitania to its historical heart. Portuguese are called Lusos by their poets; while Camoëns, who wrote the epic poem constituting the Portuguese "Aeneid," named his verses the *Lusiads*.

Lusitania, Rome's Far West, was not a wealthy or significant province. It was hardly ever mentioned by Latin historians. Yet Rome did her work well. This land is still one of the Latin group of nations, peoples, languages.

Lisbon got an early start as a port city in Roman days. Its name of Olisipo is played up by many historians as meaning the "City of Ulysses," founded by the hero of the *Odyssey* during his long wanderings in search of his home island of Ithaca. However, it is more likely that the name rises from the same place or race that gave the name of Lusitania its root.

Lusitania's connection with Rome was rudely severed by the wandering Visigoths, or West Goths, an unsettled tribe of early Germans who wandered through all western Europe before settling down in the Iberian Peninsula. Small in numbers, and lazy in rule, the Visigoths yet remained masters of the land for three hundred years until the swooping Arab fighters for the Crescent landed at Gibraltar in A.D. 711 and swept their kingdom into oblivion. The Iberian Peninsula was then submerged in the Moslem tidal wave and lost to Christian Europe for three hundred years.

How Portugal Got Its Start

Portugal, as an independent country, got its start from a romantic combination of circumstances—feudalistic chivalry and the struggle against the infidel Moors.[3]

In the eleventh century the surviving Christians of Spain began to pick away at the Moslem empire. These Christians were a small remnant clinging to the mountains of the Asturias along the Bay of Biscay. In a few decades they had cleared the north-west corner of the peninsula and set up the two kingdoms of Leon and Castile.

---

[3] The term "Moor" is interchangeable with Arab or Saracen in medieval European history. "Moor" is Spanish-Portuguese, derived from Morocco from whence their Moslem adversaries came.

In the year 1085 the King of Leon made an award that was perfectly natural and usual in the tradition of knighthood then in vogue, but which gave birth to the Portuguese kingdom. As a reward to one of his officers for a victory over the Moors, he gave him the title of count, a large segment of liberated land as his county, and his own daughter Theresa in marriage.

This count was named Henry, and he came from that embattled duchy that sired so many warriors in the age of chivalry—Burgundy in eastern France. Henry's new county was along the mouth of the Douro River. For a name he naturally took inspiration from the largest city of his domain—Oporto. In Latin days, Oporto had been called Portus Calis, or "Warm Harbor." By the Middle Ages this name had been shortened to Portugal, pronounced firmly on the last syllable.

The people of Henry's domain spoke a dialect of Hispanic Latin somewhat distinct from that of inland Spain. It was spoken along the whole western face of the peninsula, including the districts north of Portugal that to this day form part of Spain.[4] This dialect, being the court speech of the Portuguese kings, became an official language and took on strength from influences connected with its separate history. Portuguese is distinct from Spanish by virtue of its peculiar nasal vowels and emphasis on consonantal sounds in the spoken language. The written language is still, however, similar to Castilian Spanish, and the spoken word can often be understood by people on both sides of the boundary.

Henry, Count of Portugal, had as son and heir the warrior prince Affonso Henriques ("son of Henry"), who tackled the Moors incessantly. In the year 1140 he proclaimed himself King of Portugal, independent of his feudal lord of Leon, and only seven years later he captured the Moorish fortress of Lisbon. In this exploit, however, he was aided materially by a passing fleet of Englishmen bound for the Second Crusade in Palestine, who willingly pitched in to rout the infidel from these closer grounds. This incident launched a close connection of the history of the two maritime countries that ripened into an alliance only two centuries later.

---

[4] Those districts form the county of Galicia, inside whose boundaries is located Spain's great pilgrimage shrine of Santiago de Compostela.

By the early 1200's the energetic Kings of Portugal had expanded southward to round out the boundaries of the country as they stand today. They moved their capital to Lisbon, appreciating its central position and its commanding site on the great river Tagus, protected by the shadowing hills on which the Moorish fortress still stood.

One of the finest monuments of all Europe was built to honor a victory over the Moors. It is the magnificent Cistercian abbey and church at Alcobaça eighty-seven miles north of the capital. Completed in 1222, it is a complete medieval monastery copied after the famous abbey of Clervaux in France, which exists no longer. The church of this monastery is of immense dimensions— 350 feet in length, and 66 feet high—and creates an effect of awe by its simple, unadorned columns, ogival vaulting, and abstract beauty of architectural style.

Visitors to this living monument of Europe's finest medieval tradition are particularly interested in the monumental tombs inside the church containing the bodies of King Pedro I and his murdered mistress Inez de Castro. The stone carvings in pure Portuguese style are portrayals of Bible scenes, glorifying in their richness the story of Pedro's fervent love for Inez. Their tombs are placed foot to foot, manifestly so that the lovers will look on each other the first thing on Judgment Day.

Portugal's Era of Glory

Portugal's independence having been won, it soon became necessary to defend it. The King of Castile, who had swallowed up smaller Leon and its faded claim to suzerainty over Portugal, marched into the country in 1385 to oust its upstart dynasty. There followed the Battle of Aljubarrota, which was an unqualified smashing victory for Portugal. King John I was aided by five hundred English archers, who had come as a result of a treaty of alliance the Portuguese had concluded several years before in preparation for such an attack from Castile.

A year after the battle, an event took place that ranks high even now in the annals of the age when knighthood and chivalry were in full flower. A delegation came from England, headed by

Prince John of Gaunt, Duke of Lancaster, uncle of his reigning King. This expedition had sailed down across the rough Atlantic waters, which were then presumed to reach westward to the edge of the world. John brought two of his daughters and three thousand English lancers. Having concluded a treaty of friendship with Castile and espoused one of his daughters to the defeated King, he came on to Portugal. There, in the city of Oporto in 1387, was celebrated a wedding between the other daughter, Philippa of Lancaster, and King John of Portugal. At the same time a commercial treaty was signed and the military alliance confirmed.

This union was a happy one for Portugal. Of it four strong and energetic sons were born, one of them Henry the Navigator. The Queen undertook to design the new battle abbey being built in gratitude for the victory of Aljubarrota. With her English architects and masons, she supervised the creation of what is now the Abbey of Batalha, in a small town eighty miles north of Lisbon. Cloisters, a church, and a chapel are here gathered together, in northern Gothic style, with later embellishments in other motifs. The beauty and harmony of this monument to the faith and enthusiasm that had spurred Portugal into the dawn of its golden age are aptly symbolized by these buildings. John and Philippa are buried in the Founders' Chapel beneath a sculptured tomb showing them hand in hand. In the near-by Chapter House the Portuguese Unknown Soldier of World War I is entombed.

Portugal's Golden Age

The 1400's mark the epoch of Portugal's march to glory. That such a remote, marginal land should rise to wealth and power is an unusual development of the story of Europe. It can only be ascribed to the energy of its kings, the zeal of its people to make the best of their situation, and the order that had been brought to them by their swift welding into nationhood.

In 1415 King John authorized an expedition against the Moors of North Africa. The town selected was Ceuta, a Moslem stronghold opposite the Rock of Gibraltar, whose capture would

interrupt reinforcements for the weakening Moorish states in
southern Spain. The venture proved successful. Henry the Navigator took part as a young prince in it. Ceuta fell, the first prize
in the land of the infidels to be taken by the Portuguese state.

Henry was a most unorthodox type of prince. He had a
passion for the sea, inherited both from his mother and father,
and a determination to turn the seas to Portugal's benefit and
enrichment. Leaving the court of Lisbon, he betook himself to a
far corner of his country, where he could be near the sea, lose
himself in his studies, and scan the Atlantic horizon to his heart's
content. His laboratory was set up at Sagres, a village on a
bold headland on the far southwestern corner of the European
continent. To a small harbor just inside the Cape St. Vincent his
mariners and explorers began to bring their cockleshell ships.
With Henry they could gaze across to the tip of the cape, the
"Sacred Promontory" of Roman days from where the sun could
be seen setting far at sea out at the edge of the world.

Henry was no navigator himself. He was the patron and
organizer of navigating expeditions. With his wealth and influence,
he brought greater resources to the neglected science of geography
than had ever been seen before in any kingdom. He collected maps
from all possible sources. From raids on the Moors, and from
obscure libraries, he accumulated charts never before studied by
European scholars, charts that showed the course of the coast
of Africa and the existence of unknown islands out in the Atlantic.

Under Henry's encouragement, the Portuguese sea captains
began to sail with a definite purpose—to find if there were not
after all a way to get to India by heading southward around
Moorish Africa. Henry took the risk of advising his captains to
ignore the fearsome legends of Christian Europe portraying
dragons and sea monsters lurking beneath the deep ocean waters
and asserting the existence of a rim somewhere where heedless
mariners would plunge off into eternity. The legends also declared
that the seas boiled like pitch as the equator was neared. Under
this courageous policy, Portuguese mariners began to bring back
exciting stories that the new-found charts were right; that the
African coast did extend southward; and that no monsters were
to be encountered.

Thus, in the first half of the fifteenth century, Portugal took to the western ocean. The island of Madeira was discovered and settled; later the distant Azores were located and annexed. Next came the Canary Islands, and soon fearsome Cape Bojador on the African coast was approached. It took several years of courageous attempts to push the sea captains around that frowning and tempestuous headland, for the weather was hot, the stark Sahara stretched down to the sea's edge, and the rumors of boiling seas were hard to scotch.

Henry died content in 1460, long after Cape Bojador was doubled. His impetus had launched Portugal on her brave new course. His fame had extended over all Christendom, and his experiments were reported avidly by geographers in Italy, Germany, and the Netherlands. Henry had lived up literally to his vow as Grand Master of the Knights of Christ to "defend the faith, discomfort the Moors, and extend the Portuguese monarchy." Visitors to Portugal who honor this great man can best be inspired by his deeds if they visit two places—Sagres on the windswept Atlantic cape; and the magnificent castle and church of Tomar near Lisbon, the headquarters of his knightly order, containing an octagonal chapel inspired by the architecture of Jerusalem's Dome of the Rock.

Henry's work did not cease at his death. On the contrary, he bequeathed his zeal to his kinsman, the King, who sank his own wealth and energies into extending the explorations of the bold sea captains. By 1460, the latter had reached the Guinea coast, and were bringing back remunerative cargoes of slaves, ivory, and gold. In 1470 they discovered the mouth of the Congo. In 1486 Bartholomew Dias reached the Cape at Africa's southern tip, which King John II christened the Cape of Good Hope.

By this time the European world was following intently on Portugal's progress. The old trade routes to India and the East had been firmly closed off by the Turks, who ruled a solid ring of Moslem states barring the exits from the Mediterranean. Venice, Genoa and Aragon were hopelessly blockaded.

To Lisbon came the young Christopher Columbus with his plan to reach India much faster by sailing right out into the setting sun. For ten years he haunted King John's ministers, but he was put off as being a visionary. After all, the Portuguese expeditions were following a scientific path, complete with charts and distances, whereas the expatriate Genoese had only a hunch and an unproved hypothesis to go on. Portugal had no need to worry whether or not the world was round. Her sailors had only to get around the African land mass and India would be theirs.

So Spain stole the march on her little neighbor that had been so far in the lead, when Columbus was "hired" by the Spanish Queen. King John was disgusted and also very concerned. He sought the backing of the Pope to protect his investments and projects. Accordingly, in the year 1494 Pope Alexander VI issued a bull dividing the non-Christian world between lucky Spain and faithful Portugal. All lands not ruled by Christian monarchs were to be fairly claimed and possessed by these two states according to a line dividing their spheres of command, the said line to run north and south down the Atlantic four hundred leagues out at sea from Europe.[5]

Portugal then made the supreme effort to bring in the quarry she was so close to bagging—India. In 1497 a flotilla under the command of Vasco da Gama was sent out from Lisbon with the blessing of the new King Manuel I. The hopes—and commands— of the little country's destinies rode with him. The handsome fortress tower of Belem at the mouth of the Tagus, which still greets every ship standing into the port of Lisbon, was the last land of his native Portugal that Vasco trod before he set out on his fateful venture.

For two years King Manuel kept an eye on the horizon from his palace at Sintra, hoping for the first view of the returning sails bearing his hopes for the future. And his wait was rewarded. Vasco came back from India early in 1500, with irrefutable proof of the success of his voyage—silks, brocades, gold, gems, incense, ivory, and spices—objects without limit of price or value in semi-blockaded Renaissance Europe.

The elation felt by the King at this supreme event can be felt by us all today if we go to Belem and visit the glorious Jeronymos

---

[5] This line surprisingly gave Portugal land in the New World—the colony of Brazil, whose "hump" crossed far to the east of the Pope's line.

Cathedral and Monastery built by Manuel as a thanks offering for Portugal's imperial triumph. This lofty building is, furthermore, an example of architecture purely native to Portugal. The Gothic arches of the church and those lining the cloisters are of the Manueline style, richly decorated by a lacelike effect in stone, columns branching off like palm boughs, richly sculpted with mariners' ropes, serpents, tropical vines, all giving an effect of opulence and joy purely expressive of the excited atmosphere of the period. This Manueline style was later reproduced in many churches and monasteries through the length and breadth of the land of Portugal.

Wealth and power cascaded quickly into the little country on the far edge of Europe. Fleets were quickly dispatched to India, returning loaded to the gunwales with spices. Capable viceroys, including the redoubtable Duke of Albuquerque, gave Portugal primacy in the Far East, overturning at one blow the Arab domination of commerce and Turkish aspirations to create a maritime empire at its back door. The port of Goa on the Malabar Coast of India became Portugal's citadel in southern Asia, and remains down to this day a colony of the Portuguese. Venturing far afield to the east, the ambitious mariners from Lisbon repaid a thousandfold the visionary aspirations of Prince Henry. They occupied Ceylon and penetrated through the Straits of Malacca into the East Indies. They finally reached their supreme goal—the Spice Islands, known today as the Moluccas.[6] They ran across the unknown kingdom of Siam,[7] discovered a lordly island that they named "Beautiful" (Formosa), secured the foothold of Macao in China, and landed in force in southern Japan.

By 1550 Portugal was at her summit. The Indian Ocean was a Portuguese lake. From Java her fleets brought the heavenly spice—pepper; from Ceylon came cloves and cinnamon; from China came sandalwood and incense; from the far Indies came pearls; from India came silks and gems; from East Africa came ivory. All these priceless objects were unloaded on the quays of

---

[6] One of these islands, Timor, is still partly in Portuguese possession (shared with Indonesia).

[7] "Siam" is the Portuguese spelling of the original name of that kingdom.

Lisbon, whither buyers came from all corners of Europe to pay willingly the prices levied by the King of Portugal. The wealthy trade of the Orient, once in the hands of Venice, Byzantium, and Genoa, now funneled through the far western city at the mouth of the Tagus.

Sintra

Paris has its Versailles. Rome has its Tivoli. London has its Windsor. Berlin has its Potsdam; Vienna its Schönbrunn. Lisbon, too, a thoroughly European capital, has its royal country seat and it is called Sintra.

Fifteen miles north of Lisbon, Sintra is an idyllic town of steep hills, brightly tinted villas, and cobblestone streets. Its heart is a paved square confronted by a unique palace, the royal summer residence. Built in varying stages over five hundred years by kings with differing ideas, it is a joy to visit today. It is nothing like the gloomy, deserted, overstuffed palaces of northern lands. It is bright, intimate, yet first rate in architectural value. Its chief distinctness in appearance is caused by two beehive-conical chimneys that soar up high from one wing, reminding us for all the world of the same structures that crown the Seraglio Palace in Istanbul. Seen from inside the royal kitchens, these chimneys appear to be domes drawing up the ceiling to raise the smoke and steam from the royal hearths, an invention of the Saracens of ages ago.

The palace has royal rooms lined with tiles; it has patios enhanced by fountains and flowering plants. An old Moorish bath has been incorporated into it. The state dining room affords beautiful views of cozy little Sintra through the large windows. Furnishings, decorations, and coats of arms are intact in this odd building of different levels, and each room has its story.

In Sintra one has ample opportunity to gaze at the industrious people of this part of Portugal coming to market with donkey-loads of flowers and fruits, or washing their clothes at a communal laundry, or selling blossoms and straw hats. Several good hotels cater to the visitors who fall before the charm of the place.

Up above Sintra rises a crag called simply the Penha, or "the Rock." Atop it is one of the oldest buildings in the country—

a walled Moorish fort—but near-by on another crag is a sight no visitor to Portugal ever misses. It is called the Pena Palace, built only a century ago. Its charm lies in the fact that it is the best lived-in, "homey" palace that can be seen in all of Europe.

The Pena Palace is built in medieval style, with a portcullis, rock-hewn gallery, and courtyard. Its façade is completely faced with greenish-blue glazed tiles, which upon reflecting the sun give out a flash of newness and charm. Inside the palace is a small alabaster chapel and the apartments of Queen-Mother Amelia and King Manuel II just as they were left when a revolution broke out in Lisbon in 1910 and the royal occupants fled the country. Porcelain gifts, brocaded walls, furnishings from all over the world, and actual furniture used by the royal family can be admired and inspected at leisure. The palace is charmingly small. From its roof can be seen a sweeping view over the Tagus and out to the Atlantic.

The kings of Portugal lived in their palaces filled with treasures. Back in Lisbon, their collecting mania and their love of show have worked out to our benefit, especially in the case of the unique Museum of Royal Coaches. There, in a pink, one-time riding ring, are displayed over twenty intricate coaches of state, complete with exquisite leather- and wood-working, complicated steps, richly gilded panels, and beautifully constructed wheels. Coaches for children, sedan chairs, and other accoutrements for regal transportation are gathered into this collection, housed in a pink-tinted baroque building that once served as the king's riding academy.

Portugal Up to Now

Hard times that set in soon after the years of wealth and glory dragged the Kingdom of Portugal down to a sorry state during the ensuing centuries.

Vainglory and crusading zeal inaugurated this era of decline. In the year 1578 King Sebastian attempted a crusade of his own against the Moors. Sailing from his homeland with over ten thousand soldiers, he and his whole host were ambushed in the bloody defile of Alcázarquivir less than a month later. Only fifty survivors of his army are said to have ever got back to Lisbon.

This left the Portuguese throne wide open, with seven claimants eager to fill up such a rich vacuum. However, the nearest and most powerful pretender was the autocratic Philip II, King of Spain, who could not be resisted. Portugal's rising school of poets and artists was choked off by this unexpected and disastrous happenstance.

For sixty years Portugal languished as a province of Spain, during which time her rich empire was picked apart by English, Dutch, Arab, and Persian freebooters. At last, in 1640, John of Braganza, a descendant of the earlier royal dynasty through a female connection, led a successful revolution that caught the Spaniards napping. To maintain his precarious hold on the country, he lost no time in renewing the ancient alliance with England. In 1660 a new treaty was concluded, whose terms promised English aid should Spain try to invade the country, in return for which King John provided his daughter Catherine as bride for Charles II of England, adding as a dowry the strategic cities of Tangier in Morocco, and Bombay in far-off India.

Portugal remained poor and obscure during the ensuing years until the devastating earthquake of 1755 nearly destroyed Lisbon. Europe's attention was momentarily brought to the country's plight, and much aid and assistance poured in. Portugal at this time was ruled by a dictator, the Viscount of Pombal, who rebuilt the demolished center of Lisbon into its present august form of Italianate palaces and long straight streets for the various guilds and trades, connecting mosaic-lined squares into a handsome unity that intrigues Lisbon's many visitors of modern days.

New troubles came when Napoleon stretched forth his hand to upset Portuguese affairs with the same effectiveness that had upset all the other dynasties of the continent. In 1807 French troops entered Lisbon only a few hours after a British fleet had escaped bearing the royal family to safety in Rio de Janeiro.

The end of Napoleon left the country without a government, as the King lingered in Brazil until 1820. Upon his return, civil wars rent the country, after which followed several decades of uneasy peace. The kingdom was able to expand its foothold in Africa to a sizable extent and to secure world recognition for its imperial holdings around the Old World. But near-bankruptcy and internal dissension wrecked the stability of the country. King Charles II was assassinated in Lisbon in 1908. Two years later the dynasty was ousted altogether in favor of a new-fangled republic, an institution totally new to the country's long history.

An authoritarian government headed by Prime Minister Salazar, who came to power in 1928, enforced a strict rule on the chaotic republic, emphasizing financial stability, imperial reform, and astute trading with the outside world. This policy paid dividends to some classes of the country. Lisbon was extended, beautified, and enhanced by stately blocks of apartments for government workers. During World War II, Lisbon constituted a clearinghouse between the two warring blocs, being open to trade both with the Axis and the Allies. Wealth flowed in from this policy, leaving Portugal with a high national income, many luxuries in its cities, and a spic-and-span appearance of well-being, although the illiteracy of the peasantry and the tutelage of the governing class remained a flaw in these outward trappings of prosperity.

The dawn of the age of aviation brought a new lease on life to Lisbon. This city, so far off the beaten path of travelers during previous years, now became overnight a world crossroads of airlines. The first transatlantic air service, that of the "Flying Clippers" established in 1939, used Lisbon as its European terminus. This startling achievement helped make Lisbon the chief "escape hatch" for occupied Europe's refugees until American entry into the war closed off this ready exit.

Portugal's modern appeal to tourists is enhanced by two places that rank high as twentieth century attractions—the Riviera of Estoril and the pilgrimage shrine of Fatima.

Estoril

Fourteen miles west of Lisbon, connected with the capital by modern highway and speedy electric trains, is the flowery city of Estoril. Here is the Monte Carlo of Portugal.

The coastline here forms a short sunny haven similar to the Riviera of France. Running east and west, protected against north winds by the Sintra hills, and facing the warm southern sun is the "Riviera of the Sun," at the center of which sits Estoril. Beaches, villas, gardens, palaces, hotels—and a modern casino with all the attractions of Monte Carlo and a well-heeled night life—that is this modern gathering place. Travelers of today enjoy the combination afforded by this up-to-date, luxurious resort. It has now taken on the reputation of being the refuge of Europe's most fashionable monarchs-in-exile.

Farther along this coast is Cascaes, a more informal resort, with additional villas and beaches. After leaving Cascaes, the road continues to the Cabo da Roca, a reddish bluff falling steeply to the Atlantic. This marks the end of the "Riviera," but more importantly it signalizes the westernmost point of the continent of Europe. From the seething breakers of the open Atlantic at its base, three thousand miles of ocean stretch unbrokenly westward to the remote other side—the beaches of New Jersey, the harbor of New York, and the Yankee shores of New England.

Fatima

The most recently opened of Roman Catholic shrines of pilgrimage is at the tiny village of Fatima, ninety miles north of Lisbon. In a little hollow called Cova de Iria, three children saw periodic appearances of the Virgin during the summer of 1917. October 13 marked the day when the Virgin revealed her identity and asked the children to pray for sinners and to build a chapel. Popular fervor was stirred up by this event. By 1930 the apparition was officially verified by the ecclesiastical authorities. A shrine was thereupon erected and pilgrims invited from all over the world. Due to the fast growth of air travel, a large number of such pilgrims have come to Fatima while en route to Rome or Lourdes.

A replica of the Fatima church has been built in the city of Lisbon itself. However, Fatima is easily reached, because of its location near so many other important scenes of Portuguese history. Travelers can hire a modern speedy automobile and make a convenient trip to Fatima and back in one day. However, it is preferred to make a two-day trip of it and stop at several other places. For instance, on the outward ride visits can be made to Tomar for the great medieval fortress of the Templars; to Santarem, liberated by battle with the Moors in the twelfth century. Then, after paying a visit to the shrine of Fatima, visits can be made to the church at Batalha, the abbey of Alcobaça, the fishing town of Nazaré, and the spa of Caldas da Rainha, where several good hotels are located. On the following day, one can drive back by way of Obidos, the great monastery of Mafra, the royal city of Sintra and the "Riviera" towns of Cascaes and Estoril to Lisbon.

People are very reluctant to leave Lisbon, for many other drives to equally celebrated locales are available. Before leaving Portugal, everyone must take time out to go to a native café and hear the mournful traditional songs, or *fados*, sung by popular entertainers. The fados are sad recitative songs that bring to mind the Arab tradition of singing. They are sung in a mood rather than a melody.

Shopping is another attraction that makes of Lisbon an important stop in anyone's European travel itinerary. Beautiful porcelainware and glazed tiles (called *azulejos*), done in all colors and fitting together into large patterns if desired, are readily obtained. Antique furniture, glass, and silver, also objects of cork, wickerware, or carved wood, and publications from every country of the modern world are on sale in the compact shopping center of the town.

Another popular pastime in Lisbon is a bullfight, especially since Portuguese bullfighting is so much easier on the tender spirit than the Spanish variety. The bulls are harried as across the border, but at the climax, they are wrestled to a fall by a queue of gay matadors and then liberated to fight no more.

Portugal is one of those happy countries that can be visited again and again. Its history has created many things to see, and they are scattered evenly across the quiet republic, from the craggy hills of the Douro, down to the lagoons of the southern province of the Algarve. It is also one country with which Americans have never had a quarrel.

SPAIN

Trail Blazer of the New World

AMERICANS, who share the Western Hemisphere with Latin American peoples, usually like to know something about Spain, the mother country of eighteen republics in the New World. These republics have reproduced a Mediterranean civilization that can best be understood by Americans when they take a look at the traditions built up in mother Spain.

Our forefathers had many troubles with Spain, mainly due to the Spanish conviction that any others who settled in North America were trespassers. By the papal bull of 1494, any non-Christian land beyond the Atlantic Ocean was to belong to Spain, and this included the overwhelming percentage of the New World. Consequently the Pilgrims, the first settlers of Virginia, and the Yankee traders of New England were forced to keep their powder dry and an eye cocked for any Spanish police expedition coming to enforce such a claim.

Many of Latin America's early difficulties resulted from the fact that Spain has had such an unhappy history. Throughout the twenty centuries of her life, Spain has been forced to struggle with many unyielding forces—a procession of invaders, a hostile Nature, unwanted wars, dictatorial kings, a rigid class system and a faulty sense of unity.

The land of Spain, while beautiful, has too much high, barren land for its size. Its central highland of Castile, wide and treeless, divides the more fertile coastlines from each other and enforces a tendency to regionalism. The differing interests of these peripheral areas have always led the dominant, landbound Castilians to favor a strong central government by which the aspirations of the other peoples can be held strongly in check.

Spain is such a large, square peninsula that it has always proved difficult to unify. The northern coastal cities that front on the Bay of Biscay have rainy, cool weather, and conduct their trade mainly with northern Europe. That northern region is well industrialized, has important forests, and has suffered very little interruption from Moorish control.

The south of Spain, known as Andalusia, has always been affected by invasions from Africa. After being under Moorish government for five centuries, it suddenly became the funnel for the rich trade of the Americas. The loss of Spain's American colonies struck a hard blow at the prosperity of dry, semitropical Andalusia.

The northeastern corner of Spain, called Catalonia, possesses a concentration of textile industries. It has a progressive agricultural system and feels a close kinship with neighboring France. Barcelona, the capital of Catalonia, feels and looks like a European capital, and has always resisted the unifying effect of Castilian rule.

From Catalonia to Andalusia stretches Spain's long coastline on the Mediterranean, a region of mild weather where rice, oranges, and olives grow in copious quantities. Spain's long frontage on the Mediterranean—almost a thousand miles of it— running from France all the way to the Straits of Gibraltar, is the determining factor in Spanish history. For along this seashore came the pioneering Carthaginians, and after them the Romans, who brought civilization to all of Spain. The first four centuries of Spain's history connected her so closely with Rome that the stamp of Mediterranean culture has ever since overwhelmed the separatist tendencies of inland and northern Spain.

The effects of that Romanized civilization have lasted down through the centuries in a strong enough form to exert an influence on the United States, a child of northern peoples settled under a different tradition. The handsome style of architecture born in the Mediterranean—Roman-Moorish arches, weathered red-tile roofs, verandahs with flowers, patios and courtyards—

has penetrated California, Arizona, and Florida, winning popular favor with the inhabitants of those semitropical states. Spanish phrases from Mexico have peppered the speech of the American borderlands. The very name of our American currency—the dollar—was derived from Spain. Spain, in short, transferred the Mediterranean's way of life to our continent, with the result that no one who penetrates south of the Rio Grande can fail to be unimpressed with its stamp.

The story of Spain really begins with the Moors, the Arab hosts who overran the peninsula between 711 and 735. The effect of seven hundred years of struggle to evict these strangers was to harden and intensify the Spaniard's soul and to increase his religious ardor to a crusading pitch.

The character of the different provinces of Spain varies with the length of their submission to the rule of the Moslems. Only one small section escaped this fate entirely—a county on the northern coast called the Asturias.[1] The first area to be liberated from the Moors was Catalonia, the region of northeastern Spain about Barcelona. In the early 800's, Charlemagne, King of the Franks and first Holy Roman Emperor, sent an army across the Pyrenees to expel the Moors, but all he succeeded in doing was to free Catalonia—which he labeled "the Spanish March"—a frontier defense zone against the infidels.[2] It was during the retreat of one of his columns that an ambush inspired the immortal medieval epic poem "The Song of Roland," named for the prince whose detachment was wiped out in the defile of Roncesvalles.

The Spanish March later detached itself from the Franks and became independent. By the year 1000 several other small kingdoms had sprung to life in the north, each one of them a warrior state occupied with pushing back the Moorish boundaries. First of these to take the field was Leon, in northwesternmost

[1] A prince of the Spanish royal family is thus often titled "Prince of the Asturias."

[2] A march, or mark, was the name of a medieval district set up to defend an imperial frontier. Austria descends from a march set up against the Huns. Denmark's name comes from the march held by the Danes. Ruling nobleman of a march was a *markgrave*—later modified into *marquis*.

Spain, freeing Galicia and the district south of the Asturias. Next was Castile, an inland region whose warriors soon made the swiftest progress. It is interesting that the names of these new states sprang from the symbols adopted for their coats of arms— a lion for Leon, and a fortress (castle) for Castile.

To the east of Castile rose the Kingdom of Navarre, which was almost exclusively a Basque state and straddled the Pyrenees to include the southern districts of Aquitania that were peopled by Basques. East of Navarre was another Pyreneean state, called Aragon, whose expansion was rapid. Its capital was the celebrated university town of Zaragoza. In addition to Catalonia, there was also the independent state of Portugal, which, as we have seen, began life as just another Iberian state battling the Moors for survival—and expansion.

During the Middle Ages these kingdoms gradually consolidated. Many battles with the Moors originated a large number of legends that have enriched Spanish literature—particularly the story of the hero The Cid, who slew thousands of Moors by his own leadership. The Cid died in 1095.

While this warfare was going on in the north, the south of Spain prospered under a Moorish caliphate that was more en-lightened and civilized than all the courts of Christian Europe.

First city to rise to greatness under the Moslems was Cor-doba, an ancient town on the Guadalquivir River. A Syrian Prince, Abd-er-Rahman, came to Spain in A.D. 755. For two hundred years his Omayyad dynasty brought industry and pros-perity to this province of southern Spain named Andalusia.[3] The massive mosque built by a succession of Omayyad rulers is still an edifice of wonderment today. Containing 860 columns in long, straight rows, all the columns varying from each other in the type of stone, shape, and color, and rising to support horse-shoe-shaped arches, it is a place of magnificence. This mosque, as extensive in size as St. Peter's Cathedral in Rome, was once lit by 7,425 lamps hung from the ceilings. It is today a cathedral, but has not been extensively changed on the inside.

---

[3] Andalusia's name comes from the Vandals, who settled here for several decades before moving on to North Africa.

Cordoba grew to almost a half million inhabitants by the year 1000. It was purely Oriental, peopled mainly by immigrants from Syria, Arabia, and Morocco, together with a large colony of Jews. It was a center of learning, welcoming philosophers, mathematicians, medical men, and students of the occult. Its craftsmen rivaled those of Damascus in their excellence. Among their products was Cordovan leather, which still ranks high in the modern world as an article of exquisite perfection.

Silk, cotton cloth, and carpets were all introduced into Spain by the industrious caliphs of Cordoba. This era of magnificence, however, came to an end when a warrior dynasty called the Almoravides swept in from Africa and moved the Moorish capital to Seville. In later years the Moslems began to fight among themselves, as local leaders set up independent states with their own dynasties. However, these potentates were patrons of the arts to the end. The Emir of Seville constructed the beautiful Giralda minaret in 1196 and beautified his palace, or Alcázar. In the next century, when the Castilians had swept through almost all of Moslem Spain in an offensive conducted by the fervent St. Ferdinand,[4] the survivors took refuge in the Moorish state of Granada, whose leader then proceeded to build the matchless Alhambra.

The victories of Castile over the infidels gave Spain great prominence in medieval Europe, whose own legions had just been expelled from the Holy Land by other infidel rulers. The companion Kingdom of Aragon, in the meantime, having routed all Moors along its own borders, expanded out to sea, occupying the Balearic Islands and taking control of Sardinia and Sicily. Barcelona, the Aragonese port, grew to wealth and maritime power rivaling that of Genoa, Pisa, and Venice. The trade with the Levant that enriched those Italian cities gave its share of opulence to Aragon, a kingdom that became more accustomed to luxury than the austere warrior Kingdom of Castile.

---

[4] His name, San Fernando, was given to one of the early California missions by Father Junipero Serra. It is now one of the fastest-growing residential sections of Los Angeles.

Seville

Perhaps the city of Spain closest to the Mediterranean tradition is the capital of Andalusia—Seville. This is a city of style and elegance, the nearest to a picture-book Spanish town that Spain can produce. Everything is on the stately scale here.

As all lordly cities should sit beside a river, so Seville rises above its Guadalquivir,[5] greatest river of southern Spain. Freighters and small navy ships can come up this river from its mouth thirty miles distant and tie up outside the city's bull ring. This bull ring, or arena, is one of the most stately of the country. Decked out in the royal colors of red and gold, it is a perfect circle, a bowl where Spain's aspiring toreadors hope to make their biggest hit—winning the applause of the fervent Andalusian aristocratic *aficionados*. And it should be remembered that Seville is the city of the legendary Carmen, a worker in Seville's massive cigarette factory who snared the fastest-rising toreador of them all.

For five hundred years Seville was an Arab city. Its proudest relics of that productive half-millennium are the Alcázar, or emir's palace; the Gold Tower, or treasury, beside the river, which bade farewell to countless fleets heading out to the Americas; and the Giralda Tower. This latter is the emblem of Seville. Built as a minaret for the city's mosque, it now stands as the belltower for Seville's huge cathedral. Rising 305 feet on the northern side of the latter, it is decorated with frescoes and columns in pure Arab style. Its once-flat top is now a platform for a baroque steeple built in 1568, atop which floats a huge weather vane, or *giraldillo*, which gives the ancient Moorish minaret its modern name.

Seville's main streets are narrow and winding in true Arab-Oriental style. Beautiful grilled balconies jut out into the narrow passageways, and flowers adorn most window sills. Vines and trellises almost span the gap at rooftop levels. On such narrow, unpretentious streets are some of the city's finest shops and business houses.

---

[5] "Guadalquivir" was spelled in Arabic *"Wadi el-Kebir"* ("Great River").

A modern attraction of this unusual place is the Maria Luisa Park, where there was held in 1929 an Inter-American Exposition. The principal building is still standing and is a paradise for photographers because of its exquisite blue-tile facings. Possessing a semicircular colonnade around a massive paved square, each of its columns is fronted with a tiled portrayal of a Spanish province. Bridges, arched over a Venetian canal, are masterpieces of flashing blue tile.

Seville comes to life gloriously on several religious holidays each year. Most exciting of these is, of course, Holy Week, when the whole city shuts down for a period of devotion. The three days leading up to Good Friday are taken up with processions of elaborate floats, or *pasos*, portraying a scene of the Passion, or presenting a gorgeously dressed Madonna, all lit by countless beeswax candles and borne by over thirty men hidden beneath the rich drapes. As the pasos advance by fits and starts, to rest the panting bearers, they are accompanied by martial music and surrounded by members of their medieval brotherhoods, all dressed in concealing pointed hoods. The scene is an eerie portrayal of the crusading devotion of the Middle Ages. As each paso is at last borne at double time through massive doors into the great cathedral, the bands play loudly and blaringly their military refrain.

The people of Seville turn out in force for this supreme religious event of the year. This is the best time for travelers to see the beautiful Spanish women, with their clear complexions and flashing eyes, wearing the black mantillas that used to be an all-year-round headdress.

Ten days after Easter the tone changes, and Seville turns itself over to the merriment of its annual Fair. Families receive publicly at little booths. There is a burst of bullfights and dances, and colorful processions of carriages driven by the *señoritas* wearing white mantillas this time.

Seville's society ranks as high as that of any other city of Spain. And this is only as it should be, since it was once the center of the opulent gold trade with all Latin America. By royal decree, the Casa de las Indias, or Board of Trade for the Indies, controlled all commerce with the gold-bearing lands across the Atlantic. No one should miss the Archives of the Indies while in Seville, for one of Columbus' own maps is displayed there, together with other priceless relics of the exciting era when Spain ruled the world.

Granada

Second only to Seville as a treasure city of Andalusia is Granada, the last capital of the Moors. The city is filled with first-rate attractions, all revolving around the inimitable Alhambra high on its hill outside the city.

To this beautiful location, in sight of the snow-capped Sierra Nevada mountains that separate it from the Mediterranean, came Ferdinand and Isabella, sworn to their determination to expel the Moors forever from Spain. They laid siege to the city for over a year and finally managed to storm it on the second day of January in 1492.

Granada had been the peaceful capital of the last Moorish state in Spain for over two centuries. Its wealth and culture made it famed all over Europe.[6] But its days were numbered, for in those impassioned times of the early Renaissance, there was no thought that Moslems and Christians could live peacefully side by side anywhere in the world. Too much blood had disfigured the centuries for that.

In the year 1469 a marriage welded most of Spain together. Isabella, heir to the throne of Castile, was wed to Ferdinand, King of Aragon and its domains in Italy. Whereupon a united kingdom comprising all of Iberia except for the individualistic Portuguese came into sight. Isabella, known as "the Catholic," persuaded her husband to dedicate his greater riches to the capture of the thorn of Granada.

By a series of coincidences, Spain climbed to the summit of glory almost overnight. These coincidences were three: (1) the victory of Granada; (2) the discovery of America; and (3) a brilliant series of royal marriages.

The first act of this trilogy was resounding enough all by itself. The acclaim of Europe went up in unison over this triumphant

---

[6] Pomegranates got their name "apples of Granada" through the French. Grenades were also named by the French because of their resemblance to pomegranates in size and shape. "Grenadiers" as a military term came from "grenades."

climax to the seven-hundred-year struggle to reclaim Spain for Christendom. It balanced the then recent loss of all eastern Europe to the Moslem Turks.

But this acclaim died away when the balance of power in Europe was destroyed by the emergence of such a strong Spain, especially a theocratic Spain that the "Catholic Kings" determined to create. On the heels of their conquest of Granada, they decreed the expulsion of the Jews from Spain and followed up ten years later by demanding that all the remaining Moslems either get out or accept the Christian religion. These measures, taken in the heat of crusading passion, not only destroyed the base of any possible democratic development in the country, but confronted Europe with the existence of a national state whose size and accumulating wealth outweighed all the other kingdoms and principalities of the harassed continent.

Granada was indeed a jewel worth the conquering. The city became so symbolic of the victory of the Cross that Ferdinand and Isabella chose it as their burial place, and they lie today beneath a resplendent tomb in the Royal Chapel of Granada's immense cathedral.

The Alhambra of Granada can never be overlooked among the beautiful architectural masterpieces of the world. Known as "the gem of the delicate fancy of the Moor," its beauty is found in the graceful arches and decorations of its patios and chambers. The name Alhambra means in Arabic "Red Castle," and it was originally a fortress atop its forested hill. The Moorish kings developed their royal apartments within the walls as the years went by. Two large patios are exquisitely beautiful. The Court of the Myrtles, the larger of the two, has a quiet pool reflecting the delicate tracery of the arches, while the more famous, smaller Court of the Lions surrounds a well-known fountain, from which little channels lead off in the brick flooring, probably to carry off scented water. The halls and chambers, all decorated by scalloped ceilings and arches of plasterwork of infinite detail, rejoice the eye. The Alhambra, after centuries of neglect, was "discovered" by the American story writer Washington Irving in the early 1800's. His wonderment at such beauty is reflected in his inspired descriptions which evoked widespread comment in the United States of his day.

Higher on a near-by hill is the Generalife, or summer palace of the Moorish kings. Here a garden surrounds a long line of fountains, whose slender streams spurt up in perfect alignment, even after all these centuries, when turned on by an attendant for a traveler's admiration. Artificial cascades plunge down through groves of lemon and orange trees, creating a delightful retreat for Oriental-minded rulers oppressed by the torrid heat of a Mediterranean summer sun.

Granada abounds, like Seville, in churches and monasteries and goes in for solemn religious festivals as well. One of the monasteries has been made over into an informal hotel, or *parador*, complete with gardens, patios, and views over Granada's protecting range, the Sierra Nevada, or "snowy, saw-toothed range," a mountain chain whose peaks rise to 11,000 feet and have snow most of the year, even though bordering the Mediterranean.[7]

The only jarring note in this impressive city of gypsies, Arabic lore, and florid churchly architecture is a baroque palace built by King Charles V in the mid-1500's around one end of the Alhambra. Never lived in, never completed, this immense semicircular pile crowds up against the more delicate Moorish palace in acute disharmony, although giving an inkling of the symbolic majesty of the victory here of the new Spanish order over the old.

Spanish dancing, as loved by American travelers, got much of its movement from the gypsy rhythms of Granada. The flamenco style of dancing, with whirling steps, ample skirts, castanets, and blood-tingling pace, was born of the gypsies and stylized by these gracious cities of Andalusia before being passed on to Latin America and the rest of the world.

Granada symbolized for decades to come the victory that

---

[7] This name, Sierra Nevada, was given by early Spanish explorers of California to the range of that name, in honor of Spain's highest and most beautiful mountains.

inspired all Spain. Columbus named an island in the West Indies after it,[8] and the entire northwestern corner of South America was eventually formed into a viceroyalty called New Granada.[9]

Columbus, Isabella, and America

Shortly after the conquest of Granada, there came to this city of victory Christopher Columbus, who quickly seized on a hunch that launched the modern era of history and should have paid him off more handsomely.

Columbus had spent years in Portugal trying to "sell" the King there into backing him with a few ships and sailors. He evidently had never dreamed of getting backing from Spain, since Castile was a state with no maritime tradition and no fleet, a "landlubberly" warrior kingdom. And as for Aragon, it was immersed only in its Mediterranean possessions.

However, the drama of Columbus and Isabella is one that can never lose its interest, since so little documentation exists to supply the facts motivating the Queen into this unusual venture. Columbus, however, judging from his whole life's history and his character, was acting from strategy when he had his idea put before the Queen's attention. He played shrewdly on two of her obvious interests: continuing the war for the Cross by converting new realms of heathen people, such as the Indians; and achieving a fortune of gold and gems such as was known to exist in India, which would give Castile at last a chance to catch up on more opulent Aragon.

The Queen, cautious and perhaps a little narrow, failed to grasp the idea at first because of Columbus' lack of reputation; but when her advisers gave her the courage, she summoned him back from the road to France, his next possible customer, and finally gave him the backing to acquire three leaky old ships. The contract signed by the two shrewd protagonists of the unfolding American drama has many colorful provisions. As if not expecting Columbus' trip to amount to anything, the Queen granted him the title of "Admiral of the Ocean Sea," and "Captain-

---

[8] Grenada, pronounced nowadays "Gre-nay-da," is a British-owned island ninety miles north of Trinidad.

[9] Now the Republic of Colombia.

General of the Indies,"—absolute governor of all the lands he should discover. She also assented to his demand that all his heirs should be admirals in the Spanish navy.[10] But, just to be protected in case he did stumble across India, she made Columbus guarantee her a full fifth of all the treasures he found.

In late August of the same year in which Granada fell, Columbus' obscure flotilla sailed from one of Spain's most remote harbors, Palos de la Frontera.[11] He followed the well-worn Portuguese trail down to the Canary Islands for a rest and refit before tackling the unknown western ocean sea.

The voyage nearly proved to be a fiasco, as everyone had prophesied. Yet in March of 1493, Columbus safely landed again at Palos and reported to Ferdinand and Isabella, who had now set up court at the King's lovely capital of Barcelona. His treasures were mostly promises, but his few proofs galvanized all Spain. When he sailed again the same year, he captained a full fleet of seventeen vessels, manned by some of the most eager and adventurous knights of the land.

Columbus was one of the modern age's first publicists and imaginative writers. From his four voyages he brought back nothing but a handful of treasure and lurid tales of his discoveries. There is much evidence to prove that he knew he had come across some new lands, but he never let on in his report that it was anything but India that he had reached. Such a confession, without treasure to match the priceless haul being reaped by Portugal's exuberant Vasco da Gama, would have cost him his head and have been a confession of utter failure. The King and Queen were unimpressed at having missed out on the sure thing exploited by Portugal, and they lost interest in Columbus. Queen Isabella died in 1504, and Columbus followed two years after, a petitioner in the city of Valladolid, capital of Castile.

The "Catholic Kings," as Ferdinand and Isabella are called in Spain, did not advertise the voyages of Columbus. But men of science grasped eagerly at the reports brought back by the unhappy Admiral. Cartographers, gleaning the facts from his high-sounding

---

[10] His modern descendant, the Duke of Veragua, still wears this uniform.

[11] Palos is across an estuary from Huelva, port city for the rich copper-pyrites mines of Rio Tinto, not worked then.

proclamations, plotted out the new lands. One of these map-makers, living in the Netherlands, even bestowed a name on them. Having received his facts from a colleague at Florence who had learned them from a merchant-adventurer of his city called Americus Vespucius, he coined a name in the latter's honor—America.[12]

Spain Conquers by Marriage

The third coincidence that lifted Spain to hegemony over all Europe in one mighty stride was the system of marriages worked out by Ferdinand and Isabella, with results that far outweighed their original calculations, we may be sure.

They succeeded in a fantastic linking together of Europe's richest regions. Charles, their grandson, became King Charles I of united Spain in 1516; then three years later was crowned Emperor Charles V of Germany, ruler of Hapsburg dominions of illimitable extent, from Budapest to the Isthmus of Panama, from Amsterdam to the Barbary Coast of North Africa.

The only important European country outside his reach was France—and the French King was naturally alarmed. This Renaissance Prince, Francis I, entered into a series of wars and intrigues that made the epoch a fascinating period for study. At the battle of Pavia in 1526 Francis was actually captured by Charles and imprisoned for several months until he signed over many of his possessions to get out, whereupon he repudiated his promises entirely, in the spirit of his popular political contemporary Machiavelli.

Francis grasped at all straws to weaken the Hapsburg octopus that had surrounded France on every side. He made an alliance with the Sultan Solyman of Turkey, an act that horrified all Christendom, to keep Charles occupied along his Austrian borders. He sent out an explorer, Jacques Cartier, to discover lands in the New World that might turn out to be as wealthy in treasure as the Mexican bonanza uncovered by Cortez. He intrigued with Henry VIII to keep England on the sidelines.

And Francis was helped by one great unforeseen event—the outbreak of Luther's Reformation in Germany. Charles V, as

---

[12] The Florentine merchant was Amerigo Vespucci, but in Renaissance style he Latinized his professional name. Vespucci is considered to have accompanied Ojeda's voyage to Venezuela in 1499.

Holy Roman Emperor, had to take up arms against this new force threatening the heart of his dominions. Later on, another miracle occurred to upset the balance of power. Henry of England divorced his Spanish wife and led his country into the ranks of the nonconformists who were challenging Charles.

Thus Spain was dragged, willy-nilly, into this life-and-death battle of Europe. Spain's army was used to fight in Italy, the Netherlands, and Austria. Her navy was destroyed in trying to conquer Barbary. And her increasing treasure was squandered to pay for the thankless job of subduing Europe to the rule of a Hapsburg.

The Dollar, and the Armada of Imperial Spain

Spain's link with central Europe through her Hapsburg connections brought some important influences to faraway America. The sailors of the Netherlands grew familiar with transatlantic shores through voyages conducted for Charles V.[13] Venezuela almost became a German colony when put up as security by Charles V to the Fuggers of Augsburg, international bankers who gave him a loan when the Turks attacked Vienna. But more important, the dollar was born as a term of trade and made its way to America.

In what is now Czechoslovakia there is a town called Jachymov. Four hundred years ago the land belonged to Hapsburg Austria and the town was known as Sankt Joachimsthal. Silver mines had been worked there for several centuries, and a silver coin circulated in Austria known as the *Joachimsthaler,* or, as it was called for short, the "thaler." When gold and silver began reaching Spain from the Americas, it was assayed and inventoried by German and Flemish bankers for its worth in thalers. The word came to be pronounced "dólar" by the Spaniards, and with its subdivisions the "reales" and "pieces of eight" it became a term of exchange among the buccaneers and freebooters of the Caribbean.

The term dollar was so well-known that it spread to other parts of the world and not just to America. The counting unit

---

[13] This encouraged Holland to launch Henry Hudson's expedition of discovery to lands that later were colonized as "New Netherlands."

of "dollars Mex" became the staple exchange in China long before the United States was colonized. This occurred again because of the parent silver coin. When Magellan discovered the Philippine Islands, it was found that they lay within Spain's half of the globe as partitioned by the Pope back in 1494, even though they were within sight of Portugal's spice islands. Manila was linked with Spain only by a yearly treasure ship that made the lonely sail across the wide Pacific to Acapulco in Mexico. The dollar thus was carried to the Philippines as a Mex dollar, and became the unit for China, Malaya, and later, Hong Kong.

Likewise, in the 1800's, a silver dollar with the image of Austrian Empress Maria Theresa became esteemed in Africa a hundred years after it was first coined for that great monarch;[14] and until World War II Ethiopians would accept no coinage if it were not a "Maria Theresa dollar."

Philip II of Spain, heir of the Emperor Charles, is as difficult a character to define exactly as was his great-grandmother Isabella. He was fanatical, morose, cruel, and determined, yet he also had a love for Spain and a great admiration of art and beauty. He is Spain's first modern monarch. Brought up as a Spaniard, he lived all his life there in contrast to his father Charles, who hardly ever came to Spain. The spirit of Isabella was in him, in that he was a crusading warrior for the faith of Catholic Spain. He saw no merits in the Protestant Reformation and dedicated himself to defeating it at whatever cost. He saw to it that no trace of it crossed overseas to his American empire, even though such a policy meant shutting off free emigration to numberless useful colonists and confining control over that rich continent to autocratic supervision by the Casa de las Indias in Seville.

It is not generally known that Philip, when he ascended the throne of Spain, was also Prince Consort of England. In the full tradition of his great-grandmother Isabella, he had decided to "marry" England into an alliance. He landed there in 1555

---

[14] The Empress reigned from 1740–1780. She formed the League of the Three Women (with Madame de Pompadour of France and the Czarina of Russia) against that woman-hater Frederick the Great of Prussia. She was also the mother of Marie Antoinette.

to wed his first cousin Queen Mary, who at that very time was trying to stamp out the Reformation in her kingdom by burning the most prominent Protestant leaders at the stake. When Mary died in 1558, England came under the rule of a new Queen, Elizabeth, who reversed her predecessor's policy completely.

Philip's struggles with Elizabeth make for magnificent drama, but they have not been properly recounted in history without the fanatical taking of sides that is natural when describing such world-shaking events and antagonists.

Philip's reign at first was glorious for Spain. Just as the age of Elizabethan England was one of a great outpouring of literature, science, and art, so Spain enjoyed the same flowering experience. Cervantes wrote his *Don Quixote* in honor of the happy, free life in his favorite part of Castile, with the old Don vainly attacking the foibles and pomposities of the times. Artists found sanctuary in Spain, launching that great tradition that lasted far into the next century, led by Murillo, Velazquez, and El Greco. Flemish painters had been brought in by Isabella, while Philip imported Italian masters, until Spain's own artists rose to fame. Philip built, at huge cost, his magnificent Palace of the Escorial outside of Madrid, loading it with art and decorations worthy of the limitless wealth at his disposal.

For the religious conflict, Spain gave to the world another historical character who swayed the times. He was Ignatius of the Basque town of Loyola, a wounded soldier who decided to dedicate his life to fighting for his religion against the Reformation. Founder of the Jesuit order, he is now a saint, and his followers scored immediate successes in reconverting the subject peoples of the Austrian Hapsburgs.

With the Inquisition's power in Spain sufficient to prevent any Protestant leaders from preaching the new faith in Philip's homeland, and with the Moslems of the Barbary Coast triumphant over Philip's attempts to set up an empire in Africa, the King turned his attention to combatting the Reformation elsewhere. This brought him into conflict with England, for it unleashed the fires of a religious rivalry into what was basically an economic and dynastic contest between underdog, isolated England, and powerful, well-entrenched Spain.

After two decades of this rivalry, Philip decided on war to end the English challenge once and for all. Elizabeth had avoided war by outwardly disavowing the raids her sea dogs were making on Spanish gold fleets and Caribbean possessions. But when Philip decided to build a fleet to get at his adversary, Elizabeth struck first. Sir Francis Drake sailed boldly into the harbor of Cadiz, burned the fleet and sacked the city, as a raid in force to prevent a naval attack and to "singe the King of Spain's beard."

Yet the next year Philip's great Armada sailed from Spanish harbors bound for a certain victory, made up of magnificent high-pooped warships, loaded with veteran soldiers in then-modern armor, and armed with the latest cannon. Everyone knows the outcome—how English tactics plus heavy storms dispersed the Armada in the English Channel. Philip could try nothing more. He died in 1598, master of his empire, but a failure in subduing the English or his own Dutch subjects, who had successfully set up their own navy and founded their own overseas empire.

The Mysterious Decline

The foregoing events have been told in such detail because their outcome determined the future development of affairs in America. For not till she was free of fear of Spain did England dare to show the effrontery of planting colonies in North America. Only then did her business men, nobles, and religious leaders venture to invest in them. Only nine years after Philip's death, the English founded their first settlement at Jamestown.

Although the world stood in awe of Spain for two hundred years more, the country entered a long decline in world power and a period of absolutism within that brought it down from its pinnacle. No one can put his finger on the mysterious ingredient that produced such a development, except to associate it with a people tired out from playing above its strength in European wars and struggles, unable to develop a resourceful domestic life once the rich treasure from America fell away. The country was too poor in resources to support its ceaseless wars. Though gloriously rich in art, as expressed in her beautiful churches, monasteries, Roman remains, and palaces, Spain produced no industry to develop a middle class, and no patriotic element in its nobility able to shake off the privileged traditions inherited from the Middle Ages.

The years of decline saw Spain lose her grasp on her tremendous empire. An avalanche of losses, however, fell on Spain later on when her last Hapsburg King died in 1700. Immediately the Kings of Europe scrambled to annex the vacant throne, unleashing the devastating War of the Spanish Succession.[15] Mighty Louis XIV of France, the closest, won out.

For the next hundred years Spain degenerated into a satellite of France under the Bourbon "Family Compact." After losing a joint war with England in 1763, France surrendered her colonial empire, with Spain acquiring on a platter the French colony of Louisiana in North America. But the Spaniards in their turn were obliged to give up Florida to England in exchange for richer Cuba, which they had lost in battle.

Then came the period of the American Revolution. Autocratic Spain, following in France's train, found herself an unwitting ally of the Thirteen Colonies fighting against absolutism. In this war the Spaniards concentrated their energy on reconquering Gibraltar. They subjected the rocky peninsula to an exhausting four-year siege, which failed to end in victory because of insufficient sea power. When the war ended, England still held Gibraltar, but restored Florida to Spain, although a secret clause in the treaty enabled the new United States to take over from England the inland reaches of that province.

Greater disasters followed shortly afterward when Spain got entangled with Napoleon's ambitions. In 1800 the subservient Bourbon King of Spain handed back all of Louisiana to France against a vague promise of three insignificant Italian cities. In 1805 Spain sent her fleet out in unison with the French navy, only to have it mercilessly annihilated by Lord Nelson at the Battle of Trafalgar, fought almost within gunshot of the Spanish city of Cadiz.

---

[15] 1701–1714. It was called Queen Anne's War in American history.

Napoleon soon ousted the Bourbons entirely and set up his older brother Joseph in Madrid as King. Chaos then really broke out in the Spanish Empire. The colonies in America asserted their loyalty to the exiled Bourbons and set out to govern themselves. In Spain itself, the people arose with an amazing show of unity to fight for their own land, unleashing the new word "guerrilla"[16] for the first time on the world. A British army eventually expelled the French and brought back the Bourbon King, only to see this lackluster individual attempt to restore absolutism. The result was that all of South America, Central America, and Mexico fell away inside of ten years. Spain was hopelessly unable to reconquer her huge empire against the force of British sea power and the American Monroe Doctrine. In 1821 she sold Florida to the United States after long wrangling over terms, thus erasing her last toehold on the American continent.

Civil wars between two claimants to the throne took up much of the nineteenth century in Spain. A republic even came to power for two years. The *coup de grâce* to Spain's empire finally was administered in 1898 by the Spanish-American War. Cuba and Puerto Rico were lost, together with the Philippines and Guam. The next year Spain liquidated what was left to her overseas by selling her innumerable islands in the Pacific—the Marianas, the Marshalls, the Pelews, and the Carolines—to imperial Germany.

She held in her possession only the Canary Islands and some footholds in Africa. Although she was awarded a section of Morocco in the early 1900's, Spain is classed as a nonimperial power.

However, this long decline seems to have had no embittering effect on the Spanish people except in so far as it saddled them with poverty. They are unfailingly friendly and hospitable, and they go far to making Spain one of the most attractive countries to visit as a tourist.

The events of the twentieth century in Spanish history are too well-known to insert into this already overlong account. We have had to outline Spanish affairs at such extra length because

---

[16] "Guerrilla" means "a little war," fought by irregular tactics of civilian-led forces against a powerful foe.

it is one of the few European countries to have had a close contact with American history from the start.

Interesting Cruise Ports

Americans cruising to the Mediterranean often call at Spanish ports that have significant appeal. Among them the following three are the most frequently visited:

CADIZ, on the Atlantic just outside the Straits of Gibraltar. This is the port for Seville ninety miles away. It is a dazzling-white Mediterranean-type city crowded on a peninsula facing the blue ocean. The layers of history encrusting Cadiz since the days of the Phoenicians are not as much in evidence any more because of the many destructions that have wasted this strategic harbor. Visitors like to see its museum and ornate cathedral; enjoy its sea breezes and shops; stop at its modern hotel; wander through its narrow streets; and then proceed on to Seville.

MÁLAGA, an Andalusian port seventy miles inside the Straits of Gibraltar; an important port for shipping wine, olives, cork, and grain. It is the port for Granada, which lies four hours inland by motor road across the lovely Sierra Nevadas. Málaga is also a popular winter resort, enjoying the mildest winter weather of all Spain. It has a large and rich cathedral, a restored Moorish fortress called the Alcazaba—looking very much like the Alhambra on the inside—and another old fort called the Gibralfaro, popular for sunning and dining. A beach resort called Baños del Carmen, and two good seaside hotels minister to the comforts of vacationers. Málaga has bullfights, religious festivals, and interesting shops. Its wine warehouses, or *bodegas,* are also of first-rate interest.

BARCELONA, until recently the largest city of Spain, and also its most cosmopolitan. Up in the northeast corner of the country, near the French frontier, Barcelona is the most important Spanish harbor on the Mediterranean.

Despite the austerity of recent years, Barcelona maintains its gayety and appeal. Its broad boulevards are mainly devoid of traffic, but the people are always moving about on foot. A winding boulevard along the edge of the medieval city is known as the

Ramblas. Here the promenading Catalans can be watched as they keep walking all day past the shops, offices, and hotels that line this tree-shaded thoroughfare.

The Parliament, or Deputación, is an exquisite Renaissance building in the heart of the old city, with interior decorations of fine paintings showing scenes of Columbus' appearance here when he came to report to Ferdinand and Isabella. This building has some richly ornamented rooms, such as the Audiencia, or Council Chamber of medieval Barcelona, a chapel dedicated to St. George fighting the dragon, and the Hall of the Hundred, which is a relic of the days when Barcelona was capital of a self-governing Catalonia. The outside stairway leading down from these rooms is especially grand.

The cathedral, as in all Spanish cities, is a repository of art and treasures of the centuries, and should not be passed by. Barcelona's cathedral is dedicated to St. Eulalia. It is a massive structure of Spanish Gothic, built on remnants of older medieval foundations. The altar and chapels are richly decorated. On one altar there is mounted the Crucifix of Lepanto, a cross nailed to the prow of the ship led into battle by Don John of Austria, an illegitimate son of Charles V. That battle, fought in far-off Greece in 1571, chastised the Turkish fleet and finally liberated the western Mediterranean from Ottoman sea raids.

Treasures belonging to medieval kings of Aragon, and their tombs, are to be found by strolling through this central monument to Barcelona's medieval devotion—her cathedral.

Of the other things of interest that can be seen in Spain's erstwhile metropolis, no one should miss two other unusual places. One is the Church of the Sacred Family, a good example of the *art nouveau* style of architecture conceived by several Catalan architects of a century ago. This church rises up high on one side in a combination of Victorian and flaring *art nouveau*; on its other side it is "not at all," for the architect was killed in an accident and no one of his colleagues wanted to carry out his radical project. Thus today services can be held in it only on clear days, or else in its underground crypt when it rains.

The other unusual attraction of Barcelona is the Spanish People's Exposition, a reproduction of all of Spain's most typical architectural monuments created for an Ibero-American exposition in 1929. The traveler can wander through the narrow streets of old Spain, changing from province to province, and enjoying re-created façades, towers, and patios copied from all the places in Spain he may not have time to visit himself. Various handicrafts, such as metal-working and pottery-making, are carried on in small shops, with the finished articles on sale.

Most travelers who find themselves in Barcelona set aside an extra day for the drive out to the famous monastery shrine of Monserrat, a holy place so sacred in Spanish history that its name is found in most Latin American cities, and it also is memorialized by an island in the West Indies named by Columbus.

Monserrat, only twenty-two miles inland from Barcelona, has been a holy site for over twelve centuries. A chapel housing an image of the Virgin was first set up in the ninth century, and the weirdness of the mountain formation surrounding it added to its appeal. For a rugged "saw-toothed peak" (the translation of "Monserrat") rises at the head of the narrow valley, giving a backdrop of exciting proportions. The large basilica now built in honor of its richly decorated image of the Virgin was set up in the sixteenth century, and there are many other chapels, holy grottoes, and sacred figures on the mountainside above this great building. It is generally considered that Monserrat is the Monsalvat of Wagner's opera *Parsifal,* the sacred mountain in which his quest for the Holy Grail was brought to its thunderous climax.

Envoi to Spain

No one chapter like this could do justice to the richness of travel in Spain. The areas far from the shores of the Mediterranean will have to be left undescribed in our portrayal of the Middle Sea's Pageant. But many modern-day travelers will eventually want to go to Madrid; to pause in Toledo, painted so imperishably by El Greco, with its Roman bridge, and the battle-shattered Alcázar; to see the great pilgrimage center of Santiago de Compostela, the medieval cities of León, Oviedo, and Valladolid, and historic Segovia, whose Roman aqueduct has survived the centuries intact as a symbol of the noble Roman monuments that once dotted the rich and loyal province of Hispania.

SUEZ CANAL

Revivifier of the Middle Sea

VERY LITTLE IMPORTANT HISTORY was created in the Mediterranean area for three hundred years after the Battle of Lepanto in 1571. By tacit agreement of the Moslem and Christian powers, the beautiful blue Middle Sea was left as a no man's land between them.

During those three centuries of relative inaction, a stagnant commercial depression settled over the lands occupying the sea's coasts. Venice slid from her position of the world's foremost maritime power. Genoa lost her independence to her neighbors. Other ports slowly declined to impotence. Alexandria in Egypt, for instance, had sunk to less than five thousand people by the year 1830.

The Mediterranean was a dead-end sea. The Ottoman Turkish Empire wound around the entire eastern half of its shores like a slumbering dragon. The Levantine ports under its control lost their lucrative caravans from the East, because their cargoes had long since been diverted by the treasure fleets of the Portuguese. The world's commerce had taken to the open Atlantic. British, French, Portuguese, and Dutch merchant ships plodded along the well-blazed lanes around the Cape of Good Hope, bypassing the Turks and the Arabs, and in the process building up empires for themselves in India and the many Spice Islands of the Indian Ocean.

The Mediterranean Sea was blocked up as if by a plug. It was a sea leading to nowhere. Except for the depredations of the Barbary pirates, and the hot flash of war brought to its waters by Napoleon and Lord Nelson, it made little news in the European annals of the seventeenth, eighteenth, and early nineteenth centuries. It counted for nothing in the realm of world trade.

Ferdinand de Lesseps

This situation, however, suddenly began to change. Napoleon came and went, revolutionizing the political map of Europe. The industrial revolution then followed. Northern European countries began to launch fledgling industries that manufactured wide ranges of valuable new products. To keep their machines supplied, raw materials came into greater and greater demand. Ocean traffic then extended farther afield into strange distant seas seeking for these materials. Steamships were invented to enable this commerce to move faster and on a more regular basis.

This industrial revolution put northern Europe far ahead of the Mediterranean countries in population, wealth, and useful resources.

An ambitious Frenchman was undoubtedly aware of this shifting balance of world power when he traveled to Egypt in 1836 on a consular assignment. He was Ferdinand de Lesseps, of a prominent French family with business connections in Egypt. He was considerably impressed by a plan Napoleon had conceived of digging a canal across Egypt's Isthmus of Sinai to connect the Mediterranean and Red Seas. His plan had been shelved when an engineer wrongly calculated that the Red Sea was thirty-three feet higher than the Mediterranean and that locks would therefore be needed at terrific expense.

The idea of such a canal became an obsession with De Lesseps, for there seemed to be nothing else of a formidable nature to prevent such an undertaking. The distance between the two seas was only one hundred miles, and not all of that would need to be scooped out, because of several depressions that had once been the upper tip of the Red Sea. The surface of the land was flat desert, nowhere reaching higher than sixty-five feet above sea level. The terrain had been thoroughly explored, for it formed part of the land bridge between Egypt and Asia, over which invaders had poured during the centuries. Joseph and his brethren,

Moses and the Children of Israel, Jeremiah and the Christ Child, Persians, Assyrians, hosts of the Pharaohs, the Moslem Arabs, and Napoleon himself had crossed over this strategic and unbarred stretch of sand.

Egypt, which owned the Suez-Sinai isthmus, was at that time a self-governing province of the Turkish Empire. It had been turned into an orderly and progressive realm by its Albanian-born dictator Mohammed Ali. Shortly after this strong man had died, De Lesseps had reached the conclusion that he could swing the canal by his own promotional abilities. He had been informed that Napoleon's engineer had been wrong in his statistics of the varying sea levels. Thus the only problem would be to scoop out a sand ditch across the level desert. This would obviously lower the cost down to a level easily within reach of world financiers. Besides, he had learned that a canal had been dug in ancient times. Rameses the Great, fifteen centuries before Christ, had built one from the Nile delta to the Gulf of Suez that passed through the land of Goshen, where the children of Israel were then settled. Long after the canal had fallen into disuse, one of the last of Egypt's Pharaohs began to repeat the enterprise, until an oracle of the gods bade him stop lest it encourage the Persians to invade his weakened kingdom.

The Pharaoh desisted, but the Persians came anyway. Their King Darius actually finished the canal at about 550 B.C., and when it too had been dried up, the Romans once again put it into working order one hundred years after Christ. Remnants of the course of this old canal, wide enough for two triremes to be rowed abreast, can still be seen.

So in the year 1854, De Lesseps obtained the consent of Mohammed Said, the new Viceroy of Egypt, to his scheme. The French promoter was given the sole right to form a company for the purpose of making the canal, this concession to last for ninety-nine years after the completion of the project.

This was a most important step, but also the easiest one. De Lesseps' skill as a promoter was to be taxed to the utmost before the isthmus was ever cut through. He next went to Constantinople to secure the approval of the Sultan; then to Paris to call a conference of European engineers for their approval and support. This was followed by technical explorations of the site, all resulting in favorable reports.

De Lesseps, now convinced that he was on the trail of a profitable idea, appealed to the Viceroy for more support. Again Mohammed Said came through quickly, granting large tracts of lands, some mines, and a quarry to his friend. He also agreed to declare that the eventual canal was to be neutral both in peace and war, and would be open to the ships of all nations without preference.

The next step was to form the company to construct the canal, and this was quickly done. Its name was to be the Compagnie Universelle du Canal Maritime de Suez. By agreement with the Viceroy, 15 per cent of its yearly profits were to be paid to the Egyptian Government, 70 per cent to the shareholders, and 10 per cent to De Lesseps.

Publicity work was next started, with business men of Britain, France, and Germany contacted by the promoter and other enthusiasts. Yet when the 400,000 shares were put on sale late in 1858, only a little more than half of them were taken up, most of them by small French investors. This threatened to be a setback in De Lesseps' plans, but to prevent any delay in the project, the Egyptian Viceroy came forward with funds to subscribe for the unsold 176,000 shares. Accordingly, the Company signed a contract with a French construction company, and the surveys began at last.

Next step was to pick a spot on the barren coast of the Mediterranean to serve as the entrance to the canal. At length, on April 25, 1859, Ferdinand de Lesseps stood on the beach and struck the first blow of the pick which meant the start of construction. The sand and soil excavated by the twenty-five thousand workmen toiling under the broiling sun piled up a foundation for the new city of Port Said, named in honor of the beneficent Viceroy.

Water was needed badly by these working gangs. Camels were unable to bring enough for the need, so that the Company had to defer its labors in order to build another canal—one that would bring fresh water from the Nile. A depression in the isthmus was selected as a meeting point and called "Lake" Timsah. In nine months seven thousand workmen had dug the fresh water channel to this ditch. Later on in that same year, 1862, the canal was completed to the same spot twenty-five miles south of the Mediterranean. The salt waters of the Middle Sea were then allowed to fill up the new lake. A town was built on the shores of this pleasant spot amid the desert sands.

Early in 1863 Viceroy Mohammed Said was succeeded by Ismail, who turned out to be an even greater enthusiast for this enterprise that was transforming his country. In his honor the newly built town on Lake Timsah was called Ismailia.

The next year De Lesseps obtained the right from Ismail to use machine dredges in place of the slower workmen, so that the work proceeded swiftly ahead, mile by mile. At length, in the summer of 1869 the big ditch was completed, as the waters of the Mediterranean mingled with those from the Red Sea in the newly created "Bitter Lakes."

Grand Opening

Yet the commerce of the world was not to be allowed to use the canal until Ismail could complete his plans for a Grand Opening. The pleasure-loving ruler plunged into the lending market to raise funds for an Oriental-style jamboree. He commissioned the Italian composer Verdi to write him an opera and ordered an opera house to be built in Cairo within three months. The crowned heads of Europe were invited to attend its première performance. A splendid avenue was likewise laid out from Cairo to the Pyramids of Gizeh for their benefit.

When the arrangements were completed, the command opera, named *Aïda*, was put on with great splash. The honor guest was Eugénie, Empress of France, representing her absent husband Napoleon III. The young Emperor Francis Joseph of Austria, Crown Prince Frederick of Prussia, the heir apparent of the Netherlands, and lesser statesmen from all European countries were among those present in the glittering audience.

And then on November 17, 1869, the canal was declared open. The French imperial yacht *Aigle*, with Eugénie aboard, led a solemn procession of sixty-eight vessels into the cut, symbolizing the dawn of a new era.

This ostentation was in the proper spirit for such an undertaking. The Suez Canal made a hit from the start. Over seven hundred ships passed through in the first year. The world's sea lanes were shortened by thousands of miles in contrast to the old-fashioned route around the southern tip of Africa.

For instance, ships bound from north European ports to Bombay now found that they saved 4,300 miles of steaming and almost two weeks of time. Connections between Europe and China were likewise cut 3,400 miles.

Such an impact on world commerce had almost overnight results. The old sea lanes around South Africa were scrapped. Commercial navigation companies hastened to use the Suez Canal. Steamers flying the flags of all Europe funneled together at Port Said for the one-day passage through the canal that saved fourteen whole days for fast ships, and twice that time for slow freighters.

No wonder that De Lesseps' Compagnie Universelle began coining gold dividends from the start. At the same time, world shipping profited immensely by savings in operating their ships, in addition to building up extra profits through their ability to compete for new and more accessible cargoes.

Finally, the whole Mediterranean basin profited. European freight tended to cross the Alps to southern ports for transshipment. Genoa, Marseilles, and Naples began to take on a sudden new life as ships crowded into their ports for these cargoes. Austria-Hungary, an empire growing in economic strength, plunged into the investment of constructing an elaborate port at Trieste, realizing that the Adriatic Sea had become a direct road to the outside world instead of a dreamy backwater.

Passengers traveling the new route from Britain to India found that their former journey could be cut in half if they took to the railroads and traveled overland to Marseilles—or even down the entire length of the Italian boot to the sleepy village of

Brindisi, from which it was only three days of relatively smooth sailing to Port Said—entrance port to the East.

The revitalizing of the Mediterranean by this single event of opening the canal brought other momentous consequences in its train that were not so constructive. World strategy was revolutionized, for the lands surrounding the Suez Canal area took on new importance in the European balance of power.

Also, the great profits being earned by the Suez Canal company began to attract the envy of certain world powers. It seemed only a matter of time before one of them—Germany, Great Britain, France, Russia, or Austria-Hungary—would seize the canal, not only for its mounting income, but in order to shut out rivals from beating them to it and excluding the rest of the world. The Concert of Europe was becoming a rasping discord as its members fell to grabbing territories, treaties, and allies indiscriminately.

Great Britain was particularly perturbed over the strategic weak spot existing in Suez. The British had disapproved of the Suez Canal project from the start, and had done everything they could to discourage investment in it. Their distrust of everything French led them to fear this French enterprise threatening to short-circuit their mastery over the sea lanes to the East. However, when the canal opened in 1869 in spite of their efforts, the British found themselves paradoxically the chief gainers. The road to India being swifter and more secure, British steamship lines outscored those of all other countries in parading through it.

Thus Britain found herself paying most of the tolls and at the same time being reduced to dangerous dependence on a weak, unprotected, foreign-owned commercial company for her main imperial communications channels.

The British therefore took advantage of every political development to end these acute disadvantages. The first occurred late in 1875. Britain, moving like a lion, completed her move inside forty-eight hours. Hearing that the Khedive Ismail of Egypt was thinking of marketing his huge block of 176,000 shares in the Compagnie Universelle to stave off bankruptcy, Britain's Prime

Minister Benjamin Disraeli saw his chance. Having contacted the Khedive, he borrowed £4,000,000 (almost $20,000,000) from the House of Rothschild in the name of the British Government, bought the shares, and closed the deal. Britain thus became a 43 per cent shareholder in the canal Company. Parliament gasped at being bypassed so sharply, but Britain solidly approved the step, which, incidentally, proved quite profitable, as these shares have paid for themselves over and over again through the years.

In 1878 the British won from the Sultan of Turkey the right to garrison the island of Cyprus, only 230 miles off the northern end of the canal. This partly reduced the danger of a power vacuum, putting British forces nearer the pivotal area than those of any other great power.

Then, four years later, Britain took an even more decisive step. To prevent Egyptian bankruptcy and protect British holders of the nation's foreign debt, a British force landed at Alexandria in 1882 to reestablish order after an antiforeign riot had been raging for several days. Moving swiftly to Cairo, Britain, with French support, proclaimed a joint protectorate over the whole of Egypt. The principal purpose of this was to restore financial stability to the country, but as the years went on, Britain's Resident-Generals[1] extended their influence into many other fields of economic activity. Railroads were built, the Assuan Dam erected, scientific methods of agriculture pushed, fiscal reforms introduced, and integration with European financial systems completed. In 1898 Lord Kitchener advanced from Egypt up the Nile into the chaotic Sudan, as a result of which campaign a joint Anglo-Egyptian condominium was established over that vast territory reaching almost to the sources of the Nile at the equator.

Britain's presence in Egypt had an immediate effect on the administration of the Suez Canal. Tolls were reduced, pilotage taxes abolished, and various improvements in services effected. Garrisons were introduced to defend the canal against any military menace. By the end of the century the Suez Canal had been

---

[1] Most famous of them was Evelyn Baring, Lord Cromer. The French had withdrawn from any connection with the British Protectorate in 1884.

widened and deepened, over three thousand ships were using it each year, and the city of Port Said had become the greatest emporium in the Near East. Because all ships had to halt there to pay their canal tolls and load up with coal, their passengers had time to wander through this newly built city and shop for tropical as well as Oriental merchandise. The population soared up to the one hundred thousand mark, making De Lesseps' city the third in size in this one-time land of the Pharaohs.

And what of Monsieur de Lesseps? He had left the scene of his triumph in order to lead another French company that was determined to build a canal across the Isthmus of Panama. But here his capabilities proved to be a pitfall. The lessons learned in digging the Suez Canal across a flat desert were worse than useless in dealing with the tough topography of Panama. Harnessing gangs of workers to digging a sea-level ditch across the jungle-clad mountains of tropical mid-America smashed his most energetic efforts. After completing eight miles of waterway from the Caribbean, the company went bankrupt and all work stopped.

However, even though Ferdinand de Lesseps lost his fortune in this fiasco and passed away in 1894 as a pauper, his last great work was not entirely wasted. Only nine years after his death, the United States Government bought out the property of the French company and used its choice of route for its own successful canal. The United States succeeded where De Lesseps had failed because it was able to wipe out tropical diseases, install massive locks, and invent more efficient machines.

Egypt and Suez

Notwithstanding that Great Britain had taken firm hold of the Suez area and brought strategic stability to the Near East, it began to be harassed by Egypt's attitude toward all that it had done.

Politics in Cairo were anti-foreign from the start. Britain strove to placate political leaders by granting self-government and keeping out of religious matters. Yet the Egyptians remained hostile to anybody who kept them from controlling the Suez Canal themselves.

Two world wars contributed to delaying Egypt's rise to full control of the canal zone inside her territory. World strategy demanded stability, at this zone of "tender nerves," so the Egyptian politicians quickly learned that they could extract rich concessions from the British by jeopardizing that stability. Thus Anglo-Egyptian relations since 1900 were marked by a steady retreat of Britain's control from Egypt, but paradoxically, with Britain's hold on the Suez Canal firmer and tighter than before.

The first crisis in the situation came in 1914, when World War I swept over the world. Turkey joined Germany in October, whereupon Britain immediately detached Egypt and Cyprus from any further allegiance to the Sultan at Constantinople. The Turks countered by mounting an attack on the Suez Canal on February 3, 1915. British and Indian troops pushed back this stab before it could do any damage. Shortly afterward the canal area was used as a staging zone for Australian and New Zealand troops (the Anzacs) who soon arrived in strength to join in Britain's defense either in faraway France or here in the Near East.

As a shield for Suez, the British used the Anzacs to push back the Turks, not only in the Sinai peninsula, but at the Dardanelles also. The Arabs of the desert were led by Lawrence of Arabia's diplomacy to a rising against the Turks, and with their cooperation, Britain's army under General Allenby advanced across the Sinai desert—building a railway and water pipe as it went—and then pushed victoriously through Palestine and Syria to the borders of Turkey proper.

When the war ended, the British rewarded Egypt by granting her official independence in 1922 and recognizing her Khedive as a full King. Fourteen years later, in 1936, they made a final treaty providing for their withdrawal from Egypt to the Suez Canal area itself, but with certain reservations to apply in case of any outbreak of war.

These reservations soon proved of critical value, for with the oncoming of World War II Britain was in a weaker strategic position than in 1914. German and Italian bombings of the canal blocked its usefulness on several occasions. Italo-German armies under Marshal Rommel invaded Egypt from the west. For two years while Europe was under the heel of Hitler's armies, Britain was able to launch attacks on mighty Germany only from her faraway base at the Suez Canal. Convoys of armaments were unloaded at the port of Suez to sustain the savage battles in the western desert. From June to November of 1942 the Germans' front line stood at Alamein, only sixty miles from Alexandria and the Nile delta. Britain's possession of Egypt and Suez alone saved the world from a perilous setback; her strong stand kept the Germans from breaking into the Near East and striking for a union with the Japanese armies threatening India.

The end of the war brought British evacuation of all of Egypt except the zone of the Suez Canal. Political jingoism among Egypt's rival politicians led King Farouk to repudiate the 1936 Treaty five years before it was due to lapse. As the British ignored the gesture, riots in Cairo destroyed much British property the following year (including Shepheards Hotel). Despite his concurrence in this outburst of nationalistic defiance, Farouk was overthrown by a coterie of army officers in 1953. Thus Egypt was declared a republic for the first occasion in her timeless history.

Despite the ensuing strain in British-Egyptian relations, London decided to withdraw her military garrisons from the Suez Canal ahead of time. The Union Jack was solemnly hauled down after waving for almost a century over this crucial waterway in the Middle East.

What followed was a galling blow to British pride. General Nasser, leader of the Cairo regime, suddenly invaded the Zone, nationalized the Canal and dissolved the Suez Canal Company's operations in Egypt twelve years before they were due to expire.

A world crisis suddenly flared up as a result. Neighboring Israel launched an invasion of the Sinai Peninsula, followed by British and French landings at Port Said. General Nasser then blocked the Canal by ordering every tugboat, barge and dredge to be sunk where it stood.

At American instigation, the United Nations demanded and achieved a cease-fire by all parties, with their troops withdrawn from Egypt (even by Israel) by the end of 1956.

Nasser's closing of the Canal had thrust a dangerous oil shortage on all European countries. Sir Anthony Eden, architect of Britain's strike at Egypt, fell from power, while France nursed her wounds in brooding silence, unnerved because the Canal Company had been her most successful and thriving international venture.

Even after the United Nations had cleared the Canal of its obstructions, so that the channel was opened again for the commerce of the world, the world observed that one of its economic jugular veins—the sandy ditch at Suez—still lay at the mercy of a single country, a situation that would have brought paroxysms of fear and trembling to international statesmen of preceding eras.

The world crisis dissipated without achieving a definitive settlement for the future. No guarantee has been obtained from Egypt that she will keep the Canal open in peace and war to all comers, irrespective of flags, as the Viceroy Mohammed Said had committed her to doing a century before when he spurred De Lesseps' company to construct the Canal.

During the year 1960 over 16,000 vessels passed through the strategic waterway. The greatest proportion of these were British, followed by Norwegian, Liberian, Italian, French and German in that order. The principal cargo carried through is oil, the lifeblood of 20th Century industrial prosperity. Priceless cargoes of metals, rubber, jute, foodstuffs and armaments also utilize this short-cut route through the earth's bulkiest land mass.

The Suez Canal cost about $73,000,000 in 1875 values to complete. Since it takes in almost $30,000,000 every year, it has easily proved itself one of the world's most profitable ventures.

As an outcome of the hapless embroilment of this engineering enterprise with the hot fires of nationalistic fervor, the impressive statue of Ferdinand de Lesseps was dynamited into dust during the troubles of 1956. Standing for decades at the northern portal of the Canal at Port Said, it portrayed the founder gazing paternally out into the blue Mediterranean, the sea whose economic life he did more than any other one man to restore to health.

Yet homage is still paid to him by passing travelers, even if in silence, for his Canal has proved more vital to this globe of ours than he ever dreamed. His motto, blazed on the surviving pedestal of his unhappy statue summarizes the most lasting of all the successes of the Suez Canal—*"Aperire Terram Gentibus"*—"To open up the dry land to (all) peoples!"

ADRIATIC WATERS

Sunny Dalmatia

THE MEDITERRANEAN SEA has two subsidiary extensions that, like prongs, reach far away from the parent sea into the colder northlands. One of these is called the Adriatic Sea, the other the Black Sea.

The Adriatic, running straight and narrow directly up to the foothills of the Alps, is a sea lane that penetrates closer to the heartland of central Europe than any other body of water. The Black Sea, far to the east, edges up against the steppes of the Ukraine and touches the southern tip of Russia herself, where the Cossacks have their homes along the Don River.

These northward-stretching offshoots of the Middle Sea enclose a controversial peninsula, the misunderstood "dark and bloody land" known as the Balkans. On this wide peninsula there is room for four whole countries—Rumania, Yugoslavia, Bulgaria, and Albania—and parts of two others—Hungary and Turkey— plus the whole of Greece dangling farther south into the warmest waters of the Mediterranean.

This largest of Europe's peninsulas derives its name from the Balkan Mountains, which form the spine of the country known as Bulgaria. The word "Balkan" is Turkish for "mountain" and it is apt indeed, for mountains abound in every Balkan country. Some of these mountains are grand and Alpine, like the Carpathians of Rumania; others are rocky, arid, and forbidding, like the Bosnian ranges of Yugoslavia, where Tito's Partisan bands held out against the Germans for three long years.

The Balkan Peninsula abounds in valuable resources. The mines of Yugoslavia produce copper, lead, bauxite, and also very useful mercury. Bulgaria's rolling downs have always grown excellent flax, and acres of blooming roses, tended for their production of attar for perfumes. Bulgaria and Greece are large exporters of Turkish tobacco. Forests still grow almost untouched by the woodsmen in the high Carpathians of Rumania, and on the lofty Julian Alps of Yugoslavia. Petroleum—almost nonexistent in the rest of Europe—gushes forth plentifully in Rumania, and more parsimoniously in Albania.

Sprinkled through the Balkan countries are reminders of the relentless masters of olden days. Medieval castles, with dungeons, towers, and drawbridges, crown many hilltops in northern Yugoslavia and the fastnesses of Rumania's beautiful province of Transylvania. Grimmer forts, ready for instant action, are still inhabited in Albania. Monasteries rich in mosaics installed in them during the centuries of Byzantine control still exist in inaccessible valleys of southern Serbia, Albania, and Bulgaria. Mosques, with slender minarets of Arabian ancestry, cluster thickly in Yugoslav Bosnia, all over Albania, in Macedonia, and along the Black Sea coast of Rumania and Bulgaria, lands inhabited until last century by descendants of the Tartars.

Many religions and races are mixed into the veins of the people of this smilingly beautiful, yet overly warred-for peninsula. In the beginning the land was Christianized by the energetic missionaries of Justinian's Constantinople. The Greek ritual and liturgy, Greek styles of church architecture modeled on St. Sophia by the Bosporus, and the semi-Greek alphabet devised by St. Cyril and St. Methodius were adopted by the Serbs and Bulgars, Rumanians, Ukrainians, Russians, and the Macedonians and Illyrians.

However, as Constantinople's sun waned, the light from Rome grew brighter. Slavic tribes living near the Adriatic and in the corners of Balkan lands nearest to Italy were converted by missionaries from Rome.

Thus the dividing line between East and West ran down through the axis of the Balkan Peninsula. Astride the axis itself, however, the Slavs of what is now called the province of Bosnia disagreed with both rites of Christianity and practiced a form of worship that was closely identified with nature symbols, but whose details have been lost to us as a result of the Crusades launched against them by the Pope and the Hungarians. These free-believers called themselves Bogumils ("pleasing to God"), but their exact beliefs are lost to our scholars. For with the coming of the Turks in the fourteenth century, the harassed Bogumils gave up the unequal struggle and turned Mohammedan almost to a man.

The arrival of the Turks in Europe is the source of the blight that killed off Balkan progress. As dwellers on the land bridge between Turkish power and Christian Europe, the Balkan peoples found no peace and less freedom for five hundred years. The whole land fell under the Crescent except for the Mediterranean coastline of Dalmatia, and the tiny free state of Montenegro. The Albanians, many Macedonians, and some Bulgars were converted to the faith of the Prophet. The land of the Balkans was cut off from European thought almost down till our own times.

The Balkans Fenced Off From the Mediterranean

The races on the Balkan Peninsula were not given a chance to mix into a common denominator by the time the Turks arrived, and the results of such an arrested development have been dire.

Original inhabitants of this strategic land were a mysterious people, called Illyrians by the Greeks and Romans. Semicivilized by four centuries under Roman rule, they were no match for the heathen Slavs who started moving into their homeland after the fifth century. Instead they retreated into the mountains along a rugged stretch of seacoast. The Albanians of today are considered to be the descendants of the Illyrians.[1]

No one knows for sure where the Slavs came from, except to deduce that they lived for many centuries in the Ukraine and in southern Poland along the northern slopes of the Carpathians. When some great pressure hit them from farther out in space—

---

[1] Shakespeare mentions "the coast of Illyria" as the scene of the shipwreck in *Twelfth Night.*

probably an invasion by Tartars, Huns, or Goths—they packed up and followed around the Carpathian range into the almost uninhabited Byzantine lands of the Balkans. They infiltrated gradually westward as they were enticed or pushed. The Slovenes, vanguard of Slavdom, had settled in the beautiful Alpine dells of southern Austria by the seventh century. Other Slavs, ancestors of the Croats and Bosnians, had broken through to the Adriatic even before that time, burning the Roman cities and scaring the effete Roman colonists into fleeing for safety across the Adriatic.[2]

The Balkan people, though located so close to the Mediterranean's long arms, the Adriatic and Black Seas, were "fenced off" through many centuries from any effects coming from the lands across those seas. Rugged mountains shut them off from the Adriatic to the west and the Aegean to the south; while the east was plugged by the Turks and the Russians. Thus they fell prey to forces coming from the wide-open north—from hostile and feudalistic Hungary, from disdainful Hapsburg Austria, and from avaricious German lands beyond. These forces pushed their way down the blue Danube, which, like an unguarded highway, leads from Teuton lands into the very heart and soul of the Balkan nations.

Likewise, the climate is another factor shutting the Balkan peoples off from the Mediterranean. Steep mountains bring the balmy winds and the sunny zephyrs to a stop before they have penetrated over twenty miles inland from the Adriatic and the Aegean.

Thus the Balkan people derived their ways of life from cold northern influences, with the exception of their religion and their alphabet, which were derived from Mediterranean sources.

But the paradox lies in this point—that being "out" of Mediterranean affairs and racial families, they were definitely "in" the Mediterranean picture because they became a battleground between warring Mediterranean powers, occupying a land bridge over which the battling forces were smashing away to "get at" each other, thus shattering the fledgling Balkan kingdoms to bits in the process.

---

[2] One of these groups founded the Republic of San Marino in 476.

Sun-kissed Dalmatia

Sole exception to this unhappy picture of conflict was the sunny land of Dalmatia, the long, narrow, shelflike coastline of the Balkan Peninsula facing the Adriatic Sea. Here, the truly Mediterranean climate, the gorgeous scenery of mountains meeting the deep-blue sea, the rocky inlets and charming offshore islands combined to make a showplace of Nature second to no other place in Europe.

Dalmatia is the land of orange and fig trees, of ruby tomatoes and silver sardines, of lemons and cherries. It is the homeland of the maraschino cherry, by the way. Its towns are all taken right out of picture books. The water of the Adriatic is so clear that every boat in the tiny harbors seems to be floating on air. Great men like the Emperor Diocletian and Richard the Lion-Hearted figure in its long history. Its churches, squares and public buildings look as if transplanted directly from Venice, but yet not quite, for the delicate tracery of arches and rich art inside the churches were executed by Slavic pupils of Venetian masters, whose touch is quite individualistic to all who have eyes to see.

Approximately halfway down the long, narrow coast of Dalmatia is its chief port city of Split.[3] Here is a unique town, which has grown up inside a palace! The Emperor Diocletian, tired of his civil wars and his bloody persecutions of Christians in the arenas of Rome, abdicated in the year A.D. 310 and retired to the coast of Dalmatia, "to find peace and raise cabbages." He built himself a huge "palace"—rather it was a walled city, complete with arches, porticoes, straight streets and tightly clustered houses in the true Roman fashion. His marble-lined Temple of Jupiter now serves as a church, crowned with an incongruous Venetian steeple. Two hundred years after Diocletian, frantic refugees from the near-by city of Salona stampeded from the Slavs into this palace. It has remained a city to this day, with clotheslines hung out from arched Roman windows, and medieval homes resting on unchanged Roman colonnades. A modern nineteenth century city has grown up around the original walled palace, making Diocletian's last haven

---

[3] Dalmatian names given in this chapter are printed in their Yugoslav spelling. Until 1918 Split was known by its Italian-Venetian name of Spalato.

the largest port of Dalmatia. It was always a hospitable liberty port for the British navy. It is also a city once famed for its ballads and love songs honoring its pretty hill known as Mount Marijan, Split's favorite park-with-a-view.

Equally popular with travelers is the Dalmatian town of Dubrovnik,[4] 150 miles down the Adriatic coast. This city is really exquisite. To view from one's hotel window its medieval ramparts jutting out into the placid Adriatic waters—lit by a lazy moon— transports the onlooker into the most romantic picture he could conceive of. Dubrovnik is a gem of the graceful Venetian type, walled away from the steep coast, built on a peninsula that alone gives it perching space. Just offshore is the cypress-crowned island of Lokrum, an idyllic spot that Hapsburg royalty used to visit on their honeymoons.

Through a twentieth century miracle Dubrovnik came through World War II without damage, a reward for its charm that captivated all the hostile forces that held it for a time—Italian Fascists, Croatian Ustashi terrorists, the German army and navy.

This miracle gives us a glimpse at what a proud medieval city-republic looked like in the days of its glory. Just as Dubrovnik stood off the Axis invaders of today, so it held at bay the menacing Turkish armies of Sultan Solyman four hundred years ago, and scheming Venetian diplomats through several centuries. Dubrovnik's pretty charm is definitely heightened by the recollection that it was the only "torch" for oppressed southern Slavs during the era of Turkish supremacy. In this picture-book walled city the first printing press for the Slav lands of the Balkans was installed.

The fact that Dubrovnik retained its vigorous independence during the epoch of Venetian hegemony in the Adriatic is not only a tribute to its own ingenuity, but also a legend of pride shared by the Yugoslav peoples of the interior behind. Venice early "discovered" the beauteous Dalmatian coast. Her fleets took constant advantage of its sheltered bays and islands while making the long tack southward bound for the rich trade of the Levant. In the twelfth century Venice found herself opposed by an ambitious Hungarian dynasty seeking a firm outlet to the sea.

---

[4] Originally known as Ragusa.

At length the Venetians enlisted the aid of Crusaders bound for Egypt to seize the port of Zadar,[5] which was the chief base of their enemies.

The Dalmatian cities one by one gave their allegiance to Venice, except for little Dubrovnik. This town decided to bank on its own fleets and diplomats for its defense. Its well-built trading ships gave the word "argosy" to our language in tribute to their majestic appearance. For many years the Republic of Ragusa lived in alliance with Venice, importing artists, painters, and sculptors from the "Queen City" of the Adriatic to beautify its crowded city. Venetian-style loggias, markets, and monasteries were thus erected, with a charm of style that fits harmoniously into the town's quaint natural setting.

For its trade, Dubrovnik depended on its Balkan hinterland, receiving fruits and foodstuffs, minerals and grains, which it traded to Venice and Naples in return for manufactures from the Levant or from Italy.

The advent of the Renaissance, however, dealt a blow at the free city of Dubrovnik from which it failed to recover. Unlike Venice, whose imperial holdings and business investments enabled it to weather the crisis of the loss of its Mediterranean carrying trade to the Portuguese after the influx of the Ottoman Turks, Dubrovnik's sources of trade withered away. The Turks, by overrunning Serbia and Bosnia, dried up the Balkan trade that once coursed down to the Adriatic. The Turkish frontier itself was advanced to within a score of miles of Dubrovnik.

Thus the hard laws of economics whittled away the city's liberties, until it found it expedient to enter a partial union with Venice, retaining its home rule but dovetailing its business interests with the "Serenissima" government of the Queen City.

Thus Dalmatia sank back into the lethargy that settled over the entire Mediterranean during the seventeenth and eighteenth centuries. The towns along the sun-kissed shore basked in idleness, conserving their beautiful medieval buildings and toy-boat harbors, cultivating their plots of land, and tending their forts for fear of the encroaching Turkish hosts.

---

[5] Known formerly as Zara.

The Napoleonic Interlude

This decadent and stagnant idyl was sharply terminated by the advance of Napoleon Bonaparte's revolutionary armies carrying the torch of the French Revolution.

Napoleon forced Austria to surrender its entire coastline and retire back into the Alps where it had been spawned centuries before. Venice he kept for himself, but not knowing much about the Dalmatian lands he found on his hands, he conjured up an "Illyrian Republic," allied to France but free to run its own internal affairs.

This afterthought of Napoleon's turned out to be a masterstroke in world affairs. The full-flowered code of republican France —liberty, fraternity, equality—galvanized the Illyrian peoples, made up of the inhabitants of Dalmatia, Croatia, and the Slovene lands at the northern tip of the Adriatic. The Illyrian Republic lasted for only four years, but the nineteenth century literati of Croatia and Dalmatia—the thinkers, writers, artists, and political leaders—all boasted that they had received their inspiration from what they had seen and learned during its beneficent existence.

The fall of Napoleon followed the end of Illyria. Austria got back its Venetian loot. Dalmatia, from Trieste all the way down to the Black Mountain of Montenegro, became an Austrian province. Dubrovnik, like its sister towns, and Venice itself, lost its autonomy and separateness. The proud aristocratic families struck back the only way they knew how—they vowed never to have children until they won back their rights and privileges. By the middle of the nineteenth century this class had died away.

Many years later a twist of fate brought the same destiny to a Hapsburg heir. Francis Ferdinand, Crown Prince of the Austrian Empire, landed at Dubrovnik in June, 1914, and took train for his interior city of Sarajevo. A few days later he was dead by an assassin's bullet, and Austria launched the war that brought the rule of the Hapsburgs and their motley empire to its sudden end.

Kotor and Its Fjord

Continuing down the rugged coast of Dalmatia from peaceful Dubrovnik, it is only sixty miles to one of the most spectacular sights of this whole entrancing land. The shore breaks into an opening, the entrance to a majestic fjord forty miles long, leading back into the very heart of the high mountains lining the province of Dalmatia.

Sailing up this placid bay, one always feels he is approaching its end, until a tiny strait opens up and what has appeared to be a solid mountain wall turns out to be a pivot for a further extension of this singularly fjordlike bay.

The Fjord of Kotor, or Bocche di Cattaro as called by the Venetians, is named for the tiny town at its inland tip—Kotor, or Cattaro. Today this town still clusters around its medieval castle at the foot of the rocky mountain backdrop. From it a zigzaggy road, built by the Austrians, crawls up a distance of two miles to what was the perennial boundary of Venice, and later of imperial Austria. But beyond that line was not the omnipotent, ubiquitous Turkish Empire. There stood instead one of the baggy-trousered, black-capped giants of the free state of the Black Mountain— Montenegro.

The story of this remarkable state is laden with legends spun around campfires through the centuries by Yugoslav troubadours to the accompaniment of their weird instrument of one lone string —the *guzla*. They sang of the terrible battle of Kossovo back in 1389 when the Turks crushed independent Serbia on the "field of the blackbirds." It was only hollow revenge when one of the wounded warriors penetrated into the tent of Sultan Murad the Conqueror and stabbed him to death. The Turks were invincible and treated the Christian vanquished as *rayah,* or less than cattle.

Refusing such a cowards' fate, a band of Serbs left the land of their fathers, retreating for their safety farther and farther away from the Turks. Only when they reached this barren and craggy region close to the Adriatic did they find the Turks giving up the chase. The Turkish battalions instead settled down to starve out the remnant who had been pushed high up on the Tsrna Gora, or "Black Mountain."[6]

But these warriors were of stern stuff. They hung on for decade after decade, farming in tiny patches on the mountainsides and

---

[6] Translated as "Montenegro" by Venetian geographers.

raiding the Turks for weapons, ammunition, and supplies. Their ruler was their Orthodox Bishop, whose heirs handed down the sceptre from uncle to nephew. Gradually these exiles carved out a small state for themselves. Then, when great Orthodox Russia entered the European stage, the Prince-Bishops joyfully formed an alliance with the Czars. To every Turk sneer at their small and hopeless size, the Montenegrins taunted back—"We and the Russians, we make 150,000,000!"

The Balkans and World Strategy

Life was settling into a new pace of semi-stagnation for Dalmatia when suddenly the Suez Canal was thrown open to world shipping in the autumn of 1869.

The Crown Prince of Austria[7] had gone down to the official opening ceremonies for no idle reason of gala show. His government realized that Suez meant bright new horizons for Austria and a place in the world's commercial sun at last.

As international trade stampeded from its former roundabout lanes of traffic to concentrate in Mediterranean waters leading to the "new ditch" of Suez, Austria took advantage of her strategic geographic situation. She built her cities of Trieste and Fiume into first-rate modern ports. Railroads were pushed across the Alps to connect them with landlocked producing areas in the heart of Europe. Austria's whole empire funneled its trade down to the Adriatic, and soon much of Germany's followed right after. Several shipping lines were created, making the run from Trieste to Suez in three short days.

When World War I ended in 1918, a brave new era dawned for the Balkan peoples. The treaties ending this mammoth war brought justice politically to the Balkans. National states were carved out of Austria, Hungary, and Russian borderlands. A united Yugoslavia came into being, comprising Serbia, Croatia, the Slovene lands, plus Dalmatia and Montenegro too.

Economic hardships brought about by high tariffs and autarchic governments undermined the unstable Balkan states. But they

---

[7] Rudolph of Hapsburg, who later committed the tragic suicide at Mayerling.

were culturally free at long last, and able to run their own interests without kowtowing to jealous, overweening powers. It is a tribute to this system of treaties, and to the good sense of the Balkan people themselves, that World War II—Hitler's war—did not break out in the Balkans or have anything to do with the Balkans. But when Germany sucked them into her maw two years later, she inherited a hornets' nest. And Nazi rule in the Balkans succeeded in imposing a common rule of misery over the whole peninsula, uniting the diverse peoples into the same tissue of sufferings, and causing a new crop of deathless legends to spring forth centering around the modern conquering hero "Tito, Tito, our fair white violet."

The present Communist dictatorship over the Balkans is the latest phase of the struggle of the peoples of that strategic peninsula to be able to live by themselves. In their common hate of this ruthless new medievalism in their lands, they welcome the day of liberation. And thoroughly confident they are that the satraps of Moscow and of mystical Russian-Slavic hegemony will go the way of even more fierce oppressors—the Turkish Janissaries, the Austro-Hungarian hussars, the German uhlans, the Italian Fascist blackshirts, the Nazi Gestapo storm troopers.

Ever-Smiling Dalmatia

Dalmatia, the heavenly vacationland, has emerged practically unscratched from the holocausts of the twentieth century. From its experience gained between the two World Wars, it expects to become one of the favorite holiday centers for Americans while the Iron Curtain gradually dissolves away from its sunny coastland.

Cozy yachtlike steamers can whisk American travelers to Dalmatian resorts from the convenient port of Venice in only a few hours.

Dalmatia, now entirely a part of Yugoslavia, comprises such semitropical holiday centers as Opatija (once Italy's swank beach resort of Abbazia) ; Crikvenica, just a stone's throw south of Fiume; the yachting island of Loshinj (Lussin) ; the lovely little Capri-like island of Rab; the fashionable island of Hvar, where American commandoes and navy men fought amid cabanas and villas against German garrisons in bringing support to Tito's men. Lovely Korchula, an island of grapes and oranges just a few paces off the rocky coast, with its yachts, sapphire seas for swimming, fairy-tale towns and churches. Makarska and Budva, tiny but comfortable beach towns, where epic stories of wartime bravery now enliven the leisurely evenings in such romantic, blissful settings. And always Split, Dubrovnik, Kotor, as centers to go back to reunions, hiring of sailboats or cars, excursions into the interior. And no one must ever gloss over Dubrovnik's little neighbor town of Tsavtat, a tiny harbor out at the end of a peninsula, where the villas are gayest, the water clearest, and its cemetery filled to bursting with creative monuments designed by Yugoslavia's great, exiled sculptor Mestrovic.

Most splendid attraction of Dalmatia, by far, is its magnificent people. Proud, colorfully dressed, generous, friendly, they never beg. Even the children do not know the meaning of asking for handouts. The barrier of language drops before the attractiveness of such strapping, independent, handsome, industrious folk as the Dalmatians, guardians of Slavdom's window on the Mediterranean.

ISLANDS AND STRAITS

History-Kissed

RISING ABOVE THE BRIGHT-BLUE WATERS of the Middle Sea several large islands lift their mountainous heads. Like sentinels standing offshore, they have served as havens for the early navigators, buttresses against hostile invaders, and rich prizes of war. These islands have shared in the fate of the lands nearest to them; yet have remained steadily individual, harboring people who cling to their own dialects and costumes; have fought for their own ideas of how they should be governed; and carried on occupations that they learned from their ancestors of millenniums ago.

Crete of the Sea Kings

One island that launched a civilization of its own is Crete. This is the fourth largest isle of the Mediterranean, 140 miles long and about 30 wide, plugging off by its location the wide-mouthed Aegean from the rest of the Middle sea. In its center Crete rises to the lovely peak known since earliest times as Mount Ida, over eight thousand feet higher than the adjacent waters, and capped with pure snow during half the year.

Crete took an early lead over its adjacent neighbors on the mainland by becoming the center of a productive, artistic civilization, to which has been given the name Minoan. As early as 4500 B.C., contemporary with the early dynasties of Egypt, this artistic way of life began developing in Crete. The rulers of the island were all named Minos, synonymous with "palace," just as the similar name Pharaoh in Egypt was a title borne by all the rulers of that land.

Near the heart of the island was founded their capital city of Knossos, located only four miles from the sea and from the modern city of Herakleion (also called Candia). The "sea kings" who ruled Crete were an ambitious lot. Their fleets covered the eastern half of the Mediterranean, trading with all the Greek islands and the entire Levant. Conjecture identifies the Cretans with the aboriginal Sikels of Sicily and goes so far as to deduce that the Philistines of the Holy Land were emigrants from Crete. Tradition also adds that Troy was founded by Cretans, and that its semi-legendary war described by Homer in his *Iliad* took place five centuries after Crete's Minoan life had come to a sudden end.

The artists of the island of Crete won renown far back in ancient history by their beautiful utensils of gold, frescoes of a seldom equaled exactness, and furnishings as beautifully wrought as those of Egypt. Frescoes at Knossos show that the Cretans wore modern-style costumes, engaged in sports, gave their women great freedom, and had devised a system of writing that was much more comprehensive than the simple alphabet invented later by the Phoenicians.

The full impact of this richly creative civilization of Crete was never even partly understood until the destroyed palace of Knossos was excavated by Sir Arthur Evans in 1893. Up to that time only legends handed down by the Greeks hinted at this miraculous series of achievements by the unknown Minoans. Once the mysterious writing found on tablets and palace walls can be deciphered, miracles will be divulged that will bring this vague knowledge we now have into fuller focus for our more complete wonderment.

Greek legends tell of Minos as having a palace built over a labyrinth[1] in which a fearsome beast known as the Minotaur dwelt, half-man, half-bull, who demanded a yearly tribute of youths and maidens from subject peoples. Because Athens finally rebelled, the Athenians have naturally made this beast quite vivid and

---

[1] The meaning of this word is "place of the two-headed axe," the royal emblem of the Minoan rulers.

atrocious. Athens eventually sent the semi-legendary Theseus, who slew the Minotaur and then eloped with the king's beauteous daughter Ariadne, who had facilitated his victory. However, archaeologists have reduced this legend to a more factual basis. The Minoans did breed huge bulls, shown on their frescoes of a stature to make modern Spanish fighting bulls look like midgets. The Minoans are believed to have been descended from Jupiter and beautiful Europa, a maiden who was brought to Crete on the back of a bull. However, the bulls of Minos were used in the palace courtyard for sport. One such challenge is well preserved on the frescoes at Knossos. It shows youths facing the dynamic charge of one of the huge bulls, seizing his horns at the precise second of impact, being tossed high by the bull's bucking head, turning a somersault in mid-air and landing squarely on the bull's back. This was naturally an exciting sport, and undoubtedly most of the Athenian novitiates were unable to master it at the first try, thus giving birth to the legend that they were fed to the bull, whom, to make more terrifying still, they named the Minotaur.

One of the most priceless of artistic treasures found at Knossos was a statuette of a bull-leaper wrought in pure ivory, somehow dropped by fortunate chance amid the debris by some hurried looters.

The close identification of bulls with the kings of Crete is another link connecting the Minoans with ancient Egypt, where bulls in the later dynasties became sacred, and then godlike, and finally were worshiped in a merger with Osiris, a bull-headed deity called Serapis.

Another legend having to do with Crete pays tribute to the possibility that the Minoans experimented with aviation. Daedalus, an artisan of the court, fashioned wings of wax in order to arrange a quick escape from some intrigue then affecting his welfare. He and his son Icarus actually took off, became airborne, and soared out to sea. Here legend parts from acute realism, as would be testified to by numberless aviators of the last war. Legend stated that the closer someone got to the sun, the hotter the air became, whereas wartime aviators with their electrically heated costumes would chorus otherwise. Thus the wax on Icarus' wings was supposed to have melted and tossed the helpless youth into the drink, while Daedalus, sagely flying lower, managed to make Sicily.

Another interesting legend connects Crete with the lost continent of Atlantis. Egyptian geographers described such a magnificent civilization in a way to place it where Crete is located. Plato, retelling the story centuries later, locates the lost continent out beyond the Pillars of Hercules.

At any rate, the magnificent reign of Minoan Crete came to an abrupt end about 1500 B.C. In the centuries before this time, invasions by Achaeans from Greece had caused much trouble, particularly since the gold-working Cretans were at a loss against the iron weapons of the newcomers. The Dorians, who came down later from the Balkans, wrought much havoc likewise. The learning the Achaeans took back from Crete led them to construct the first civilized towns of Greece—Mycenae and Tiryns in the near-by Peloponnesus. Probably these invasions, coupled with a series of earthquakes, brought about the culminating events that wrecked the palaces, ports, and homes of what is still a miraculously modern, even if half-mysterious, civilization.

Crete then sank back into obscurity as a colony for a long parade of foreign masters. First the Dorians, then the Phoenicians, the Athenians, the successors of Alexander the Great, next the Romans, and finally the Byzantine Empire. All these rulers were content to dominate the two chief ports of Canea and Herakleion, leaving the country people to themselves, so that the rural Cretans of today are still definitely of a Minoan cast, tall, lean, and slight-bearded.

For 150 years the Saracen sea raiders held the coast of Crete, rebuilding Herakleion into a fortress town that they renamed Candia. In A.D. 974 they were chased out in turn by the Byzantines, who resumed their control over this citadel of their empire until the disastrous capture of Constantinople by the Fourth Crusade in 1204. Thereupon the Venetians, chief mariners of that diverted expedition, immediately appropriated Crete for themselves, and it served them well as a way-station, outfitting base, trade emporium and colony for over four centuries.

The Venetians were expelled only after the Turks had besieged them for twenty-four years in the fort at Candia. By the time the Turks had won, in 1669, they had become such a weak power that Crete mostly went its own way for two more centuries, until the rise of an independent Greek kingdom on the mainland began to act as a magnet. After 1890 the Cretans launched several revolutions that were so successful that the European powers interfered to prevent any Turkish reprisals. By the year 1900 the only symbol left of Turkish sovereignty was its flag flying over Suda Bay.

Through these troubled times the islanders produced their first hero of international stature since Daedalus—Eleutherios Venizelos. This revolutionary-turned-statesman was called to Athens in 1910 to administer Greece itself, at a time when the little kingdom was harassed by its inability to expand against the Turks. Venizelos' program was to bury the hatchet with the Balkan states to the north, woo them as allies, and establish the Balkan League with Serbia and Bulgaria. Inside of two years he had gone to war with the Turks and proclaimed the annexation of Crete.

Crete's latest epoch of glory came in April of 1941 when Nazi Germany selected her as a laboratory for a new experiment in air attack developed by Hermann Goering. An entire airborne division was dropped on the island, suffering colossal losses, but finally forcing the outnumbered British, Greek, Australian, and New Zealand defenders to clear out. The world trembled at the appearance of this ruthless and squandered onslaught. But it turned out that Crete had absorbed the blow for the world. The Nazis had no more such air divisions.

Visitors to Crete today can go by small Greek steamers to the port of Candia, now renamed Herakleion, and motor to Knossos for an investigation of the achievements of the sea kings. They should also tour the countryside to gaze up at serene Mount Ida, to photograph the countless stubby windmills, to greet the proud inhabitants, who still wear the Turkified native costume, and to buy the olives, almonds, and oranges produced by this lovely island at the southern tip of Europe.

Cyprus, the "Sentinel Isle"

Three hundred miles to the east of Crete, tucked away in the northeastern tip of the Mediterranean Sea, stands the island of Cyprus. No small isle is this, either, for it is 140 miles long, and lined with a formidable mountain range in its interior.

Cyprus has not dominated history as Crete once did, for it has been too influenced by events on the mainland close at hand. Only 45 miles off the island's north coast rise the mountains of Asia Minor, now a part of the Republic of Turkey. And off to the eastward, only 65 miles away, can be seen on very clear days the high-pointed peaks of the Lebanon Mountains, located in the twin republics of Lebanon and Syria. And facing south, Cyprus is only 230 miles away from Egypt and the Suez Canal.

The energetic peoples of antiquity who dwelt on those three segments of the mainland, together with the Cretan sea kings to the west, early discovered Cyprus. They regarded it as an important source of the valuable metal that gave the island its name—copper. Copper was fashioned by the artisans of Antioch, Damascus, and Tarsus on the near-by Asia Minor shore into weapons and statues of durable bronze.

While the original peoples of Cyprus were a mixture of all the elements that cruised the seas or crossed over from the mainland—Phoenicians, Cretans, Egyptians, Syrians, and Assyrians—they early got to the point where they considered themselves Greeks, relying on the culture and the trade brought from the energetic Greek city-states of the distant peninsula. Twelve independent city-states sprang up in Cyprus alone. While they had to bend the knee to the all-powerful Persian Empire when it overran the entire Levant, they held on to their identity until Alexander the Great made them Greek again.

Through the ages the usual procession of conquerors came to Cyprus as to Crete. The Saracens of the Moslem world held the island for a century, until the Byzantines came to free it once again. Then history, however, began to trace a different and individual pattern for Cyprus.

Richard the Lion-Hearted, sailing eastward to join the Third Crusade and reconquer Jerusalem from Saladin, paused in Cyprus in 1191, snatching it from the Greeks in the process. After marrying a local princess named Berengaria, he sold the island to the powerful Knights Templar, who in turn got rid of it to a French knight who as the last "King of Jerusalem" was now throneless. Thus there grew up the strange anomaly of an independent feudal kingdom reigning in a Moslem corner of the world, maintaining a purely European standard similar to the chivalric court of France. Such a pointless era came to an end with the dying out of the dynasty and the absorption of Cyprus into the Venetian Empire in 1434.

Cyprus under Venetian rule was outwardly prosperous, sitting astride the rich trade lanes from the Levant. The Venetian court carried on the same style of pomp as was noticed by Shakespeare when he chose Cyprus as the locale for several scenes in his *Othello*. The villain Iago began entwining the hapless Desdemona in his intrigues when he found time hanging heavily on his hands during those languorous, easygoing days of feudal Cyprus.

At length, as it must and did to all the lands of the Levant, the heavy hand of the Turks fell in 1573. Among the few natives who escaped from the island at its fall was a talented young artist who found his fortune in faraway Spain, where he was known simply as El Greco ("The Greek").

Cyprus languished as a forgotten province of the monolithic Turkish Empire for three hundred more years. During this stagnant period almost a fifth of its inhabitants became Moslems.

Meanwhile the world changed. The French Revolution and the age of steam ushered in the liberal nineteenth century, consolidating Europe into national states participating in a shaky "balance of power." Turkey in the meantime grew weaker and "sicker." Suddenly Cyprus found herself "liberated," but only halfway so. At the Congress of Berlin in 1878 the diplomats shuffled their chess pieces about, and Disraeli chose to take control of Cyprus because it was the closest available land to the newly opened Suez Canal.

In deference to Turkey, Disraeli proclaimed Cyprus to be under "British administration" only. Complete separation from Turkey was postponed until 1914, when the Sultan threw his country into World War I on the side of the Germans.

Cyprus thus played, for almost three-quarters of a century, the role of "the sentinel island" guarding the northern approaches to Suez. Its Cypriot inhabitants enjoyed partial self-government, with the freedom to trade with or migrate to the British Empire's more prosperous corners. The island was in effect a quiet backwater, with the usual poverty, overcrowding, and lack of "life" that characterize such has-been Mediterranean lands. This condition led to a gradual rise of political action on the part of the Cypriots to unite with Greece, culminating in a tense guerrilla war. In 1959 the British conferred independence on the island, reserving military bases for themselves and strict cultural and government guarantees to the Turkish minority.

Visitors to Cyprus usually land at the medieval fortified port of Famagusta, or at the roadstead of Larnaka, and motor into the central hills, where the picturesque capital city of Nicosia is located. Many travelers are seeing Nicosia more than in previous years since its little airport has become a strategic crossroads for aviation lanes owing to the establishment of Israel as an independent state.

Cyprus still grows its wine grapes, raisins, oranges, and olives; trades with the British garrison; welcomes the new tourists; and experiments with its new independence under a strict constitution, and plays the role of a full member of the United Nations.

Rhodes, "Bride of the Sea"

One of the loveliest islands imaginable to be found anywhere in the Mediterranean is Rhodes. Surrounded by deep-blue Aegean waters, its mountains are covered with wildflowers and thick vegetation. Semitropical flowers are in evidence all year round— the scarlet altheas, purple bougainvillaea, and roses in limitless profusion. In summer its landscapes are brightened by millions of butterflies. On many a deserted hilltop stand ruins of graceful temples. This surely seems a land native to the nymphs and dryads of ancient Greece.

Rhodes is the second of all the Aegean islands in size, subordinate only to Crete, which lies seventy miles southwest. Rhodes is sixty miles long, located far over in the southeast corner of the Aegean world, its nose nuzzling the nearest projection of Asia Minor flung out to meet it.

The sunshine from its combination of dry air, blue sea, and dense vegetation casts a beneficent light over the whole island, a phenomenon which impelled the earliest of its ancient peoples to dedicate it to Apollo, the god of light.

The island's chief city, bearing the same name, is a delightful, quiet Greek town lying beside three microscopic harbors, the center one of which was built by the Knights of St. John in the Middle Ages to protect their typically feudalistic town. The extreme tip of the island was made into a summer resort by the Italians, complete with luxury hotel, diving boards, immense church, and stupendous public buildings.

Rhodes first became noted in history when its sea kings took over control of the Aegean waves from the descendants of the Minoans and from the penetrating advance guard of the Phoenicians.[2] Settled by the energetic Dorians of Greece, and by refugees from Crete, the Rhodians were the supreme navigators among all the Greeks until the rise of Athens in the seventh century before Christ. The earliest known naval codes for administering a fleet have descended from these people, and their principles were adopted by the British navy in its formative days as a guide to framing a code of its own.

Wealth poured into Rhodes during the centuries of sea traffic. As an ally of Athens, a veteran of the Trojan War, and the ruler of the Aegean, Rhodes amassed the treasure with which to erect its great Colossus, the Colossus of Rhodes, which Herodotus proclaimed as one of the wonders of his ancient world.

The Colossus stood for so short a time that very little is known of its exact size and location. It was a statue of Apollo holding aloft

---

[2] Cecil Rhodes, the diamond tycoon of South Africa, probably derived his name from an ancestor who had fought during the medieval sea battles near Rhodes, or had been a Crusader. Thus Rhodes' own colonies of Rhodesia in the heart of Africa carry on the spelling of ancient times.

a flaming torch as his symbol. Its height has been exaggerated by time, and likewise its location as standing astride the entrance to Rhodes' harbor. Built in the fourth century before Christ, after twelve years of labor, it was overthrown in 227 B.C., toppled by an earthquake into the sea. Three hundred years later the biggest pieces were recovered and carried away by a shrewed merchant on three hundred beasts of burden.

Rhodes, whose name is believed to have come from its wealth of roses, remained a center of education and navigation throughout ancient times. Julius Caesar, while heading here in his youth to attend school, was captured by pirates on the way, and he turned to a military career in order to avenge himself for this humiliation.

The island shared the fortunes of Greece and Crete, except for an absence of Arab conquest, until the thirteenth century. Then, having been conquered by the Crusaders, who had in a cowardly manner seized Constantinople, it was later taken by the homeless Knights of St. John of Jerusalem to be their citadel for making another stand against the Moslem hordes.

This knightly Order had a very interesting development, and we shall meet it again in Malta. In fact, it is not yet extinct.[3] During the First Crusade, in the eleventh century, the Order was founded by the initiative of the republic of Amalfi as a group of men giving aid and comfort to wounded fighters in the Holy Land. It was dedicated to John the Baptist, whose hand was its holiest relic. It contrasted with the companion Order of Knights Templar, whose duty was to defend the Temple at Jerusalem. The Knights Hospitalers, as the Order came to be called, were compelled to abandon the Holy Land in 1290 when the Arabs captured their last stronghold of Acre. They retreated to Cyprus and later to Rhodes, when they found the latter a more defensible haven.

By this time they had grown to power and wealth, inheriting the estates of many slain knights. They lost no time in building a fortified city on Rhodes that is still a marvel of medieval architec-

---

[3] In 1950 the vestigial Order was given custody of Italian airplanes over and above the amount permitted by the Peace Treaty as a dodge to allow Italy to secure newer models for herself. The Order is officially governed from Vatican City and maintains its original status as a quasi-holy order.

ture. The Order was divided into nationalities, or *langues* ("tongues"), each one having its own hospice, or *auberge,* governed by a master of that nationality. Spain was represented by the langues of Aragon and Castile; France by Auvergne, France, and Provence; Italy and Germany each had a hospice for themselves. The langues were each given a sector of the fortifications to defend. Supreme ruler was the Grand Master, an official recognized as the equal of many European temporal rulers, and high in standing with Christian Europe as the commander of the most valiant fighting force for the Cross.

However, the Turks finally proved too much for them. Solyman the Magnificent, on ascending the throne, set for himself the immediate task of ousting this insolent group of warrior nobles who had almost chased his fleet from the seas. Solyman managed to beat down the defenses of Rhodes in 1522, but in the tradition of the chivalrous Saladin before him, he offered honorable terms to the Knights for their surrender. Accordingly, the surviving Knights, with all their possessions and archives, marched out of the city and set sail for France. By the terms of the surrender, Solyman was prevented from destroying their city or tampering with the islanders' religion for a score of years.

Rhodes, so close to Turkish Asia Minor, remained tightly in the possession of the Sultans for almost four hundred years.

Its release from the Turks came in not too glorious a manner. In 1911 an Italian fleet appeared off the harbor and demanded the surrender of the Turkish governor, Italy then being at war with Turkey. When the peace treaty was signed the next year, Italy kept Rhodes and its adjoining twelve islands[4] as a "guarantee" until the Turks should abandon all their holdings in Libya. Then World War I took place, after which Italy decided to stay on a while longer, until Mussolini bluntly announced, with no bones about it, that he was there to stay. During the ensuing occupation, the island was intensively developed to attract tourists. Roads were built, ruins excavated, the hot springs of Kalithea developed, and the fine Hotel of the Roses built. The Hall of the Grand Masters of

---

[4] Named the Dodecanese ("Twelve Islands") by the Venetians.

the Order of St. John was likewise restored into an elegance that would have astounded those less privileged warriors.

But the Rhodians were hostile to this alien occupation. Their Orthodox priests took to the path of passive resistance against the new order. Liberation only came after three years of starvation and bombardment during World War II. Italy's surrender to the Allies caused the Germans to seize Rhodes' and pack the Italian garrison into prison camps. A little war between British and German commandoes lasted fitfully until V-E Day. When the war ended, they surrendered to the British, who in turn handed Rhodes and the Dodecanese over to Greece, a reunion devoutly wished by both the mother and daughter peoples after a separation of half a millennium.

Rhodians of today entertain their visitors by giving choral dances in peasant costumes and boots and by selling antique-type pottery in rustic designs of blue and green.

The Aegean "Isles of the Blest"

The colorful legends of golden Greece come vividly to life on all of the little islands that stand like steppingstones across the Aegean Sea, connecting Greece with Asia Minor. One of the most entrancing voyages imaginable is that to be enjoyed on a small steamer cruising amid these myriad specks of land. They are all the tips of extinct, submerged volcanoes. Rock-bare and steep, they show glorious profiles when lit by the roseate setting sun or by the brilliant moon. They act as beckoning fingers, one always in sight of the other. All but the tiniest of them possess a whitewashed central village, crowded together into an inaccessible spot, surrounded by stunted trees. They can be reached only by donkey-back from some tiny beach, except for the larger islands that boast an auto or two of ancient vintage that can careen over primordial "roads" to some holy spot of olden times.

The Aegean Sea is the branch of the Mediterranean that is the most deeply steeped in the glories of Greek history. Here the

---

[5] Britain's appreciation of the value of strategic Rhodes is told by Winston Churchill in *Closing the Ring* of his memoirs.

ancient islanders got in trouble with the capricious gods, who were constantly bending down to interfere with mortal affairs and to run off with helpless maidens. Its waters have been criss-crossed ceaselessly by the frail craft of the olden war fleets and by the trading flotillas of antiquity's most magnificent cities.

The Aegean is a squarish sea that extends from Crete in the south to Macedonia in the north. Its islands are divided into three groups—the Dodecanese, the Cyclades, and the Sporades.

The Dodecanese include large-sized Rhodes and a dozen smaller islets. One of them is Cos, where Hippocrates, the father of medicine, lived and taught. On another, Patmos, to the north, St. John in his exile saw the vision that led him to write the Book of Revelation.

The Cyclades were so named because they form a circle surrounding the tiny island of Delos. In Athenian times the island of Delos was so sacred to Apollo as his birthplace that no pirate would possibly despoil it. Thus, its temple to Apollo was chosen as the depository of the rich treasure of Athens and her allies. Today, almost the entire surface of Delos is strewn with marble fragments and ruined classic structures.

Most unusual of the Cyclades is Thera, a crescent-shaped crater with brilliantly-striped cliffs, famed for its hospitable people and an idyllic little town. Melos to the northwest gave its name to the lovely fragmentary nude, the "Venus de Milo." The island of Paros is entirely composed of a translucent marble. Largest of the Cyclades is Naxos, producer of figs and raisins, and the island where lovely Princess Ariadne, daughter of the King of Crete, was abandoned by ungrateful Theseus after their flight. But by far the most popular of all the Cyclades is arid little Mykonos. Almost in the very heart of the archipelago, this friendly isle attracts streams of travelers to its two beaches, new hotels, its picturesque walled town, its many chapels, picture-book windmills, and its homes of skilled weavers turning out woolen cloth on hand looms.

The Sporades lie in the northern Aegean, and are so called because they are "strewn" across its waters. Among them is Skyros, where the poet Rupert Brooke was buried after being wounded in the Dardanelles battles of 1915; and Samothrace, whose excavations yielded the "Winged Victory" from some looted or buried ship. Samothrace, for some capricious reason known only to themselves, was turned over by the Nazis during the war to be occupied by the Bulgarians, a landlocked people who nourished a traditional hatred for the Greeks.

On the mainland at the northern end of the Aegean Sea lies Macedonia, frontier kingdom of Alexander the Great, where the conqueror was born in 356 B.C.

Salonica, chief port of Macedonia and second city of modern Greece, lies at the uppermost tip of the sea.[6] Forming a side of its bay is the three-pronged peninsula of the Chalcidice, at the extreme eastern promontory of which cluster the remote monasteries of Mount Athos, resting on steep cliffs high above the azure sea, forbidden to females of all species, and reached only by elevated baskets, or by an arduous ride on donkeyback.

On the eastern shores of the Aegean, off mountainous Asia Minor, lie three very large islands. Mitylene, or Lesbos, was the home of Sappho and Alcaeus, poets who lived seven hundred years before Christ. Chios boasts of being the home of Homer. Samos, almost touching the Turkish shore, was the birthplace of the philosopher Pythagoras.

The shore of Asia Minor itself belongs to modern Turkey. But its marshy valleys and silted-up bays were once fertile fields surrounding the wealthy cities of St. Paul's time and before. Civilization is vastly enriched by the work and creations of these destroyed urban centers. The seven churches "which are in Asia," named by the Book of Revelation, were all among those vanished places. Up in the northern corner of Asia Minor, where the Dardanelles pours into the Aegean Sea, lies the hill bearing the ruins of the seven successive cities of Troy. Pergamum, once a rich city, now but a vacant site, gave its name to parchment, which it pioneered in manufacturing. The region of Lydia nearby was the age-old Kingdom of Croesus, antiquity's richest man. Halfway down the Asia Minor coast is a city sprung again to life in the nineteenth century—Smyrna, famous for figs and tobacco, and as an export outlet for rugs, angora and mohair, as well as Turkish

---

[6] The city to which were written the two Epistles to the Thessalonians.

produce of all kinds. The modern Greeks, in attempting to re-create Asia Minor's dependence on Greece, held on to Smyrna after World War I until 1922, when they were forced out by the Turkish armies of Mustapha Kemal Atatürk.

Also in Asia Minor near the sea was Ephesus,[7] powerful city of wealth, whose magnificent Temple of Diana was one of the Seven Ancient Wonders. Farther south still is the silted-up harbor where Miletus, another metropolis, once stood. And near the southwestern tip of Asia Minor, facing the island of Cos, once stood Halicarnassus, whose tomb to its King Mausolus originated the word "mausoleum," so glittering was its grandeur, entitling it to be another of the Seven Wonders. Herodotus, father of history, himself was born in Halicarnassus in 484 B.C.

What a productive and creative corner of the world this was until waves of barbarian invaders overturned its wealthy and prosperous life! The scope of our civilization is so enriched by what these ancient philosophers, mathematicians, scientists, cartographers, poets, inventors, sailors, artisans, architects, and writers forged in their cultural laboratories around this Aegean Sea that no one can possibly calculate the debt owed to their pioneering.

Today the entire galaxy of Aegean islands belongs to Greece except for two,[8] once again, after long struggles and contests, reunited to their motherland, for whom and by whom they were given the collective name of Archipelago, or "Greece above the sea."

Over on the other coast of Greece, in what is known as the Ionian Sea, lie several other large islands famed to world annals. Zante is a great producer today of currants;[9] Ithaca is the legendary home of Ulysses and Penelope; and Corfu to the north is lined with caves, ruins, and sites of events that once rocked the daily life and times of the ancients.

In those Ionian waters were fought two naval battles that have shaped the fate of the world—Actium, thirty-one years before

---

[7] To which St. Paul wrote his Epistle to the Ephesians.

[8] Imbros and Tenedos, left to Turkey as protection for the near-by Dardanelles.

[9] The word "currant" comes from Corinth, ancient owner of the island and exporter of the sweet product.

Christ, where Anthony and Cleopatra were whipped by Augustus, restoring order and government to Rome; and Lepanto, where Christian nations smashed the Turks in 1571, freeing the western Mediterranean from Moslem attack from that day on.

Malta, "The Buttress Island"

Out to the west, almost a day's steaming from Greek waters, the Mediterranean narrows down to its "throat," where the island of Sicily reaches across to within ninety miles of Carthage on the northern tip of Africa. Guarding that strategic opening in the Middle Sea stands the tiny island group of Malta, a relic of the actual land bridge that once stretched across the opening and linked primordial Africa with Europe. Malta is not volcanic as are the Aegean isles, but is a low-lying, undulating bit of land that alone was left above the sea after the series of terrible geologic convulsions smashed the land bridge and made the Mediterranean one continuous salt sea.

Malta is only seventeen miles long and nine wide. Even with its "suburban" isle of Gozo added, it is a speck on the Mediterranean map. Yet its extreme strategic value is what has made it a prize for the maritime powers of Mediterranean history to hold.

Not only by its location has Malta tempted the navies of surrounding lands. It also has a superb haven, its famed Grand Harbour, which penetrates in two prongs deep into the island from its northeast shore. On the ridge of land between those prongs stands the baroque and picturesque capital city of Valetta.

From the very first moment of arrival, a traveler is impressed with the charm and "difference" of Malta. The Grand Harbour is lined with rising parapets and battlements on both sides, built by the Knights of the Order of St. John in true medieval fashion. The harbor's waters are cleft by quaint little boats resembling Venetian gondolas and called *dghaisas* in the native language. In Valetta, the narrow, straight streets are faced with hundreds of enclosed balconies, of glass and wood, resembling the carved, secluded balconies of the "harem" countries of North Africa. On all street corners are booths selling British confections and cigarettes, for Valetta always has its complement of British seamen to serve, men whose blondness is conspicuous in this sunlit, almost semitropical, island.

Outside the powerful walls of Valetta, the whole landscape of Malta unfolds. There are no trees or high mountains to cut off the view over rolling hillsides, crowned with towns of limestone houses, dominated by massive, baroque churches. The fields in between the towns are divided by numberless stone walls weaving back and forth. And over all is the bright-blue Mediterranean sky, giving a radiant light to the unusual scene.

The people are very friendly and interesting. Many of the women wear their stiff, encompassing *faldettas*, coifs of black cloth whose origin is obscure. Church bells make for a constant symphony as they sound from different distances. Little donkey-carts, herds of goats, and darting small automobiles add to the bustling semi-Oriental quality of the atmosphere. The Grand Harbour is always host to some large naval vessel, cruise ship, or passenger liner. The other prong of the bay, called by the natives Marsamxett,[10] is usually filled with destroyers and pleasure craft. Lining this pretty blue bay are the residential apartments and villas of the suburb known as Sliema. Malta's luxurious hostelry, the Phoenicia Hotel, also faces this bay from outside the walls of Valetta.

This scene of bustle, this overcrowdedness stemming from the existence of 270,000 people on this island of only ninety-five square miles, the myriad churches with their bells proclaiming the faith of Rome, and the presence of British naval staffs on every hand, contrasted with the Arabic language of the people, make for a charming combination of impressions, which adds to the delight of every visitor. Is it Africa or is it Europe? Is it East or West? This little island blends the strains of both in its striking individuality and self-attachment.

By Act of Parliament in 1801, Malta is a part of Europe. But by verdict of history, it is made up of equal parts European and African, and has been possessed by empires from both of the opposing shores.

---

[10] Note the "Marsa" of this name—the Arabic word for "bay" that appears in so many Mediterranean place names.

In Malta, there are remains of all the civilizations and cultures that have affected the fate of this tiny spot above the sea. Prehistoric inhabitants have left stone tombs and fossilized cart tracks. The Phoenicians and Carthaginians, who first colonized Malta, contributed the curious Arabic medley of speech that is the Maltese language. The Romans are memorialized by an excavated villa, complete with artistic fragments and mosaic floors. Most of the grand buildings of today's Malta were erected by the powerful, wealthy Order of St. John's noble knights. And the British give reminders of their presence on every hand, in royal arms, public buildings, and all the paraphernalia of a great naval base.

Malta's ancient name of Melita is supposed to have been the origin of the word for "honey" in Greek and Latin lands. For, even today, one of the most typical products of the island to be bought as a souvenir is a jar of honey flavored by that delightful tang of wild thyme that so captivated Cicero and the other noble Romans.

Malta's role in ancient history was undistinguished until its first great rendezvous with ancient annals occurred in A.D. 58—when St. Paul was shipwrecked on the island. Up to that time it had been a trading harbor for Phoenician craft, a base for Carthage's naval control of the Mediterranean, and then a Roman prize after the wars with Hannibal. St. Paul's tempest-tossed ship was wrecked in a pretty bay at the northern corner of the island, a place where "two seas meet." A statue of the apostle now gazes out on the placid view.

This whole story is beautifully told in detail in the last chapters of the Book of Acts. Once arrived, Paul galvanized the island's attention by healing himself of snake-bite, and the Melitans received the homeless band with the typical friendliness that is so deep in their make-up of today. The Bible refers to them as "barbarous," meaning that they were not Greco-Romans, as was conspicuous even then after two hundred years of Roman rule.

The capital of Malta in those days was a large city in the middle of the island, known today as *Mdina*, the Arab word for "city," or *Notabile* in Latinized heraldic language of the Knights of Malta. St. Paul was welcomed there by the Roman governor

Publius, whose father he immediately healed of a "fever and bloody flux." Paul lingered in Malta for three whole months, evidently with good results, for there is evidence that the Christian tradition was firmly laid during his stay. Many people turned to the new faith, and the island has been a stronghold of the Roman rites of Christianity through all its vicissitudes. Despite the Semitic nature of the population, they held on to their religion all through the later days of Arab occupation, at a time when their kinsmen in near-by Africa were turning wholesale to the newer preachings of Mohammed, Prophet of Mecca.

The seventeenth century, super-baroque cathedral in the congested walled town of Mdina supposedly stands on the site of the palace of Publius, a wing of which Paul is supposed to have consecrated as the first church in Malta. Outside the walls there are some extensive catacombs that can be easily visited, catacombs that give strong evidence of the early hold taken by Christianity after Paul's departure, and also silent testimony of the sufferings endured by the early churchmen when persecutions were ordered from Rome.

Malta then relapsed into many centuries of obscurity. Roman rule was succeeded by Byzantine occupation and then by an Arab conquest that lasted for almost 250 years. Malta was restored to Europe in 1090 by Roger de Hauteville, a Norman warrior of the band who had liberated Sicily, whereof the island existed as a dependency from then on, governed first by Frenchmen from Anjou and then by the Kings of Aragon, until the advent of the great events of the sixteenth century. These events catapulted the forgotten island into the midst of a renewed outbreak of the great struggle between the Cross and the Crescent.

The Knights of the Hospitalers' Order of St. John of Jerusalem, having been evicted from their stronghold of Rhodes by Sultan Solyman the Magnificent in 1522, sailed to France, trying to find a new home. But King Francis I, who was then allied to the Turks, gave them no support and made no offer. It was the Emperor Charles V who finally gave them the dubious gift of the island of Malta, and the African port of Tripoli, for the annual tribute of one falcon paid to the Viceroy of Sicily.

The Knights were dismayed at this new homeland, for the island had fallen into decay. It had only ten thousand inhabitants, and was exposed to the wrath of any Turkish fleet that was headed for the narrow straits of Sicily. But they had no choice in the end. Bringing their treasures of documents, battle flags, precious metals, and the full strength of their high-born membership from France, they settled on the Grand Harbour and built two strong forts.

And just in time, too. For in 1553 they had to give up Tripoli to the Turks. Then, in 1565, the Knights had to stand up and be counted when Solyman decided that they were to be erased from the map of the Mediterranean.

For four months in the hot summer of that year a Turkish force of sixty thousand men assaulted the two forts of the beleaguered, isolated Knights, whose total strength could not have exceeded ten thousand. The Turks overran the whole island and finally broke down by sheer weight of numbers the fort of St. Elmo at the harbor's mouth after every defender had died in its defense. They performed acts of savagery to overawe the other fort and threw their total strength into the fight, regardless of their heavy losses. Not until the slothful Viceroy of Sicily bestirred himself to send a relief fleet across the few miles of sea to Malta did the weakened Turks pack up and sail away for home.

Surveying their costly victory, the Knights determined that they would have to build a stronger citadel. They thus chose the present site of Valetta for it. Immediately, the wealth and the praises of Europe poured in on them. Both Catholic and Protestant Europe understood the valor of the defense of Malta, and what it meant for the safety of divided, defenseless Europe. The Knighthood, or, as it was called, "the Religion," became known in the far corners of Europe, and its emblem of the Maltese cross was adopted by knights and potentates of many small European baronies.

Valetta, named for the defending Grand Master de la Valette, was built in its entirety between 1570 and 1585. The soft limestone of the island was shaped into the expensively decorated palaces, *auberges*—or homes of the langues—churches, and public buildings of the new city. The ensuing two centuries marked the high point in the power of this Order, a holdover from the vanished days of feudalistic Europe and the lost Crusades. The Religion was a quasi-military, quasi-religious group of celibate knights of undisputed noble family, bound together in the twin tradition of militancy and hospitaling, deriving income from properties in every country of Europe. Novitiates, or "postulants," who wanted to join this prestigious band had to attest their noble lineage by exacting "proofs," many of which are on display in Valetta's library in the shape of coats-of-arms, letters from European kings and queens, and long personal applications.

The Order began to grow top-heavy with wealth. To enshrine its chief relic, the dead hand of St. John the Baptist, it built a conventual church that outdid many of the cathedrals of Europe in size and luxury. Now called the Co-Cathedral of St. John,[11] it is a sight to make the visitor gasp once he has stepped inside. Its every inch is part of a combined presentation of glitter, gorgeousness, and wealth that can never fail to impress. Each side chapel was enriched by a different langue in an effort to outdo the other langues. The floor is paved with marble mosaic slabs bearing the coats of arms of Europe's noblest families. On the ceiling is a magnificent painting by Mattia Preti.

Equally ostentatious is the adjoining Palace of the Grand Masters of the Religion. A foursquare baroque mansion of immense size, surrounding a delightful courtyard, it comprises many spacious rooms in which several branches of Malta's present government are adequately housed. The governing chamber of the Council of the Order is hung with magnificent Gobelin tapestries and is one of the most charming artistic rooms in all Europe. The Maltese Parliament has chosen that room for its meeting place. The long corridors are lined with paintings of the Grand Masters, and of the sovereigns of pre-Napoleonic Europe, paintings donated by themselves to their sovereign brothers, the Grand Masters.

Matchless among all the rooms in the palace, however, is the armory, or the huge, long, high-ceilinged room that was once the infirmary, or hospital, of the Religion. Here there is assembled

---

[11] The principal cathedral of Malta is at Mdina.

a collection without any equal in value or completeness of Europe's finest arms and armor, worn and used by the Knights since the days of the Crusades. Shields, cutlasses, coats of mail, leggings, helmets, swords, lethal hand weapons, spears, and gold-inlaid suits of armor used in Richard the Lion-Hearted's time—all are found in this one hall. The peaked metal helmets like those worn by Cortez in Mexico are lined on the walls here almost by the hundreds. And sombrely interspersed in the display are the Oriental, Mongolic types of braided armor, rounded shields, fierce helmets, and lethal scimitars abandoned by the Turks after the great siege.

The throne room is another burst of splendor. Walls brocaded by Europe's finest artisans, and decorated with frescoes showing every detail of the horrendous siege of 1565, line this extensive room, in which stand the thrones placed for the monarchs of Great Britain in case they hold any convocations in Malta.

The anachronistic rule of the Religion over Malta was brought to a sudden, abrupt end by Napoleon Bonaparte, who stopped by on his way to conquer Egypt in 1798. He expelled the Order, looted its palaces of their precious metals, and thoroughly antagonized the people, who had originally welcomed him. Only two years after Napoleon had gone on, the people rose up and barricaded his French garrison inside Valetta, calling in the British fleet to rid them of the French entirely. From 1800 down to the present day, Malta has been an important part of the British Empire, conferred on Britain in 1814 by "the love of the Maltese and the voice of Europe," as an inscription has it.

During the nineteenth century the British navy used Malta as its chief Mediterranean base. The island gained fame from the important personages, royal and noble, stationed here from time to time. The opening of the Suez Canal added immensely to its value and it became a port of call for merchant ships stopping for fuel and cablegrams on their way from Britain to India.

Yet this prosperity of modern times suddenly gave way to the old law of "survive or be killed" that descended on Malta from the skies during World War II. Beginning with the summer of 1940, the island was raided almost daily, first by the Italian air force, then by the deadly German Stukas. Over 1,200 different raids peppered Valetta's harbor, and 3,000 alerts were called. This unprecedented attack, mounted with savagery and inhuman persistence, would have reduced the overpopulated islands to starvation but for the gallant sacrifices of the British merchant navy, fighting ships, and air force, aided by American equipment.[12] Malta was weakened, but never put out of action. But for Malta's never-say-die part in the war, it is hard to conceive how the African campaign could have been won so completely and promptly by the Allies.

In gratitude for Malta's game stand, the King of Great Britain awarded the George Cross to the entire population, an event unique in the annals of heraldry. Then, in 1964, the islanders were granted independence inside the British Commonwealth.

Today, Malta is an ideal tourist spot, with so much to see and so much of Europe's treasure to explore in the archives of its Order. It is also a source of much excellent lace to be shopped for. The bombings spared most of the finest monuments of the glorious era when Malta's chivalric knights outbuilt and outshone their sovereign kinsmen of Europe.

Sardinia

Lying in the "dead heart" of the western Mediterranean is the seldom visited, almost unknown island of Sardinia. This island for some mysterious reason has played small part in world history even though putting up with the usual parade of conquerors and occupiers. Travelers seldom if ever bother to go there, and it is completely off the lanes of world tourist travel.

It is reached most regularly by overnight steamer from Rome's port of Civitavecchia. Sardinia is the second largest island[13] in the Middle Sea, and has a population of almost a million hard-working peasants. It has several large cities, of which the most

---

[12] On one occasion the aircraft carrier *Wasp* approached within four hundred miles and launched a rescuing air group. At other times tankers crept in through the air blockade.

[13] Largest, of course, is Sicily.

extensive is the capital of Cagliari. It has coal mines, extensively developed by the Fascists, mysterious watchtowers dating from days in the long past, mountains, pretty bays, and a lovely subtropical climate on its southern coasts.

However, its chief distinction is that it gave its name to sardines, which have always been one of its most important exports. It contributes olive oil, fruits, minerals, and coal to the Italian trade balance. But there is little that is distinctive or natively created to cause travelers to take the extra exertion of journeying out specially from Italy.

Sardinia is 150 miles long and almost 60 miles wide. Its southern coast stretches to within 80 miles of North Africa, while its northern tip is separated by only a three-mile strait from its sister island of Corsica. Its people speak a language that is a mixture of Italian and the Catalan introduced during its five centuries of rule by the Kings of Aragon.

Sardinia, however, played a perceptible role in Italy's struggle for unification and freedom. When detached from Spain after the great horse-trades following the Bourbon acquisition of the Spanish throne, it was assigned in 1720 to the Dukes of Savoy, who had played a role in history as useful allies of the Austrian Hapsburgs. These Dukes, reigning from the north Italian city of Turin, immediately took the title of Kings of Sardinia, and one of them later found Sardinia a useful place of refuge when Napoleon swallowed up his Italian kingdom.

Later, the Kings of Savoy-Sardinia led the fight for unifying the collection of Italian duchies, principalities, and weak kingdoms into the present-day united country. They finally succeeded in 1860. One of them, Victor Emmanuel II, became the first King of Italy. His grandson, however, made the mistake of tolerating Mussolini too long and paid for it with his throne and the loss of his dynasty's century-old position.

Cagliari was reduced to ruins by Allied bombardments in World War II, resulting from the German use of its airport as a base for bombing the vital convoys snaking along from Gibraltar to Malta. This sea-air battle lasted for two years. However, when

Italy capitulated in 1943, Sardinia expelled its Nazi garrison by its own efforts as its contribution to victory.

Corsica, Isle of Vendettas

Corsica is a colorful island of mountains and azure sea, dear to the lovers of "noble bandits" and fighters for freedom. It has a charm for tourists as a wilder continuation of the Riviera, from which it is detached by only sixty miles of blue sea.

Corsica is separated from Sardinia to the south by the narrow Strait of Bonifacio, but it is of a completely different character from that more placid and more bulky island. Corsica is all mountain and sea, with no appreciable resources or overpopulation. Its people have lived on very little through the ages, but are suffused with the energy and ingenuity that would be expected of those who live in a more richly endowed stretch of scenery.

Eighty miles long from north to south, equidistant from the Riviera and from the Tuscan coast of Italy, Corsica has played little part in world history except through the headlines produced in other countries by its several outstanding sons. Corsican fighters took part in the European wars of the eighteenth century. Their proud guerrilla leader, Pasquale Paoli, led a persistent backwoods rebellion against the lethargic Genoese for twenty years. And his inspired admirer, Napoleone Buonaparte, grew up in Corsica only to sprout the indefatigable energy and the matchless gift for leadership that launched a new era into European politics and statecraft.

Nowadays Corsica is a quiet department of France. Its Italian-speaking inhabitants quickly learn French and rise to positions of importance in the motherland. Belonging to France has served to siphon off from its home acres much of the turbulent spirit of this lovable people.

It takes only six hours by steamship, or fifty minutes by airplane, from Nice across to Ajaccio, little port city of Corsica. Here, a typical Italianate town of stucco houses, palm-lined streets, colonnaded buildings, and floreate parks welcomes one with a native placidity spiked by a French cosmopolitan flavor. After one has paid his dutiful visit to the house where Napoleon was born, he is free to motor out along the beautiful coastline to the resort or village where he chooses to settle down for a few days of carefree rest in true semitropical languor.

However, such an enjoyable pursuit as welcoming tourists is comparatively new as an occupation for the Corsicans. Their whole tradition is one of rebellions and fighting, either abroad or at home. "Vendetta" is a word coined by the local patois-speakers of the island to describe their chief occupation of former days—avenging slights on family honor, and perpetuating feuds inherited from medieval days.

The Corsicans, a mixture of all the races of the western Mediterranean around a core of the early, unknown settlers of the island, were left in relative peace by the Carthaginians, the Romans, and the Saracen freebooters, until the Pisans came in the twelfth century. Pisa's energetic sea fighters recruited willing Corsicans to fight in their galleys against the Moslems, while the folks back home were gradually reduced to paying tribute to the saucy city at the mouth of the Arno. Pisa was succeeded in the thirteenth century by the haughtier Genoese, who laid heavier tribute on the primitive islanders. This tribute, followed by centuries of neglect, is what led the Corsicans to go on the warpath in the eighteenth century. This is what brought the unhappy island to the notice of Europe at large. Their guerrilla chieftain Paoli had a knack for enlisting sympathy abroad, and he reaped rich rewards by attracting a British fleet to his aid.

This intrigue is what undoubtedly precipitated a sudden change in the island's fortunes. For in the year 1768 the weary and weak Genoese Republic gladly sold its rights over Corsica to its potent neighbor, King Louis XV of France. And only a few weeks later the child Napoleone Buonaparte[14] was born at Ajaccio, a French citizen from his birth, with the opportunities of a powerful motherland at his disposal.

Napoleon left his home town of Ajaccio in 1786 never to return, but his opprobrious nickname of "the Corsican" blazoned the fame of his native island across the far reaches of Europe.

---

[14] In France, Napoleon spelled his surname as "Bonaparte."

The many ensuing years brought little change to the story of the island, until Mussolini fastened his ambitions on it as a bit of his "unredeemed Italy." In 1942 his legions were allowed to overrun the island by Hitler in revenge for the Allied landings in French North Africa. The Fascist soldiers cowered in Corsica until Italy herself surrendered, whereupon they lent assistance to Free French commandoes in expelling the Nazi garrison from its last toehold in battered Bastia.

It should be mentioned here that several islands lie in the narrow waters between Corsica and Italy. These islands, once held as vassals of Pisa, were annexed by Florence when she swallowed up Pisa, and have remained Tuscan ever since. Largest of the islands is Elba, famed as a source of iron through the ages, and as a temporary home for Napoleon in 1814 by grace of the powers of Europe. Perhaps the tiniest is Monte Cristo, an uninhabited rock made deathless to romantic novel-readers the world over by the masterpiece of Alexandre Dumas concerning a supposed treasure found there by his hero "the Count of Monte Cristo," who shouted those enviable words—"The world is mine!"

The chief port on the Italian mainland across from Corsica is Leghorn, which enjoyed a short heyday during the eighteenth century as a prosperous international settlement controlling the maritime trade of Florence.

Majorca and the Balearics

One more island group in the Mediterranean remains to be observed, and this one is perhaps more significant than the others because of the favorable publicity it has received in America as an escapist paradise for taxpayers.

Majorca, largest island of the group as its name signifies, is an exquisite island about forty miles square, inhabited by a race of proud and artistic people speaking the Catalan idiom of Barcelona. Its principal city is Palma, a historic town of one hundred thousand containing some very artistic buildings.

Modern sun-seekers like Majorca most for its mild and little varying climate, coupled with its attractive low prices for hotels and amusements. It is still a fact that hotel rooms can be found for less than $10 a day including meals, and villas for $100 a month complete with servants, but not including food. The islanders industriously produce all their own meat, fruit and vegetables, and hire themselves out at low wages, although they find it hard to make a living or to pay for anything imported.

These Majorcans produce a very fine lace, which is all made by piecework at home by unmarried young ladies. They stage several lively fiestas during the year, the chief of which is scheduled for Palm Sunday. Particularly entrancing are the surviving peasant dances, enacted by wandering troupes on demand.

Life in Majorca is easygoing and uneventful. But the cosmopolites vacationing there give excellent society, and there is always a new excursion or a new sport to fill each few days. The rugged mountain scenery lends grandness to the view from every hotel balcony or from every villa's terrace.

Palma, as the island's center, has all the attractiveness of its Spanish sister cities on the mainland. Its profile is dominated by its soaring Gothic cathedral, built in the thirteenth century with all the fervor of a people rejoicing over liberation from long centuries of Moorish rule. Inside this lofty building a rose window has an unusual property of shaping the rays of the sun into circular shafts that fall on the stone floor in the form of perfect circles of rich blue, green, or gold.

Another building of Palma is the Lonja, or "Exchange," built in 1426 to serve as a trading place for the rich maritime trade carried on by the seamen of Majorca. Today it is a museum, its interior graced by six spiral columns of particular elegance. From its four towers a splendid view over the closely crowded city can be enjoyed.

The Royal Palace near-by was once a Moorish structure called the Almudaina, and is now a government office building. The streets of old Palma are filled with charm of all varieties— the busy everyday life of the attractive people, little shops and stalls where bargains can be unearthed without any searching, the fruit vendors, the bright-eyed children and, in odd contrast, the bobbing streetcars painted a rich orange color.

Up above the city's inland limits rises the Hill of Bellver, capped by the colonnaded, battlemented royal castle that is a popular goal for leisurely promenaders heading for a lovely view.

There are many other sights of attractive appeal in Majorca outside of the city of Palma. The main trip for visitors leads into the surrounding mountains, through the fertile valleys lined with almond trees and olive groves. Fifteen miles from Palma is the beautiful, secluded town of Valldemosa, which clings to a massive Carthusian monastery built in stages through recent centuries by its industrious monks. Chief interest in Valldemosa for modern-day travelers is its vivid memory of the composer Chopin and his author friend George Sand, who spent the winter of 1838 here trying to find a warm climate for Chopin's frail health. They took a suite comprising several one-time cells facing richly planted gardens and a superb view out over the valley. The big building is now a museum, centering about the Chopin mementoes of pianos, manuscripts, and testimonials, and an elementary pharmacy organized long ago by the Carthusian monks.

Beyond Valldemosa the road winds high above the sea along majestic cliffs. On one side of the road is the vista over the enchanting deep-azure sea, with pinnacles and breath-taking sheer sides enhancing its foaming shores. On the other side of the road are endless groves of the oldest olive trees in the world, so old that their trunks are gnarled in the most agonizing and fantastic shapes, yet they still bear the useful fruit that yields the valuable oil export of the island.

Passing the former Hapsburg estate of Miramar,[15] the road leads to the handkerchief-sized landlocked bay of Sóller, and the pretty, tile-roofed city of the same name lying three miles inland. Sóller is a veritable garden of orange and lemon trees, snugly protected from the outside world by Majorca's highest peak, Puig Mayor, six thousand feet high and often capped with snow.

Returning to Palma by rapid electric train, one can start out later on drives through the semitropical plains to such old-time romantic towns as Pollensa, Alcudia, Inca, Manacor, and to the fashionable beach of Formentor, favored hideaway of celebrities.

---

[15] This name inspired Archduke Maximilian to give his marble palace at Trieste the same lovely title.

Another "must" is to drive forty miles across the island from Palma to Drach on the far coast, where there are several caves containing underground lakes of brilliant transparency, comfortably admired by gliding over them in gondolas.

The other Balearic Islands are of less interest because they are flatter, smaller, and windier. Minorca, thirty miles to the northeast, has a landlocked bay at Port Mahon prized by the British and French navies over the years, and with several attractive towns. The other islands of Formentera and Ibiza are smaller editions of Majorca, but without the indefinable charm of the greater island.

The Balearic Islands, located only 132 miles off the coast of Spain, have been attached to that country's fortunes throughout the ages. They are best reached by overnight boat or by short plane ride from Barcelona.

Their name signifies "slingers," and was given to them by the Carthaginians, who held their earliest inhabitants in healthy respect because of their matchless skill at using that effective primitive weapon. Carthage enlisted bands of these slingers to fight in her armies against the Greeks and Romans.

When the Romans ejected the Carthaginians, they found such delight in Majorca that they built the city of Palma in testimony of the "palm of victory" and made it a favorite resort of theirs. After the Romans, the Visigoths held the islands in tribute until the corsairs from North Africa planted the flag of the Crescent over them in the ninth century. For four hundred years the islanders enjoyed the benign rule of these outsiders who introduced the arts of weaving and learning as practiced in Andalusia and Morocco. The tolerance of their rule is evidenced by the fact that no forced conversions to Islam were made during that time.

However, the growing resentment of the Kingdom of Aragon on the mainland opposite to having a Moslem outpost so near its capital city of Barcelona led to an expedition being sent out in 1232 by King Jaime I. The Moors were ousted with little difficulty. In the years following, the islands became incorporated with Aragon and, following Ferdinand and Isabella, with united Spain.

Majorca, because of its size and its fortress at Palma, escaped depredations from wandering navies, but little Minorca was less protected. In 1531 it was cruelly ravaged and despoiled by the Turkish corsair Barbarossa in revenge for the equally cruel Spanish destruction of Tunis.

In the eighteenth century Minorca fell under British naval rule for various periods, because of its closeness to Toulon, whence the sea dogs of Albion could keep a close check on the movements of the French fleet in those days before wireless and radar.

Minorca was split again from its neighbor during the Spanish Civil War of 1936-1939. Larger Majorca joined the Franco side from the start, whereas Minorca stood firm for the Republic down to the very end.

Thus the islands of the Mediterranean have played a commanding role in the great story of the peoples of the inland sea. Most of them lie apart from the heavily traveled lanes of twentieth-century voyaging, and for that reason they have retained their charm and separateness, a distinctness that gives an added blend to the racial groups of which they form an annex. They possess many artistic relics, and some of them have quite modern tourist facilities and comforts.

Those travelers who have not the time or good fortune to set foot on any of these islands often have the favorable chance to gaze at them from the seaward, or from the air above, with opportunity to admire their beauty and graceful outlines as they pass by. Mute and secluded as they now stand, their existence has played one role at least that has vital import for our age—they were beacons to the daring early mariners who stood out boldly to sea, steering toward the faint trace of land on the far horizon.

THE PILLARS OF HERCULES AND MOROCCO

IT IS NOW TIME to sail out of the Mediterranean, and what better way than to follow the course charted by the ancients—through the Pillars of Hercules?

Ancient mariners who felt at home in the landlocked Middle Sea disliked the rough ocean outside the Mediterranean and considered it an unfriendly and frightening body of dangerous waters. The Greeks, with their perennial imitators the Romans, feared the unknown world beyond their sea, and they conveniently adapted a handy legend to give them an excuse for staying safely inside the comforting limits of their Mediterranean.

The Phoenicians and the Carthaginians, however, had not been so coy or so overawed by the narrow exit into the outside world. The Phoenicians had sailed through the Strait of Gibraltar almost a thousand years before Christ and plodded both north and south along the tidal shores. The Carthaginians had traded down the coast of Africa and stood boldly out into the open ocean.

But the Greeks were excited by mixed sentiments on beholding the passage. Their earliest navigators were thrilled by the glorious sunsets seen through the strait.[1] To the Greeks the bright colors of sunset signified happiness and fortune. Greek writers located the "Isles of the Blessed," the happy continent of Atlantis, out there in the wide unknown, basking under such rich and glowing colors. They also set the legendary gardens of the Hesperides, a place of problemless happiness, in this general area.

---

[1] Residents of Berkeley, California, can appreciate such a scene by admiring their sunsets seen through the "slot" of the Golden Gate.

However, a frightening element neutralized these sentiments, since the Greeks reasoned that ordinary mortals would be doomed if they tried to pry into such heavenly secrets. They told of an unhappy titan named Atlas, brother of Jupiter, who rebelled against the head god and was sentenced eternally to stand out in the west and support the weight of all the heavens on his broad, titanic shoulders. This he was solemnly doing when one day he mistakenly looked upon the head of Medusa the Gorgon, being turned forthwith to stone. His robust body became a mountain range, his feet steep cliffs, and his hair and beard a thick forest atop the crests. To this day those mountains—the Atlas range—still hold up the heavens; and both the lost continent of Atlantis and the great Atlantic Ocean have been named after this hapless titan Atlas.

Many years later Hercules, coming by on one of his missions, paused to cut a passage for himself through these mountains. Proud of this achievement, he named the two edges of his opening after himself and, before heading home, snatched up the golden apples of the Hesperides,[2] which are considered to be the oranges of Spain.

Thus a legend, created to explain away a fear, was turned back upon itself. Hercules' Pillars, instead of opening a passage, were rather interpreted as marking a limit, a bound across which no one dared trespass. The Greeks named the northern pillar, rising on the European shore, Calpe; that on the southern, or African, side was christened Abyla.

The Arabs, who later took possession of these pillars, gave them the names that have come down to us—for Calpe, Gibraltar, (Jebel-al-Tarik); for Abyla, the Jebel Musa.

The Strait of Gibraltar

The Strait of Gibraltar is a geographic phenomenon almost without parallel in its strangeness and in its influence on history. But for it, the Mediterranean would be a super-briny lake. Its narrow width of nine miles has for centuries, until the opening

---

[2] The Hesperides' name in Greek means "Daughters of the Evening"—another reference to this land of the ancients' far west.

of the Suez Canal, been the only connection between the immense, landlocked Middle Sea and the outside oceans of the world. The strait is the only opening in the solid front of the Old World from Denmark down to the tip of southern Africa.

Two currents squeeze through this amazing cleft between the continents. The one on the surface represents the Atlantic flowing into the Mediterranean to replace the heavy evaporation that goes on from the inland sea's entire surface. The other is deep down beneath and is a reimbursing flow of water from the cool depths of the Mediterranean into the vacuum caused above.

Yet the strait is too narrow to permit any tides to pass through. The Atlantic tides, which reach fourteen feet at near-by Cadiz, and sometimes higher in Lisbon, dwindle to a matter of inches inside the strait. The Mediterranean is thus tideless, mirror-clear because of little silt, and very salty; the Atlantic is high-tided, more opaque because of its silt and sediment, and less heavily salted.

A common misconception held by non-travelers is that the Rock of Gibraltar stands at the edge of the strait. This is, alas for the romantic, inexact, for the Rock is tucked inside the Mediterranean entrance. As another surprise, the Rock is faced completely away from the sea! The bristling mane and head of the lion-shaped Rock gaze across the flat, sandy soil leading to Spain!

The Rock is made up simply of a tilted ledge of limestone topped by a rough ridge. It is cavernous inside, holding reservoirs of drinking water fed from concrete-paved catchments on various steep sides of the fortress rock. Its head reaches fourteen hundred feet in height, and around its chest are punctured big holes from which cannon can shoot.

Dotting the shoulders of the Rock are military barracks, huts, and scattered buildings. Gibraltar Town on the flanks below is a free-and-easy little place known to thousands of sailors of Britain's navy. It has row upon row of shops displaying the wares of all the world, without tariff or duty surcharges. It has a cemetery in which are buried many of the dead of Trafalgar. Its chapels, canteens, and clubs are filled with seamen taking it easy in this rock-girt linchpin of Britannia's Empire. Chief way of spending time for a casual visitor is to clop-clop by buggy down to Europa Point for a view across the strait toward Ceuta,[3] or back around to the other side of the Rock for a swim in the Mediterranean and a halt to see if some of the elusive Barbary "apes" will make an appearance. These apes, which are really small monkeys, are the only such animals native to Europe and are deliberately spoiled and pampered, for their disappearance would, if tradition means anything, presage the departure of British power from Gibraltar.

Oddly enough, one of "Gib's" chief sights is its airport. When World War II came, and Gibraltar was Britain's only base inside hundreds of miles of hostile lands, an airport was hurriedly built by prolonging a tiny prewar racecourse far out into the bay until it furnished a runway. Eisenhower, Churchill, General Giraud, and countless luminaries of the wartime forces touched down on this tiny speck of friendly soil.

From Gibraltar, Spain can be clearly seen. Just across the boundary line is a town, appropriately enough named La Linea, complete with bull ring. Directly across the five-mile-wide bay is the larger town of Algeciras, which is the beginning of the Spanish railroad system, connected by through trains with Seville and Madrid.

To a land power like Spain, it might seem incongruous that a foreign power should hold on to the tiny peninsula of Gibraltar hanging down from the huge mainland of Spain. And that is why the Spaniards have been trying to get it back for 250 years. During the American Revolution, when Britain was preoccupied with its war across the ocean, Spain concentrated her entire energies on besieging the Rock and starving out the British from their toehold. For four years this grim and time-consuming effort went on, but the British held out. Spain, rather than getting the Rock back when the peace treaty of 1783 was signed, got Florida instead!

---

[3] At this point, fifteen miles away.

Gibraltar's name originated with Tarik, the Arab leader who led the hosts of Islam across the strait in A.D. 711 after conquering North Africa. It means "Tarik's Mountain."

Britain's role began a thousand years later, in 1704, when her forces seized the harbor and Rock as a blow against the new Bourbon King of Spain. To Britain, as a sea power, this Rock and harbor are a natural and necessary type of possession. Small enough to be administered by naval men, strategic enough to watch over the vital strait, it is to them no problem to anybody, and actually a boon to Spain, since over twenty thousand Spaniards cross into it daily to be employed in jobs that pay much better than anything they could do at home.

Leaving the Bay of Gibraltar, steamers reach the strait very quickly. Following the shore of Europe westward for three miles, they reach the narrowest point at Tarifa's[4] lighthouse on the right, marking the southernmost tip of Spain. The shorelines of Europe and Africa then begin to draw apart again, and soon the end of the short outlet from the Mediterranean world is attained. The headland up the Spanish coast to the north is Cape Trafalgar, off which Nelson won his smashing victory of 1805 over the French-Spanish navies, murmuring as he died aboard his flagship, the *Victory*,[5] "England expects every man to do his duty." Beyond the cape lies the port of Cadiz.

The headland on the African side is Cape Spartel, beneath which lies Tangier. Those capes mark the end of the strait, facing out into the open Atlantic.

Tangier

Africa's "watchdog city" outside the Strait of Gibraltar is Tangier. This colorful Moorish town has been an African window on Europe—and a European look-see into Africa—down through the ages. It is only a two-hour crossing by steamer from Gibraltar

---

[4] Tarifa is supposed to have given us our word "tariff," from the dues levied by the Moors when they held both sides of the strait.

[5] This old frigate has been preserved and can be visited in the naval port of Portsmouth, England (only twenty miles from the port of Southampton).

or Algeciras, and a railroad connects it with the big cities of Morocco to the south.

Tangier is a drawing card for an even more significant reason. Europeans with money to spare invested it in real estate in this little enclave of old-time laissez-faire. The world's moneys were freely exchanged on the streets of Tangier without worries as to blocked accounts, black markets, or embargoes. Why? Because for fifty years Tangier enjoyed the strange status of being a free "international city," belonging to no country and administered by the consuls of nine European nations.

This anomaly among the world's political units grew from its strategic location at the doorstep of the Strait of Gibraltar. No European nation, particularly Britain, could tolerate any other country's annexing it. So, by process of universal agreement, it came to be governed by so many countries that it belonged to none—except to the Empire of Morocco, whose Sultan was always recognized as its official sovereign, and whose local governor, or *Mendoub,* exercised jurisdiction over the native Moors living in it.

This picturesque, rag-tag type of government devised by international agreement for this anachronistic but strategic zone is now a matter of history. It can be found in detail in any of the guidebooks surviving from those days, for its separate status was doomed as soon as Morocco was given its independence by France in 1956. Two years later the Sultan reannexed his fair city, his "window on Europe," while respecting its separate financial status and free zone privileges. However, this arrangement turned out to be merely a stopgap. The proud Moroccans eventually demanded its complete integration into the motherland, and by 1960 Tangier reverted to the status of a Moorish provincial port town. Along with it came the whole "International Zone" including Cape Spartel with its powerful lighthouse perched on the northwestern "shoulder" of Africa.

Travelers landing here find the city charming. Its core is the old Moorish casbah of tightly crowded, whitewashed square-roofed houses rising up the slopes from a tiny bay. Around this old city and its minaretted mosques extends the modern town of fine hotels, banks, apartment houses, palm-lined drives, parks, and gardens, sports fields, and wealthy homes. The finest residential district lines the cliffs facing the strait, across which can be clearly seen the lovely profile of the hills of Spain.

Inside the walled Moorish city it is interesting to promenade through the winding alleyways as in Algiers. In the heart of the town is the Petit Socco, or smaller market square, where the cosmopolitan groups of the city mix, bargain, argue, and loaf, in true African style. The larger market, or Grand Socco, stands at the corner of the walled city facing the business district of the new town. Here, every Thursday and Sunday, an animated market takes place, with foodstuffs, flowers, and bargains of all kinds offered by the Arabs of the vicinity.

One should also see the Sultan's Palace, or governors' mansion, which is now a rug-making school and a museum of old treasure chests. From the roof a splendid view can be had over the strait; and a café for taking refreshments in Moorish style is open to all.

Tangier has held on to its Moorish flavor despite its having the most chequered history of all Moroccan cities. Founded by the Phoenicians and Carthaginians, it was built up by the Romans into the city of Tingis, capital of the province of Mauretania, which was Rome's name for Morocco. However, Roman occupation was merely a veneer; the Visigoths and Vandals erased all traces of civilization, until they themselves were swallowed up by the Arab conquest of the eighth century. The city then became a bone of contention between the Moors of Morocco and the Moors of Spain for several centuries. Then suddenly, in 1471, a Portuguese expedition swooped down and captured the city. For almost two hundred years afterward, Tangier was thus subject to a Christian power, only to be suddenly traded over to another when in the year 1661 Portugal handed it as a free gift to Great Britain in the form of a dowry for a Portuguese princess. However, Britain was passing through a weak period under her "Merry Monarch," and her forces evacuated Tangier in 1681 after a series of menaces from the Moors.

The international period of the city's history stemmed from a custom the European powers had in the nineteenth century of stationing their diplomats accredited to the Moorish Sultan in this easily protected city rather than sending them into the chaotic interior. The international statute and the status of the Free Zone "growed" naturally from this practice into the recently-lapsed elaborate arrangement.

Tangier is a popular winter resort for Europeans because of its mild weather and accessible location. It has given its name to a distinct type of local orange, which is now known throughout the world as a tangerine.

Fez, Religious Heart of Morocco

If we enter Morocco by going south from Tangier, we can get to understand this mysterious country more quickly, for we will see in the proper order the cities most representative of its different epochs and cultures. Fez, magnificent city of fervent Islam, is Morocco's earliest Moslem capital and its most typical-looking walled city.

Morocco is an exciting land to visit. Having entered the world of international life only in this twentieth century, it has changed little since the time of its heyday. Morocco offers a curious paradox—there it is perched on the strategic, accessible northwest shoulder of Africa, and thus the nearest of all African lands to America. It is the farthest advanced of all Islamic lands into the Western world. Yet, despite this advantageous natural position, Morocco played no part in the great explorations of the Atlantic Ocean that coasted past its front door. Instead, it felt isolated, being so far from the source of its religion and culture—Arabia. Known in Arabic as Maghreb el Aksa, or the "westernmost land," it clung to isolation and inbred fanaticism. Thus, even though it was grazed by the imperial thrust of Europe on several occasions, it was able to escape the full blast of this force and to stay aloof from the world's affairs—until the twentieth century.

Probably the principal cause of this curious isolation has been the lack of unity of the people of Morocco. The inhabitants are still mainly Berbers, the original settlers who were not uniformly Moslemized by the early Arab invasions of the seventh century, and who maintained their own tribal organization. The Atlas Mountains have an effect of dividing Morocco in two, while their side-valleys tend to enforce tribalism. Instead of a competition between tribes, tending toward progress and innovations, the competition seems to have been in reverse—to remain more traditional, more fanatical to one's own idea of religion, more separated from new thoughts, than one's neighbors.

During the first two hundred years of Moslem Morocco, the chief city of the land remained the Roman town of Volubilis.

The site of this town with the prosperous-sounding name was uncovered only a half-century ago, and travelers of today can enjoy the restoration of much of this Roman town, which, in the third century after Christ, was Rome's frontier outpost in Mauretania. Roman rule did not extend much farther south of Tangier than to this region around Volubilis. The town eventually went the way of all rich Roman settlements in North Africa— looted and decimated by Berber revolts, plundered by Vandals, and felled by earthquakes. Yet today, in a little museum outside the city's beautiful restored triumphal arch, can be seen some pretty bronze statues like those at Pompeii, also gold jewelry, fragments of mosaics, lamps, lost coins, and fractured columns.

Volubilis' last act of grace was to contribute its population to colonize the new Arabic city of Fez, built fifty miles away as Islam's first new-built settlement in this "westernmost land." It was a peculiar custom of the early days of Mohammedanism to ignore heathen, infidel cities and build totally new ones consecrated from their birth to the Prophet of Mecca. Thus the fervent early believers erected Cairo in Egypt, Bagdad in Mesopotamia, Kairouan in Tunisia, Cordoba in Spain—and Fez in Morocco.

A hundred years after the Moslem conquest, a descendant of the Prophet himself, named Idris, arrived in Volubilis and by his fervor converted the Berber tribes to his way of strong faith. When he was poisoned by an envoy from the Arabic caliphs, he was buried in a valley near-by, around which a holy city named after him simply Moulay Idriss has sprung up. This ancestor town of Fez is still so holy to the fervent Moslems of Morocco that no Jew or Christian can live there, and the few tourists who come to see it may enter only by day, being rigorously excluded from the precincts of the holy man's sanctuary.

Idris' son, Idris II, founded Fez and conquered a large part of Morocco. His thoroughness in building the city's walls, and in encouraging Berber peoples to come and live there started it off on an era of prominence that made it the glory of medieval Morocco.

Fez lies 225 miles south of Tangier by road and slightly farther by rail. It is on the main North African trunk line railroad from Casablanca to Algiers and Tunis, and thus was gazed at by many American G.I.'s taking the long ride toward the Tunisian battlefields in 1943.

By the mid-1300's, when Europe was in the thraldom of the Middle Ages and America not yet discovered, Fez was a prosperous city of two hundred thousand, recognized as the cultural center of all North Africa and southern Spain. We who go to Fez today can see the city just as it looked and worked in its heyday.

Fez is today a city in three parts—Fez-el-Bali, or the "Old City"; Fez-el-Djedid, or the "New City"; and the European settlement outside the walls. Inside both old and new Fez, travelers must leave their cars and launch out by foot through the succession of narrow streets, so typical of all Moslem towns. Pretentious mosques, scattered through such a holy capital, rise on all sides, but no infidel is permitted to enter them. Moroccan mosques are thus more fanatically regarded than in Egypt, Syria, Tunisia and other Moslem lands where infidels can go through them at their leisure.

However, outsiders can go into a *medersa*, of which there are several inside this city. A medersa is part mosque, and part an academy of Moslem law and theology preparing students for careers in government, religion, or the judiciary, all of which are closely connected in Moslem tradition and governed solely by the Koran.[7]

Fez also attracts attention by its magnificent gateways, gateways that look like the most stately fancy of the *Arabian Nights.* Through them go all the sundry types of a Mohammedan city— the proud Berber chieftain, the turbaned city dweller, the barefooted waterseller, the heavily-veiled, silent-shod women, the mer-

---

[7] The University of El-Azhar in Cairo is of this same tradition.

chants from other cities carrying many of their wares on their back or on that of a plodding donkey, mullahs, or holy men, and sad-eyed little children enjoying so few years free of the responsibilities and taboos of adulthood.

Visitors can spend one day or a week in this enchanting and unusual Mohammedan city. Despite its age and its ups-and-downs, and its off-chilly weather, it has remained through the centuries the intellectual, religious, and artistic capital of the land; and its inhabitants are more tutored, cultured, well-mannered, trade-minded, adroit, courteous and diplomatic than the people of any of its rival Moorish cities.

A fine hotel called the Palais Jamai exists inside the walled city, housed in a palatial Moroccan home.

The enchanting life of this city is the principal interest for all visitors. The muezzins calling from the numberless minarets, the men shuffling into a mosque, the bazaars teeming with bargains and treasures, and the holy mystic silence outside the sacred tomb of Idris II, founder of the city, all proclaim that this is Morocco at its best and most typical. The scene looks so strangely Oriental —so much like Arabia, Persia, even India—that it is with a start that we remember that Fez is only 126 miles from the Atlantic Ocean.

Shopping is the second preoccupation for all foreigners visiting Fez. The principal items to shop for are jeweled ornaments, brocades and embroideries, beaten copper tabletops, trays, platters, objects of Moroccan leather (a product of excellence through the ages), pottery, rugs, and antique weapons.

When the visit to Fez is reluctantly over, we can feel that we understand the Moorish mind, conditioned to its way of life unchanged through the centuries, and can continue toward the newer, more modern sections of this paradoxical country—an Oriental land on the Atlantic, an African land in a northern latitude, or as Marshal Lyautey so briefly summed it up—"a cold country under a hot sun."

Meknes—Versailles of Morocco

Only seventy-five miles west of Fez, and scarcely twenty miles south of Volubilis, sits Morocco's second imperial city—Meknes—

high on its hilltop above the fertile plain that nourishes Fez and Volubilis.

However, Meknes did not reach its glory until the seventeenth century. Before that time Morocco went through several conquests. The Idris dynasty of Fez lasted only a century before being overrun in 1053 by the Almoravides, a puritanical Moslem sect that rolled up from the desert to the south. This dynasty was in turn overwhelmed in 1147 by the Almohades, a Berber movement from the heart of the Atlas that occupied the same territory and spread even to Tripoli. These dynasties performed the function of at last uniting the "westernmost land" under a single government. In the way they left it, it remained until our times—a Berber country converted to Islam, containing several great cities of Spanish-Moorish art and civilization, and owing allegiance to a government that tried to combat separatism by identifying itself with the religious goals of Islam.

In the thirteenth century a new wave of Arab immigration into Morocco overthrew these Berber rulers and attached the country once more to its North African neighbors, under the tutelage of a Bedouin dynasty called the Merinides. This period brought on a stage of disintegration. Arab words and traditions were introduced to engulf the Berber customs, and a purer form of Islam was taught by the many medersas founded by the new Sultans.

After the Merinides came a period of chaos resulting from the collapse of the Moorish kingdoms of Spain, whose desperate refugees poured into Morocco, an unstable force of religious desperadoes. Mohammedan fanaticism took a new turn in revenge against the Christian victors, and a wave of warrior saints gained the upper hand in various sections of the divided country. At this time the Sultans took on the title of the "Sherifian Empire," a symbol of the holy mission of their government—to stand as the guardian, or *Sherif,* over the holy places of the Mohammedans.

The present Alaouite dynasty of Morocco came to the front in 1666 under Moulay Rechid, who expelled the Saadite sect from the southern capital of Marrakech.[8] His son, Moulay Ismail, how-ever, became Morocco's first Grand Monarch in the style of his contemporary Louis XIV of France, and the whole country rocked under his energy.

Moulay Ismail reigned for fifty-five years, from 1672 to 1727. Imposing a reign of terror on his country, he unified it, but main-tained his rule by a mercenary army of Negroes brought from the Sudan across the desert. To house these strangers, he built castles and fortresses across the land; and to give honor to his palace guard and to exalt himself, he chose Meknes for a new capital.

Thus, under this one Sultan, Meknes was changed from an oasis city of mediocre importance into an imperial center. Today this city is a sight to pause for when traveling from Fez to the coast. Its pretty setting in a fertile valley, and its Fez-like appear-ance with high, thick walls that weave around a terrain ample enough for a far greater metropolis, are enhanced by impressive Oriental gateways.

Among the thirty thousand slaves set to work by Ismail were three thousand Christian captives, who labored on the mosques, palaces, stables, and pools inside the walls. Because this great enterprise was carried on at the same time that Louis XIV was erecting his monumental palace city outside Paris, Meknes is often referred to as the "Versailles of Morocco." But it has no artistic creativeness, and after Ismail's inevitable death his great city began to decay, although the great gateways and monumental-sized ruins are of first-rate interest. Like this city, the whole country slipped into disorganization after Moulay Ismail's reign.

Down to the twentieth century the prevailing situation was chaos, while the Sultans, despite their noblest efforts, gave up the task of ruling their realm beyond the closest suburbs of their chief cities.

---

[8] Marrakech had been capital of the country for so long that it had given its name to the country in the eyes of the Europeans. Until 1925 its European name was Morocco City. Its name was spelled "Marruecos" by the Spaniards —and carried over into Italy as "Marocco"—thus becoming "Maroc" in French, and "Morocco" in English.

Before leaving Meknes, one can visit a prison where Christian slaves were kept confined and observe from a distance the shrine of Sidi Aissa, one of those Moorish saints whose cult is treasured by the fervent fidelity of this odd extremity of Islam. Sidi Aissa founded a self-flagellating sect whose reunions became a brawl of shouting, contortions, bloodletting, mayhem, and self-torture, including the eating of serpents and ground glass. The more modest rites of these ceremonies are often staged for groups of tourists outside Morocco in the oasis towns of Algeria, principally Biskra.

Rabat, Morocco's Modern Capital

It is only eighty miles by excellent road from Meknes to the resplendently modern city of Rabat, the capital of French Morocco, a city of first-rate interest located on the Atlantic Ocean at the mouth of the River Regreg.

Now a pleasant city of one hundred thousand people, Rabat set the style for all the new Moroccan cities—a French-type settlement complete with gardens, pretty homes, modern hotels, arcaded office buildings and shops, palm-lined boulevards, and a profusion of clubs—rising outside the walls of the tinier native city, which was left to live in its own Arab way, subject to a few sanitation improvements and police measures.

Thus the Boulevard Lyautey, Rabat's main avenue, is a delight to foreign travelers. Two or three hotels, together with more modest hostelries, offer all the comforts and delights of Paris life and cuisine.

On the southern outskirts of this twentieth century city stand the Royal Palace and the Home of the former French Residents-General. The Sultan's Palace is new, built in proper regal style by the French in faultless Arab architecture. Visitors can see the gardens, walk inside the patios, photograph the palace guardsmen in their bright-red pantaloons and tunics, and even catch a sight of the Sultan driving to his private mosque if it happens to be a Friday.

Rabat's most artistic and impressive monuments, however, date from the Middle Ages, when the Moors made it one of their strongest coastal citadels.

The thing to do in Rabat is to enter the native city down by the ocean and stroll through its *souks,* or colorful open-front bazaars, where the usual profusion of Oriental handicrafts can be shopped for (and the price agreed on) at leisure. Beyond the souks are the Oudaias Gardens lying inside a high-walled citadel built in the 1100's by the Almoravide Sultans. It is entered by the usual magnificent gateway, with much to see inside—the old medersa made into a museum of Moorish art, the formal gardens, a promenade along the top of the walls giving a fine view of the city, and a shop for Moroccan rugs, brassware, leather work, and jewelry. For refreshment, there is a Moorish-type café on the far side of the walls, located high above the Regreg River just above its mouth in the Atlantic Ocean.

This Oudaias citadel is a lovely place in which to rest and muse on the significant story of this unique land of Morocco, all the while enjoying the view, especially at sunset. The ocean across the bar at the river's mouth is the same Atlantic which on the opposite shore washes the tidal islands of Georgia and the Carolinas. If it is wintertime, the walls of the gardens will be lined with storks, the identical birds that like to nest on Danish chimneytops and Dutch windmills, but fly down to Morocco to pass the winter.

Rabat's story has had much to do with the development of modern Spain and the voyages of discovery out into the Atlantic Ocean.

Ironically, Rabat originally was a suburb[9] of the crowded, whitewashed city of Salé huddling on the far side of the Regreg River from which we are sitting. Rabat grew up as a camp for warriors defending the city and then as a rallying point for troops being gathered to fight Christians in Spain. In the twelfth century the Oudaias citadel was built as a fortress commanding this important spot.

A half-century later, at the time Richard the Lion-Hearted was leaving England for his Crusades, the Moslems won the great victory of Alarcos over the Castilians. In celebration, Sultan Yacoub el Mansour renamed the place Rabat el Fath, or "Camp of Victory," and launched himself into an enterprise of building

---

[9] Rabat in distant Malta is likewise the "suburb" of Mdina.

the hugest mosque in the world, whose minaret would surpass the Giralda of Seville and the Koutoubia of Marrakech built by his fathers. He was half finished when he died, whereupon, as is so customary in Moslem lands, his work fell into the discard. The minaret, called the Hassan Tower, can be easily seen from our vantage point, rising up from beside the river. One hundred forty feet high, its spire only is lacking. Everyone should mount it, climbing the easy internal ramp, which was made wide enough for three horsemen to ride up abreast. At its feet stand long lines of columns, all that have been left by earthquake and pillage of the greatest mosque in the world that was never finished.

Salé and Rabat were later peopled by disgruntled refugees, the half-Christianized Moriscoes of Spain, expelled by Philip III in 1608. They took avidly to piracy, a trade that had already sprung up in this sheltered river mouth, taking advantage of the loaded Spanish treasure ships wallowing homeward from America off these coasts. Portuguese merchantmen, following more closely inshore on their route back from India, were likewise fair prey. These rowdy corsairs became so dreaded in their depredations that the "Sally Rovers" had to be evaded by following a more inconvenient course farther off the coast.[10]

From Rabat it is only twenty-five miles up the shore to the excellent harbor of Kenitra, built by the French at the mouth of Morocco's principal river, the Sebou, which flows all the way from the central Atlas ranges. "Port Lyautey," as it was known then, was occupied by the American Navy on the first day of the great landings on the Moroccan coast in 1942, and has remained a naval air base ever since.

Just outside Rabat extends the parklike Forest of Mamora, whose thick oak trees produce some of Africa's finest cork for the markets of the world.

No one can stay long in Rabat without hearing occasionally reverent mention of Marshal Lyautey. Every visitor also wonders how this beautiful French-style city happened to grow up in such a Moorish land, and how it is that France's stamp of culture is

---

[10] Robinson Crusoe tells of being attacked and captured by "Sally Rovers" in the opening chapters of his adventures.

so extensively ingrained into this ancient and still Moslem territory. The work of Marshal Lyautey will best give the answer to that fascinating story, which all took place in our own century.

How the French Came to Morocco

Four hundred years ago two Christian nations tried to conquer Morocco and failed. They were Portugal and Spain, who felt that the proximity of such a fanatical Moslem state was an uncomfortable menace to their own welfare.

After two centuries of struggle, they succeeded in holding on to a mere handful of coastal villages. Neither of those two countries had the strength or will to subdue such a large and fanatical people as the Moroccans, so that by the dawn of the twentieth century Spain's and Portugal's interest had dwindled away almost to nil.

However, more-powerful European states were fastening their eyes on Morocco for strategical and commercial reasons. They were embarrassed by the existence of this chaotic realm on such an important site, commanding the south side of the Strait of Gibraltar and fronting on sea lanes running to the new European empires in farther Africa.

These nations were primarily France, Britain, and Germany. The French were closely concerned because of their large neighboring colony of Algeria, whose pacification was continually jeopardized by incursions and smuggling from the Moroccan side of the frontier. The British had historic trading rights and interests and, besides, had taken the stand that no strong country should get preponderance in the land across from Gibraltar. Germany, for her part, was in an expansionist mood looking for new markets to conquer.

After 1900 French diplomacy began to take definite steps to end the uncertainty over Morocco. The energetic Foreign Minister Théophile Delcassé bought off any possible Italian rivalry by a treaty giving Italy a free hand in Libya. In 1904 France and Britain cleared the air by leaving Morocco to the former and Egypt to the latter without competition from each other. France then won Spain's consent by awarding her a sphere of interest along

Morocco's Mediterranean littoral. All was now prepared for a French protectorate over the Sherifian Empire to be proclaimed, when Germany suddenly overturned the applecart.

The Kaiser, cruising in his yacht, sailed into Tangier harbor on March 31, 1905, landing with conspicuous pomp. Pretending to be the Protector of Islam, the Kaiser made a speech saying:

"I am making this visit in honor of the independent and sovereign Sultan of Morocco, a Morocco that will remain freely open to pacific relations with all nations, without monopoly or annexation, on the basis of absolute equality."

Germany was too strong an empire to be ignored. France's plans were swept into the wastebasket, and an international conference was called for the next year.

This Algeciras Conference was one of those international gatherings in which the United States played a full part. President Theodore Roosevelt exercised a strong influence from a distance to thwart the demands of the Germans. When the conference adjourned, it had made a compromise that helped the French start rolling again. It declared Morocco independent but entrusted police supervision to the French and Spanish and allowed France to guard her Algerian border without any interference.

The French were soon able to take the next step. When a French engineering party working at Casablanca to build its first docks was attacked by rioters, an insurrection against the authorities almost wrecked the city. Immediately a Franco-Spanish force landed and occupied the port. General Lyautey, in turn, advanced across the opposite frontier from Algeria to protect Frenchmen in the Oudjda district.

The next year civil war broke out in Morocco, as the Sultan was declared deposed by his brother in Marrakech. The usurper attacked the French, only to be defeated. Fleeing to Fez, he found himself the brunt of an uprising by Berber tribesmen. Soon the situation of the Sultan was impossible. At his call for help, a French expedition hastened inland and took the city.

The fall of Fez in the early summer of 1911 brought the Germans to life again. The Kaiser sent the warship *Panther* into the southern harbor of Agadir. The French then became so resentful over this interference that Europe rocked with the threat of war. Headlines in American papers splashed the name of this faraway country—that was really not so very far away—across the vision of the crowds enjoying the summer on the beaches directly across the ocean from Agadir.

Britain and the world stood by France in this crisis, so the Germans agreed to "negotiate." As soon as they were bought off by a grant of a huge block of land in the French Congo, they removed all objections to a French protectorate over Morocco. Accordingly, on March 30, 1912, the Sultan at Fez signed a treaty granting France authority over Moroccan trade, finances, foreign affairs, and internal order.

General Lyautey came to Fez as the first "Resident-General," only to be isolated inside the walled city by the rioting multitudes. In the nick of time, reinforcements came to his aid, whereupon the attackers melted away. Lyautey, on leaving Fez to his successor, set the motto for the new regime by saying:

"Be like iron for the respect due to France. . . . Respect their religion, their pious establishments, their women and customs. In short, *Ne les embêtez pas!*"[11]

It was Lyautey who chose Rabat as the site for his mission and for the residence of the Sultan from that day on.

Who was this remarkable colonial administrator whose name is now a hallowed byword in France for a wise and skillful governor of a proud and independent empire?

Maxime Lyautey was a career officer who had spent his life in Algeria studying the ways of the Moslems. He determined to apply to Morocco a twentieth century technique to pacify and administer the country without disturbing its social or religious ways.

Accordingly, the Sultan was left in charge of the administration of the natives. Local officials, observed by French administrators, applied Moslem law to their localities. In the name of the Sultan, Lyautey began to expand into the Atlas Mountains, winning the Berber tribes to an alliance without having to use his army.

---

[11] Translatable only approximately as "Do not do anything to make them get stubborn."

Roads were extended and markets built to systematize trade and communications.

His work was so successful that it had been well grounded by the time World War I broke out. The French Government gave Lyautey permission to withdraw his forces to the coast, but the general replied laconically, "I will hold Morocco for France."

And he did. During the long war that followed, he sent almost all his troops back to the mother country, yet continued his penetration into the farthest reaches of his territory. By 1932, French control had extended out into the desert beyond the Atlas, and the pacification of Morocco was declared complete.

Lyautey died in 1926 and was first buried in a simple mausoleum at Rabat. Now he reposes in the Invalides at Paris with Napoleon. In this time when imperialism and colonialism are under close scrutiny everywhere, world students must take into account the unmistakable and astonishing task accomplished by the French in so few years. Physically the country has been transformed with new cities, mines, electrified railways, a network of good roads, many schools, hospitals, native academies, factories, and, not leastly, great ports like that at Casablanca. Yet native life has not been visibly changed, in that its cities, occupations and tribal organizations have been left untouched. Agriculture, forestry, handicrafts and sanitation have been brought up to a European standard or minimum.

To foreigners, the greatest miracle is that travel is now so relatively safe and easy. They can motor safely from city to city, or up into the high Atlas, whose peaks reach close to thirteen thousand feet high. They can laze in comfortable hotels in native towns, or in desert oases. They can wander through the souks, observe Moorish arts and crafts, and purchase the increasing output of native souvenirs and art objects.

Morocco can be reached by air from Paris, or Lisbon, or Madrid, in a few hours; it is connected by rail with Algeria and Tunis; it is on the main line of surface travel from Spain via the Gibraltar-Tangier ferry, and it is one of the chief ports of call on all Mediterranean cruises.

In short, Morocco has been put on the map of the world with a twentieth century respect for the artistic and creative way of life of this paradoxical people who prefer to exist as did their ancestors of ten centuries ago.

Casablanca, Morocco's "Americanized" City

Everyone has heard of Casablanca, the Moroccan port supposedly a center of intrigues and unsolved mysteries. However, they may not be so aware of the more palpable facts about this "Atlantic window" of French Morocco. For instance, it is not always appreciated that whereas Casablanca as recently as 1907 was only a small, walled Arab town, it now is a fast-growing metropolis of a half-million people, of whom at least 150,000 are Europeans. Back in 1907 there was no harbor—just a bend in the coast where ships were unloaded by hand-rowed lighters that could only cross the reefs when the ocean was sufficiently calm. Today Casablanca has a full-sized deep-water harbor, protected by a mile-long breakwater and served by the most modern of piers, wharves, and warehouses. And whereas Casablanca was just an isolated little locality at the beginning, it is now the hub of railroads and highways leading to the farthest corner of Morocco —through the great Atlas ranges and out on to the Sahara plateau beyond.

Such a twentieth century port was naturally a prize of first-rate value during the war. That is the main reason why the Allied landings in North Africa were concerned with seizing Casablanca's vital port and communications nexus. This done successfully, Casablanca then served as the great port of debarkation for troops, supplies, and munitions that eventually led to the opening of the Mediterranean, the expulsion of the Axis from Africa, and the conquest of Italy.

Casablanca has expanded so rapidly that its French builders like to talk of it as an "Americanized city." For such a modern town and port to have been constructed so speedily and efficiently despite the handicaps of two world wars smacks of American methods and achievements. However, the French settlers stress that something new has been added, something they call a "Latin grace." In other words, a city of beauty has been created as well as a city of commerce and industry.

When going ashore at Casablanca, this is certainly a talking-point in comparison with many American and British port cities. The principal streets and avenues are lined with French-type modern buildings, faced with colonnades and Parisian embellishments, and often rows of palms along the middle. The public buildings are all designed in superb Arabic style that sublimates anything the Moors themselves have evolved for their own commercial centers. The cafés, newspapers, theatres, hotels, and shops are all on the Parisian style—and tempo.

Instead of one native quarter, Casablanca actually has two. The Old Medina is comprised of the original town rebuilt after the bombardment of 1907. The old town joins the new city at the Place de France, surely Casablanca's most interesting spot, for here all the paraphernalia of a modern European city—taxis, restaurants, office buildings, and modern-dressed people—are mixed with the Arabian Nights costumes, veiled women, watersellers, and impassive robed individuals who just sit and contemplate the passing parade. Then, the French have built a completely separate New Medina a few miles away, complete with mosques, narrow streets, public market squares, and bazaars, to accommodate the vast accumulation of native settlers who have flocked to this city for jobs in its busy industries and harbor activities.

Casablanca has a square once dedicated to Marshal Lyautey, and a palace for the Sultan (which he seldom if ever uses), whose gardens are as beautifully laid out and ornamented with tiled tea-houses and Arab "orangeries" as could be found in any caliph's palace in Damascus or Bagdad.

Modern Casablanca stretches out along its Atlantic coast for several miles. It has beaches modeled on Plage de Paris, a huge swimming pool one thousand feet long on the very edge of the ocean, filled and refreshed by every tide, and it has a modern hotel called the Anfa on a beautifully landscaped small hill. Here was the scene of President Roosevelt's conference with Prime

Minister Churchill in January of 1943, when the two statesmen forced the feuding French generals De Gaulle and Giraud to shake hands publicly, and where they announced their doctrine of unconditional surrender as the only basis for peace, an announcement that gave great heart to the suppressed multitudes of Europe and enabled them to take a more relentless stand against the Nazi-Fascist armies of occupation.

The Anfa Hotel stands on the highest hill anywhere near town, a gentle rise that gives a pleasant view of the whole city and its modern residential suburbs, together with the rocky, low Atlantic shore. Americans can well muse at this shoreline, which is the first bit of land to rise above the ocean in three thousand miles of billowy expanse from the similar low land of the Carolinas and Virginia opposite.

Travelers who come from Rabat to this city find the approach to Casablanca most interesting. The distance is only fifty-six miles and can be covered in less than two hours. Over this flat countryside the road passes many typically Moroccan scenes. The primitive native huts, conical-shaped lean-to's of reeds and brush, called in the native tongues *noualas,* are similar to the commonplace huts of the great Sudan area beyond the desert. Heavy masses of prickly cactus surround each of these small farms, representing Nature's most effective fencing apparatus. On some modern houses along the road, storks can be seen perching grandiloquently. In the fields the helpful little white birds, called *piqueboeufs,* ride on the backs of the cattle, conveniently pecking annoying insects off, or else following respectfully behind the plowers' masters as they turn over the soil. And on the roads, dromedaries can often be seen plodding along with a heavy load for market.

On the way between the two cities, every motorist should stop at the little resort city of Fedala, because on its majestic, curving beach the first wave of American landing craft hurtled in out of the ocean on the early morning of November 7, 1942. Their surprise was so complete that they captured the entire German Armistice Commission billeted at the Miramar Hotel. Today a plaque commemorates that event on the beach itself, and the hotel offers pleasant, sea-cooled accommodation and other hospitality.

As Casablanca comes into view, it is an impressive sight of white skyscrapers, industrial chimneys, and great factories that proclaim this city to be the "New York of Morocco," or, as the French say, the most striking accomplishment of France overseas.

Casablanca was selected as the chief port site for Morocco because of its tradition as a trading post for a selected few European merchants during the past three hundred years. The Portuguese had originally seized the town, but then were forced out by the Moors in the eighteenth century. The Portuguese and Spanish merchants had called their trading post the "White House," and the Moroccans accepted this name when they rebuilt the town. Thus, Casablanca it has remained ever since. During the nineteenth century and the early years of the twentieth, it became the principal place for dealing with Moorish traders for wool, goatskins, and grain. Thus, when the Sultan authorized a French company to modernize the port here in 1905, it drew down on the engineers and laborers the fire of the fanatical resistance of the neighboring tribes, which resulted in the bloody riots of 1907 and the landing of the French forces that eventually established the Protectorate. This head-start as the bridgehead of the French regime, and its nearness to the new capital of Rabat, are what determined the growth of the harbor of Casablanca into what Lyautey visualized —the pride of French technicians and engineering skill on this neglected coast of northwest Africa.

Marrakech—the Southern Capital

No one can leave Morocco without visiting Marrakech, the picturesque capital of the land for four centuries, and its southern city at the gates of the Sahara.

Situated 150 miles inland and south from Casablanca, Marrakech is a vivid contrast to the great port city—for it is a Moorish oasis, surrounded by eleven miles of reddish-rose walls, dominated by its lovely Koutoubia minaret[12] and peopled by a greater cross-

---

[12] The Koutoubia was designed by the same dynasty that erected the Giralda Tower at Seville.

section of Berbers and inland natives than can be found in any other city of the country.

The best way to reach Marrakech is by electric train, since the countryside is flat and uninteresting, except for the wild-flowers that spring up during the winter rains. Upon approaching it, one sees the first ranges of the Middle Atlas on the horizon. This may be the travelers' first view of the Atlas ranges, since they lie far inland from the coast in most of Morocco and only come toward the Atlantic in this southern region of the land.

During the winter and early spring, snow sparkles on the crest of these noble peaks, making for a lovely backdrop to subtropical, palm-girt Marrakech.

Upon arriving, most visitors transfer immediately to the unique Hotel de la Mamounia, built in tropical style with balconies and terraces and located in a magnificent park of orange trees, bougainvillea and subtropical vegetation.

The things to see in this city comprise entirely the native architecture, the enticing bazaars, and the magnificent show of native life.

The Koutoubia minaret is a typical monument of pure Arabesque style. Over two hundred feet in height, reddish-rose in color, it has sculptured faces, a rim of blue tile around the top, and a tiny spire surmounted by golden balls.

Marrakech is an odd combination of market place and holy town. It grew up in earliest days as a trading center between the plainsmen and the caravans from across the Atlas. Its name is a Berber term for "keep moving," because of its continuous crowds and teeming traders even in those days. However, the Almohad dynasty, upon making this city their capital in the 1100's, began to make it a religious monument of their fanatical faith. In the 1200's it became resplendent under the reign of the Sultan Yacoub-el-Mansour (the Victorious Jacob), who erected the Koutoubia mosque and minaret, and administered his whole empire from here. Later the Saadian rulers, the local Sultans who controlled southern Morocco during the troubled times of the sixteenth century, built mosques, finished the walls, and made Marrakech the unusual city we see today. The city's greatest patron, however, was Sultan Ahmed "the Golden," who in the late 1500's brought treasure from the faraway Niger, from Timbuktu, and from desert oases for miles around, to lavish on Marrakech. He designed the tombs for his family that are today gems of Hispanic-Moorish art. They can be visited in their original glory—marble tombs of Ahmed and his son, in a lovely room surrounded by twelve columns of Italian marble and walls of tiles and lacy sculptings, at the foot of which are buried the Sultan's relatives. The roof is a dome of gilded cedarwood.

The souks or bazaars will occupy much time of the visitor, since their offerings include unusual items brought from the Sahara region—scimitars and old arms, Oriental jewelry, as well as fine Moroccan leather produced in the city itself.

However, by far the most exciting thing to do in Marrakech is to go at sundown to the great market square, bearing the resoundingly romantic African name of the Djemaa-el-Fna, where the native life reaches a fascinating climax. After a long day of trading for the most trifling of necessities—empty cans, amulets, roasted sausage, herbs, old bottles and bric-a-brac—the Berber people from the mountains gather into circles to be amused by Africa's most traditional entertainers—acrobats, magicians, snake-charmers, wailing storytellers, mountain dancers, musicians with weird ancient-designed instruments—all performing in circles surrounded by the motley peoples of western Africa—Arabs in brightly striped hoods, Chleuh tribesmen in bright blue, Oriental Jews in Levite black, Haratin clansmen from the Sahara, and Negroes from the far Sudan half-naked in their linen pantaloons.

This unstaged spectacle of unmatched interest, seen at sundown with a backdrop of the graceful Koutoubia, makes for one of the highest experiences of pure travel enchantment that can be found in this twentieth century world.

Morocco has still more things to see—seaside towns, skiing resorts in the Atlas, oases in the desert, mountain villages, French army posts in strange tribal areas, and magnificent Oriental cities built in the purest form of medieval Arabic art. It will exercise a growing appeal to American travelers as the years go on, because of its nearness as the rampart of the Oriental Moslem world closest to America, as well as its unspoiled, unchanged way of life stemming from a thousand years of incubation and inbred development unhampered by outside conquest, and because it is the most varied of all North African lands, with more scenery, a greater network of highways, and a more motley population producing a greater profusion of excellent handicrafts than any other Moslem country in the world.

The Atlas Mountains and the great Sahara Desert shut off Morocco from the rest of Africa and make of it an island of civilization in the northwest corner of the great African continent. Yet modern methods of travel and modern efficiency will make it possible for hardy adventurers of the future to push out from Morocco's farthest outposts across the still undefined southern boundary and out along the caravan trails leading to that legendary trading emporium on the other side of the desert, beside a great river named after its black tribes the Niger, a city known since the days of Carthage as Timbuktu.

ATLANTIC OUTPOSTS

Madeira, the Canaries, and the Azores

THE INFLUENCE OF THE MEDITERRANEAN does not by any means end where its continental outposts—Portugal and Morocco—fall away into the wide Atlantic. The Mediterranean world has outlying sentinel positions—islands lying out in the wide ocean, remnants perhaps of legendary Atlantis. These island groups are three—Madeira, the Canaries, and the Azores. They are as distinctly a part of the Middle Sea as if they lay snugly inside the Pillars of Hercules, for they enjoy a Mediterranean climate; they have a gentle Mediterranean way of life; and they belong to two Mediterranean countries—Portugal and Spain.

Madeira and the Canaries are salubrious winter resorts, semitropical lands of beauty designed by Nature for luxurious loafing and convalescing. The Azores, farther out in the deep blue, are "unsinkable aircraft carriers," naval bases of great value, and also a steppingstone to America, which made them first a valuable cable station and now a strategic aviation base.

These island groups, far enough out at sea to be unknown to medieval Europe, were nevertheless discovered and settled by the energy of Prince Henry the Navigator during the fifteenth century, so that they were able to serve as bases for the further voyages of his sea rovers. Columbus lived on an islet off Madeira for ten years, compiling information from the tales of returning mariners; and on his first famous voyage to America, he spent three weeks outfitting and watering in the Canary Islands.

Let us take a look at these beautiful sea-girt lands—these tops of volcanic peaks reaching far up from the oceanic bottom to above the foamy Atlantic. Beginning with the ones nearest to the Mediterranean, we arrive first at Madeira.

Madeira, "Flower Garden of the Atlantic"

Picture a lovely island only 37 miles long and 12 miles broad, which rises precipitously out of the warm Atlantic to a peak 6,150 feet above the sea. Being the top of an extinct volcano, its soil is rich, its vegetation is a profuse green, and some of its beaches are jet-black volcanic sand.

Its nearest mainland neighbor is the Moroccan coast of Africa 340 miles away to the east, but its principal commerce is with the mother country, Portugal, whose capital city of Lisbon is 535 miles northeastward. In relation to America, Madeira rises from the ocean 2,760 miles east by south of New York.

Madeira's holiday atmosphere and flowery mild winters make it invariably a port of call on Mediterranean cruises operating from New York in the winter months. Travelers approaching it by sea find its rugged scenery magnificent. During the middle of winter, they can espy the rare treat of crisp snow tipping the higher peaks, even though the aroma of spring flowers can be sniffed from the lower reaches of the slopes. On coming closer they can sense the appeal of the balmy climate and see the quaint tiled roofs and the tinted fronts of the houses of Funchal, the chief city, rising up the steep sides of the island as if to form an amphitheatre around the small, deep bay that is the island's only harbor.

Madeira has almost 300,000 people, of whom over 80,000 live in Funchal,[1] which is a semitropical edition of Lisbon in its general appearance. It has the same mosaic-patterned sidewalks, gaily colored buildings, avenues of palms or jacaranda trees, and flowery displays as those of the mother city on the mainland.

The island has been famed throughout its history for the famous Madeira wine produced from the vineyards that line the

---

[1] Funchal was named by the first settlers "the place of fennel" because of the profuseness of that herb on the hillsides.

terraces scooped out of the steep slopes of the mountainsides. Aged in casks stored in Funchal warehouses, or *bodegas*, it can be bought, sampled, or tasted by all visitors and carried away in bottles packed into gaily colored wicker containers woven by the industrious women of the island.

Madeira's second most important source of wealth is its embroideries. Linen, imported from Ireland, is assigned to women on a piecework basis. They skillfully embroider this material in their homes, turning it over to Funchal stores for sale in the form of doilies, handkerchiefs, tablecloths, blouses, or napkins, as well as for export all over the world.

Next comes the tourist trade, an enterprise that engages most of the Madeira islanders in one way or another. Several good hotels—among them the internationally famous Reid's Palace —and many pensions are open all year round in Funchal. The tourist trade comes mainly from Britain and northern European countries, as Americans come here only on Mediterranean-bound cruise liners. Madeira fills the function of serving as a "Bermuda" for British travelers seeking warmth and color and carefree semi-tropical holidays in this closest of such lands to their misty cities.

Madeira's hospitality extends to conserving three of its lazy, antique forms of transportation which add immensely to its appeal to vacationing travelers. Where else in the world can a holiday-goer find bullock-hauled sleds, or wicker "toboggans," or portable hammocks? Yet they are all available in Madeira.

The need for getting around the rugged island in nabob style brought about these short cuts to comfort back in the old colonial days, but the people of Madeira have the good sense to hold on to them despite the onslaught of modern automobiles. Their tenacity is paying off, for the tourist trade is crowding the wine and embroidery industries for the position of top money-earner in the island's exchequer.

These old-fashioned, home-grown "vehicles" are unfailingly intriguing to newcomers. When someone wants to go sightseeing leisurely in Funchal, a bullock-sled is the thing. This is actually a sled, although it looks like a gay carriage with a fringe on the top. Yet it is mounted on handsome, curved runners instead of wheels and is towed by two patient bullocks. The streets of Funchal are paved with smooth cobbles, and the sled coasts along easily and smoothly, prodded now and then by passing over a tallow bag thrown down by an attendant. Who cares about speed? The bullocks will get you there sooner or later.

Much more unique, however, is Madeira's own tropical toboggan. People ride up by automobile to the panoramic outlook of Terreiro da Lucta 2,670 feet up the mountainside above the capital city. After enjoying the view and a lunch at the restaurant, the fun begins of coming down by toboggan. Picture a cozy seat on a wicker platform, the whole fastened to flat runners. Two "runner boys" holding the contraption back with ropes run alongside as the toboggan slides down the steep inclines over a cobblestone trail. Visitors need do nothing more than sit back and let gravity give them leisurely propulsion. While descending they can gaze at the superb view, admire the tinted villas, arbors and flower gardens that rival those of Naples, and coast lazily down into Funchal's main street.

More antique, but still to be found—and hired—are "cross-country hammocks" that date from far back in Madeira's comfortable history. What can be more relaxing than lying in a fluffy hammock that is slung from a long pole borne by two agile men? This form of traffic is specially designed for reaching the steeper slopes and upper heights of the mountainous island. However, these hammocks are gradually growing extinct as motor cars begin to force roads out to most parts of craggy Madeira.

To those who linger for a while on Madeira, various scenic drives are offered. Only twelve miles west of Funchal there is a superb sight—a black cliff rising out of the ocean to a sheer 1,900 feet. Hardier souls can look down at the tossing sea from its summit, standing at an altitude twice as high as the Eiffel Tower. Other drives follow the coast through colorful little fishing villages, where it is possible to stop and muse for a while, buying flowers, making friends with the hospitable townsmen, and inspecting the homes and churches of this simple setting. The countryside is full of picture-making possibilities, scenes of grandeur or homely shots of peasants hauling their produce on donkeyback or lolling outside their thatched cottages. On all sides can be seen the intricate system of terracings, which, like tattoo scars, climb every mountainside laboriously. On these narrow shelves, some only two feet wide, the people of Madeira grow most of their food, grain, vegetables—even bananas and sugar cane.

Madeira has every facility for sports and entertainment, including a golf course, casino, open-air movie theatres, and social events with music and dancing.

This lovely island was first put on the maps of Europe in the year 1418, when a Portuguese sea captain named Gonçalves Zarco landed at its offshore satellite of Porto Santo, twenty miles to the northeast. He was sent out by Prince Henry on assignment, for legends had reached the royal ears, of an island in this vicinity. A hundred years before, a ship bearing two eloping British lovers was wrecked on the island, and the little village of Machico is supposed to have commemorated the couple by a fragment of the cross marking their burial place. A sailor who managed to escape on a home-made craft of some kind was later captured by the Moors and related his story to a fellow-captive, who was able to hand it down after his escape to freedom.

Zarco also discovered the main island of Madeira and gave it its name, which means simply "wood." Unfortunately, most of the timber has disappeared through the centuries, probably due to the growth of wine culture and the terraces that give the vines room to take root.

Columbus married a young lady whose father was Governor of Porto Santo, meeting her in Lisbon and following her out to this island, which in those days was the farthest-flung outpost of Europe. His house is still on display to visitors who go over to Porto Santo.

When the Portuguese found this little archipelago, it was totally uninhabited. During the fifteenth century, settlers were brought from Portugal and from the Spanish Netherlands, and later on there was an influx of Moorish captives and Negro slaves. Madeira has always belonged to Portugal, and is an integral province of the mother country.

The Canary Islands

Slightly different, more tropical and closer to Africa in comparison with Madeira, and belonging to Spain are the seven mountainous Canary Islands.

Lying 150 miles due south of Madeira, the closest one inshore is only 80 miles off the Sahara coast of Africa—a strip of land owned by Spain that is south of Morocco and dependent on the Canaries for its government.

The two islands of the Canary group most frequently visited by vacationers are Grand Canary and Teneriffe. The other five—Lanzarote, Fuerteventura, Comera, Hierro, and Palma—are usually seen only by those who spend some time on the central two.

Largest of them all is Teneriffe, whose culminating peak of the same name, rising to twelve thousand feet, stands as a beacon from far out at sea, especially in winter when thick snow covers its summit and flanks.

Capital of the archipelago is Santa Cruz on Teneriffe Island, a town that is typically Spanish in its stately beauty and general layout. It has several good tourist hotels to accommodate its regular influx of winter visitors. The balmy breezes from Africa keep the southern shores of the island warm and cozy, encouraging bananas, oranges, almonds and luscious flowers to grow profusely in the gardens and along the roads.

The people of the islands are an industrious and friendly strain of the Spanish race. They bring their produce and their basketware into the towns for sale at the lively markets, which constitute such an unfailing attraction for visitors.

The second largest island is Grand Canary, situated across a deep channel twenty miles Africa-ward from Teneriffe. This almost round island is steep and volcanic as is its neighbor. On its northeastern flank sits its principal city of Las Palmas, while its northerly point protects the best harbor in the Canaries—Puerto de la Luz. Ships connect this town with Seville in Spain every week, while direct air service to Madrid also operates regularly.

Las Palmas is a smaller city but a more modern business center than Santa Cruz on Teneriffe Island. It likewise has hotels and pensions, a beach, and many sports facilities. Both islands have good roads that parallel the narrow shore, and trails leading into the side valleys. The warm, carefree atmosphere of both, their richness in tropical fruits, and their sunny weather convince historians that these were the "Isles of the Blessed" sung about by Homer and described by Plato.

The Canaries weren't named after the well-loved canary birds, but instead gave these birds their name. The word is considered to mean "wild dogs," and was possibly bestowed on the islands by the earliest Portuguese navigators, who were feeling their way down the African coast toward fearsome Cape Bojador, which lies only a few parallels of latitude to the southward. Since these islands were inhabited by a backward but warlike tribe of Africans called Guanches, the Portuguese didn't bother to colonize or claim them, especially after the King of Castile had asserted a positive title to them inherited from some shipwrecked sailors of a century earlier. Thus Castile took possession of these islands in the early fifteenth century.

Warfare with the Guanches on the island of Grand Canary finally extinguished the tribe and also the wild dogs. As for the little brown finches that winter in this balmy land, they gradually acquired the name of "canary island birds"[2] and were introduced into Europe by being carried away as caged songsters by early transatlantic sea captains.

Columbus led his three tiny vessels hither from Spain before attempting the hazardous ocean crossing. His investigations had worked out the fact that suitable winds blew westward in this southerly latitude. Thus he made a good start, on leaving this lovely haven, by being blown across the intervening arm of the Gulf Stream and well south of that area of dangerous calms called the Sargasso Sea, which had inspired earlier pioneers with fear and forebodings. This "sea," described as being a mass of clawing seaweed, dangerous monsters, and deadly calms, is nothing more than the basin of unruffled water enclosed within the en-

---

[2] The yellow color of today's canary birds was bred into them later by German fanciers.

compassing arms of the Gulf Stream. Later navigators called it the region of the "horse latitudes."[3]

Columbus' skillful navigation avoided that tricky patch of ocean and fetched him up against the Bahama Islands over two thousand miles due west of the Canaries. He knew enough of the ocean winds to chart his return voyage far to the northward, where different breezes would carry him quickly, even if turbulently, homeward.[4]

The Canary Islands are scenically exquisite. They stand as friendly mountain beacons saluting the passing ocean liners bound out from Europe to the faraway lands of South America and South Africa beyond the equator.

The Azores

Far to the north and westward lie the nine Azores Islands, scattered astride the Great Circle route bearing direct from Gibralter to New York.

The Azores are in the latitude of Lisbon, 850 miles to the west, thus being about one-fourth of the way across the Atlantic between Europe and America. They were discovered by the Portuguese in 1434, during a voyage by Captain Gonçalo Velho on a mission for Prince Henry. Mysterious maps had been appearing in various Italian and Catalan towns, describing some "islands of sea birds" out in the Atlantic, and Henry probably was convinced by one that was explicit enough for him to locate their approximate position before anyone else could possibly seize them. A map drawn by the ancient Alexandrian cartographer Ptolemy had stated pointedly

---

[3] "Horse latitudes" supposedly originated as a name from the fact that becalmed Spanish galleons forced their horses to jump overboard to lighten ship and save water.

[4] Columbus' blazing of this northward orientation led to a Spanish ship's discovering Bermuda in 1575 (the storm-tossed isles were named after its captain, Juan de Bermudez) ; it also explains the reason for Spain's founding of St. Augustine in Florida, as early as 1565, as a fortress and base for protecting the narrow exit route from the Gulf of Mexico for Spanish treasure fleets endeavoring to avoid the pirates infesting the other channels leading out of the Caribbean.

that seven such islands existed. The Moors of Morocco were also quite familiar with them, judging by their rudimentary charts found by Henry. The Carthaginians are supposed to have been the first voyagers actually to land there, as indicated by some Punic coins found on Corvo Island, but these are now nowhere to be seen in any museum.

The islands were discovered one by one during the fifteenth century; then peopled by Portuguese, Flemings, Italians and later by castaways; settled into established towns and villages reminiscent of Portugal; and annexed to the mother country, as they have remained down to the present day.

As if in tribute to the earlier sketchy maps, the islands were given the name of Azores (meaning "Hawks"), as evidence of the discovery of the same islands' connection with flocks of sea birds, as had been indicated by the mysterious other explorers.

The islands lie in three groupings running from southeast to northwest. The first group is comprised of the two discovered earliest, lying nearest to Europe—Santa Maria and São Miguel (or St. Michael). The central group comprises five smaller islands lying close together—Terceira, Graciosa, São Jorge (St. George), Pico and Fayal. Off to the northwest, farthest toward distant America, lie Flores and Corvo. The names of these volcanic peaks were chosen aptly by their discoverers and were bestowed either in honor of saints or in description of the beautiful appearance they made from out at sea.

Of the 280,000 inhabitants of this mid-ocean archipelago, approximately half dwell on the island of São Miguel, whose chief city of Ponta Delgada is the business center of the islands. Ponta Delgada has recently become the chief safe harbor because of a sturdy breakwater completed during the war. It is a compact and pleasant town resembling Funchal in Madeira, with Portuguese architecture, quiet streets, and brightly colored stucco houses. A deserted chapel has some exquisite wood-carving on the walls done by unknown early settlers. It has a few small hotels and an international business colony, making for a quiet social life.

A museum exists in Ponta Delgada housed in a former convent. On display are statues carved by local talent, a stuffed whale, a two-headed calf born on the island and likewise stuffed, and much lace work and handicrafts of the islanders, together with a complete set of elaborate paintings giving historical tableaux of Portuguese history.

The island is fifty-five miles long and has quite a bit of variety for such a small area. East of Ponta Delgada is a resort area of foaming hot springs, many of them medicinal, in a region appropriately called Furnas. On the other end of the island is located a lake in an extinct volcanic crater bearing the romantic name of Seven Cities.

São Miguel has taken energetically to the cultivation of pineapples, which in this latitude have to be grown in greenhouses. Each pineapple plant takes almost a year and a half to nourish into a bloom. When full-grown the fruits are husky and black-skinned from the smoke that is pumped into their greenhouses to force their growth. They, together with their canned juice, make for a luxury export to Europe that, it is hoped, will balance the once-heavy trade in oranges that featured Azores' trade balances until the trees were killed off by a mysterious blight three decades ago.

São Miguel's smaller sister island of Santa Maria is exceedingly mountainous in its small area of eighty-five square miles, with colorful little towns hugging its wider valleys, but it is practically the best known of all because of its large international airport built during the war. Until 1946 a heavy traffic in passenger planes as well as in bombers winging their way to Europe used this pioneer field, which housed a population of several hundred American troops. Today it is only a civilian field, surpassed in importance by a larger military base recently constructed on Terceira Island.

Terceira (so named because it was the third to be discovered in the Azores) lies ninety miles northwest of São Miguel. Being less rocky than the other islands, it offers scope for a large agricultural and cattle production, as well as for the important airport of Lagens. This airdrome is of significant value to the American Air Force, since all-year-round weather conditions permit the heaviest bombers to alight here for fuel on the long hop to Europe when the shorter northern route is closed in by winter fogs. Portugal gave us the rights for this base during the closing months of the war, then extended it as a concession to keep our Air Force in Germany supplied, and finally re-extended it when she, as a member of the North Atlantic Treaty Organization, became an ally of the United States.

The most stately of all the islands in appearance is Pico—planted in the center of the chain of nine—well-named for its symmetrical peak that rises to the lofty height of seven thousand feet, highest point in all Portugal, and indicative of the monumental forces that could push a volcano up such a fabulous distance from the bottom depths of the Atlantic. Pico's inhabitants are skilled in hunting whales and are considered to be principally Flemish in origin.

Sheltered by this massive mountain, the adjacent smaller island of Fayal furnishes the Azores' one-time chief harbor of Horta, located across a four-mile strait from Pico's magnificent profile. Horta was made a mid-ocean cable station in the late nineteenth century, and thus was the island's chief city for a few years until Ponta Delgada's trade overtook it because of its larger and richer hinterland.

The two outflung islands of Flores and Corvo are small and scantily populated. They possess hot springs, but are without roads or harbors, and are occupied mainly with pasturage.

The history of the Azores has been a story of patient struggle and isolation. While semitropical in general climate, the islands suffer from stiff winds and fogs, and have not built up any tourist trade, not only because of the weather, but also because of their greater distance from the motherland Portugal. Its inhabitants were Portuguese and Flemings at the start. When Portugal became part of Spain in 1580, the Spaniards took an interest in the Azores, building a fortress on Terceira and stationing their fleet in the vicinity in order better to defend the homing treasure fleets. A civil war broke out in the next century when the Portuguese took necessary measures to expel this garrison.

In the eighteenth century the British fleet began discovering the advantages of rendezvousing in Azores waters for the purpose of checking any French or Spanish squadrons that might attempt to seize the islands as a prize in the imperial struggles going on in America and India during those embattled decades.

The limited agricultural output of the islands and the decline of the whaling industry hit the Azores hard during the nineteenth century. Since 1880 the population has remained relatively stationary as hundreds of families abandoned their windy homeland for richer pickings abroad. Many of them went to Portugal's former colony of Brazil, where they were quickly absorbed into the population. Hundreds of whaleboatmen signed on with New England whaling ships and at the end of their voyages settled down in Massachusetts coastal cities to seek a more remunerative living from fishing and sailing. Still others, who signed on passing sailing ships as expert mariners, "hit the beach" in Hawaii to work in sugar fields, or else, in California, where they built up Monterey's sardine-fishing industry. The overwhelming majority of the Portuguese population in the United States is thus Azorean in origin.

Other Azores farmers took the short voyage to Bermuda, the nearest mid-Atlantic island to them, where they have since taken control of the vegetable- and truck-gardening industry on that warmer and more accessible island.

In World Wars I and II German submarines lurked in the lee of these lofty islands, while British diplomacy worked in both wars, on the strength of Portugal's ancient alliance with Britain, to keep the islands safely on the Allied side. The development of world aviation has now come in its turn to give the crowning touch to the Azores' strategic location in mid-Atlantic, keeping them under the close guard of diplomatic chancelleries of all the world's capitals.

EAST OF SUEZ

Arabia, Iraq, and the Persians

Ship me somewheres east of Suez,
  Where the best is like the worst,
Where there aren't no Ten Commandments,
  An' a man can raise a thirst.

IN SUCH A SHORT QUATRAIN Rudyard Kipling summarized the explanation of the vast difference existing in the thoughts and standards of the multitudes who live "east of Suez"—in other words, beyond the end of the Mediterranean.

One line in Kipling's verse—"Where there aren't no Ten Commandments"—is literally a summing up of the great difference between Europe and Asia.

This means that "east of Suez" the unhappy lands and peoples of Asia have been subject to the rule of force instead of the rule of law throughout their history. The Oriental standards of government by favoritism, nepotism, and "squeeze" have been handed down from century to century without being tempered, except by influences from without. The trend of other peoples toward national states was of no concern at all to these lands of the Middle East[1] until our own times in the mid-nineteenth century. Now this concept has been borrowed by educated governing classes in order to work political miracles among the supine masses, who see

---

[1] Middle East is a term applying to the lands around the Persian Gulf and Caspian Sea (Iran, Iraq, Afghanistan, Pakistan, and the Caucasus), and it should be distinguished from the Near East, which, strictly speaking, is identical with the Levant.

nationalism as a negative force to help smack down the foreigner rather than as a way to consolidate their own countries.

In short, the lands east of Suez are not permeated with the doctrines of individual dignity, service to others—or the Golden Rule—or equality before the law,[2] as are the states of Europe and those in America, the daughter of Europe. The struggle to live and the distrust of governing authorities—who have the power to confiscate, to tax, and to cause no end of botherment—are instead the ever present thoughts in the minds of the millions. Consequently, there is no natural popular barrier against the doctrines of Communism, or the organization of a Soviet state, as there endemically is deep down in the make-up of almost every European. For, after all, the Soviet state, which borders directly on the Middle East, has made more material progress and has evolved more startling twentieth century technological wonders than have any of the smaller peripheral countries. And the coaxings of Red propaganda—preaching salvation to the individual—are like honey to the ears of individuals who for centuries have had no such kind attention from the oligarchies or autocratic potentates of their own nationalities.

"East of Suez" can include the entire continent of Asia and its dependent islands. However, for the purpose of our interest, "east of Suez" applies only to those lands lying beyond the eastern rim of the Mediterranean that have felt an influx of ideas and a cultural influence through their contact with the civilizations that have lived along the actual coasts of the Middle Sea.

For it is a palpable fact that the great dynamic impact of the cultural movements originating on the shores of the Mediterranean throughout the ages has set up waves of motion that have ringed their ways farther and farther back into the barren and mountainous landlocked regions to the east. Races that have long since disappeared, together with those who are still anxious for a more progressive life, have been gilded with shafts of light from the

---

[2] This statement is not meant to overlook the lofty achievements of certain religions, such as Hinduism, Buddhism, and some sects of Islam. However, even though individuals and groups inside these religions have evolved noble motives and ideals, the national and tribal states have not adopted or acted toward these at all times on a government basis.

Mediterranean aura and have been ennobled by what they have absorbed.

This region "east of Suez" includes the great peninsula of Araby; the rivers Tigris and Euphrates, together with the salt sea called the Persian Gulf into which they flow; the mysterious land of the Caucasus at the far tip end of the Black Sea, where the Armenians and the Georgians live; the high plateau of Iran, or Persia; the incubation zone of our race in central Asia surrounding Samarkand and Tashkent; and the valley of the Indus River inside the gates of India. This whole region was once forged into an empire by the armies of Alexander the Great, for Alexander had merely followed a trail connected through the centuries with the Mediterranean empires.

Christianity for a time grew to be a unifying force resolidifying these interconnected lands of Alexander's dead empire. Christian missionaries, bearing the Syriac rite from their center at Antioch,[3] penetrated into Persia, and even to southern India, where their converts carried on the message through the centuries down to the Portuguese conquest 1500 years later. However, Christianity was blotted out everywhere else in this whole land mass by the total victory of Mohammedanism. Not only Christianity and paganism, but the ancient nature-worshiping religion of Persia—Zoroastrianism—were drowned in this irresistible flood.[4] However, it is one of the most significant facts of world history that the Moslem surge went only as far overland—and no farther—as Alexander's armies had marched. Up to the Indus River and over the treeless steppes of central Asia to the end of civilized settlement, the equalitarian doctrine of the Prophet of Mecca swept. And there it was halted—either by the Hindu masses of India, or by the Buddhist nomads of Turkestan, who had never known the effect of Hellenism or Mediterranean ideas.

Centuries later, Arab mariners carried the flags of Islam to the South China Sea, but that is far outside the scope of our story.

---

[3] Antioch is the place where the disciples of Jesus "were first called Christians" (Acts 12:26).

[4] Remnant of the Zoroastrians are the Parsee sect in India's seaport city of Bombay, who fled from Persia to carry on the old religion.

Today, the Mediterranean's hinterland beyond Suez is totally Moslem—except for the island of the Armenians, who are independent Christians, and their neighboring people, the Georgians, who have associated themselves with the Orthodoxy of Holy Russia.

The Arabs

Bearers of the doctrine of Mohammed to the far corners of the Old World were the Arabs, originally one of the Near East's most backward desert peoples. A Semitic race confined to the sandy wastes of Arabia, a people akin to the Assyrians, the Babylonians, the Chaldeans, the Phoenicians and Syrians, and the ancient Hebrews,[5] they were an inarticulate association of wandering nomads during the entire ancient classic period. Worshiping pagan idols and desert deities, they counted for naught until one of their own number—Mohammed—galvanized the entire world with his revolutionary new religion that he called Islam—"Peace with God."

Mohammed lived in an obscure city called Mecca, located in an oasis of Arabia only forty miles inland from the Red Sea. He had traveled in Syria and Palestine, and knew the Jewish and Christian religions well. His purpose was to distill what he considered the finest points of those religions, to take lessons from their prophets—particularly Abraham (Ibrahim), Jacob (Yacoub), David (Daoud), and Jesus (Issa)—but to shun the idolatrous practices which horrified him. He wrote a holy book called the Koran, into which he poured all his thoughts and beliefs, and also a code of social laws, adding strict *do*'s and *don't*'s. He forbade idol-worship to the absolute extreme of outlawing the drawing of any image—even of a flower—in art or architecture. He interdicted the drinking of alcohol. And he conveniently abandoned the Christian teaching of "love your enemies" and "do good to those who persecute you" by authorizing his followers to kill infidels in a holy war as the surest transition to paradise.

Mohammed's radical new teaching stirred up his home town of Mecca to such a hostile degree that he was chased out of it by the irate priests and citizens. This event, which took place in

[5] Hebrew tradition classes the Arabs as descendants of Ishmael, Abraham's son by the bondwoman Hagar.

the year A.D. 622, is called in Moslem history the Hegira, or flight, to the city of Medina, and registers as the year 1 on the Mohammedan calendar.

Ten years later Mohammed died at Jerusalem. Only a few years afterward the new doctrine swept the thinkers and masses of Arabia. The old pagan gods were dashed into the discard, and the rabid flocks of devotees smashed Christian statues and figures as equally detestable idols. Inside of a century, the new religion swept into the great area which had been partly Hellenized by Alexander the Great, and partly Christianized by latter-day missionaries. Christianity was stamped underfoot, one of the most significant events of all history. For with the loss of its holy places and the decimation of its Levantine rites, Christianity had to turn Westward, its Western rites of Constantinople and Rome taking pre-eminence in the direction of the movement's spread. Christianity became a European religion instead of a Mediterranean imperial faith. In its place, controlling the one-time strongholds of primitive Christianity all over Asia,[6] the new Asiatic, Arabian faith of Islam took hold and soon eradicated all traces of the original teachings of the early Christians.

With the lightning-like sweep of the Moslem hordes went in their train the Arabic way of life. The Koran was written in Arabic, the conquering hosts were Arabs, and the successors of the Prophet, called Caliphs, were of course descendants of Mohammed.[7] Thus the Arabic script, the Arabic style of worship and the Arabic language covered the whole of the Middle East. The proud language and civilization of Persia went down before the Arabized religion, as did the inheritance of the peoples of the Indus River valleys. The acceptance of Islam by various races made them instantly equal with and indistinguishable from other members of the faithful; but they were likewise separate from their kinsmen who clung to the old ways. Thus, in India,

---

[6] Of "the seven churches which are in Asia," mentioned in Revelation, all the towns became forgotten sites by the year 1000.

[7] Mohammed's heir was his daughter Fatima, although many Moslems honor the usurping Caliph Omar; Islam has suffered from deep rifts and feuds over which of these two—Omar or Fatima—was the rightful Caliph and successor of Mohammed.

the peoples of the Indus and of the desert turned to Mohammedanism, scrapped the caste system and the taboos of the Hindu gods, forgot their original language and culture for the Arabic, until this sense of separateness, enforced through the centuries by subsequent predominance over the Hindus under the Mogul emperors, led to the present-day division of India. The Moslem sections are now a separate dominion under the name of Pakistan.

The Arabs have a baffling outlook on life, so far as the European observer is concerned. They can be faced with the modern inventions and progressive social improvements of the whole world and yet change not a whit in their simple ways of living in a fatalistic manner of *Inchallah*—"As Allah wills it"— including a contentment with unsanitary, laborious ways of living. Their women remain satisfied with their *purdah,* and the farmers cling to the Biblical methods of cultivating the soil. Under this fatalistic code of thought, the Arabs have carried on the way of life that suits them best down through the ages, resisting the Crusaders, the fierce Tamerlane, the traders of the nineteenth century, the colonial powers and armies of the twentieth. Some of the richest farmlands of ancient times they have allowed to fall into eroded desert, while proud cultured capitals of antiquity have disintegrated into heaps of rubble.

The Arabs, having always lived in desert surroundings, early learned the ways of becoming adjusted to their environment, surviving by preserving the oases and following the seasonal rains with their flocks. They have learned how to trade; how to execute articles of lovely craftsmanship; how to transport wares by caravan across the desolate miles of sand; how to build important cities where their trade routes cross.

While their religion is a great leveler, uniting all believers into one equalitarian fraternity, strong differences among the Arabs can be discerned by students of the Near East. The perennial economic tug-of-war between the nomads of the desert and the dwellers of the sown has brought about periods of turmoil and civil war. The Arabs of the desert, nomads who are called Bedouin, cherish a distrust of the more effete and secular townsmen, many of whom have adopted the dress, languages, and luxuries of the European. In some states the Bedouin predominate—in the Kingdom of Jordan, and most emphatically in the land known as Saudi Arabia.

The Kingdom of the Yemen on the southern tip of Araby is also a strict, puritanical state, although submitting to the government of a town-bred dynasty of absolute rulers. Yemen is considered to be the land where coffee originated during the far-back Middle Ages. Coffee first attracted the attention of the medieval world upon being brought by Arab dhows up the Red Sea via Yemen's port of Mocha, from which the berries took their first name.

The Arab Kingdom of Iraq represents a state governed by the "townsmen" of the two cities of Bagdad and Mosul.

Arabia and its northern rim, the Fertile Crescent, have been influenced by Mediterranean cultures only in so far as trade is concerned. Arab sailors and traders took their priceless spices, musk, incense, gold, hides, perfumes, and jewels to Egyptian ports for sale to Venetian and Genoese purchasers, while Mesopotamian caravans bearing equal wealth from the Persian Gulf ports trekked over the burning sands to Levantine ports on the same errand. European ideas and products were brought back, but in a small quantity that affected only the royal families and richer townsmen of the trading cities.

Arabia's masses remained untouched and unimpressed with the currents of world thought then being generated by the creative currents of the great Middle Sea.

In recent years Araby of the past has spanned the centuries to become the center of twentieth century expansion. The peoples of this perplexing region have been yanked from the traditional age of the camel to the era of aviation without passing through any of the stages in between. America's experiment of training nomadic Arabs into skilled petroleum workers is something new that needs to be studied as an example of what may be achieved all over this once-forgotten segment of the world.

Thanks to this fantastic empire of oil, the Middle East has now become a projection of the Mediterranean world. Pipelines running from Iraq and Arabia to Syrian and Lebanese ports; airlines connecting Bagdad, Bahrein, Teheran, and Dhahran with Cairo, Lydda, and Damascus; and tanker routes from Basra to the Suez Canal are ties that are binding the Persian Gulf firmly and tightly to the Middle Sea. Thus the world can now see clearly into that once-ignored domain of Araby. It must watch intently, for that oil wealth and that warm body of water known as the Persian Gulf have attracted the spotlight of the world's most powerful empires and peoples—for better or for worse only the future can decide.

THE MEDITERRANEAN
AND AMERICA

THERE CAN BE VERY LITTLE DOUBT left by now of the fact that the Mediterranean has contributed bountifully to the enrichment of American civilization. All the Scenes of this Pageant have combined to prove how big a proportion of America's wonderful heritage has been derived from what the Mediterranean peoples achieved.

All the factors leading up to the actual discovery of America came through forces that were built up inside the Mediterranean system.

However, after the year 1600, the center of gravity of Old World affairs shifted back to Europe, and the Mediterranean basin entered a long period of stagnation that we have mentioned several times during the course of our story.

Due to the inactivity of Mediterranean powers during this period, the North American continent became settled by expeditions from England and France. Because Spain was too weak to enforce her monopoly to ownership of the new continent, the English were able to found their thirteen colonies one by one on the neglected coast of North America, while the French staked out their claims northward in Canada. The foundation stones of the American union were thus of northern European origin, not Mediterranean. Anglo-Saxon principles of law and government took root and began to flourish, while parallel systems of culture, activities, and social organization grew alongside them.

Consequently the early American cities, such as Boston, New York, Philadelphia, and Charleston, by the time of the Revolution resembled small English towns in their layout and architecture.

They had no similarity to Mexico City or Buenos Aires, settlements laid out in the Roman manner with narrow, straight streets, close-huddling houses, hidden patios, and imposing central plazas. At the same time the local colonial governments, with their self-assertive legislatures, were a far cry from the undemocratic assemblies in the French and Spanish colonies. The churches of North America were patterned on the English parish church system, with simple rural meetinghouses designed in a Georgian motif, rather than tending toward the imposing basilican-style temples and cathedrals that were erected in Spanish and French lands as symbols of authority and eminence.

Thus, the American Revolution and the ensuing foundation document of the Constitution were forged in the northern European tradition—yet with an odd extra factor included. The eighteenth century French philosophers were liberally copied and quoted by the Founding Fathers in their effort to protect the unique American liberties within the novel form of a republic. Jefferson, Franklin, Adams, and the others had been obliged to go back to ancient Athens for an authoritative, respected concept of free government that could operate without a monarch; but at the same time they improved on Athens by preserving the basic Anglo-Saxon freedoms and respect for law already enjoyed in America.

Thus, on the foundation stone of their English rights, the early American patriots erected a façade of classical appearance, borrowing from Greek precedents in the form they understood them. These precedents were perhaps too Arcadian and Utopian, but they did transmit the elements of popular government that the Athenians had made a pass at developing.

Almost as an outward symbol of this new concept of liberty buttressed by ancient path-finding, early American statesmen leaned to the classical style for the new public buildings that were soon set up to house the growing independent government of the United States. The Capitol Building at Washington, begun in 1795, was developed from such a plan. This plan lumped together the finest flowerings of Mediterranean architecture—the Greek fluted column, the Roman arch, and the Renaissance dome. The very name for the building—the "Capitol"—was taken bodily from ancient Rome, whose Capitoline Hill was the center of the republican city's solemnities, the "end of the Sacred Way" for all processions and triumphs doing homage to the Roman people.

From the Capitol the gospel spread to all the corners of the nation. State capitols, mansions, and office buildings leaned on this example, so that a dome became almost a hallmark of a state house, and Georgian-Greek pillars the badge of an executive mansion.

When the nation decided to do special honor to its first President, the Father of His Country, it erected the first specially built obelisk of modern times. The simple expression of ancient Egyptian art representing majesty and consecration—a pointed obelisk, without adornment or flourishes—still stands in honor of George Washington almost within sight of the ancestral acres where he lived the happiest days of his life. Later on, when Abraham Lincoln in turn came to be obsequized, his Memorial was modeled on the most beautifully chaste classic-style building that has yet been evolved on this planet—a Greek temple. Still later, Thomas Jefferson's Memorial was modeled along similar lines, except for the addition of a dome and a rounded colonnade, making it suggestive of the ancient Roman Pantheon.

America owes a heavy debt to Mediterranean civilization for the art and the music that it is now taking and readapting to the modern times into which we have entered.

Another cultural aspect that has been heavily borrowed from Mediterranean leadings is the wide field of public shows and theatrical entertainments. Our northern European ancestors had no experience in such things, but the Mediterranean peoples, thanks to the head start obtained by living in a land of long rainless summers and balmy weather the year round, evolved festivals and spectacles that are still the envy of many of our modern showmen. Our very words "theatre," "stadium," and "colosseum" were taken bodily from Greece or Rome, because those peoples perfected the art of public mass shows almost to a modern standard.

Theatres owe such a debt to Greek pioneering that they still borrow heavily from classical models to carry on their work of today. "Cyclorama," "tragedy," "comedy," and "drama" are Greek words, as are "chorus," "orchestra," and many others. "Thespian" and "Terpsichorean" are adjectives pertaining to forms of show business that have no modern synonyms. Theatres have often borrowed their actual names from classical showplaces. This practice was expanded to an unprecedented scale when movie theatres the length and breadth of the land began adopting such Greek or Roman names as:

"Odeon"—a Greek word for a place where songs are sung.

"Delphi"—the gathering place in Greece famous for the oracle of Apollo.

"Apollo"—named from the same source.

"Coliseum"—a simplified spelling for Colosseum, or "colossal" outdoor theatre of late Roman days.

"Alhambra"—probably chosen because of architectural resemblance to Granada's Moorish gem.

"Alcazar"—castle or palace of Arab countries; an architectural style of Oriental plushness, together with an idea of a fancy gathering place.

"Rialto"—the gathering place of the crowds in medieval Venice—the Rialto Bridge, where the active business of the day was transacted.

"Tivoli"—a frivolous resort of ancient and modern Rome, famous for a waterfall, cool groves, and a Cardinal's expensive gardens and cascades.

"Rivoli"—a pleasant Arcadian spot in northern Italy made famous by a Napoleonic battle.

"Arcadia"—the province of ancient Greece famed for its gentle pastoral life.

"Palace"—a suitable name, but harking back to Rome's Palatine Hill, site of palaces and villas of the emperors and consuls.

The list is endless and could be expanded indefinitely.

Origins of Many of Our Institutions

Perhaps the debt owed by our modern civilization to the peoples of the Mediterranean can best be brought into true focus by mentioning several phases of our everyday life in connection with their origins in the far-back Mediterranean world.

BUSINESS INSTITUTIONS: The pace of modern business is purely twentieth century, and many of our present techniques are native-grown and designed. However, the basic structure of commercial dealings as we know them today rests on practices worked out by trial and experiment during the past centuries. Stocks and stock-selling, for example, can be traced back to Renaissance England, whose companies of "merchant adventurers" sold out shares of a new venture on the order of a system worked out previously in Venice. The phrase "when one's ship comes in" stems from the habit in Venice and other Italian cities of financing a commercial trading expedition by chartering a ship and selling shares in her outward cargo. If the ship came back with priceless products from the East, a rich profit was made. If, however, the ship was wrecked, or captured by Barbary pirates, then everyone suffered a loss and had to try to start again.

Banking on the modern scale got its first start in Florence during the times of the Medici. The florin of those days was the stablest coin of Europe. Lending, pawnbroking, and the issuing of checks are practices first worked out in Renaissance Italy.

As for merchandising and advertising, these most modern of industries can trace their vitality back to the shrewd individualists and publicists of olden days. Clever trading is still a staple profession in all the countries bordering on the Mediterranean. The concept of establishing standards of excellence and reliability was also worked out in ancient times in such cities as Bagdad, Damascus, Cordoba, and Venice.

EDUCATION: The idea of popular education is definitely an Anglo-Saxon concept. However, the forms of pedagogy and instruction used in teaching in most institutes come from classic styles. The "academy," or "lyceum," used in ancient Greece to teach candidates for government has been taken over by our higher institutions of learning. Blackboards are direct descendants from the ancient habit of writing records on tablets, so that "they who run may read." Most terms used in education have been borrowed by early modern instructors from Greek or Roman parallels—"curriculum," "scholastic," "diploma," "graduation," etc.

LITERATURE: Almost all our literary forms were first worked out by classic or medieval literary pioneers. The indulgence in philosophies and exercises of the mind was a noble pursuit of ancient Greeks and Romans. Drama was born, reared, matured, and perfected to its modern degree by the Greeks and then copied by the Romans. Epics were first worked out by these same people, then relied on by medieval troubadours who recited national folk tales in the form of legendary embellishments, from which they were handed down by wandering singers and players in all the folk gatherings of Western Europe.

The troubadours also founded the art of telling a good story, although they received much headway from the Arabs' love of the same type of entertainment. Love tales, or "romances," took their name from the troubadours' practice of singing these tales in Latin, a romance tongue. Novels were born late—in early eighteenth century Italy—but quickly adopted and adapted by French and English writers of the same century. Essays, so popular in ninteenth century English literature, were copied after the Italian novella of an earlier period.

THE LAW: The legal profession, and the law courts, have borrowed liberally from Roman customs and codes. Our basic law, even though it is English common law, includes many systematic organizations and terms dating from Rome. The structure and phraseology of our court systems are also Franco-Roman, brought by the Norman conquerors to Britain. Thus, while our jury is mainly a Saxon institution, its name is Franco-Latin, meaning "they who are sworn." The judge, while a democratic official bound by legal precepts, has the solemn title of "decider" borne by the autocratic Roman and French judges, who usually sit in trios and interpellate a code rather than defend the purity of the sources of law as the Anglo-Saxon system requires.

DIPLOMACY: The whole institution of modern diplomacy is an outgrowth of the practice developed by the Republic of Venice of sending representatives to other states to study commercial practices and to strengthen Venice by scenting out any activity that might turn out to be hostile. In other words, Venice hoped to use wit and shrewdness to play off against the powerful armies that the kingly states had at their disposal. Later, this Venetian system was taken over by the kings of Europe, who made their envoys their personal representatives at each other's courts. "Diplomacy" comes from the Greek word used by early ambassadors, "diploma," meaning the card of recommendation carried by each ambassador as his protection and introduction.

Military Affairs: Modern military methods are a fearsome thing, being largely the product of technology and invention far surpassing in scope the methods worked out by the Romans and Spaniards for their more picayunish conflicts. Yet military terminology is replete with Latin words and even later French terms, coined by Bourbon France's military strategists from earlier Mediterranean precedents.

"Castle," "fort," "cavalry," "artillery," and "armor" are words that first saw the light during Roman military operations, as did the words "military," "army," and "navy" themselves. "Ballistics," "strategy," and "engine" are likewise classical words. Ballistics is the science of bullets, or "balls," coming from the Low Latin word for small pellets used as slung projectiles. "Strategy" is a Greco-Latin word for route-planning, or "science of the road." "Engine" was originally a cumbersome machine worked by springs or cords to throw rocks or to batter down walls. Our word "mile" comes from the distance covered by a thousand paces of a Roman soldier (*milia passuum*).

An interesting offshoot of this military-inspired heritage is the width of our modern standard-gauge railroad tracks. This inconvenient width, namely, 5 feet, 8½ inches, was adopted because the earliest wooden tracks put down for coal-wagons in early Britain were of this odd gauge. It is believed that the gauge came from medieval carts, which were copied directly after Roman chariots that had exactly this same width between their wheels. Visitors to Italy today can notice the high-wheeled load carts used by the peasants, all of which have only two wheels like a chariot, and the breadth of one of our standard railroad tracks.

Our word "standard" likewise comes from Roman practices. Each military unit carried its emblem on the tip of a pole—either as a pennant or a stiff metal or wooden insignia. Because the unit held great mystic pride in the reputation of its insignia, the word "standard" came to mean an unimpeachable evidence of the worth of a certain thing. From this same practice came the evolution of our national flags as the most portable emblems of the identification of a military or other political division.

In further connection with the emblems of Roman military bands, their commonly accepted insignia for their largest unit—the legion—was an eagle. As a symbol of might and victory, the eagle descended through the ages, reappearing on the escutcheons of many royal dynasties and noble warriors. This association probably influenced the founding fathers of the United States to adopt the eagle as the symbolic bird on the great seal. But for this traditional association, it would have been more sensible to choose the turkey or some other American bird as the national shield-bearer!

SPORTS: Our track meets are modern reincarnations of the more deadly clashes between champions of rival cities or armies. The Olympic Games, of course, are a still nobler re-creation of the finest of physical competitions of ancient Greece, when athletes outpointed each other in honor of the Olympian Zeus, whose temple and statue made up one of the Seven Wonders of the Ancient World. Their only reward for victory in those faraway days was a laurel wreath—and presumably the favor of Zeus. Even further back than the Games, however, Greek legends built up the half-divine Hercules as a protagonist of physical strength and keenness.

COOKERY: The Mediterranean countries deserve signal honor for their vital contribution to the piquancy of modern cuisines. But for the skill derived from the lands of the Middle Sea, our mealtimes would be as heavy and dull as were those of our not-too-distant forebears of northern Europe.

The French, master chefs of all time, have developed an art of cookery that borrows heavily from the Turkish in the form of spiced pastry, sweetmeats, piquant sauces, transformed meats, and well-mixed *plats du jour*. The Turks in turn got their luxurious way of dining from the Persians and the Arabs.

American pastries, seasonings, cheeses, gravies, and assortments have been endlessly enriched by the French. That one factor explains the principal variation of American cuisine from the original English and modern New England school of cookery with which we started out in history.

CLASSIC NAMES: No country in the world pays such honor to the Mediterranean as does the United States. The map and the gazetteer sing the glories of faraway locales around the shores of the Middle Sea.

Significantly, however, the classic names adorning the American map were not bestowed in most cases by rhapsodic travelers returning from contact with the lovely scenic paradises of the Mediterranean. Instead, they were selected by idealistic farmers and merchants who had never left the United States, but who were inspired by the role played by such places in the simpler, seemingly more democratic, days of antiquity. By re-creating on the landscape of the retreating wilderness the gilded name of a city sung by Homer or Virgil, the pioneers hoped to baptize their fledgling new homes with the glitter of immortality that was reflected by their august namesake cities.

Thus Syracuse, New York, pays honor to Sicily's one-time metropolis, where lived Archimedes. It has the classical spelling, and not that of the modern Sicilian port of "Siracusa," whose first emigrants could not have reached new Syracuse until at least eighty years after the city's establishment. Near Syracuse there stand Rome and Utica, also with their neoclassic spellings.

Athens, Sparta, Troy, Alexandria, Antioch—also Bethlehem, Venice, and even Medina—have been transplanted to America without exchanging any direct settlers. Fame, and the aura of the centuries, achieved this swift adoption between continents.

Toledo, Ohio, bears a name bestowed by an admirer of the city's symbolic prestige in Spain as the Moslem and Christian center of that country, whose liberation by The Cid in 1085 was an event worthy of commemoration on the forested shores of the Maumee River where it flows into Lake Erie.

All of the Renaissance metropoles of Italy are well reproduced in the United States—Florence, Milan, Pisa, Modena, Genoa. Portugal's capital of Lisbon is also copied in Maine and New Hampshire, possibly out of the sympathy felt by the pre-Revolutionary colonials over the city's disastrous earthquake of 1755. The Spanish town of Cadiz is likewise included among American names, possibly because of colonial pride over its sacking by Drake in 1586 as a precaution against the assembling of the Armada.

Crete and Mount Ida, Lebanon and Mount Hermon, Sharon and Mount Carmel have been reproduced in various states, lifted bodily from their classic roots. Ithaca, an undistinguished Greek island, is the name of a lovely university city in New York State thanks only to Homer's description of it as the shining goal for the Odyssey of Ulysses. What town could have been more lovingly named than Olympia in Washington? That city's beautiful location on Puget Sound surrounded by forests and mountains had nothing in common with Greek Olympia except a similar expression of excellence and veneration.

Early settlers who came to the Mississippi River compared it immediately to antiquity's most divine and fruitful river—the Nile. Ambitious but educated promoters named Memphis in Tennessee after the vanished, destroyed capital on the Nile, thinking of its geographical position at the head of the Nile delta, and of its one-time greatness as the commercial and governmental center of the first civilization in world history. At the same time other visionary migrants had founded Cairo in Illinois, deeming its location at the confluence of the Ohio with the Mississippi as the correct head of the river's bottomland delta. Cairo, though pronounced differently than in Egypt, honors the modern capital of that ancient land, even though in appearance hardly any two cities could ever be more opposite. In Illinois, Cairo's importance has even spread into its hinterland, which has taken on the name of "Egypt" since before Civil War days.

Out in Utah, the pious Mormons procured ideas from their Bibles whenever they wanted particularly suitable names. The climax they reached in this regard is the great scenic region known as Zion National Park. To the simple Mormon farmers and emigrants of a century ago, the soaring beauty of the eroded red and white peaks of that desert corner of their state could symbolize only Zion, the center of Old Testament solemnities, the Promised Land of the Hebrews in exile.

Indianapolis and Minneapolis took their suffixes from a smaller town founded a hundred years before this expanding classic revival—Annapolis in colonial Maryland.

These classical borrowings and embroiderings have, of course, been vastly extended in scope by the liberal use of Spanish names in California, Arizona, New Mexico, Texas, and Florida, and French names in the Great Lakes region. Such factors go far toward explaining why the nomenclature, the names on the face of the land of America, makes our country one of the most exciting in the whole world to explore and understand.

Religion

This cannot be the place to go more deeply into the contribution of Mediterranean peoples to the religion of America than has already been done in the various preceding Scenes. However, this work would not be complete without repeating that American civilization was founded on a religious inspiration, a combination of the simple Christian doctrines that came from distant Palestine, supporting the sublimated political institutions of the Athenian and Roman republics.

Christianity and Judaism both came entirely from a Mediterranean origin. However, both have gone through great permutations, metamorphoses, and reforms before being landed on the shores of America.

Thus, in a religious as well as in a cultural way, the United States is not a Mediterranean country or a Mediterranean civilization. It is a product of Western civilization, planted by north European peoples, built up on the institutions they themselves brought over bodily and nourished into a new strength and virility—and then refined, leavened, and beautified by the grace and lightness evolved by the Mediterranean peoples. Our country is thus the heir of the finest of all the divisions of the Western world, a fusing of the tastes of north and south.

How to Go to the Mediterranean

No one can very long resist the beauty and glamor of the Mediterranean lands. Americans have been traveling through them for many years. All travelers in the future should include a peep at the Mediterranean at one or more points of any European itinerary they intend to pursue.

Cream of the travel crop is the Mediterranean cruise, a two-month trip that takes travelers luxuriously to a whole succession of the finest and most history-kissed lands in the Middle Sea. This, however, should be merely an introduction. Once this general once-over has been enjoyed, one will know which parts of the Mediterranean basin he will wish to see again a second time and at greater leisure.

Those who visit Europe on a vacation trip can easily include the Riviera and Italy as their introduction to the Mediterranean. Others on the second trip will want to see Spain and Sicily. And everyone should plan on that further and never-to-be-missed trip—a cruise down the Dalmatian coast and through the Greek islands, regions of charm, splendid climate, and scenes steeped deep in history.

Almost every corner of the Middle Sea is always in season. It is never too hot or too cold to see any of these places, though there are preferences to be exercised whenever a traveler is in a position to choose his season or his itinerary.

One thing must always be done by any traveler who is planning to go to this magnificent region. He should study in advance an outline of the history and the cultures of the countries he intends to visit—which should then be placed against the whole backdrop of the closely-interrelated Mediterranean story. He should know which languages are spoken, try to pick up a few elementary words of courtesy in each one of them, set straight in his mind who were the various races who affected the development of the places on his itinerary—and try to understand what they have done toward making more rich and more purposeful our ways of life in the United States. He will then never feel at a loss anywhere, and he will be appreciably more at home everywhere, for he will know the things that count the most.

The glamor, the color, the fire and dash of all the events that have taken place in the vivid history of the Middle Sea combine to do more than make up a history or a dreary recitation of dynasties. They instead unite their brilliance to create the spectacle that we have just attended—the parade of the entire Pageant of the Mediterranean.

THE END

Index

A

Abraham, 52, 351
Acre, 42, 45, 287
Acropolis, 71, 72, 75–79, 83
Adriatic Sea, 183, 185, 259, 266, 269, 270, 271, 272, 274
Aegean Sea and Islands, 73, 76, 78, 84, 87, 147, 268, 269, 286, 289–92
Aeneas, 104, 121, 205
Agrigento, 92
Alamein, 23, 264
Albania, 266, 267, 268
Alcobaça, 220, 231
Alexander the Great, 17, 30, 54, 77, 81–82, 85, 146, 281, 283, 291, 350, 352
Alexandria, Egypt, 17, 18, 22–23, 43, 82, 152, 254, 261, 264, 364
Algiers, 157, 199 ff., 210–11, 322
Alhambra, 236, 240 ff., 251
Amalfi, 109 ff., 112, 287
Amerigo Vespucci, 176, 244 and footnote
Antioch, 82, 283, 364
Appian Way, 115, 118, 128, 129
Arabs, 47, 48, 55, 57–58, 60, 67, 153, 154, 161, 175, 200, 209, 210, 228, 254, 256, 263, 287, 296, 316, 320, 350–55
Aragon (Catalonia), 96, 112, 223, 233, 234, 236, 239 ff., 242, 252, 296, 301, 307
Architecture, 3, 6, 23, 76, 77, 107, 125, 166, 233–34, 357
Argos, 86
Arles, 191
Armenians, 30, 350
Assisi, 172
Assyrians, 29, 48, 54, 121, 146, 256, 283, 351
Atatürk, Mustapha Kemal, 150, 162, 292
Athens, 70, 74–76, 78–79, 80–86, 88, 93, 279, 280, 281, 286, 290
Atlantic Ocean, Scene XVIII, 336–
47; *also* 310 ff., 319, 323, 342–43
Atlantis, 281, 309, 387
Atlas Mountains, 197, 198, 202, 204, 310, 328, 335
Attica, 72, 75, 78, 84
Augustus, Emperor, 104, 115, 125 ff., 191, 293
Austria and Austrians, 184, 185, 244 ff., 252, 259, 269, 271, 273, 274, 275
Avignon, 136, 193
Azores, 223, 336, 343–47

B

Baalbek, 34 ff.
Babylonians, 52, 54, 72–75, 82
Bagdad, 38, 161, 317, 330, 354
Baldwin of Flanders, 55, 155
Balearic Islands, 236, 304–307
Balfour Declaration, 56, 59
Balkan Countries, Scene XV, 166–77; *also* 142, 147, 160, 266 ff.
Barbarossa (Kheir-ed-Din), 112, 194, 210, 211
Barbary Coast, Scene XI, 197–213; *also* 245, 247
Barcelona, 206, 233, 236, 243, 251–52, 307
Basilicas of Rome, 133, 135 ff. and footnote, 137 ff., 140
Batalha Abbey, 221, 231
Beatitudes, Mount of the, 61
Beirut, 24 ff., 32 ff., 43–44, 73
Belem, Portugal, 224–25
Benghazi, 212
Berbers, 208–209, 316–17, 318, 320, 327
Bethel, 43, 68
Bethesda, 64
Bethlehem, 43, 55, 56, 67–68, 127, 364
Bible, The, 24, 33, 37, *et passim;* Book of Acts, 295 ff.; Book of Revelation, 290, 291, 352; *see also* Scene III, 41–69
Biskra, 202, 322

The Cast of Mediterranean Peoples Today

(In order of their appearance in the Scenes)

The following political chart of the modern Mediterranean world will serve to show what our Cast of Mediterranean Peoples looks like, following 150 generations of intermittent pageantry—and how the map of the Mediterranean has changed from the single world of the Roman Empire to the forty or more separate states of today.

Scene	Country	Capital	Area Sq. Miles	Population	Official Language	Currency
	*New York State	Albany	50,000	16,782,304	English	Dollar
I	Egypt	Cairo	386,000	25,032,000	Arabic	Egyptian Pound
	Sudan	Khartoum	968,000	11,037,000	Arabic	Pound
	Ethiopia	Addis Ababa	350,000	21,600,000	Amharic	Ethiopian Pound
II	Lebanon	Beirut	4,000	1,719,000	Arabic	Lebanese Pound
	Syria	Damascus	66,000	4,421,000	Arabic	Syrian Pound
III	Israel	Jerusalem	10,000	2,062,000	Hebrew	Israeli Pound
	Jordan	Amman	34,740	1,607,000	Arabic	Jordan Dinar
IV	Greece	Athens	50,000	8,216,000	Greek	Drachma
	Bulgaria	Sofia	43,000	7,766,000	Bulgarian	Lev
	Rumania	Bucharest	92,000	18,059,000	Rumanian	Leu
V	Sicily	Palermo	9,927	4,721,000	Italian	Lira
VII	Italy	Rome	116,000	48,735,000	Italian	Lira
	San Marino	San Marino	38	2,410	Italian	Lira
VIII	Turkey	Ankara	297,000	25,932,000	Turkish	Turkish Lira
IX	Switzerland	Berne	16,000	5,230,000	French-German-Italian	Franc
X	France	Paris	213,000	44,847,000	French	Franc
	Monaco	Monaco	1	20,442	French	Franc

	Country	City	Area	Population	Language	Currency
XI	Algeria	Algiers	847,552	10,625,000	French	Franc
	Tunisia	Tunis	48,000	3,880,000	Arabic	Dinar
	Libya	Tripoli	679,000	1,153,000	Arabic	Pound
XII	Portugal	Lisbon	36,000	8,510,240	Portuguese	Escudo
XIII	Spain	Madrid	196,000	29,894,000	Spanish	Peseta
	Andorra	Andorra	191	6,500	Catalan	Peseta & Franc
XV	Yugoslavia	Belgrade	96,000	18,582,000	Serbo-Croatian	Dinar
	Hungary	Budapest	36,000	9,911,000	Hungarian	Forint
	Austria	Vienna	32,000	7,021,000	German	Schilling
XVI	Cyprus	Nicosia	3,570	528,000	Greek	Pound
	Rhodes	Rhodes	545	95,000	Greek	Drachma
	Crete	Candia	3,225	462,000	Greek	Drachma
	Malta	Valetta	95	306,000	Maltese	Pound
	Corsica	Ajaccio	3,367	244,000	Italian	Franc
	Sardinia	Cagliari	9,283	1,383,000	Italian	Lira
	Balearics	Palma	2,000	419,000	Spanish	Peseta
XVII	Gibraltar	Gibraltar Town	2	23,000	English	Pound Sterling
	Morocco	Rabat	190,000	10,330,000	Arabic	Dirham
XVIII	Canaries	Las Palmas	2,800	807,000	Spanish	Peseta
	Madeira	Funchal	308	269,000	Portuguese	Escudo
	Azores	Ponta Delgada	888	338,000	Portuguese	Escudo
XIX	Iraq	Bagdad	117,000	6,700,000	Arabic	Dinar
	Iran	Tehran	628,000	20,042,000	Persian	Rial
	Saudi Arabia	Riyadh	413,792	6,159,000	Arabic	Rupee
	Kuwait	Kuwait	1,950	210,000	Arabic	Rupee
XX	*United States	Washington	3,022,387	179,323,175	English	Dollar

* Yardstick for comparison. Figures approximate for convenience.

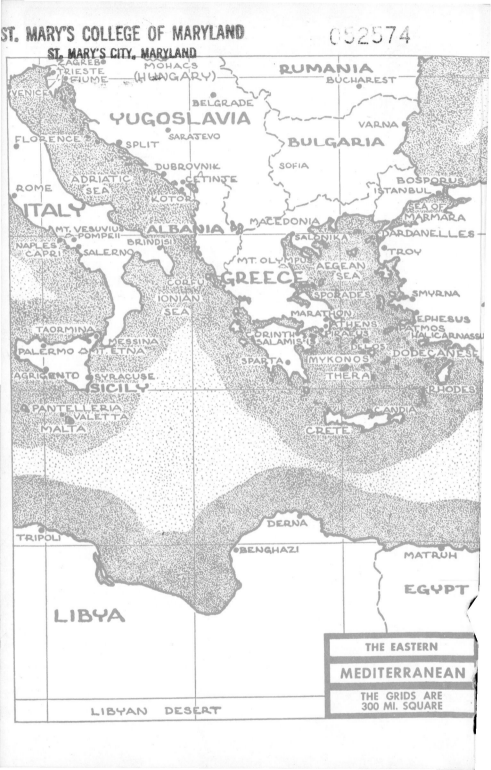

THE EASTERN
MEDITERRANEAN
THE GRIDS ARE
300 MI. SQUARE